Foundation XML and E4X for Flash and Flex

Sas Jacobs

friendsof

DESIGNER TO DESIGNER™

an Apress® company

Foundation XML and E4X for Flash and Flex

Credits

I'd like to dedicate this book to my Grandma Lucy, who died while I was writing it. You are a beautiful person, and I miss you very much.

CONTENTS AT A GLANCE

CONTENTS

ABOUT THE AUTHOR

Sas Jacobs is a web developer and author who works with Flash, Flex, and XML. Sas has written several books on these topics and has spoken about them at conferences such as Flashforward, webDU, and FlashKit. Nowadays, Sas works as a software developer in the area of e-learning, where she tries to share her passion for all things ActionScript.

When she's not working, Sas loves traveling, photography, running, and her son.

.

ABOUT THE TECHNICAL REVIEWER

Kevin Ruse is the principal of Kevin Ruse and Associates Inc., a web and print design and consulting firm based in Santa Clara, California. Kevin has been a trainer in web development and graphic design in a variety of environments, including De Anza Community College and the University of California, Santa Cruz. Kevin has also taught the staff and faculty at Stanford University and University of California, Berkeley.

Kevin is an Adobe Certified Instructor and a Certified Training Partner for the Altova XML Suite of software and the <oXygen/> XML editor. He currently teaches the following languages and software: Flex, Fireworks, Flash, Dreamweaver, Photoshop, InDesign, Acrobat, Quark XPress, JavaScript, ActionScript, MXML, XML, XSLT, DTD/Schema, ColdFusion, HTML, XHTML, and CSS.

Kevin is the author of *Web Standards Design Guide*, a college textbook. He is an enthusiastic instructor who maintains a strong belief that with patience, determination, and guidance, all individuals can reach their maximum potential.

ABOUT THE COVER IMAGE DESIGNER

 **Corné van Dooren** designed the front cover image for this book. After taking a brief from friends of ED to create a new design for the Foundation series, he worked at combining technological and organic forms, with the results now appearing on this and other books' covers.

Corné spent his childhood drawing on everything at hand and then began exploring the infinite world of multimedia, and his journey of discovery hasn't stopped since. His mantra has always been, "The only limit to multimedia is the imagination," a saying that keeps him moving forward constantly.

Corné works for many international clients, writes features for multimedia magazines, reviews and tests software, authors multimedia studies, and works on many other friends of ED books. You can see more of his work at and contact him through his web site, www.cornevandooren.com.

If you like Corné's work, be sure to check out his chapter in *New Masters of Photoshop: Volume 2* (friends of ED, 2004).

ACKNOWLEDGMENTS

Thanks again to all the people at friends of ED for your hard work in putting this book together. You're a great team and, as always, it has been a pleasure working with you.

INTRODUCTION

This book started out as an update to my first book on Flash and XML. Originally, the idea was to update the content with the changes to XML in ActionScript 3.0. However, when it came to drafting the table of contents, I realized that there was a whole audience of Flex developers who would also benefit from a book about XML and ActionScript 3.0. Hence, this book was born!

So, my plan is for this book to cater to both audiences: Flash designer/developers and Flex developers. I've included common code approaches, as well as topics that are specific to each package. I've tried to show readers how to achieve the same XML results in both software packages.

This book is best suited to people who have limited experience in the areas of XML and ActionScript 3.0. It is really pitched at introductory level users who are keen to learn more about ActionScript 3.0. The book is purposely simple in its approach, showing how to achieve common tasks required for working with XML in Flash and Flex. The Flash sections show function-based approaches, whereas the Flex sections show how to work with custom classes.

I hope that you find this book useful and that it whets your appetite for working with XML in your SWF applications. Hopefully, you'll find that the power and simplicity of XML will inspire you in your Flash and Flex development efforts!

Layout conventions

To keep this book as clear and easy to follow as possible, the following text conventions are used throughout:

- Important words or concepts are normally highlighted on the first appearance in *italics*.
- Code is presented in `fixed-width` font.
- New or changed code is normally presented in **`bold fixed-width font`**.
- Pseudo-code and variable input are written in *`italic fixed-width font`*.
- Menu commands are written in the form Menu ➤ Submenu ➤ Submenu.
- Where I want to draw your attention to something, I've highlighted it like this:

> *Ahem, don't say I didn't warn you.*

- Sometimes code won't fit on a single line in a book. Where this happens, I use an arrow like this: ➥.

```
This is a very, very long section of code that should be written all
➥on the same line without a break.
```

Chapter 1

INTRODUCTION TO XML

If you work in the web design or development area, you've probably heard of XML. It's the basis of all modern web sites, but how many of us actually know what it really means?

This chapter introduces XML and explains why it is such an important standard for exchanging information. I'll cover some of the basic concepts behind XML, including the rules governing the structure of XML documents. I'll also review some of the uses for XML and the reasons you might need to use it in your SWF applications. You'll see some examples of XML documents and, by the end of the chapter, have a solid understanding of XML and its related concepts.

If you're already familiar with XML and are comfortable generating XML documents, feel free to skip forward to Chapter 3. If not, read on! You can download the resources referred to in this chapter from http://www.friendsofed.com.

What is XML?

Let's start by answering the most basic question of all: what is XML? It's very difficult to provide a short answer to this question. The people who invented XML, the World Wide Web Consortium (W3C), provide the following definition for XML in their glossary at http://www.w3.org/TR/DOM-Level-2-Core/glossary.html.

Extensible Markup Language (XML) is an extremely simple dialect of SGML. The goal is to enable generic SGML to be served, received, and processed on the Web in the way that is now possible with HTML. XML has been designed for ease of implementation and for interoperability with both SGML and HTML.

I think the definition is very accurate if you already know about XML, but it doesn't really explain XML to a novice. Let's go back to basics and see what that definition really means.

Understanding XML

XML describes a format that you can use to share information. By itself, XML doesn't do anything other than store information. It's not a programming language, so you can't use it to create stand-alone applications. XML simply describes information. XML documents need humans or software packages to process the information that they contain.

XML stands for Extensible Markup Language, which is a little misleading, because XML is actually a metalanguage, so you can use it to create other markup languages. That's what the word *extensible* means in the acronym. The term *markup* means that the languages you create use tags to surround or mark up text, which you'll be familiar with if you write Extensible Hypertext Markup Language (XHTML).

In fact, XHTML is one of the languages created by XML. We call XHTML a *vocabulary* of XML. It was created when HTML was redefined according to XML rules. For example, in XHTML, all tags must be in lowercase. This requirement doesn't apply to HTML.

Think about the tags you use in XHTML, such as <p></p> and <h1></h1>. These tags mark up information that will display on a web page. You use these in a very specific way, according to some predefined rules. For example, one rule says that you can't include <p></p> tags in the <head> section of a web page.

It's possible to make up your own XML vocabulary or work within a group to create an industry-wide language based on XML. By agreeing on an XML vocabulary, groups can share information using a common set of markup tags and structures. Chemical Markup Language (CML), for example, allows scientists to share molecular information in a standardized way. There are specific rules for structuring CML documents and referring to molecular information. MathML is another vocabulary of XML that describes mathematical operations. But you don't need to work with an existing vocabulary to include XML in your applications. It's possible—in fact, very likely—that you'll create your own XML structures to suit the particular needs of your application. You'll see this as we work through the examples in the book.

So what type of information can you store in an XML document?

Storing information in XML documents

XML documents work best with structured information, similar to what you would find in a database. Examples include lists of names and addresses, product catalogs, sales orders, an iTunes library—anything with a standardized format. Like a database, XML documents can show hierarchical relationships. Instead of breaking the information into tables and fields, elements and tags describe the data. By nesting tags inside each another, you can create a hierarchy of parent and child elements.

The following code block shows some sample XML elements. You can see the hierarchical relationship between the elements, and the tag names describe their contents.

```
<contact>
  <name>Sas Jacobs</name>
  <address>123 Red Street, Redland, Australia</address>
  <phone>123 456</phone>
</contact>
```

The code sample describes contact details, similar to what you would see in an address book. Most of us have an address book that we use to store contact information about our friends and colleagues. You might have the information in a software package like Outlook or Outlook Express. It might also exist on your mobile phone.

Your address book contains many different names, but you store the same information about each contact: name, phone number, and address. The way the information is stored depends on the software package you've chosen. If the manufacturer changes the package or discontinues it, you'll need to find a new way to store information about your contacts.

Transferring the information to a new software program is likely to be difficult. You'll need to export it from the first package, rearrange the contents to suit the second package, and then import the data. Most software applications don't share a standard format for contact data, although some can share information. You must rely on the standards created by each company.

As an alternative, you could use an XML document to store the information. You could create your own tag names to describe the data. Tags like <contact>, <phone>, and <address> would provide clear descriptions for your information. Any human who read the document would be able to understand what information the document held.

Because the address book XML document has a standard format, you could use it to display your contacts on a web page. Web browsers contain an XML parser to process the XML content. You could also print out your contacts, or even build a SWF movie in Flash or Flex to display and manage your contacts.

Your friends could agree on which tags to use and share their address books with each other. You could all save your contacts in the same place and use tags to determine who had contributed each entry. When you use a standardized structure for storage, you have endless choices about how to work with the information.

So if XML is so useful, how did it all start?

XML, in the beginning

XML has been around since 1998. It is based on Standard Generalized Markup Language (SGML), which was in turn was created out of Generalized Markup Language (GML) in the 1960s. XML is actually a simplified version of SGML.

SGML describes how to write languages, specifically those that work with text in electronic documents. It is also an international standard: ISO 8879. SGML was actually one of the considerations for HTML when it was first developed.

The first XML recommendation was released in February 1998. Since then, XML has increased in popularity and is now a worldwide standard for sharing information. Human beings, databases, and many popular software packages use XML documents to store and exchange information. Web services and RSS feeds also use an XML format to share content over the Internet.

The W3C developed the XML specification. The W3C also works with other recommendations such as HTML, XHTML, and Cascading Style Sheets (CSS). Detailed information about the XML specification is available from the W3C's web site at http://www.w3.org/XML/. The current specification is XML 1.1 (Second Edition), dated 16 August 2006. You can view this specification at http://www.w3.org/TR/2006/REC-xml11-20060816/.

The W3C has also created a family of related recommendations that work together to create an independent framework for managing markup languages. The other areas covered by recommendations include XML schemas, which describe the structure and syntax of an XML document; XML stylesheets, which allow the transformation and output of XML content; and XPath, which describes how to navigate or locate specific parts of XML documents.

When it created XML, the W3C published the following goals at http://www.w3.org/TR/REC-xml/#sec-origin-goals:

1. XML shall be straightforwardly usable over the Internet.
2. XML shall support a wide variety of applications.
3. XML shall be compatible with SGML.
4. It shall be easy to write programs which process XML documents.
5. The number of optional features in XML is to be kept to the absolute minimum, ideally zero.
6. XML documents should be human-legible and reasonably clear.
7. The XML design should be prepared quickly.
8. The design of XML shall be formal and concise.
9. XML documents shall be easy to create.
10. Terseness in XML markup is of minimal importance.

In other words, XML should be easy to use in a variety of settings, by both people and software applications. The rules for XML documents should also be clear so they are easy to create.

An XML example

The following code block shows a simple XML document with address book data containing a single contact. If you've worked with XHTML, you'll see that the elements are written in a similar way.

```
<?xml version="1.0"?>
<phoneBook>
  <contact id="1">
    <name>Sas Jacobs</name>
    <address>123 Some Street, Some City, Some Country</address>
    <phone>123 456</phone>
  </contact>
</phoneBook>
```

The information is stored between tags, and the names of these tags are descriptive—for example, <name>, <address>, and <phone>. The casing of the opening and closing tags is consistent. The hierarchy within the document shows that the information relates to a single <contact> element. You can use any names for these elements, as long as you follow the rules for constructing XML documents. These rules are presented in the "Structuring XML documents" and "Understanding well-formed documents" sections later in the chapter.

Now that you know a little more about XML, you may be wondering why it is so important and why might you want to use XML as a source of data.

Why XML?

Quite simply, XML is simple, flexible, descriptive, accessible, independent, precise, and free! Let's look at each of these advantages of XML in turn.

Simple

The rules for creating XML documents are very simple. You just need a text editor or another software package capable of generating XML formatted data. The only proviso is that you follow some basic rules so that the XML document is well-formed. You'll find out what this means a little later in the chapter, in the "Understanding well-formed documents" section.

Reading an XML document is also simple. Tag names are normally descriptive, so you can figure out what data each element contains. The hierarchical structure of elements allows you to work out the relationships between each piece of information.

Flexible

One key aspect of XML is its flexibility. As long as you follow some simple rules, you can structure an XML document in any way you like. The choice of tag names, attributes, and structures is completely flexible so you can tailor it to suit your data. You can also agree on an XML vocabulary so you can share information with other people. A Document Type Definition or schema describes the "grammar," or rules for the language.

XML documents provide data for use in different applications. You can generate an XML document from a corporate software package, transform it to display on a web site using Extensible Stylesheet Language Transformations (XSLT), share it with staff on portable devices, use it to create PDF files with Extensible Stylesheet Formatting Objects (XSL-FO), and provide it to other software packages. You can reuse the same data in several different settings. The ability to repurpose information is one of XML's key strengths.

> *XSLT and XSL-FO are two related XML recommendations. Both of these recommendations describe how to change or transform an XML document into a different type of output. You might use an XSLT stylesheet to create HTML or text from an XML document. You could use XSL-FO to create a PDF document.*

The way XML information displays is also flexible. You can display any XML document in any XML processor, perhaps a web browser, to see the structure of elements. You can also use the document to display the following:

- A printed list of summary data
- A web page displaying the full details of each element
- A SWF movie that allows you to search the XML content

Descriptive

Because you can choose your own tag names, an XML document becomes a description of your data. Some people call XML documents *self-describing*.

The hierarchy of elements means that XML documents show relationships between information in a similar way to a database. For example, the hierarchies in the address book document tell us that each contact has a name, address, and phone number, and that we can store many different contacts.

Accessible

XML documents separate data from presentation, so you can have access to the information without worrying about how it displays. This makes the data accessible to many different people, devices, and software packages. For example, the sample address book XML document could be accessed in the following ways:

- Read aloud by a screen reader
- Displayed on a web site
- Printed to a PDF file
- Processed automatically by a software package
- Viewed on a mobile phone

XML documents use Unicode for their standard character set, so you can write XML documents in any number of different languages. (The Unicode standard is maintained by the Unicode Consortium; see http://www.unicode.org/.) A SWF application could offer multilingual support simply by using different XML documents with equivalent content.

Independent

XML is platform- and device-independent. It doesn't matter if you view the data on a PC, Macintosh, or handheld device. The data is still the same, and people can exchange it seamlessly. Programmers can also use XML to share information between software packages that otherwise couldn't easily communicate with each other.

You don't need a specific software package to work with XML documents. You can type the content in just about any software package capable of receiving text. You can read the document in a web browser, text editor, or any other XML processor. XML documents can provide a text-based alternative to database content. In the case of web services, XML is an intermediary between you and someone else's database.

XML doesn't have "flavors" that are specific to a single web browser (like CSS), version, or operating system. You don't need to create three different versions of your XML document to handle different viewing conditions.

Precise

XML is a precise standard. If you want your XML document to be read by an XML parser, it must be well-formed. Documents that aren't well-formed won't display. You're probably wondering what *well-formed* means. We'll cover that a little later, in the "Understanding well-formed documents" section.

When a schema or Document Type Definition is included within an XML document, an XML processor can validate the content to make sure that the document structure conforms to the structural rules you've established. XML documents with schemas provide standards, so there is only one way that the data they contain can be structured and interpreted.

Free

XML is a specification that isn't owned by any company or commercial enterprise. This means that it's free to use XML—you don't have to buy any special software or other technology. In fact, most major software packages either support XML or plan to support it in the future.

So why should you use XML in your Flash and Flex projects?

Why is XML important in Flash and Flex?

XML is an important tool for all web developers. Many people consider XML the *lingua franca* of the Internet as it provides the standard for data exchange among humans and machines in many different settings.

An understanding of XML is essential for Flash and Flex developers for the following reasons:

- XML is one way for Flash and Flex developers to store content that powers SWF movies.
- Flex uses a vocabulary of XML, called MXML, to describe interfaces.
- XML provides a mechanism for working with data that is disconnected from a database or the Internet.
- ActionScript 3.0 contains features to make working with XML much easier than in previous versions, so it's a sound alternative to plain-text files for content.

XML as a SWF data source

Storing content outside a SWF application means that clients can update their own content without needing to learn either Flash or Flex, or contact the developer each time they want to make a change. It's also possible to provide client tools that make it easy to generate the content automatically.

Developers will understand the importance of storing information for SWF movies in an external data source. Doing so allows the content of a SWF application to change without the need to recompile it each time. Simply update the source document to update the information within the application.

There are many possible sources of external data: text files, databases, and XML documents. While it's possible to create external text files for a SWF file, it's more practical to use an XML document, which can include the data and describe the hierarchical relationships between the data.

Although a developer or client can create an XML document by hand, it's easier to generate the content automatically. With the assistance of a web server and a server-side language like PHP, Visual Basic .NET (VB .NET), or ColdFusion, databases can easily generate XML content suitable for a SWF application. You'll see how this can be done in the next chapter. In terms of security, it's good practice to use an XML layer between a user and database.

Many software packages are capable of exporting their content in an XML format. The most recent versions of Microsoft Office allow you to save Word, Excel, and Access documents using either Microsoft's XML vocabularies or your own. Using standard business tools to generate XML content allows clients to take control of their own application content.

For SWF applications that need to be portable, XML is an excellent choice as a data source. An XML document is usually small in file size, making it easy to include on a CD, DVD, or handheld device.

MXML in Flex

In order to get the most out of Flex, developers need a good understanding of XML. Flex uses an XML vocabulary called MXML to describe application interfaces. MXML is a markup language that provides the same role in Flex applications as XHTML does in web pages.

MXML consists of a set of tags that correspond to ActionScript 3.0 classes. Because MXML is a vocabulary of XML, it must follow the same rules and be well-formed. I'll cover this term in more detail later in the chapter.

ActionScript 3.0 and XML

ActionScript 3.0 greatly simplifies the process of working with XML documents compared with earlier versions. XML is a native data type in this version of ActionScript, making it much easier to work with in both Flash and Flex.

If you've worked with XML in an earlier version of ActionScript, you'll be used to writing complicated expressions and looping through collections of nodes to locate specific information in an XML document. The new process means that you can target content in an XML document by using element names instead. This change is significant and makes working with XML content much easier than in earlier versions of ActionScript. I have found that ActionScript 3.0 has saved me hours of development time when it comes to working with XML content. You'll find out more about the changes to ActionScript in Chapter 3.

ActionScript 3.0 also includes a full implementation of the ECMAScript for XML (E4X) standard, ECMA-357 (see http://www.ecma-international.org/publications/files/ECMA-ST/Ecma-357.pdf). Because ActionScript 3.0 adheres to international standards, you can take advantage of any existing knowledge you have in this area. Learning E4X means that you'll be able to apply the same skills when working with JavaScript.

Now that you appreciate why XML is important to Flash and Flex developers, let's look more closely inside an XML document.

XML document sections

It's important to understand exactly what the term *XML document* means. This term refers to a collection of content that meets XML construction rules. The *document* part of the term has a more general meaning than with software packages. In Flash or Flex, for example, a document is a physical file. While an XML document can be a physical file, it can also refer to a stream of information that doesn't exist in a physical sense. You can create these streams from a database using a web server, and you'll see how this is done later in the book. As long as the information is structured according to XML rules, it qualifies as an XML document.

An XML document is divided into two sections: the *prolog* and the content, or *document tree*. The content exists inside the *document root* or *root element*.

Document prolog

The document prolog appears at the top of an XML document and contains information about the XML document as a whole. It must appear before the root element in the document. The prolog is a bit like the <head> section of an XHTML document.

The prolog consists of the following:

- An XML declaration
- Processing instructions
- Document Type Definitions (DTDs)

XML declaration

The prolog usually starts with an XML declaration to indicate to humans and computers that the content is an XML document. This declaration is optional but if it is present, it must appear on the first line. At a minimum, the declaration appears as follows:

```
<?xml version="1.0"?>
```

The minimum information that must appear inside an XML declaration is an XML version. The preceding declaration uses version 1.0.

> *At the time of writing, the latest recommendation is XML 1.1. However, you should continue to use the* version="1.0" *attribute value for backward-compatibility with XML processors, unless you specifically need version 1.1. For example, XML 1.1 allows characters that can't be used in XML 1.0 and has slightly different requirements for namespaces.*

The XML declaration can also include the encoding and standalone attributes. The order of these attributes is important.

Encoding determines the character set for the XML document. You can use Unicode character sets UTF-8 and UTF-16 or ISO character sets like ISO 8859-1, Latin-1, or Western European. If no encoding attribute is included, it is assumed that the document uses UTF-8 encoding. Languages like Japanese and Chinese need UTF-16 encoding. Western European languages often use ISO 8859-1 to cope with diacritical characters, such as accent marks, that aren't part of the English language.

The encoding attribute must appear after the `version` attribute. Here are some sample declarations that include an encoding attribute:

```
<?xml version="1.0" encoding="UTF-8"?>
<?xml version="1.0" encoding="UTF-16"?>
<?xml version="1.0" encoding="ISO-8859-1">
```

The `standalone` attribute indicates whether the XML document uses external information, such as a DTD. A DTD specifies the rules about which elements and attributes to use in the XML document. It also provides information about the number of times each element can appear and whether an element is required or optional.

The `standalone` attribute is optional. When it's included, it must appear as the last attribute in the declaration. The value `standalone="no"` can't be used when you are including an external DTD or stylesheet. Here is an XML declaration that includes this attribute:

```
<?xml version="1.0" encoding="UTF-8" standalone="yes"?>
```

Processing instructions

The prolog can also include processing instructions (PIs). Processing instructions pass information about the XML document to other applications that may need that information in order to process the XML.

Processing instructions start with the characters `<?` and end with `?>`. You can add your own processing instructions or have them generated automatically by software packages. The first item in a processing instruction is a name, called the processing instruction *target*. Processing instruction names that start with `xml` are reserved.

One common processing instruction is the inclusion of an external XSLT stylesheet. An XSLT stylesheet transforms the content of an XML document into a different structure, and I'll cover this topic in more detail later in this chapter, in the "Understanding XSL" section. A processing instruction that includes an XSLT stylesheet must appear before the document root. The following line shows how this processing instruction might be written:

```
<?xml-stylesheet type="text/xsl" href="listStyle.xsl"?>
```

Processing instructions can also appear in other places in the XML document.

Document Type Definitions

DTDs, or DOCTYPE declarations, can also appear in the prolog. A DTD provides rules about the structure of elements and attributes within the XML document. It explains which elements are legal in the XML document, and tells you which elements are required and which are optional. In other words, a DTD provides the rules for a valid XML document and explains how the document should be constructed.

The prolog can include a set of declarations about the XML document, a bit like an embedded CSS stylesheet in an XHTML document. The prolog can also include a reference to an external DTD as well as or instead of these declarations. The following shows an external reference to a DTD:

```
<?xml version="1.0"?>
<!DOCTYPE phoneBook SYSTEM "phoneBook.dtd">
```

All the other content in an XML document appears within the document tree.

Document tree

Everything that isn't in the prolog is contained within the document tree. The tree contains all of the content within the document. The section "Structuring XML content" explains exactly what items appear here.

The document tree starts with a document root or root element. An XML document can have only one root element. All of the content within the XML document must appear inside the document root. In HTML documents, the <html> tag is the root element. This is a rule of a well-formed document.

Whitespace

XML documents include whitespace so that humans can read them more easily. Whitespace refers to spaces, tabs, and returns that space out the content in the document. The XML specification allows you to include whitespace anywhere within an XML document except before the XML declaration.

> XML processors can interpret whitespace in an XML document, but many won't actually display the spaces. If whitespace is important, there are ways to force an XML processor to display the spaces using the xml:space attribute in an element. I'll leave you to research that topic on your own if it's something you need to do.

Namespaces

XML documents can get very complicated. One XML document can reference another XML document, and different rules may apply in each case. XML documents can also summarize content from multiple sources. For example, you might combine several different XML documents into one.

It's possible that an XML document will contain elements that use the same name but that come from different locations and have different meanings. For example, you might use the <table> element as part of an XHTML reference in a document about furniture, which also needs to use a <table> element as a description of the type of furniture.

In order to overcome this problem, you can use *namespaces* to distinguish between elements. Namespaces associate each XML element with an owner to ensure it is unique within a document, even if there are other elements that use the same name.

Each namespace includes a reference to a Uniform Resource Identifier (URI) as a way to ensure its uniqueness. A URI is an Internet address, and each URI must be unique in the XML document. The URIs used in an XML document don't need to point to anything, although they can.

You can define a namespace using the xmlns attribute within an element. Each namespace usually has a prefix that you use to identify elements belonging to that namespace. You can use any prefix that you like, as long as it doesn't start with xml and doesn't include spaces.

Here is an example of using a namespace:

```
<FOE:details xmlns:FOE="http://www.friendsofed.com/ns/">
  <name>Sas Jacobs</name>
</FOE:details>
```

In the <details> element, the FOE prefix refers to the namespace http://www.friendsofed.com/ns/. You can also use this prefix with other elements and attributes to indicate that they are part of the same namespace, like this:

```
<FOE:address>
   123 Some Street, Some City, Some Country
</FOE:address>
```

This prefix indicates that the <address> element also comes from the http://www.friendsofed.com/ns/ namespace.

You can also define a namespace without using a prefix. If you do this, the namespace will apply to all elements that don't have a prefix or namespace defined. It is referred to as the *default namespace*.

In an XHTML document, the <html> element includes a namespace without a prefix:

```
<html xmlns="http://www.w3.org/1999/xhtml">
```

The namespace then applies to all of the child elements of the <html> element; in other words, all of the remaining elements in the XHTML document.

It isn't compulsory to use namespaces in your XML documents, but it can be a good idea. Namespaces are also important when you start to work with schemas and stylesheets. ActionScript 3.0 provides mechanisms for working with namespaces when dealing with complex XML documents in SWF applications.

You can find out more about namespaces by reading the latest recommendation at the W3C site. At the time of writing, this was the Namespaces in XML 1.1 (Second Edition) recommendation at http://www.w3.org/TR/xml-names11/.

Structuring XML documents

XML documents contain both information and markup. The information about the document appears in the prolog, as discussed in the previous section. You can divide markup into the following:

- Elements
- Attributes
- Text
- Entities

- Comments
- CDATA

Let's look at each of these items in turn, starting with elements.

Elements

Each XML document contains one or more elements, and they will usually make up the bulk of the document. Elements, also called *nodes*, identify and mark up content. At the very minimum, an XML document will contain one element: the document root.

Elements serve many functions in an XML document:

- Elements mark up content. The opening and closing tags surround text.
- Tag names provide a description of the content they mark up. This gives you a clue about the purpose of the element.
- Elements provide information about the order of data in an XML document.
- The position of child elements can show their relative importance in the document.
- Elements show the relationships between blocks of information. Like databases, they show how one piece of data relates to others.

Writing elements

As in XHTML, XML tags start with a less-than sign (<) and end with a greater-than sign (>). The name of the tag appears between these signs: <tagName>.

> *Although they are often used interchangeably, the terms element and tag have slightly different meanings. A tag looks like this:*
>
>   <tag>
>
> *An element looks like this:*
>
>   <tag>Some text</tag>
>
> *An element usually contains both an opening tag and a closing tag, as well as the text node in between those tags.*

If an element contains information or other elements, it will include both an opening and closing tag: <tag></tag>. An empty element can be written using a single tag: <tag/>. So, *<tagname></tagname>* is equivalent to *<tagname/>*. (In XHTML, the <img/> and <br/> tags are examples of empty elements.)

As explained earlier, you can include whitespace anywhere within an XML document, so you can split elements across more than one line, as shown here:

```
<contact>
   Some text
</contact>
```

13

Naming elements

Element names must follow these rules:

- Element names can start with either a letter or the underscore character. They can't start with a number.

- Element names can contain any letter or number, but they can't include spaces. In addition, there cannot be a space between the opening angle bracket (<) and the element name.

- Although it's technically possible to include a colon (:) character in an element name, it's not a good idea, because colons are used when referring to namespaces.

It's best to use a meaningful name that describes the content inside the tags. This element name:

```
<fullName>Sas Jacobs</fullName>
```

is more useful than this one:

```
<axbjd>Sas Jacobs</axbjd>
```

> Notice that I've used camel case in the first example, where I capitalize the first letter of every word in the tag name except for the first: `<fullName>`. This naming practice is common among developers and can help to make the name more readable.

It's also a good idea to be careful not to add extra spaces between the tag names and the contents. For example using this form:

```
<fullName>Sas Jacobs</fullName>
```

is preferable to using this one:

```
<fullName> Sas Jacobs </fullName>
```

If you needed to sort using the contents, the extra space in the second example would distort the sort order.

Populating elements

There are unlimited variations in the content that you can store in an element. The following element contains two tags and some text:

```
<tag>Some text</tag>
```

Elements can include other nested elements and text. They can also be empty, without any text or elements.

You call an element inside another a *child* element or *child* node. Not surprisingly, the element that contains the child is called the *parent*.

```
<parentTag>
  <childTag>Text being marked up</childTag>
</parentTag>
```

The family analogy continues with *grandparent* and *grandchild* elements, as well as *siblings*.

You can also mix the content of elements, which means they can contain text as well as child elements, as in this example:

```
<parentTag>
  Text being <childTag>marked up</childTag>
</parentTag>
```

The first element

The first element in an XML document is called the *root element*, *document root*, or *root node*. It contains all the other elements in the document. Each XML document can have only one root element. The last tag in an XML document will almost always be the closing tag for the root element.

XML is case-sensitive. For example, the tags <phoneBook> and </phonebook> are not equivalent and can't be used to open and close the same element. This is a big difference from HTML, and one of the changes introduced with XHTML.

It's possible to modify the opening tag of an element to include an attribute.

Attributes

Attributes provide additional information about an element to clarify or modify the element. Attributes are stored in the opening tag of an element after the element name.

Writing attributes

Each attribute consists of a name and a related value, as shown here:

```
<tagname attributeName="attributeValue">
  Text being marked up
</tagname>
```

The value of an attribute appears in quotation marks (quotes) and is separated from the attribute name with an equals sign. It doesn't matter whether you use single or double quotes. You can even mix and match the quotes in the same element, like this:

```
<tagname attribute1="value1" attribute2='value2'>
```

Use double quotes where a value contains an apostrophe.

```
<person name="o'mahoney">
```

Use single quotes where double quotes make up part of the value.

```
<photo caption='It was an "interesting" day'>
```

An attribute can't include tags within its value.

An XHTML image tag is a good example of an element that contains multiple attributes.

```
<img src="logo.gif" width="20" height="15" alt="Company logo"/>
```

There is no limit to the number of attributes that can appear within an element, but attributes inside the same element must have unique names. When you are working with multiple attributes in an element, the order isn't important.

Naming attributes

Attribute names follow the same naming conventions as elements: you can't start the name with a number, and you can't include spaces inside the name. Some attribute names are reserved, so you shouldn't use them in your XML documents. Reserved names include the following;

- `xml:lang`
- `xml:space`
- `xml:link`
- `xml:attribute`

Notice that all of these names have the `xml` prefix, indicating that they're within the XML specification. These attribute names are called *qualified names*. You can use the unqualified versions of these attribute names. So, `lang`, `space`, `link`, and `attribute` would be fine.

Structuring attributes as elements

You can rewrite attributes as nested elements, as follows:

```
<contact id="1">
  <name>Sas Jacobs</name>
</contact>
```

The preceding XML fragment could also be written in this way:

```
<contact>
  <id>1</id>
  <name>Sas Jacobs</name>
</contact>
```

There is no one right way to structure elements and attributes. The method you choose depends on your data. The way you're going to process the XML document might also influence your choices. For example, some software packages have more difficulty working with attributes than they do working with elements.

Text

Text refers to the content in an XML document that is marked up by the tags. Text is any nonelement information stored between opening and closing element tags. In the following line, the text Sas Jacobs is stored between the `<fullName>` and `</fullName>` tags:

```
<fullName>Sas Jacobs</fullName>
```

Unless you specify otherwise, the text between the opening and closing tags in an element will always be processed as if it were XML. This means that special characters such as < and > must be replaced with the entities `&lt;` and `&gt;` to prevent an error in the XML processor. Entities are discussed in the next section. An alternative is to use a CDATA declaration to present the information, as explained a little later, in the "CDATA" section.

Entities

Character entities are symbols that represent a single character. In HTML, character entities are used for special symbols such as an ampersand (&) and a nonbreaking space ( ). Table 1-1 lists the common entities that you'll need to use.

Table 1-1. Entities commonly used in XML documents

Character	Entity
<	&lt;
>	&gt;
'	&apos;
"	&quot;
&	&amp;

Character entities replace reserved characters in XML documents. All tags start with a less-than sign, so it would be confusing to include another one in your code, like this:

```
<expression>3 < 5</expression>
```

To avoid causing an error during processing, replace the less-than sign with the entity <:

```
<expression>3 &lt; 5</expression>
```

Some entities use Unicode numbers. You can use numbers to insert characters that you can't type on a keyboard or choose not to type because they conflict with an XML parser (such as <). For example, the entity é creates the character é—an e with an acute accent. The number 233 is the Unicode number for the character é.

You can also use a decimal or hexadecimal number to refer to a character. For more information about this topic, see http://www.w3.org/TR/REC-html40/charset.html#h-5.3.1.

Comments

Comments in XML work the same as in XHTML. They begin with the characters <!-- and end with -->.

```
<!-- here is a commented line -->
```

Comments are a useful way to leave messages for other users of an XML document without affecting the way the XML document is processed. In fact, software that processes XML always ignores comments in XML documents.

The following are the only requirements for comments in XML documents:

- A comment can't appear before the first line in an XML declaration.
- Comments can't be nested or included within tag names.
- You can't include --> inside a comment.
- Comments shouldn't split tags; that is, you shouldn't comment out just an opening or closing tag.

CDATA

CDATA stands for character data. CDATA blocks mark text so that it isn't processed as XML. For example, you could use CDATA for information containing characters that would confuse an XML processor, such as < and >. Doing so means that any < or > character contained within the CDATA block won't be processed as part of a tag name.

CDATA sections start with <![CDATA and finish with]>. The character data is contained within square brackets [ ] inside the section.

```
<![CDATA[
  3 < 5
  or
  2 > 0
]]>
```

Entities will display literally in a CDATA section, so you shouldn't include them. For example, if you add < to your CDATA block, it will display the same way when the XML document is processed, rather than as a left-angle bracket character.

The end of a CDATA section is marked with the]]> characters, so you can't include these inside a CDATA block.

A simple XML document

So far, I've explained the structure and contents of XML documents. Now it's time to put this knowledge into practice to create a complete XML document.

The following listing (provided as the address.xml file with this chapter's resources) shows a simple XML document based on the address book example introduced earlier in the chapter. I'll use this example throughout the rest of the chapter.

```
<?xml version="1.0" encoding="UTF-8"?>
<phoneBook>
  <contact id="1">
    <name>Sas Jacobs</name>
    <address>123 Red Street, Redland, Australia</address>
    <phone>123 456</phone>
  </contact>
```

```
      <contact id="2">
        <name>John Smith</name>
        <address>4 Green Street, Lost City, Greenland</address>
        <phone>456 789</phone>
      </contact>
    </phoneBook>
```

The first line declares the document as an XML document with UTF-8 encoding. The declaration is not required, but it's good practice to include it on the first line. A software package that opens the file will immediately identify it as an XML document.

The remaining lines of the XML document contain elements. The first element <phoneBook>, the document root, contains the other elements <contact>, <name>, <address>, and <phone>. There is a hierarchical relationship between these elements.

There are two <contact> elements. They share the same *parent* <phoneBook> and are *child nodes* of that element. They are also *siblings* to each other. The document uniquely identifies each <contact> element using an id attribute.

The <contact> element contains the <name>, <address>, and <phone> elements, and they are *child elements* of the <contact> tag. The <name>, <address>, and <phone> elements are *grandchildren* of the <phoneBook> element.

The last line of the document is a closing </phoneBook> tag, written with exactly the same capitalization as the first tag.

In this document tree, the trunk of the tree is the <phoneBook> tag. Branching out from that element are the <contact> elements. Each <contact> element has <name>, <address>, and <phone> branches.

Figure 1-1 shows the relationships between the elements in the phone book XML document.

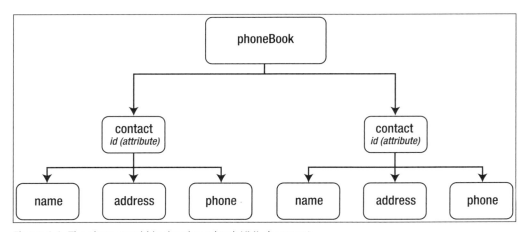

Figure 1-1. The elements within the phone book XML document

In this example, I've created my own element names. These names are descriptive, so it's easy to figure out what I'm describing. If I want to share the rules for my phone book XML document with other people, I can create a DTD or XML schema to describe how to use the elements.

I can view this, or any other XML document, by opening it in a web browser, as browsers contain XML processors. Figure 1-2 shows the address.xml file displayed in Mozilla Firefox.

Figure 1-2. An XML document opened in Firefox

You can see that Firefox adds coloring to make the document tree easier to read. Most recent web browsers do this. Firefox also adds minus signs so that you can collapse sections of the document.

Throughout this chapter, I've referred to the rules for creating XML documents. These rules ensure that you'll create documents that are well-formed.

Understanding well-formed documents

Correctly constructed XML documents are said to be *well-formed*. The W3C created this term to provide rules that people and software packages must follow when constructing XML documents, and it has a specific technical meaning.

Well-formed documents meet the following criteria:

- The document contains one or more elements.
- The document contains exactly one root element, which may contain other nested elements.
- Elements nest correctly within each another.

- Each element closes properly.
- Opening and closing tags have matching case.
- Attribute values are contained in quotes.

Let's look at each of these rules in a little more detail.

Element structure

An XML document must have at least one element: the document root. It doesn't need to have any other content, although it usually will.

The following XML document is well-formed, and it contains the single element <phoneBook>:

```
<?xml version="1.0"?>
<phoneBook/>
```

Of course, this document doesn't contain any information, so it's not likely to be very useful.

It's more likely that you'll create an XML document where the root element contains other elements. The following listing shows an example of this structure:

```
<?xml version="1.0"?>
<phoneBook>
  <contact id="1">
    <name>Sas Jacobs</name>
    <address>123 Red Street, Redland, Australia</address>
    <phone>123 456</phone>
  </contact>
</phoneBook>
```

This XML document contains a single <contact> element with other child elements. As long as all of the elements appear inside a single root element, the document is well-formed.

Element nesting

Well-formed documents close elements in the correct order. In other words, child elements must close before their parent elements, and nested elements must close in the reverse order of their opening.

The following line is incorrect:

```
<contact><name>Sas Jacobs</contact></name>
```

The <contact> element opened first, so it should close last, as follows:

```
<contact><name>Sas Jacobs</name></contact>
```

Element closing

A well-formed document closes all elements correctly. In the case of a nonempty element, the element closes with an ending tag, which must appear after the opening tag and the element content.

```
<name>Sas Jacobs</name>
```

A forward slash character (/) appears at the beginning of the closing tag.

You can close empty elements by adding a forward slash to the opening tag, as follows:

```
<name/>
```

XHTML elements such as `<br/>` and `<img/>` provide a good illustration of this rule.

You can also write empty elements with a closing tag immediately after the opening tag, as shown here:

```
<name></name>
```

This example is equivalent to the preceding one.

Element opening and closing tags

As XML is case-sensitive, opening and closing tag names must match their case exactly. The following examples are incorrect:

```
<name>Sas Jacobs</Name>
<Name>Sas Jacobs</name>
```

The correct form is like this:

```
<name>Sas Jacobs</name>
```

or like this:

```
<Name>Sas Jacobs</Name>
```

Quotes for attributes

All attribute values must appear inside either double or single quotes, as follows:

```
<contact id="1">
<contact id='1'>
```

If your attribute value contains a single quote, you'll need to use double quotes, and vice versa. Use a form like this:

```
<contact name="O'Malley"/>
```

or like this:

```
<contact nickname='John "Bo bo" Smith'/>
```

You could also replace the quote characters inside an attribute value with character entities, as follows:

```
<contact name="O&apos;Malley"/>
contact nickname='John &quot;Bo bo&quot; Smith'/>
```

See the earlier section on "Entities" for more information about which character entities you can use in an XML document.

Documents that aren't well-formed

If you try to work with an XML document that is not well-formed, the XML processor will not be able to parse the document and will generate an error. For example, opening a document that isn't well-formed in a web browser causes the error shown in Figure 1-3.

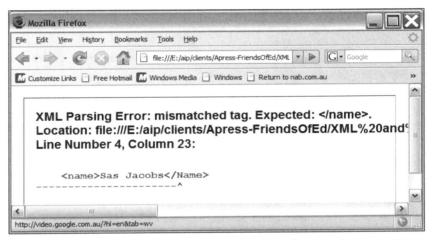

Figure 1-3. Firefox displays an error when you try to open a document that isn't well-formed.

In this case, the error message shows that the closing element name `</name>` was expected.

You can test this with the file `address_not_well_formed.xml`, included with this chapter's resources. Try opening it in a web browser to see the error.

You'll also see an error if you try to work with a document that isn't well-formed in a Flash or Flex application.

As long as you follow the rules outlined in this section when creating XML content, you'll generate well-formed XML documents.

> The term well-formed *doesn't have the same meaning as the term* valid *when applied to an XML document. A well-formed document follows the rules outlined in this section. A valid document is one that is constructed correctly according to the rules contained within an XML schema or DTD. It is possible for a document to be both well-formed and invalid.*

XML, HTML, and XHTML

The terms XML, HTML, and XHTML sound similar, but they're really quite different. XML and HTML are not competing languages. They complement each other as technologies for managing and displaying online information. XML doesn't aim to replace HTML as the language for web pages. XHTML is a hybrid of the two languages, with more robust construction rules than HTML.

Understanding HTML

HTML was designed as a tool for sharing information online in web pages. It defines a set of tags that describe structure and web site content. HTML has been around for a long time. When it was first created, HTML didn't have very robust construction rules. In fact, the rules for working with HTML are a little inconsistent. Some tags, such as `<font></font>`, must be closed; others, like `<br>` and `<p>`, do not need to be closed.

Because of these inconsistencies, it is possible to include major errors in an HTML document and still have the page display correctly in a web browser. For example, in many browsers, you can include two `<title>` tags, and the page will still load. You can also forget to include a closing `</table>` tag, and the table will still be rendered in many browsers.

The HTML language includes formatting instructions along with the information. There is no separation of the presentation from the structure and content in a document.

HTML is supposed to be a standard, but in the past, it often worked differently across web browsers. Most web developers knew about the problem, and they created different web sites so that they appeared the same way in Internet Explorer, Opera, Firefox, and Netscape for both PCs and Macs.

Like XML, HTML comes from SGML. Unlike XML, HTML is not extensible. You're stuck with a standard set of tags that you can't change or extend in any way.

How is XML different from HTML?

Unlike HTML, XML deals only with content. XML describes the structure of information, without concerning itself with the appearance of that information.

Using XML, you can create any element to describe the structure of your data. An XML document can show relationships in your data, just as a database can. This just isn't possible in an HTML document, as the HTML tags don't imply any data relationships. They simply deal with structure and formatting.

XML documents don't deal with the display of information. If you need to change the way an XML document appears, you can change the appearance by using CSS or Extensible Stylesheet Language (XSL). XSL transformations can also reorganize, sort, or filter XML content. You can even use them to create XHTML from an XML document, or to sort or filter a list of XML elements.

XML content is probably easier to understand than HTML content. The names of tags normally describe the data they mark up. In the sample `address.xml` file, tag names such as `<address>` and `<phone>` describe exactly what data each element contains.

You can use an XML structure to display information directly in a web page. However, it's more likely that you'll use the XML document behind the scenes as a data source. It can provide the content for a web application or a SWF movie.

Compared with HTML, XML is much stricter when it comes to constructing markup. There are rules about how to write tags, and you've seen that all XML documents must be well-formed before they can be processed.

A DTD or XML schema can also provide extra rules for the way that elements are used. These documents determine whether XML content is valid according to the rules of the vocabulary. The rules for construction can include the legal names for tags and attributes, whether they're required or optional, as well as the number of times that each element must appear. In addition, schemas specify what data type must be used for each element and attribute.

Where does XHTML fit in?

XHTML evolved so that the useful features of XML could be applied to HTML. The XHTML specification became a recommendation in 2000 and was revised in 2002 (see http://www.w3.org/TR/xhtml1/).

The W3C says that XML *reformulated* HTML into XHTML. XHTML documents have much stricter construction rules and are generally more robust than their HTML counterparts.

The HTML specification provides a list of legal elements and attributes within XHTML. XML governs the way that the elements are used in documents. Together, they merge to form XHTML. One example of this merging is that the HTML <br> tag must be rewritten as <br/> or
</br>. In XHTML, web designers can't use a single <p> tag to create a paragraph break, as is permissible in HTML.

Another difference between HTML and XHTML is that you must write attribute values in full. For example, the following HTML is acceptable:

```
<input type="radio" value="JJJ" checked>
```

In XHTML, this must be written as follows:

```
<input type="radio" value="JJJ" checked="checked"/>
```

The following list summarizes the main changes from HTML to XHTML:

- You should include a DOCTYPE declaration specifying that the document is an XHTML document.
- You can optionally include an XML declaration.
- You should include a namespace declaration in the opening <html> element.
- You must write all tags in lowercase.
- All elements must be closed.
- All attributes must be enclosed in quotation marks.
- All tags must be correctly nested.
- The id attribute should be used instead of name.
- Attributes can't be minimized.

It's no accident that some of these changes are the same as the rules for well-formed XML documents.

The following listing shows the sample address.xml document rewritten as an XHTML document:

```
<?xml version="1.0"?>
<!DOCTYPE html PUBLIC "-//W3C//DTD XHTML 1.0 Transitional//EN"
"http://www.w3.org/TR/xhtml1/DTD/xhtml1-transitional.dtd">
<html xmlns="http://www.w3.org/1999/xhtml">
<head>
  <title></title>
</head>
<body>
  <table>
  <tr>
    <td>Sas Jacobs</td>
    <td>123 Red Street, Redland, Australia</td>
    <td>123 456</td>
  </tr>
  <tr>
    <td>John Smith</td>
    <td>4 Green Street, Lost City, Greenland</td>
    <td>456 789</td>
  </tr>
  </table>
</body>
</html>
```

Notice that the file includes both an XML declaration and a DOCTYPE declaration, as well as a namespace in the <html> element. You can see the content in the address.htm file included with this chapter's resources.

You're probably used to seeing information like this in web pages. A table displays the content and lists each contact in a separate row. Figure 1-4 shows how this document appears in Firefox.

Figure 1-4. An XHTML file displayed in Firefox

I've rewritten the content in XHTML so it conforms to the stricter rules for XML documents. However, the way the document is constructed may still cause some problems. Each piece of information about my contacts is stored in a separate cell within a table. The <td> tags don't give me any clue about what the cell contains. I get a better idea when I open the page in a web browser.

Because this web page is essentially an XML document, I could use it as a data source for a Flash or Flex project. However, in this example, the addresses appear inside generic <td> tags that indicate the document structure. The tags don't specifically label each piece of data and indicate their relationships. I can't easily identify which column contains the names and which contains the phone numbers. The XHTML document doesn't inexorably link the name information with the first column of the table. If I used Flash or Flex to extract the content, I would experience difficulties if the order of the columns changed.

XHTML controls the way the information is structured on the page. I can make some minor visual adjustments to the table using stylesheets, but I can't completely transform the display. For example, I can't remove the table and create a vertical listing of all entries without completely rewriting the XHTML source.

Each time I print the document, it will look the same. I can't exclude information such as the address column from my printout. I don't have any way to filter or sort the information. I am not able to extract a list of contacts in a specific area or sort into contact name order.

Compare this case with storing the information in an XML document. I can create my own tag names and write a schema that describes how to use these tags. When I view the document in a web browser, the tag names make it very clear what information they're storing. I can apply an XSL transformation to change the appearance of the document or to sort or filter the contents. I can display the document as a table or as a bulleted list. I can sort the items into name order or by phone number. I can even filter the contents so that only a subset of contacts appears.

XML isn't a replacement for XHTML documents, but it certainly provides much more flexibility for working with data. You're likely to use XML documents differently from how you use XHTML documents. XML documents are a way to store structured data that may or may not end up in a web page. You normally use XHTML only to display content in a web browser.

Understanding related recommendations

As you saw earlier in the chapter, XML works with other recommendations from the W3C that provide additional functionality. Although there are many other recommendations, two areas are of particular importance: DTDs/XML schemas and XSLT. Let's take a brief look at both, starting with DTDs and XML schemas.

Understanding DTDs and XML schemas

DTDs and schemas perform the same role: they describe the rules for a vocabulary of XML. They provide information about the element names, their attributes, how many times they can appear and in what order, and what type of data they must contain.

> In addition to the two approaches discussed here, there are other ways to describe valid XML documents. You can use alternative schema languages, such as Relax NG and Schematron. However, these approaches are not recommendations from the W3C.

If you have either a DTD or an XML schema, you're able to determine whether an XML document is valid according to its construction rules. This process is called *validation* and is usually carried out automatically by a software package.

An XML schema, sometimes called an XML Schema Definition (XSD) file, uses an XML format to describe these rules. The W3C created this vocabulary of XML.

A DTD is an older method and uses a different method for writing validity rules. HTML and XHTML files include a DTD declaration at the top of the file to indicate which version of the language they use. This declaration allows a validator to determine whether the web page is valid.

The following code listing shows a simple XML schema that describes the rules for the XML vocabulary used in the address.xml file. You can find this file saved as addressSchema.xsd with the chapter resources.

```
<?xml version="1.0"?>
<xsd:schema xmlns:xsd="http://www.w3.org/2001/XMLSchema">
  <xsd:element name="phoneBook">
    <xsd:complexType>
      <xsd:sequence>
        <xsd:element ref="contact" maxOccurs="unbounded"/>
      </xsd:sequence>
    </xsd:complexType>
  </xsd:element>
  <xsd:element name="contact">
    <xsd:complexType>
      <xsd:sequence>
        <xsd:element name="name" type="xsd:string"/>
        <xsd:element name="address" type="xsd:string"/>
        <xsd:element name="phone" type="xsd:string"/>
      </xsd:sequence>
      <xsd:attribute name="id" type="xsd:integer" use="required"/>
    </xsd:complexType>
  </xsd:element>
</xsd:schema>
```

It's easy to understand the rules for this language from this schema document. To start with, the schema uses an XML structure and is a well-formed document.

The schema describes a <phoneBook> element that is a complexType element, meaning that it contains other elements. The attribute value unbounded means that it can contain any number of <contact> elements.

The `<contact>` element contains three other elements—`<name>`, `<address>`, and `<phone>`—each of which dictates that the contents of the element should be a string. The `<contact>` element also has a required attribute called `id`.

Of course, there is more to the language than this simple file, but it gives you a starting point for understanding XML schemas.

Understanding XSL

Another important recommendation from the W3C is that for XSL. This recommendation covers two areas: XSLT stylesheets and XSL-FO. An XSLT stylesheet transforms one XML document—the source document—into a second type of document, called the transformed document. You might use an XSLT stylesheet, for example, to convert an XML document into an XHTML document for display in a web browser. XSL-FO stylesheets specify output for an XML document and might be used, for example, to output the content as a styled PDF file.

An understanding of XSLT is important because it allows XML documents to be rewritten for different purposes. It could allow XML content from one database to be transformed to a different structure, suitable for import into another software package.

XSLT transformations take place because of the rules written into an XSLT stylesheet. Unlike CSS, an XSLT stylesheet doesn't deal with the formatting of content. Rather, it can change element names and structures, perform simple calculations, and even sort and filter the content in the source document.

The following code listing shows an XSLT stylesheet that transforms the `address.xml` file into an XHTML page, displaying the contacts in an unordered list. You can find the XSLT stylesheet saved as `listStyle.xsl` with the other chapter resources.

```
<?xml version="1.0"?>
<xsl:stylesheet version="1.0"
  xmlns:xsl="http://www.w3.org/1999/XSL/Transform">
<xsl:template match="/">
  <html>
  <body>
  <h1>Phone Book</h1>
  <ul>
  <xsl:for-each select="/phoneBook/contact">
    <li><xsl:value-of select="name" /></li>
  </xsl:for-each>
  </ul>
  </body>
  </html>
</xsl:template>
</xsl:stylesheet>
```

This stylesheet creates some simple HTML code and creates one `<li>` element for each `<name>` element in the source XML document. Again, there's a lot more to this recommendation than this simple example shows, but it does give you an idea of how XSL works.

Summary

In this chapter, you learned about XML and the contents of XML documents. You also learned about the differences between XML, HTML, and XHTML. You should now understand the advantages of working with XML as a data source for your SWF applications.

The importance of XML cannot be overstated. It allows organizations and individuals to create their own mechanisms for sharing information. At its most simple, XML provides a structured, text-based alternative to a database. More complex uses of XML might involve data interactions between corporate systems and outside consumers of information. The most important thing to remember is that an XML document can provide a data source for many different applications.

The widespread adoption of XML by major software companies such as Microsoft and Adobe ensure its future. Most of the popular database packages provide XML support. If it's not already there, you can expect XML to be part of most software packages in the near future.

In the next chapter, we'll look at some of the different ways to generate XML content for use in Flash and Flex applications. You'll see the role of server-side languages like PHP, ASP .NET, and ColdFusion in creating content from databases. I'll also demonstrate how you can create XML content from Office 2007 software packages.

Chapter 2

GENERATING XML CONTENT

Before you can start working with XML content in Flash and Flex applications, you'll need to create the XML documents that you want to use. These can be stand-alone physical XML files or content from a database. Remember that an XML document may simply be a stream of information generated electronically.

The easiest way to create XML content is to save a text file with an .xml extension. You can also use a web server to create either a physical XML document or a stream of XML information from a database. You can even generate the content from existing data in another software package such as Microsoft Office.

In this chapter, I'll cover all of these possibilities. I'll show you how to write your own XML content by hand and demonstrate the use of an XML editor. I'll also explain how to automate the process of creating XML documents by using a web server, some server-side processing, and a database. We'll do this with ASP .NET, PHP, and ColdFusion. I'll finish by giving you an overview of generating content from Microsoft Office 2007.

Each of the XML documents that you create for your SWF applications is likely to have unique content and to use a different structure. These documents may use an existing vocabulary of XML, or you may decide on your own tag names. The only thing that your XML documents will have in common is the rules that you use to create them. At the very minimum, all XML documents must be well-formed, a concept covered in the first chapter of this book.

You can download the resources used for this chapter from http://www.friendsofed.com.

We'll start by looking at how you can use a text editor to create physical XML files.

Authoring XML documents in a text editor

There are many different approaches that you can use to author physical XML files. For example, you can use a text editor like Notepad or SimpleText. You can also use an HTML editor like Adobe HomeSite or an XML editor such as Stylus Studio 2008 XML. You can even work with a web design tool like Dreamweaver.

We'll start with a look at how you might use a text editor to write a physical XML document.

Using text and HTML editors

You can use a text editor to create a physical XML file by writing every line in the software package using your keyboard. Text editors provide no automation, so this process could take a long time if you're working with a large document.

If you're working with an existing XML vocabulary, you'll need to be familiar with the language-construction rules so that you use the proper element names in the correct way. As you learned in Chapter 1, an XML schema or a DTD describes these rules, and the process of checking is called *validation*.

If you are creating your own XML elements to describe the data, you can just type the tag names and structures as you need them. You'll need to keep track of the structure and element names yourself. When you've finished entering the content, you can then save the file with the extension .xml.

Text editors are easy to use and either free or very cheap. Their main problem is that they don't offer any special functionality for XML content. Text editors don't help you identify documents that are not well-formed. They don't provide error messages if tag names don't match, if you've mixed up the cases of your element names, or if you've nested elements incorrectly. Many text editors don't automatically add code-coloring to the elements in your document so you can visually check your markup.

In addition, text editors don't include XML-specific tools. So, if you're using an existing XML vocabulary, you can't automatically check your XML document against a DTD or XML schema to make sure that it is valid according to the rules of that vocabulary. A text editor can't apply an XSLT stylesheet transformation to change the output of an XML document. In fact, you may not find any errors in your XML documents until you first try to work with the document in another application, and that's usually too late!

Flex Builder is an example of a text editor that allows you to work with XML files. You can use it to create and edit an XML document. However, unlike when you're working with MXML documents, Flex Builder doesn't add coloring of tags in standard XML documents. Also, it also doesn't include XML-specific tools other than those specifically designed for working with MXML.

As an alternative, you can use an HTML editor like Adobe HomeSite (http://www.adobe.com/products/homesite/) or AceHTML (http://software.visicommedia.com/en/products/acehtmlfreeware/) to create XML documents. One advantage of these software packages over text editors is that they can automate the process a little. They add coloring to opening and closing tags to make it easier to read your content. Some also add the XML declaration automatically. HTML editors often come with extensions for working specifically with XML documents. These might add the correct declarations to the file and auto-complete your tag names. As with a text editor, you'll still need to type in most of your content line by line. Most HTML editors don't include tools to validate content and to apply transformations. You can expect that functionality only from an XML editor.

Using XML editors

An XML editor is a software program designed to work specifically with XML documents. You normally use an XML editor to enter your XML content manually, similar to the way that you use a text or HTML editor. Most XML editors include tools that auto-complete tags, check for well-formedness, validate XML documents, and apply XSLT transformations. In addition to creating XML documents, you can use XML editors to create XSLT stylesheets, DTDs, and XML schemas. You're not limited to working with only XML-structured content. It isn't mandatory to use an XML editor when creating XML documents, but it's likely to save you time, especially if you work with long documents.

XML editors include both free and "for purchase" software packages. If you plan on spending time creating physical XML documents by hand, I recommend that you invest the time to learn more about an XML editor.

Common XML editors include the following:

- Stylus Studio 2008 XML (http://www.stylusstudio.com/)
- Altova XMLSpy 2008 (http://www.altova.com/products/xmlspy/xml_editor.html)
- XMLBlueprint XML Editor (http://www.xmlblueprint.com/)
- <oXygen/> (http://www.oxygenxml.com/)
- Microsoft XML Notepad (http://www.codeplex.com/xmlnotepad)
- XMLEditPro (freeware) (http://www.daveswebsite.com/software/xmleditpro.2.0/)
- XMLFox (freeware) (http://www.xmlfox.com/)

To give you an idea of the advantages of using an XML editor, I'll show you how Stylus Studio 2008 XML works.

Using Stylus Studio 2008 XML

Stylus Studio 2008 XML is a full-featured XML editor that you can try before buying. It allows you to create and edit XML, XSLT, and XML schema documents. It can check that a document is well-formed, validate an XML document against an XML schema or DTD, and apply an XSLT transformation.

In this section, we'll look at some of the features of Stylus Studio 2008 XML as an illustration of what's possible with an XML editor. If you want to follow along, download it and install it on your computer. It's a PC-based tool, and your PC will need to have the Java Virtual Machine installed. You can download a seven-day trial version of the software. Those of you working on a Macintosh will need to get hold of a PC if you want to try out the features shown here.

Figure 2-1 shows the Stylus Studio 2008 XML window. If you've worked with Flex Builder, you'll find parts of the layout familiar. On the left side of the window, you can see a list of all projects. Projects allow you to work with a set of related files, and they are really an organizational tool. Stylus Studio 2008 XML includes an Examples project containing many different types of sample documents.

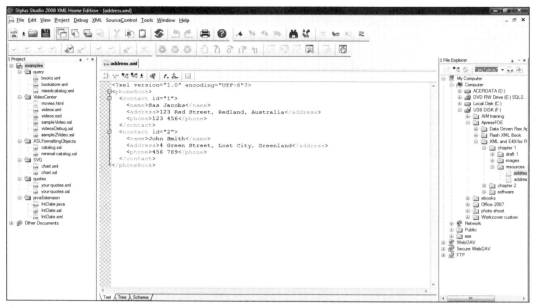

Figure 2-1. The Stylus Studio 2008 XML window

The right side of the window contains the File Explorer, which allows you to locate files on your computer or by FTP. You can drag files from the File Explorer on the right to a project on the left side of the window, or you can double-click to open a file that isn't part of a project.

The middle of the screen contains any documents that are open. In Figure 2-1, you can see the address.xml file. We used this file in Chapter 1, and you can find it with the Chapter 2 resource files. Notice that Stylus Studio 2008 XML automatically adds coloring to the content to make it easier to view the elements and attributes in the document. You can collapse and expand elements by clicking the minus and plus signs to the left of the document.

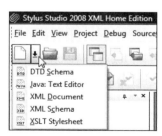

Figure 2-2. Options available when creating a new document with Stylus Studio 2008 XML

When you create a new document, Stylus Studio 2008 XML allows you to choose from a range of different document types. You can create a standard XML document, an XML schema or DTD, or even a stylesheet, as shown in Figure 2-2.

If you choose to create a standard XML document containing data, the software automatically adds the following XML declaration at the top of the file:

```
<?xml version="1.0"?>
```

You can assign an XML schema, DTD, or XSLT stylesheet to the document through the XML menu. Stylus Studio 2008 XML will then add the relevant directives to the file.

You can use Stylus Studio 2008 XML like a text editor in Text view, which you can see in Figure 2-1. In Tree view, it shows the document structures graphically. You can see the address.xml file displayed in Tree view in Figure 2-3. Notice that I've expanded all of the elements in the file.

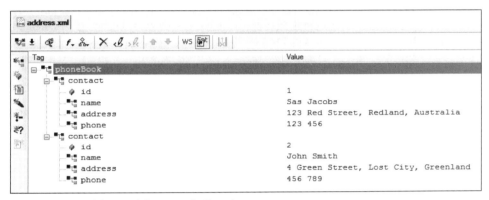

Figure 2-3. The address.xml document in Tree view

Tree view removes the markup from the document and displays the content in a hierarchy of tags, showing the values on the right of the screen. This layout makes it easy to determine the document structure. You can collapse and expand each area with the plus and minus signs to the left.

If you open an XML document that has an associated XML schema or DTD, you'll be able to see the details in Schema view. I've done this with the document addressSchema.xml, as shown in Figure 2-4. This file contains the same markup as in the address.xml file but includes a reference to the addressSchema.xsd file. You can find both files with your resources for this chapter.

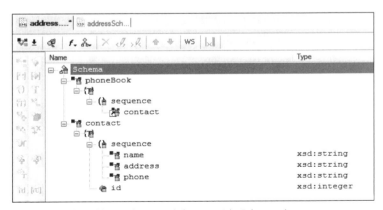

Figure 2-4. The addressSchema.xml document in Schema view

In Figure 2-4, you can see the details of the associated XML schema in Schema view. The figure shows the details of the <phoneBook> and <contact> complex elements, as well as the simple elements <name>, <address>, and <phone>. You can see the data types of the simple elements listed on the right side of the view.

If you open an XML schema document in Stylus Studio 2008 XML, you'll be able to view more detailed information about the schema. The software generates a diagram of the element structure and element properties. Figure 2-5 shows the file addressSchema.xsd in Stylus Studio 2008 XML. You can see that I've selected the <name> element from the schema. The diagram highlights this element and displays the properties for the element at the bottom left of the window. The Properties area shows the type of element selected, as well as details about how many times the element occurs and if it is nullable. In this case, we are viewing a string element that can occur exactly once and cannot have a null value.

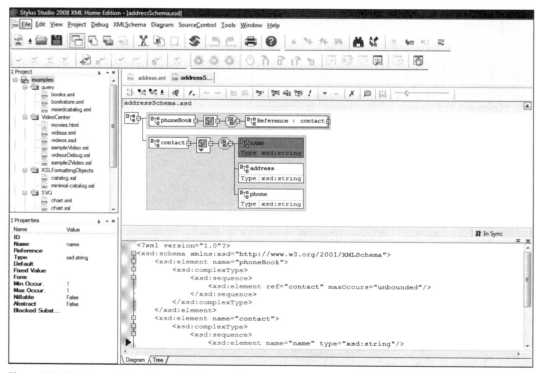

Figure 2-5. Viewing an XML schema in Stylus Studio 2008 XML

Another useful feature in most XML editors is auto-completion of tags. As you enter elements in an XML document, you'll notice that Stylus Studio 2008 XML completes the closing tags for you. After you type the characters </, the software inserts the correct closing tag. Not only does this save you some typing, but it also ensures that the file is well-formed.

Stylus Studio 2008 XML also helps with tag hints as you make modifications to the document content, as shown in Figure 2-6.

Other important features of a good XML editor are these abilities:

- Checking that a file is well-formed
- Validating an XML document against a schema or DTD
- Transforming an XML document using an XSLT stylesheet

Stylus Studio 2008 XML offers all of these features when you work with an XML document.

In Text view, you can check and validate an XML document using buttons in the toolbar that appears above the document. This toolbar contains two buttons: one with a yellow check, which will review the XML for well-formedness, and a second button with a green check, which will validate the document against its XML schema or DTD. You can also access these options from the XML menu at the top of the screen.

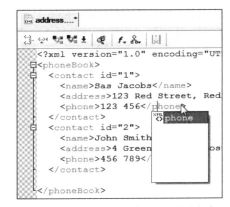

Figure 2-6. Stylus Studio 2008 XML helps out with tag suggestions as you edit an XMIL document.

You can check that a document is well-formed by clicking the button with the yellow check, or by choosing XML ➤ Check well-formed. If your document is not well-formed, you'll see an error message that will help to pinpoint the problem. Figure 2-7 shows an error where the XML document is missing the matching closing </phone> tag from the first <contact> element. You can see the error highlighted at the bottom of the window. In addition to the error message, Stylus Studio 2008 XML adds a pointer to the line containing the error.

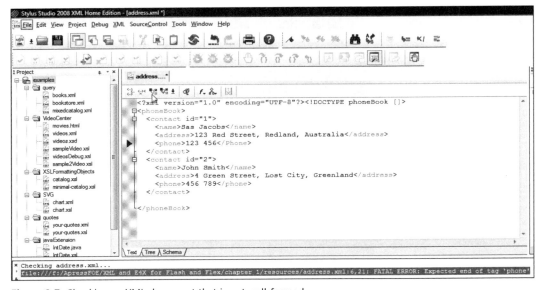

Figure 2-7. Checking an XML document that is not well-formed

39

If you want to see this feature in action for yourself, open the address.xml file in Stylus Studio 2008 XML and change it to introduce a deliberate mistake. You could change the case of one of the closing tags, or you might remove the quotation marks from an attribute. When you check the file for well-formedness, you'll see an error message.

Stylus Studio 2008 XML can also check that an XML document is valid against its DTD or XML schema. If you're checking against a schema, you'll need to associate the document with the schema first by choosing XML ➤ Associate XML with Schema. Once you've created the association, you can test for validity by clicking the button containing the green check on the center window toolbar or by choosing XML ➤ Validate Document.

If the XML document is valid according to the XML schema, Stylus Studio 2008 XML will report this with the message The XML document address.xml is valid in the output section at the bottom of the window. If the document is not valid, you'll see an error message relating to the invalid content. I haven't provided an example here, but you might want to try out validity checking with the addressSchema.xml file. Try adding extra elements out of sequence or deleting one of the required elements.

Finally, if you're going to transform your XML document with an XSLT stylesheet, you can use Stylus Studio 2008 XML to create the stylesheet as well as to preview the transformation before it is applied. You can associate an XML document with a stylesheet by choosing XML ➤ Associate XML With XSLT Stylesheet. This action will add a stylesheet reference at the top of the XML document. You can see an example saved in the resource file addressStylesheet.xml. This XML document references the XSLT stylesheet listStyle.xsl, which is also included with the chapter resources. The transformation in the file displays the contents as an XHTML list. Once you've added a stylesheet reference to your XML document, choose XML ➤ Preview in Internet Explorer. Stylus Studio 2008 XML will apply the transformation and provide a preview of the transformed output. You can see the transformation provided by listStyle.xsl in Figure 2-8.

Figure 2-8. Previewing a transformed XML document

The transformed content appears at the bottom left of the window. You can see the names of the contacts displayed in an unordered XHTML list.

The preceding examples demonstrate some of the ways that an XML editor can help you to work with XML documents. A full-featured product like Stylus Studio 2008 XML can save you time by checking, validating, and transforming your documents with the click of a button.

If you don't want to take the time to learn another software package and you already own Dreamweaver, you might be surprised to know that it contains many of the XML editor features that you've just seen.

Working with Dreamweaver

You can also use a package like Adobe Dreamweaver as an XML editor. When you first install Dreamweaver, it offers itself as the default editor for XML and XSLT files. If you open one of these file types in Dreamweaver, it will automatically appear in Code view. Dreamweaver will add tag coloring to make it easier to work with the file.

Figure 2-9 shows how the address.xml resource file appears when opened in Dreamweaver. The Code view provides the same coloring functionality as other HTML and XML editors. It also shows line numbers to the left of the window.

Figure 2-9. Viewing an XML document in Dreamweaver

As with other types of Dreamweaver files, you can preview an open XML file in a web browser. If you have added a reference to an XSLT stylesheet, previewing in a browser will apply a transformation to the XML document. You can see the effect in Figure 2-10 as Dreamweaver previews the address.xml file in Firefox. This XML document doesn't have an associated XSLT stylesheet.

You can also validate an XML document in Dreamweaver using the command File ➤ Validate ➤ As XML. If you don't have a referenced schema, Dreamweaver will check that the file is well-formed instead. If the file contains errors, Dreamweaver will report them, as shown in Figure 2-11. This example shows the output where the addressSchema.xml file contains more than one <phone> element. I've highlighted the error in the screenshot. If you own Dreamweaver, you might want to try this for yourself.

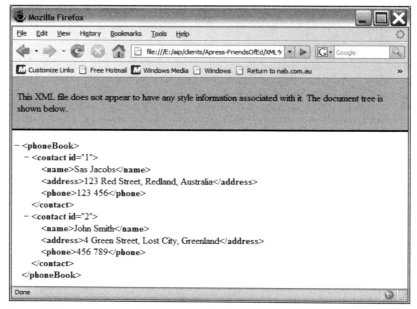

Figure 2-10. Previewing the XML document in Firefox using Dreamweaver

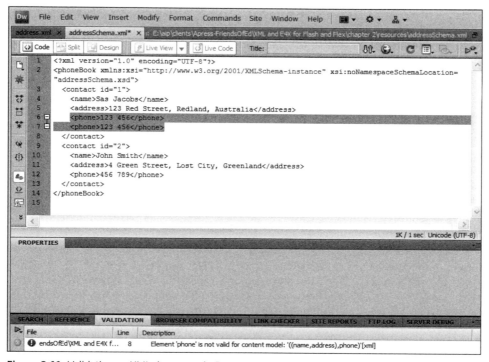

Figure 2-11. Validating an XML document in Dreamweaver

If you already use Dreamweaver for your web development work, this software package might be a good alternative to an XML editor when it comes to working with XML. You won't need to spend extra time or money on a new software package.

Instead of creating an XML document by hand in an XML editor, you might want to use a more automated approach and generate content from a database.

Generating XML content from a database

Databases are similar to XML documents in that they store structured information. This makes a database an ideal source for generating XML content. While it's possible to query a database and return records in other ways, generating content in XML format allows you to preserve the hierarchical structure and relationships in the document.

Using XML as an intermediary is a good idea because of its flexibility. You can generate either physical files or information streams, both in XML format. This means that it is easy to repurpose the database content to suit different situations.

Working directly with records from a database means that you need to remain connected to the database to access the content. Saving the records in a physical XML document allows you to use the records while you are disconnected, perhaps on a handheld device or within a SWF movie running from a CD or DVD. You can use the same content to populate a web application using an XML information stream from the database.

So how do you go about creating an XML document from a database?

Using a web server to generate XML content

You need to use a web server and some server-side code in order to convert records from a database into XML format. You'll need to write web pages that convert to XML format using a server-side language like ASP .NET, PHP, or ColdFusion. The server-side file will query the database, receive the records, and generate the XML structure. It will either return a stream of XML-formatted information or save a physical XML document.

To use this approach, you'll need to have a web server capable of processing the server-side language. This might be Internet Information Server (IIS), Apache, or ColdFusion. You'll also need to use a database like Access, MySQL, SQL Server, or Oracle to store the information.

In the following sections, I'll show how you can generate XML content from a database using ASP .NET, PHP, and ColdFusion. We'll generate an XML stream similar in structure to the resource file address. xml from a database. My intention is to provide a walk-through, rather than a complete tutorial. The aim here is not to make you an expert in each server-side language, but rather to give you a brief introduction to show you how to generate XML in this manner. If you need to carry out this task on a regular basis, you might want to further develop your skills in this area.

You can use any database to provide the content. To make the example simpler, I'll use an Access database for all three examples. It contains a single table called phoneBook, made up of ID, contactname, address, and phone fields. This database is saved as addresses.mdb with your resources for this chapter.

43

> *Some of the examples ahead contain concepts that are quite challenging for begin-ners. If the examples are more than you need at this stage, feel free to skip ahead to a later section.*

We'll start by looking at generating an XML information stream with an ASP .NET page written in VB .NET.

Working with VB .NET

In this example, we'll use a VB .NET page to generate an XML stream from the database. I'm going to show you the declarative code for the page, but bear in mind that I've used a code-behind page to keep my VB code separate from the interface. You can find the pages getAddresses.aspx and getAddresses.aspx.vb with the other resource files for this chapter. The getAddresses.aspx.vb page contains all of the code.

Before we get into the details of the code, if you're going to work through this example, you'll need to compile the application so that the page will work correctly. You can do this in Visual Studio using the command Build ➤ Build Solution or by publishing the web project with Build ➤ Publish [Project Name]. You choose the second option once you've finalized the files and are ready to copy them to their final location.

The getAddresses.aspx page works with the getAddresses.aspx.vb page to generate an XML docu-ment from the content in the Access database. The ASP .NET page consists of only a page declaration, as the content is generated by the code-behind page. There are no other elements, as you don't need to generate XHTML content to display in a web browser.

The page declaration for the getAddresses.aspx file appears here:

```
<%@ Page Language="VB" AutoEventWireup="false"
  CodeFile="getAddresses.aspx.vb" Inherits="getAddresses"%>
```

The getAddresses.aspx.vb page generates an XML stream containing the details of each contact in the address book. Because the focus of this book is on Flash, Flex, and XML, I'll show this entire code-behind page and explain it afterward, rather than stepping through how to create it from scratch. The following shows the content of the getAddresses.aspx.vb file:

```
Imports System.IO
Imports System.Xml
Imports System.Data
Imports System.Data.OleDb

Partial Class getAddresses
  Inherits System.Web.UI.Page
  Protected Sub Page_Load(ByVal sender As Object,
      ➡ByVal e As System.EventArgs) Handles Me.Load
    Dim dbConnString As String = ConfigurationManager.
      ➡ConnectionStrings("addresses").ConnectionString
    Dim dbConn As New OleDbConnection(dbConnString)
    Dim objCommand As OleDbCommand
```

```
            Dim objDataReader As OleDbDataReader
            Dim strSQL As String
            Dim addressesXMLDoc As XmlTextWriter =
              ➥New XmlTextWriter(Response.OutputStream, Encoding.UTF8)
            Response.ContentType = "text/xml"
            strSQL = "SELECT * FROM phoneBook ORDER BY contactname"
            dbConn.Open()
            objCommand = New OleDbCommand(strSQL, dbConn)
            objDataReader = objCommand.ExecuteReader()
            addressesXMLDoc.Formatting = Formatting.Indented
            addressesXMLDoc.WriteStartDocument()
            addressesXMLDoc.WriteStartElement("phoneBook")
            While objDataReader.Read()
              addressesXMLDoc.WriteStartElement("contact")
              addressesXMLDoc.WriteAttributeString("id",
                ➥objDataReader("ID"))
              addressesXMLDoc.WriteStartElement("name")
              addressesXMLDoc.WriteValue(objDataReader("contactname"))
              addressesXMLDoc.WriteEndElement()
              addressesXMLDoc.WriteStartElement("address")
              addressesXMLDoc.WriteCData(objDataReader("address"))
              addressesXMLDoc.WriteEndElement()
              addressesXMLDoc.WriteStartElement("phone")
              addressesXMLDoc.WriteValue(objDataReader("phone"))
              addressesXMLDoc.WriteEndElement()
              addressesXMLDoc.WriteEndElement()
            End While
            addressesXMLDoc.WriteEndElement()
            addressesXMLDoc.Flush()
            addressesXMLDoc.Close()
            objDataReader.Close()
            dbConn.Close()
        End Sub
    End Class
```

The page starts by referencing the relevant namespaces that you'll need. The System.Xml namespace provides the XML functionality for the page and allows you to access the XML document-construction methods that you'll use.

The Page_Load event creates the XML document so that the content exists when the page finishes loading. The subroutine starts by declaring the variables needed. The first variable refers to the connection string for the Access database. The connection string is saved in the config.xml file for the application with the name addresses. If you want to create your own example, you'll need to specify a connection string in that file.

The page creates a database connection object called dbConn, which uses the addresses connection string. It also creates a variable to store the SQL statement that you'll need to extract the records from the database table, called strSQL. In this case, you're issuing a simple SELECT statement: SELECT * FROM phoneBook ORDER BY contactname. The VB .NET page will iterate through the database records using a DataReader, referenced with the object objDataReader.

The page uses an XmlTextWriter object to create and structure the XML document. It specifies that the output will be an information stream, rather than a physical file, by using Response.OutputStream, and that it will use UTF-8 encoding. The page also sets the content type of the document to text/xml so that it can generate the correct type of output.

The code sets the value of the strSQL variable and opens the database. It creates a command object to issue the SQL statement to the database, and then executes the DataReader object to access the returned content.

After the page makes the database call, it creates the XML document. It starts by setting the format of the document to indented and writes the start of the XML document using the WriteStartDocument() method of the XmlTextWriter. The page writes the root element using the following line:

```
addressesXMLDoc.WriteStartElement("phoneBook")
```

It passes the name of the element, phoneBook, to this method.

The code loops through the DataReader, creating the relevant XML nodes from the database records. The page uses the WriteStartElement(), WriteEndElement(), WriteAttributeString(), and WriteCData() methods to generate the XML content, passing the relevant element names and values.

```
addressesXMLDoc.WriteStartElement("name")
addressesXMLDoc.WriteValue(objDataReader("contactname"))
```

After looping through the returned records, the subroutine writes the closing root element and uses the Flush() method to write the content to the XmlTextWriter(). It then calls the relevant Close() methods on the DataReader and database connection.

You could add some more stringent error handling to manage the database connection and respond if no records are returned. I haven't included this type of error handling here for brevity. Feel free to alter the example if you wish.

You can view the contents of the getAddresses.aspx page by right-clicking it and choosing View in Browser. You can also press F5 to view the page if you have allowed debugging in the web.config file, or press Ctrl+F5 if you have disabled debugging.

This is an example of an XML document that doesn't exist in a physical sense. It doesn't involve saving a physical file with an .xml extension. Instead, the server-side file creates a stream of XML data that can be consumed by a SWF file. If you view the file in a web browser through the web server, you'll see that it looks like a normal XML document, as shown in Figure 2-12.

This action is possible because the page sent its content type appropriately, using the following line:

```
Response.ContentType = "text/xml"
```

If you try this example yourself, you'll need to make sure that you use a page address starting with http://localhost rather than the file path of the page. Using an address in this format will ensure that the web server processes the file contents before sending the results of the processing to the web browser.

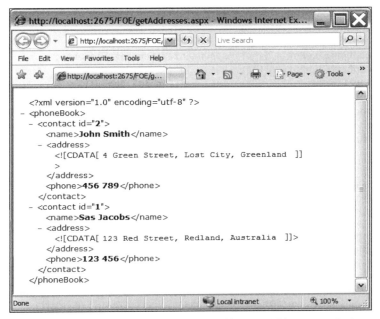

Figure 2-12. Viewing an XML stream generated by VB .NET in Internet Explorer

You can find the files discussed here with the other chapter resources.

Another popular server-side approach is the use of PHP, which we'll look at in the next section.

Working with PHP

We'll re-create the previous example using PHP to generate the XML content. Again, you would need to use this page with the appropriate database connection code, which I haven't provided. This example appears in the resource file getAddresses.php. The complete page follows, with the explanation afterwards.

```php
<?php
header('Content-Type:text/xml');
include 'dbConn.php';

$xml = new DomDocument('1.0', 'UTF-8');
$root = $xml->createElement('phoneBook');
$root = $xml->appendChild($root);
$sql = 'SELECT * FROM phoneBook ORDER BY contactname ';
$result = mysql_query($sql);
if ($result) {
  if (mysql_num_rows($result) > 0) {
    while ($row = mysql_fetch_array($result)) {
      $id = $row['ID'];
      $name = $row['contactName'];
```

```
            $address = $row['address'];
            $phone = $row['phone'];
            $contactElement = $xml->createElement('contact');
            $contactElement = $root->appendChild($contactElement);
            $contactElement->setAttribute('id',$id);
            $nameElement = $xml->createElement('name',$name);
            $nameElement = $contactElement->appendChild($nameElement);
            $addressElement = $xml->createElement('address', $address);
            $addressElement = $contactElement->appendChild($addressElement);
            $phoneElement = $xml->createElement('phone', $phone);
            $phoneElement = $contactElement->appendChild($phoneElement);
        }
    }
    echo $xml->saveXML();
    ?>
```

The first line declares the content type for the document—in this case, text/xml. I've assumed that the database connection code appears in a file called dbConn.php so the second line of the file includes that file in the code. You'll need to create this file yourself if you want to work through this example.

The next line creates a new version 1.0 DomDocument object with UTF-8 encoding. This is your XML document. The file uses the createElement() and appendChild() methods to create the structure for the start of the XML document. The createElement() method requires the name of the element as the first argument and has an optional second argument that indicates the content for the element. In this case, the line specifies that the root element is called <phoneBook> and doesn't add any content.

The page declares a variable, $sql, containing the SELECT statement to retrieve the appropriate database records. It uses the same SELECT statement as in the previous example: SELECT * FROM phoneBook ORDER BY contactname.

The page then queries the database, storing the results in $result. If the query returns records, the page loops through them, retrieving the ID, contactname, address, and phone fields, and storing them in variables. The code then creates the relevant XML elements using the createElement() method, beginning with the <contact> element. It appends each new XML element to the correct parent element after it is created. The <contact> element also has an attribute called id, added by using the setAttribute() method, and passing the name and value for the attribute.

Finally, the page finishes by writing the XML document to the screen using saveXML(). If you viewed the page through a web browser, you would see the file structure shown in Figure 2-12.

As with the previous example, this page could include some error handling to deal with an empty record set or a database error. However, the intent here is to show you how to generate simple XML content, rather than to give you a lesson in writing robust PHP pages. You can find this example saved as getAddresses.php with the other chapter resources.

To finish this section, we'll look at using ColdFusion.

Working with ColdFusion

We'll complete this example by using ColdFusion to generate the same XML content. Again, you would need to use this page with the appropriate database connection code, and I've called it addressesConnection in the example.

This example appears in the page getAddresses.cfm with your resources. As before, the explanation follows the complete page listing.

```
<cfprocessingdirective suppresswhitespace="yes" pageencoding="utf-8">
  <cfquery name="addresses" datasource="addressesConnection">
    SELECT * FROM phoneBook ORDER BY contactname
  </cfquery>
  <cfxml variable="addressXML">
    <phoneBook>
      <cfloop query="addresses">
        <cfoutput>
          <contact id="#ID#">
            <name>#contactname#</name>
            <address>#address#</address>
            <phone>#phone#</phone>
          </contact>
        </cfoutput>
      </cfloop>
    </phoneBook>
  </cfxml>
  <cfoutput>#addressXML#</cfoutput>
</cfprocessingdirective>
```

The page starts with a `<cfprocessingdirective>` root tag that tells ColdFusion how to process the page. It contains two attributes: suppresswhitespace, which suppresses excess whitespace in the document, and pageencoding, which sets the page encoding. The remaining code for the page appears between the opening and closing `<cfprocessingdirective>` and `</cfprocessingdirective>` tags.

The SQL SELECT statement appears between opening and closing `<cfquery>` tags. The opening `<cfquery>` tag includes a name attribute and a datasource attribute, which is set to the connection addressesConnection. As with the other examples, you would need to set up the addressConnection database connection in order to make this file work correctly.

ColdFusion reads the content from the database fields using # # symbols around each field name. The page creates an XML document containing the values from the SELECT query using the `<cfxml>` tag. This tag creates a ColdFusion XML document object, and it has an attribute variable with a value of addressXML. You'll be able to use this name to generate the XML document once it is created.

The `<cfxml>` tags enclose the structure for the XML document. The code starts with the root element `<phoneBook>`. It uses a `<cfloop>` tag to add the results from the SELECT query. Each variable appears inside the # # symbols within a `<cfoutput>` element. Every contact appears inside a `<contact>` element, which includes an id attribute as well `<name>`, `<address>`, and `<phone>` child elements.

The final step in the ColdFusion file is to output the `addressXML` variable. The page uses the `<cfoutput>` element to create the XML stream. If you ran this page through ColdFusion Server, you would see the same output as in the previous two examples.

That's it for our brief look at generating XML content from the server. The techniques that I've touched on here are important. If these topics are new to you, it's probably a good idea to research them further and spend some time learning how to write the appropriate code.

Another approach for generating XML is to use a software package such as Microsoft Office 2007.

Generating XML from other software packages

Many other software packages are capable of exporting their content using an XML format. This functionality allows for data exchange between unrelated applications. Recent versions of Microsoft Office also provide this functionality. I'll focus on the Microsoft Office applications in this section.

For Microsoft Office to be a source of XML content, you need the right version of the software suite on either a PC or a Macintosh. Office 2003 and later versions provide support for PCs, while Office 2008 for Macintosh provides the same features. You can generate XML documents using Microsoft Word or Excel, and for PC users, Microsoft Access.

Using Microsoft Office to generate XML documents for SWF applications can be very useful. Clients can maintain their own application content using familiar tools like Word and Excel. By providing them with some simple instructions and an XML schema, you can leave them to get on with creating and modifying the content for their applications. They don't need to learn to use an XML editor or a package like Dreamweaver.

Excel 2007, Word 2007, and PowerPoint 2007 for PC all use XML as their default file format, called the Office Open XML format. These packages in Microsoft Office 2008 for Macintosh use the same format. If you understood these XML vocabularies, you could write an entire Office document in a text editor, although once you see the languages, you'll realize that this approach would be very cumbersome!

Using the Office Open XML format means that you can both generate and open XML content in these software packages. The only requirement is that the XML documents you work with are well-formed. Office 2003 and above for PC and Office 2008 for Macintosh support the use of XML schemas and XSLT transformations.

Because I'm a PC user, I'll give you a brief look at how you can generate XML from Microsoft Office 2007, but the process should be similar on a Macintosh. I'm not going to go through every XML feature in each package, but I will give you an overview of some processes that might be useful.

Getting started with XML in Excel 2007 and Word 2007

You'll find the XML features in only the stand-alone version of each package or in the Professional version of Microsoft Office 2007. By default, the XML options aren't displayed in Excel and Word, so you'll need to display them in the Ribbon of both packages before you start work. You can do this by clicking the Microsoft Office button and selecting either Word Options or Excel Options.

Figure 2-13 shows how you would change this setting in Microsoft Office Word 2007. In the Popular category of the Word Options dialog box, check the Show Developer tab in the Ribbon option. Once you select this option, Word 2007 adds the Developer tab, which contains the XML options shown in Figure 2-14.

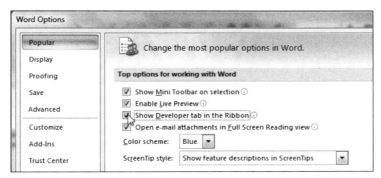

Figure 2-13. Showing the Developer tab in Microsoft Office Word 2007

You can display the XML Structure pane on the right side of the window by clicking the Structure button. This pane provides additional XML functionality.

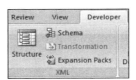

Figure 2-14. The XML options available in the Developer tab of Microsoft Office Word 2007

You can work with an XML schema using the Schema button or an XSLT transformation with the Transformation button. The Transformation button is grayed out in Figure 2-14 because no transformation has been added to the file. Finally, you can add an expansion pack by clicking the Expansion Packs button. An *expansion pack* is a collection of files that make up an XML solution.

Generating XML from Word 2007

The stand-alone and Professional versions of Word 2007 provide tools that you can use to work with XML documents. There are two ways to use these editions to generate XML documents from Word 2007:

- Create a WordML document, which uses Microsoft's own word processing XML vocabulary.
- Generate your own XML structure by adding an XML schema or XSLT stylesheet into the mix.

Creating an XML document in Word using Save As

The simplest way to generate an XML document from Word 2007 is to use the File ➤ Save As command, select the Other Formats option, and choose Word XML Document as the file type. This option creates a WordML document.

WordML is Microsoft's XML vocabulary for describing Word documents. It describes attributes about the document, the content in the document, and the formatting applied to elements of the document. Figure 2-15 shows how to save a document in this format. In this case, the file news.docx will be saved as a Word XML document named news.xml.

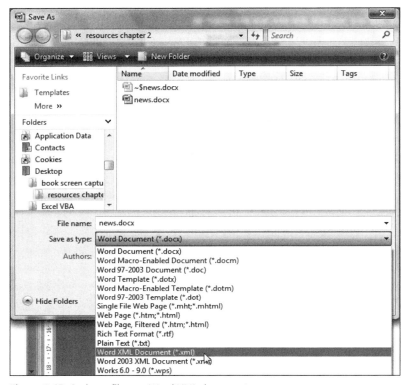

Figure 2-15. Saving a file as a Word XML document

The news.docx file contains a news item with the following three lines:

```
July 4, 2008
Fireworks extravaganza!
US expats in Australia celebrated the 4th of July with firework
➡demonstrations throughout the country.
```

I've included this file with the resources for this chapter if you want to have a look.

Saving the document using the Word XML Document format generates a WordML representation of this document. You can see the XML generated by Word in the resource file news.xml. You will need to open this file in Notepad or an XML editor to see the content that Word generates. Don't double-click, as that will just open the file in Word 2007. This behavior is because of the processing instruction on the second line of the XML document.

The generated XML file contains information about the document and the formatting settings, as well as the content itself. That's why the document is so long, especially when compared with the length of the original document.

The following listing shows the first few lines of the generated document:

```
<?xml version="1.0" encoding="UTF-8" standalone="yes"?>
<?mso-application progid="Word.Document"?>
<pkg:package xmlns:pkg="http://schemas.microsoft.com/office/2006/
xmlPackage">
<pkg:part pkg:name="/_rels/.rels" pkg:contentType=
"application/vnd.openxmlformats-package.relationships+xml"
pkg:padding="512"><pkg:xmlData><Relationships xmlns=
"http://schemas.openxmlformats.org/package/2006/relationships">
```

This listing contains only a small amount of the generated content from the news.xml file. The second line is a processing instruction that tells the document to open in Word. If you open the document in Notepad and scroll down, you'll see that there are many lines before you get to the actual content inside the original document. Feel free to repeat the test yourself to see the enormous amount of WordML generated by Word.

If you knew how to write WordML, you could create a document in an XML editor and open it in Word. You could also edit the WordML from the Word document in your XML editor as an alternative way to make changes to the document. However, both of these processes are likely to be cumbersome.

The size of file generated is restrictive and would be unwieldy if used in a SWF application. It would be difficult, even with the XML changes introduced in ActionScript 3.0, to navigate through the document to locate the content. The SWF application would need to load a lot of extra content to access the original three lines.

An alternative for SWF applications is to specify your own XML structure by including an XML schema. This approach allows you to streamline the generated content.

Creating XML content in Word by using a schema

Attaching a schema to the Word document will allow you to specify your own structure, which means you can reduce the number of XML elements created from the document. You can use the schema to ensure that the generated document is valid according to your language rules. You could also transform the content with an XSLT stylesheet.

In this section, I'll briefly show you how to generate your own XML content by using an XML schema. You need to follow these steps to create an XML document in Word 2007 using a schema:

1. Create a schema for the XML document.
2. Create a Word 2007 document that uses the schema.
3. Mark up the Word document with the XML elements from the schema.
4. Save the data only from the document in XML format.

The result will be a valid XML document with fewer lines compared with its WordML relative.

I'll walk you through these steps with a simple example. This section will provide an overview; it isn't intended as a tutorial. You can find all of the files that I refer to with the resources for this chapter.

To start, I used an XML schema to describe the XML structure for the news item file you saw earlier. An XML schema provides information about an XML vocabulary. It lists the elements that are valid in an XML document, their type, and any rules relating to their construction.

The file newsSchema.xsd contains the complete schema. I'm not going to explain how to write a schema from scratch here, as that's beyond the scope of the book, but the content follows:

```
<?xml version="1.0"?>
<xsd:schema xmlns:xsd="http://www.w3.org/2001/XMLSchema">
  <xsd:element name="news">
    <xsd:complexType>
      <xsd:sequence>
        <xsd:element name="newsDate" type="xsd:string"/>
        <xsd:element name="newsTitle" type="xsd:string"/>
        <xsd:element name="newsContent" type="xsd:string"/>
      </xsd:sequence>
    </xsd:complexType>
  </xsd:element>
</xsd:schema>
```

In this schema, the root element <news> contains the elements <newsDate>, <newsTitle>, and <newsContent>. There can be only one of each of these elements, and they must be included in the order specified. The elements all contain string data.

I've created a simple document called newsXMLOutput.docx to demonstrate the process. If you have Word 2007, you can open the file to see how it looks. The process is easiest if you click the Structure button in the XML group to display the XML Structure pane.

The process of adding a schema is straightforward. You start by choosing the Schema option from the Developer tab. Click the Add Schema button, as shown in Figure 2-16. This screenshot shows that the schema is already attached.

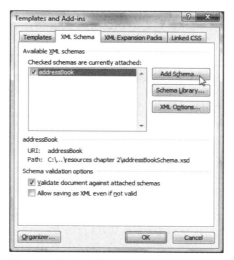

Figure 2-16. Attaching a schema to a Word 2007 document

To attach the schema, you need to navigate to the correct file. Enter a URI or namespace for the schema and an alias when prompted. The URI doesn't need to reference a file or URL; it just needs to be a unique value in the application. The alias is a shorthand name that Word uses to refer to the schema. I entered the value addressBook for both settings. Click OK to close the dialog box

To use the schema to generate simplified XML content, the application needs to know that it should output only the data from the file, not the XML tags. After you've attached the schema, set this option by clicking the XML Options button. Check the Save data only check box, as shown in Figure 2-17. Selecting this option means that the formatting and meta-information will be excluded from the output.

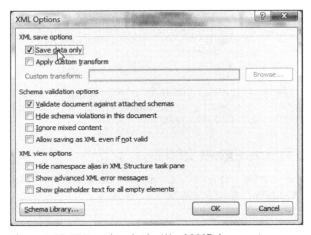

Figure 2-17. XML options in the Word 2007 document

You need to apply the XML elements for the schema to the Word document. You do this by selecting the text in the document and dragging an element from the schema to the selection. Start by high-lighting all of the text and drag the root element, news. Then select the date and drag the newsDate element to the selection. Repeat the process for newsTitle and newsContent. Figure 2-18 shows how the document appears after applying the elements.

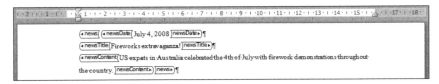

Figure 2-18. The document marked up with XML tags in Word 2007

This document maps to the attached XML schema. Figure 2-18 shows the XML elements from the schema applied to the content in the file. They are the purple tags that surround the content. If you can't see these tags, click the Structure button in the XML group of the Developer tab to display the XML Structure pane. Make sure that the Show XML tags option in the document is checked.

You can generate XML consistent with the schema by saving in Word 2003 XML format. Choose the File ➤ Save As command, select the Other Formats option, and choose Word 2003 XML.

The generated XML document is saved as newsXMLOutput.xml with this chapter's resources. It contains the following XML structure:

```
<?xml version="1.0" encoding="UTF-8" standalone="no"?>
<news xmlns="http://www.aip.net.au/wordNewsXML">
  <newsDate xmlns="">July 4, 2008</newsDate>
  <newsTitle xmlns="">Fireworks extravaganza!</newsTitle>
  <newsContent xmlns="">US expats in Australia celebrated the 4th of
    July with firework demonstrations throughout the country.
  /newsContent>
</news>
```

Compare the structure and content of this XML document with the one that didn't use a schema, newsWord.xml. You'll see that the tag names in this document are more descriptive, and it is significantly shorter than the equivalent WordML document. This document is more suitable for use in a SWF application than its WordML cousin.

Word 2007 is useful for generating XML content for nonrepeating items such as the document you saw in the example. If you have repeating or list-based items, you might consider generating XML content from Microsoft Office Excel 2007 instead.

Generating XML from Excel 2007

Again, I'll give you a brief overview of how to create XML content from an Excel spreadsheet, rather than working through an exercise step by step. First, though, you must understand the type of XML that Excel will generate.

Excel document structures are very rigid. They always use a grid made up of rows and columns. This means that the XML content generated from Excel must match this layout. If you generate XML content from Word, it's possible to include elements within other elements or text. For example, you could display the following mixed XML elements using Word:

```
<title>
  This is a title by
  <author>Sas Jacobs</author>
</title>
```

In Excel, the smallest unit of data that you can work with is a cell. Cells can't contain other cells, so you can't generate mixed elements in the same way that you can in Word. Any XML document generated from Excel will include a grid-like data structure so it is suitable for generating list-based XML content.

Generating an XML document in Excel using Save As

As with Word, the easiest way to create an XML document from Excel is to save it using the Spreadsheet 2003 XML file type. Saving as this type of document creates output written in SpreadsheetML, Microsoft's spreadsheet XML vocabulary.

To illustrate this process, I've included the file addresses.xlsx with your resources for this chapter. This file is shown in Figure 2-19.

	A	B	C	D
1	ID	**Name**	**Address**	**Phone**
2	1	Sas Jacobs	123 Red Street, Redland, Australia	123 456
3	2	John Smith	4 Green Street, Lost City, Greenland	456 789

Figure 2-19. A simple Excel 2007 document

This document is a representation of the content in the address.xml file that you saw earlier. It contains two addresses. Use the Save As command and select the Excel Spreadsheet 2003 XML file type to generate SpreadsheetML to describe the document.

You can see the output from this process saved in the resource file addresses.xml. You'll notice that, as with Word 2007, this simple Excel 2007 document generates a large SpreadsheetML document. The following code block shows the few first lines of the generated XML document:

```
<?xml version="1.0"?>
<?mso-application progid="Excel.Sheet"?>
<Workbook xmlns="urn:schemas-microsoft-com:office:spreadsheet"
 xmlns:o="urn:schemas-microsoft-com:office:office"
 xmlns:x="urn:schemas-microsoft-com:office:excel"
 xmlns:ss="urn:schemas-microsoft-com:office:spreadsheet"
 xmlns:html="http://www.w3.org/TR/REC-html40">
 <DocumentProperties xmlns="urn:schemas-microsoft-com:office:office">
  <Author>Sas Jacobs</Author>
  <LastAuthor>Sas Jacobs</LastAuthor>
  <Created>2008-04-28T00:34:09Z</Created>
  <LastSaved>2008-04-28T00:35:34Z</LastSaved>
  <Company>Anything Is Possible</Company>
  <Version>12.00</Version>
 </DocumentProperties>
```

As you can see, because the code describes attributes of the file as well as the structure of the document, the resulting XML is very long and complicated. As with Word 2007, you can simplify this process by using an XML schema to structure the output.

Creating XML content in Excel using a schema

If you wish to specify your own format for the XML generated by the Excel 2007 spreadsheet, you'll need to attach an XML schema to the document. Excel converts the schema to a document map that describes the structure of XML documents that can be exported from the workbook. As with Word, you must specify which spreadsheet data maps to each element in the document map.

Excel works with data in a grid, so that gives a clue about the best type of XML data to import and export with Excel. You will experience difficulty if you try to work with complex content with mixed elements—those containing both elements and text. Instead, expect to work with and generate grid-like XML documents.

The example in this section uses the following XML schema. This schema describes the phone book XML document you saw in Chapter 1, and it is saved in the file addressSchema.xsd with the other chapter resources.

```
<?xml version="1.0"?>
<xsd:schema xmlns:xsd="http://www.w3.org/2001/XMLSchema">
  <xsd:element name="phoneBook">
    <xsd:complexType>
      <xsd:sequence>
        <xsd:element ref="contact" maxOccurs="unbounded"/>
      </xsd:sequence>
    </xsd:complexType>
  </xsd:element>
  <xsd:element name="contact">
    <xsd:complexType>
      <xsd:sequence>
        <xsd:element name="name" type="xsd:string"/>
        <xsd:element name="address" type="xsd:string"/>
        <xsd:element name="phone" type="xsd:string"/>
      </xsd:sequence>
      <xsd:attribute name="id" type="xsd:integer" use="required"/>
    </xsd:complexType>
  </xsd:element>
</xsd:schema>
```

The file addressesWithDocumentMap.xls already has this XML schema applied. This was done through the XML group in the Developer tab. If you can't see this tab, you'll need to display it using the instructions provided earlier in this chapter.

To view the XML map, click the Source button in the Developer tab to display the XML Source pane. I added the schema by clicking the XML Maps button at the bottom of the XML Source pane and navigating to the XML schema document.

Figure 2-20. The document map in the XML Source pane

The Excel 2007 file addressesWithDocumentMap.xls is included with the other chapter resources. Figure 2-20 shows how the document map for this file appears in the XML Source pane.

I applied the elements from the document map to the data in the Excel workbook. I selected all of the data and dragged the <phoneBook> element to the selection to set the root node for the file. As the column headings in this workbook are the same as the element names in the XML schema, Excel automatically associates each element in the document map with the correct columns. If this were not the case, I would need to select each column and match it with the relevant element by dragging and dropping. Figure 2-21 shows how the worksheet appears with the document map applied.

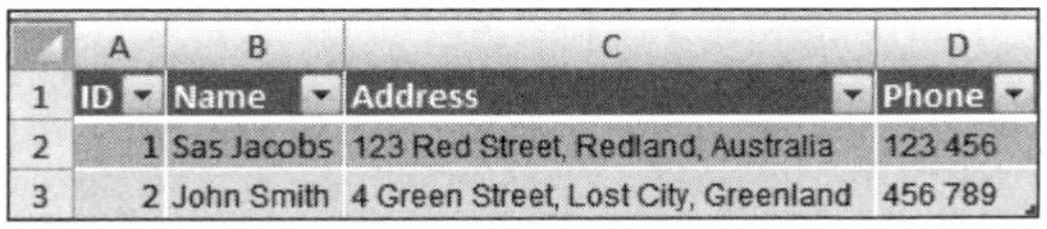

	A	B	C	D
1	ID	Name	Address	Phone
2	1	Sas Jacobs	123 Red Street, Redland, Australia	123 456
3	2	John Smith	4 Green Street, Lost City, Greenland	456 789

Figure 2-21. The Excel document with document map applied

You can export simplified XML from any worksheet where the content has been mapped according to an attached document map. Click the Export button in the XML group of the Developer tab to generate the new XML document.

I've exported XML content from `addressesWithDocumentMap.xlsx`, and you can see the results in the resource file `addressesExported.xml`. The contents of this file follow:

```
<?xml version="1.0" encoding="UTF-8" standalone="yes"?>
<phoneBook>
  <contact>
    <name>Sas Jacobs</name>
    <address>123 Red Street, Redland, Australia</address>
    <phone>123 456</phone>
  </contact>
  <contact>
    <name>John Smith</name>
    <address>4 Green Street, Lost City, Greenland</address>
    <phone>456 789</phone>
  </contact>
</phoneBook>
```

The file looks almost identical to the XML document that you saw earlier in the chapter. The only difference is the missing attribute from the `<contact>` element. As with Word 2007, applying a schema to the Excel document greatly simplifies the XML content exported.

The final Office package that I will cover in this section is Microsoft Access 2007 for PC.

Creating XML content with Access 2007

Access 2007 works a little differently when it comes to XML compared with the other Office applications. Getting data out of Access and into an XML document is easy—you just export it in XML format. The XML documents that are generated come from the structure of the table or query exported. The names of the fields in the table or query are used to name the elements in the resulting XML document, so you do not need to attach a schema to simplify the content.

To export an entire table or query, right-click the object name and choose Export. Select the XML File option. Figure 2-22 shows this process with the Access database `documents.accdb`.

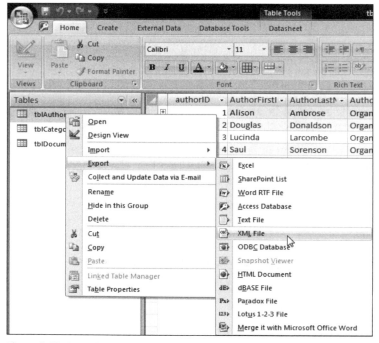

Figure 2-22. Exporting a table in Access 2007

You'll be prompted to choose which files to export: the data (XML), a schema (XSD), and presentation of the data (XSL). You can choose any one or all of these options.

Access 2007 generates an XML document based on the table or query structure. You can see an example in the `tblAuthorsExported.xml` resource file, which follows. Try exporting the `tblAuthors` object yourself to see this result.

```
<?xml version="1.0" encoding="UTF-8"?>
<dataroot xmlns:od="urn:schemas-microsoft-com:officedata"
  generated="2008-04-28T09:11:06">
  <tblAuthors>
    <authorID>1</authorID>
    <AuthorFirstName>Alison</AuthorFirstName>
    <AuthorLastName>Ambrose</AuthorLastName>
    <AuthorOrganisation>Organisation A</AuthorOrganisation>
  </tblAuthors>
  <tblAuthors>
    <authorID>2</authorID>
    <AuthorFirstName>Douglas</AuthorFirstName>
    <AuthorLastName>Donaldson</AuthorLastName>
    <AuthorOrganisation>Organisation B</AuthorOrganisation>
  </tblAuthors>
```

```
        <tblAuthors>
          <authorID>3</authorID>
          <AuthorFirstName>Lucinda</AuthorFirstName>
          <AuthorLastName>Larcombe</AuthorLastName>
          <AuthorOrganisation>Organisation C</AuthorOrganisation>
        </tblAuthors>
        <tblAuthors>
          <authorID>4</authorID>
          <AuthorFirstName>Saul</AuthorFirstName>
          <AuthorLastName>Sorenson</AuthorLastName>
          <AuthorOrganisation>Organisation D</AuthorOrganisation>
        </tblAuthors>
      </dataroot>
```

As you can see, these exported Access files don't require a schema to be smaller than their Word and Excel equivalents. The elements in the XML document take their names from the field names in the table or query. Access replaces any spaces in field names with an underscore (_) character. If you don't want to use the default field names in the table, you can always write a query that creates more user-friendly names.

The only thing added by Access is the <dataroot> root element. It contains a namespace reference and an attribute called generated. This attribute represents a timestamp for the generation of the XML document.

As you can see from the previous sections, each of the Office applications works with particular data structures. Word 2007 works best with nonrepeating information, a bit like filling in a form to generate the XML elements. Excel 2007 best suits grid- or list-based data structures that don't include mixed elements. Access 2007 works with relational data, and you can either export an entire table or write queries to specify which data to export.

You've seen several different ways to generate XML content for use in SWF applications. There's one important point to consider about this type of content: validation of the XML document

Validation and XML content in SWF applications

In this chapter, I've shown you different ways to generate XML content that you can use as a data source in SWF applications. Provided that the document you create is well-formed, you'll be able to use the data it contains when you build SWF applications in Flash or Flex.

ActionScript uses an XML parser to process loaded XML content. It allows you to iterate through each part of the document once loaded. The ActionScript XML parser will generate errors if it has to process XML content that is not well-formed, but it will do this only at runtime.

The ActionScript processor is not a validating XML parser. When a SWF application loads an XML document that references an XML schema or DTD, the processor is not able to determine whether the XML document is valid according to that schema or DTD.

So, if you're working with a predetermined XML vocabulary, you can't rely on Flash or Flex to check that the content is valid according to its DTD or XML schema. Instead, you'll need to use other tools or mechanisms to make ensure that the XML content is valid before loading it into the SWF application.

Summary

This chapter described several ways to create XML content for use in SWF applications. We started by looking at some tools that you can use to write an XML document manually. The most useful class of tools is XML editors, as they can automate several processes. They can check that documents are well-formed, validate them according to an XML schema or DTD, and apply an XLST transformation. As an example, I demonstrated this functionality in Stylus Studio 2008 XML.

I also showed some basic approaches for generating XML content from a database with server-side code. The chapter includes simple examples using VB .NET, PHP, and ColdFusion. It doesn't provide a comprehensive guide, so you may want to research the topic more thoroughly if you're going to use one of these approaches.

We finished by looking at how you might generate XML content from Office 2007 documents. I didn't cover every method possible, but you saw the different types of content that you can generate from these software packages. You saw that adding a schema to either Word 2007 or Excel 2007 allows you to control the structure of the file generated.

The next chapter looks at the new ActionScript 3.0 approaches to working with XML content. I'll cover the new E4X ActionScript 3.0 classes, and you'll see examples of how to work with each class in both Flash and Flex.

Chapter 3

ACTIONSCRIPT 3.0 AND XML

So far in this book, you've been introduced to XML and seen some different ways to generate XML content for SWF applications. In this chapter, you'll learn about the role of XML in ActionScript 3.0. If you have been coding with ActionScript 2.0, be prepared to forget any previous experience you have with ActionScript and XML, because things have changed radically.

ActionScript 3.0 completely reworks the XML class and also introduces a new XMLList class. Both represent a leap forward for developers, as the changes will speed up the development process greatly. The new functionality is based on ECMAScript standards and is referred to as E4X.

Another major change is that XML is now a native data type. This means that you can declare and explicitly assign content to XML objects, in much the same way that you would with strings and numeric types.

You'll learn about these new ActionScript 3.0 features in this chapter. You can download the resources for this chapter from http://www.friendsofed.com.

Differences between ActionScript 2.0 and 3.0

If you've worked with earlier versions of ActionScript, you'll be familiar with the ActionScript 2.0 XML class. Unfortunately, you'll need to forget what you've previously learned, because ActionScript 3.0 changes things quite significantly. The good news is that the new approaches make life much easier for developers.

ActionScript 3.0 includes completely new XML functionality based on the E4X specification, ECMA-357. E4X is an extension to ECMAScript (JavaScript) specifically targeted at working with XML documents. It is a standard, managed by an international body called the European Computer Manufacturers Association (ECMA), which allows an XML document to be defined as a JavaScript object or, in our case, an ActionScript object.

E4X is implemented in a number of different areas, including a full implementation within ActionScript 3.0. Unfortunately, there is only limited support for E4X in JavaScript within current web browsers.

In ActionScript 3.0, you can target content in an XML object by using methods of the XML class to write E4X expressions. You can also use some shorthand expressions that are similar to XPath, and I'll cover those in the next chapter.

E4X expressions allow you to target the content in an XML object by writing paths that refer to node and attribute names. If you've ever had to write paths or loop through XML content using ActionScript 2.0, you'll welcome this functionality with open arms!

The introduction of E4X to ActionScript 3.0 has the following advantages:

- ActionScript 3.0 now uses a standardized approach.
- E4X usually produces far less code to parse XML content compared with ActionScript 2.0.
- E4X expressions are simple and are generally easier to understand than the equivalent ActionScript 2.0 expressions.
- E4X is easy to learn, especially for developers with experience in XPath.

You can find out more about E4X by reading the specification at http://www.ecma-international.org/publications/standards/Ecma-357.htm. If you want to know more about the XPath specification, you can find it at http://www.w3.org/TR/xpath, although it's not essential for using E4X in Flash and Flex.

E4X introduces several new classes to ActionScript 3.0, as follows:

- XML: This class works with XML objects.
- XMLList: This class works with an ordered collection of XML content and may involve more than one XML object.
- XMLListCollection: This class is a wrapper collection class for the XMLList class.
- QName: This class represents the qualified name of XML elements and attributes.
- Namespace: This class works with namespaces.

> *The old ActionScript 2.0* XML *class has been renamed to the* XMLDocument *class for support of legacy applications. Using this class for new SWF applications is not recommended.* XMLNode *is also available as a legacy class.*

We'll take a closer look at these new classes in this chapter. Before we start though, let's look at XML as a native data type in ActionScript 3.0.

XML as an ActionScript data type

ActionScript 3.0 includes XML and XMLList as new complex data types. This means that you can write XML inline within ActionScript code. If you are working with Flex, you can also use a tag-based approach to create literal XML content.

Writing XML inline within ActionScript

If you've worked with ActionScript 2.0, you're probably familiar with passing a string to the XML constructor to create an XML object, as shown here:

```
var strXML:String = "<phoneBook><contact>Sas</contact></phoneBook>";
var phoneBookXML:XML = new XML(strXML);
```

While you can still create XML content in this way, ActionScript 3.0 allows you to write XML inline within ActionScript code using a literal value, as shown here:

```
var phoneBookXML:XML = <phoneBook>
  <contact id="1">
    <name>Sas Jacobs</name>
    <address>123 Red Street, Redland, Australia</address>
    <phone>123 456</phone>
  </contact>
</phoneBook>;
```

In this case, I've created an XML object with <phoneBook> as the root element. The object contains a single <contact> element. Notice that I don't need to use quotes around the XML content, and it can be split onto different lines. The phoneBookXML object has a data type of XML, not String.

The only requirement for creating an XML object in this way is that the content must be well-formed. This requirement also applies if you're passing a string to the XML constructor method. (If you're not sure what *well-formed* means, refer to Chapter 1.)

You can write a path to locate the root element in an XML object by using the object name. In this example, I can use the name phoneBookXML to reference the root of the XML object, <phoneBook>. The root node is the starting point for most of the XML methods covered in this chapter.

You normally create an XMLList object by applying an E4X expression to an XML object. You'll find out more about these expressions later in this chapter and in the next chapter.

Writing XML with the XML tag in Flex

You can use the `<mx:XML>` tag in Flex to work with literal XML content in an XML data model. This tag compiles the data into an XML object, which you can work with using E4X expressions.

You can either add the content directly to the `<mx:XML>` tag or specify an external document source. The following block shows how to declare the content of an `<mx:XML>` element explicitly:

```
<mx:XML id="phoneBookXML">
  <phoneBook>
    <contact id="1">
      <name>Sas Jacobs</name>
      <address>123 Red Street, Redland, Australia</address>
      <phone>123 456</phone>
    </contact>
  </phoneBook>
</mx:XML>
```

This example is equivalent to the ActionScript variable created in the previous section. As with the ActionScript 3.0 equivalent, the content inside an `<mx:XML>` tag must be well-formed XML.

One advantage of using the `<mx:XML>` tag is that you can specify an external document as the content using the source attribute, as shown here:

```
<mx:XML id="phoneBookXML" source="assets/address.xml"/>
```

This `<mx:XML>` element loads content from the `address.xlm` file in the `assets` folder of the Flex project.

Be careful with this approach though, as the `<mx:XML>` tag compiles the data into the SWF file, rather than loading it at runtime. You can't modify the external XML document and expect the application to update the content automatically. If you need that functionality, you must load the content using one of the methods shown in Chapter 5. For simplicity, in this chapter we'll keep working with static XML content stored in the SWF application.

Next, let's look at the new ActionScript 3.0 E4X classes.

Overview of the new ActionScript 3.0 classes

Before we explore the new classes in detail, it's useful to understand the general purpose of each one, as well as the way the classes interact with each other. I'll provide a brief summary of the new classes here.

The ActionScript 3.0 XML class

The ActionScript 3.0 XML class allows you to work with XML content. As mentioned earlier, this class implements the E4X standard for working with XML documents. In the previous section, you saw that it was possible to declare an XML object and assign a value using ActionScript.

An XML object contains a single root node with some optional child nodes. An XMLList object is a collection of XML content or nodes. It doesn't have a root node as a container for the other elements.

The XMLList class

You can create an XMLList through various E4X expressions and methods of the XML class. For example, you can use the children() method of an XML object to return a collection of all child nodes of an element. You can also use an E4X expression to create a list of nodes matching certain criteria, with the expression acting as a filter for the XML content.

The XMLList class represents an ordered collection of XML elements. Many of the XML class methods that you'll see shortly return an XMLList. One useful feature of an XMLList is that you can assign it as a dataProvider for Flex components.

The difference between XMLList and XML objects is that the XML object is a single object containing any number of child nodes, whereas an XMLList is a collection of one or more objects. However, the distinction blurs somewhat, because an XMLList object containing a single item is treated in the same way as an XML object.

So how can you tell whether you're working with an XML object or an XMLList object? If you call the length() method, the value will always be 1 in the case of an XML object. An XMLList can have any other value, although an XML class method returning an XMLList with a single element will also show a value of 1.

The XMLListCollection class

If you're working in Flex, it's useful to assign the XMLList to an XMLListCollection object and use that as the basis for data binding. The XMLListCollection provides additional methods for working with the XMLList content, and the binding is monitored for changes. This isn't the case if you bind an XMLList.

You'll usually use an XMLListCollection object as the dataProvider property for another component. In addition to XMLList methods, it contains methods for sorting data, adding items, and editing items.

The QName and Namespace classes

You'll use the QName and Namespace classes when you work with XML content that falls within a specific namespace. Remember that namespaces associate XML elements with an owner, so that each element name is unique within the XML document. You can create a QName object to associate an element with a specific namespace or to identify the element uniquely with a string.

Now let's look at the new classes in more detail, beginning with the XML class.

Working with the XML class

The XML class class allows you to work with XML documents. XML documents must have a single root node and be well-formed before they can be parsed by either Flash or Flex.

You can either declare the XML content within your SWF application or load it from an external source. You saw the first option earlier in this chapter. You'll see how to load external content in Chapter 5.

Each XML object can include any or all of the following node types, called *node kinds*:

- An element
- An attribute
- A text node
- A comment
- A processing instruction

To understand the XML class a little better, let's look at its properties and methods, and work through some examples of how they might apply in both Flash and Flex.

Properties of the XML class

The XML class class has five static properties that determine how the XML content is treated. These properties are listed in Table 3-1. Because they are static properties, they determine the overall settings for XML objects in your SWF applications, rather than applying to a specific instance.

Table 3-1. Static properties of the XML class

Property	Type	Description	Default value
ignoreComments	Boolean	Determines whether to ignore comments when the source XML content is parsed	true
ignoreProcessingInstructions	Boolean	Determines whether to ignore processing instructions while parsing the XML document	true
ignoreWhitespace	Boolean	Determines whether to ignore whitespace when parsing the XML document	true
prettyIndent	int	Determines the amount of indentation, in spaces, when prettyPrinting is set to true	2
prettyPrinting	Boolean	Determines whether whitespace is preserved when the XML document displays with either the toString() or toXMLString() method	true

We'll look at the effect of these properties in an example using the following XML object:

```
<phoneBook>
  <contact id="1">
    <name>Sas Jacobs</name>
    <address>123 Red Street, Redland, Australia</address>
    <phone>123 456</phone>
  </contact>
</phoneBook>
```

We'll work through examples in both Flash and Flex, starting with Flash.

Working with XML properties in Flash

Follow these steps in Flash:

1. Open Flash and create an XML object called phoneBookXML. Assign the preceding XML content to this object, as shown here:

```
var phoneBookXML:XML = <phoneBook>
  <contact id="1">
    <name>Sas Jacobs</name>
    <address>123 Red Street, Redland, Australia</address>
    <phone>123 456</phone>
  </contact>
</phoneBook>
```

2. The toXMLString() method of the XML class provides a string representation of the XML object. Add the following lines below the XML object:

```
XML.prettyPrinting = false;
trace(phoneBookXML.toXMLString());
```

This example turns off the prettyPrinting property so you can see unformatted XML content.

3. Test the SWF file using the Ctrl/Cmd+Enter keyboard shortcut. Figure 3-1 shows the output from this simple ActionScript code. As you can see, the content renders without indentation or any spacing that would make it easier to read.

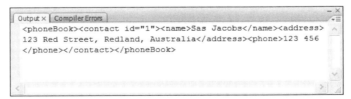

Figure 3-1. Tracing the XML object without comments or pretty printing

4. Modify the code as follows:

```
XML.prettyIndent = 4;
XML.prettyPrinting = true;
trace(phoneBookXML.toXMLString());
```

You've turned on the prettyPrinting setting and set an indent of four spaces. Figure 3-2 shows how this content appears in the Output panel. The output now uses pretty printing to lay out the content. It includes four characters of spacing between indented lines because of the prettyIndent and prettyPrinting property settings.

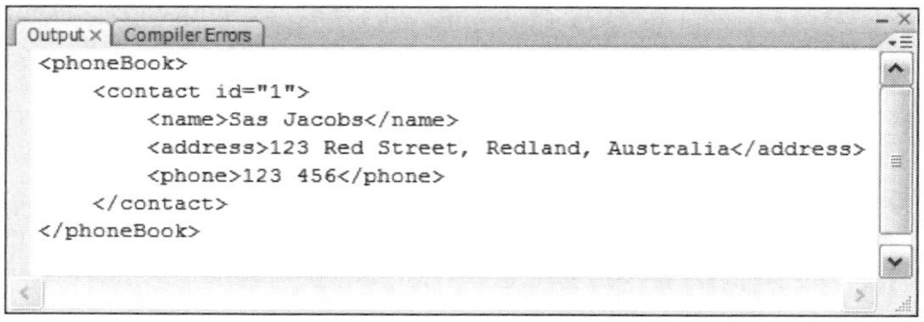

Figure 3-2. Tracing the XML object with pretty printing

You can find the file used for this example saved as xmlObjectStaticProperties.fla with this chapter's resources.

Working with XML properties in Flex

You can re-create the preceding example in Flex by creating a project and application file, as follows:

1. Add the XML content to the application in an <mx:XML> element:

```
<mx:XML id="phoneBookXML">
  <phoneBook>
    <contact id="1">
      <name>Sas Jacobs</name>
      <address>123 Red Street, Redland, Australia</address>
      <phone>123 456</phone>
    </contact>
  </phoneBook>
</mx:XML>
```

2. Modify the <mx:Application> element to add a creationComplete attribute, as follows:

```
<mx:Application xmlns:mx="http://www.adobe.com/2006/mxml"
layout="absolute" creationComplete="initApp(event)">
```

3. Add the following <mx:Script> block:

```
<mx:Script>
  <![CDATA[
    import mx.events.FlexEvent;
    private function initApp(e:FlexEvent):void {
      XML.prettyPrinting = false;
      trace(phoneBookXML.toXMLString());
    }
  ]]>
</mx:Script>
```

The script block imports a FlexEvent as that object is passed within the initApp() function. It creates the initApp() function, which sets the prettyPrinting static property to false. As with the previous example, it displays the XML content using toXMLString().

4. Debug the application to see the output in the Console view, which will look similar to the output shown in Figure 3-1.

5. Replace the prettyPrinting line with the following code:

```
XML.prettyIndent = 4;
XML.prettyPrinting = true;
```

6. Debug the application again. This time, you'll see the same effect as in Figure 3-2, with the XML content formatted and easy to read.

You can find the MXML application saved in the resource file xmlObjectStaticProperties.mxml.

In addition to the static properties, the XML class also has a number of methods.

Methods of the XML class

You can access content within an XML object by using E4X expressions, as discussed in the next chapter, or by using methods of the XML class. Many of these methods return an XMLList object. There are also a number of methods that developers can use to create and modify XML content, which are covered in Chapter 8.

The most common methods of the XML class can be divided into the following categories:

- Methods that help to locate XML content
- Methods that find out information about XML content
- Methods that modify XML content

We'll start by looking at methods for locating XML content.

Locating XML content

The XML class class includes many methods that allow you to parse an XML object to locate specific information. This information is always treated as a String data type, so you'll need to cast any values that should be treated as numbers or dates.

As I mentioned, there are two ways to access content from an XML object: use the XML class methods or use E4X expressions as a kind of shorthand. In this chapter, we'll focus on using XML methods, and the shorthand E4X expressions are covered in Chapter 4. In most cases, you can use either approach to locate values within your XML content. However, the following methods of the XML class don't have an equivalent E4X expression:

- Locating the parent with the parent() method
- Using comments() to access the collection of comments in the XML object
- Using processingInstructions() to access the collection of processing instructions

Table 3-2 shows some of the most common methods that allow you to access content in an XML document. These methods also apply to the XMLList class.

Table 3-2. Methods of the XML class that assist in locating XML content

Method	Description
attribute(attributeName)	Returns the value of a specified attribute as an XMLList. The attribute name can be a string or a QName object.
attributes()	Returns a list of attribute values for a specified node as an XMLList.
child(propertyName)	Returns the child nodes of a specified node matching the supplied name.
children()	Returns all children of the specified node as an XMLList.
comments()	Returns all comments within an XML object.
descendants(name)	Returns all descendants of an XML object as an XMLList.
elements(name)	Lists the elements of an XML object as an XMLList. This method ignores comments and processing instructions.
parent()	Returns the parent of the specified XML object as an XMLList.
processingInstructions(name)	Returns processing instructions.
text()	Returns all text nodes.

Let's look at examples of some of these methods.

Instructions for the code samples

The code samples for both Flash and Flex are identical, but you need to add the code at different locations in the Flash and Flex files.

For the Flash examples, follow these steps:

1. Open up a new Flash document.

2. Add the contents of the authors.xml document to an XML object called authorsXML on an Actions layer. Here are the first two lines, to get you started:

```
var authorsXML:XML = <allAuthors>
  <author authorID="1">
```

3. Add the ActionScript lines shown in the following examples below the declaration for the XML object.

Follow these steps for the Flex Builder files:

1. Create a new project and application file using File ➤ New ➤ Flex Project.

2. Create an assets folder for the project and add the XML document authors.xml.

3. Add an <mx:XML> element and set this XML element as the source for the XML object, as shown here:

```
<mx:XML id="phoneBookXML" source="assets/authors.xml" />
```

4. Add the following creationComplete event to the <mx:Application> element:

```
creationComplete="initApp(event)"
```

5. Add the following <mx:Script> block containing the initApp() function above the <mx:XML> object:

```
<mx:Script>
  <![CDATA[
    import mx.events.FlexEvent;
    private function initApp(e:FlexEvent):void {
      //add testing lines here
    }
  ]]>
</mx:Script>
```

6. In the examples that follow, replace the //add testing lines here content with the code samples. Because you'll be using trace() statements, you'll need to debug rather than run the Flex application.

The complete Flex code follows:

```
<?xml version="1.0" encoding="utf-8"?>
<mx:Application xmlns:mx="http://www.adobe.com/2006/mxml"
  layout="absolute" creationComplete="initApp(event)">
  <mx:Script>
    <![CDATA[
      import mx.events.FlexEvent;
      private function initApp(e:FlexEvent):void {
        //add testing lines here
      }
    ]]>
  </mx:Script>
  <mx:XML id="authorsXML" source="assets/authors.xml" />
</mx:Application>
```

The authors.xml file contains information about several authors and the books that they've published. We'll use the content as an XML object to demonstrate the most important methods listed in Table 3-2.

To start, we'll look at the attribute() and attributes() methods.

Working with attribute() and attributes()

You can use the `attribute()` method to locate a specific attribute in an element. You need to provide the path through the document tree before calling the `attribute()` method. Remember that the name of the XML object is equivalent to its root node.

```
trace(authorsXML.author[1].attribute("authorID"));
```

This expression finds the `authorID` attribute of the second `<author>` element. The expression starts by referencing the `<authorsXML>` root element using `authorsXML`. It then locates the second author using `author[1]`. You use the number 1 because the list of elements is zero-based, so the first author is `author[0]`. The expression uses the `attribute()` method, passing the name of the attribute, `authorID`. When you test the SWF application, the Output panel should show the value 2, as shown in Figure 3-3.

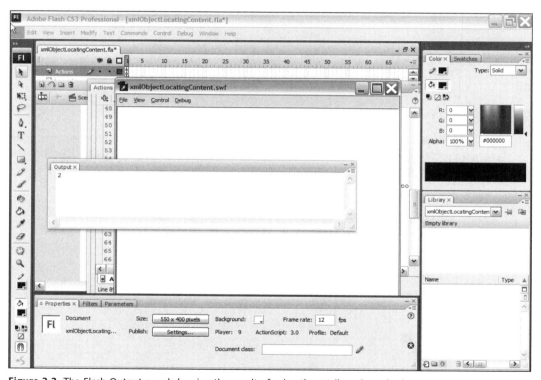

Figure 3-3. The Flash Output panel showing the result of using the attribute() method

If you need to access all of the attributes of an element or collection of elements, you can use the `attributes()` method, as follows:

```
trace(authorsXML.author.attributes());
```

This expression will display the output 1234, because these are all of the attribute values in the `<author>` elements of the authorsXML object.

You can access individual attributes from this collection by specifying an index. For example, to find all attributes of the first <author> element, use the following:

```
trace(authorsXML.author[0].attributes());
```

Testing that expression will display the value 1.

Finding child elements

You can find the child elements of a parent element by calling the child() method and specifying the name of the child element to locate. Here is an example:

```
trace(authorsXML.author[2].books.book.child("bookName"));
```

In this case, the expression finds all of the <bookName> elements associated with the children of the third <author> element. Remember that the first author is at position 0. Notice that you need to specify the element structure from the root element, including the <books> and <book> elements. The expression produces the following output:

```
<bookName>Bikes as an alternative source of transport</bookName>
<bookName>Entertaining ways</bookName>
<bookName>Growing radishes</bookName>
<bookName>Growing tulips</bookName>
```

The output provides a collection of all of the <bookName> elements for this author. You could assign this expression to an XMLList object to work with it further.

The children() method accesses all children of a specific element. The following expression finds all children of the fourth author:

```
trace(authorsXML.author[3].children());
```

It produces the following output:

```
<authorFirstName>Saul</authorFirstName>
<authorLastName>Sorenson</authorLastName>
<books>
  <book ID="2">
    <bookName>Bike riding for non-bike riders</bookName>
    <bookPublishYear>2004</bookPublishYear>
  </book>
</books>
```

Notice that it finds the <authorFirstName>, <authorLastName>, and <books> child elements.

Finding descendants

The descendants() method allows you to access all of an element's descendants, including text nodes. The returned content includes the child elements, grandchildren, and every element at lower levels in the XML object. Here is an example of using this method:

```
trace(authorsXML.author[3].books.descendants());
```

77

This expression finds all descendants of the <books> element of the fourth author. It produces the following output:

```
<book ID="2">
  <bookName>Bike riding for non-bike riders</bookName>
  <bookPublishYear>2004</bookPublishYear>
</book>
<bookName>Bike riding for non-bike riders</bookName>
Bike riding for non-bike riders
<bookPublishYear>2004</bookPublishYear>
2004
```

Notice that each descendant is listed in turn, starting with the complete <book> element, then the <bookName> element and its text, followed by the <bookPublishYear> element and its text.

It's also possible to pass the name of an element to match within the descendants() method, as shown here:

```
trace(authorsXML.author[3].books.descendants("bookPublishYear"));
```

This expression returns the value 2004.

Finding elements

The elements() method lists all of the elements of the XML object, ignoring comments and processing instructions. Unlike the descendants() method, elements() doesn't return the text nodes separately. You can see how this works by testing the following expression:

```
trace(authorsXML.author[3].books.elements());
```

This time, you'll see the following output:

```
<book ID="2">
  <bookName>Bike riding for non-bike riders</bookName>
  <bookPublishYear>2004</bookPublishYear>
</book>
```

Compare it with the earlier output from the descendants() method to see the difference.

Finding the parent element

The parent() method returns the complete parent element for the child path specified. Here is an example:

```
trace(authorsXML.author[0].books.parent());
```

This expression returns the first <author> element, complete with all of its children:

```
<author authorID="1">
  <authorFirstName>Alison</authorFirstName>
  <authorLastName>Ambrose</authorLastName>
  <books>
    <book bookID="1">
      <bookName>Shopping for profit and pleasure</bookName>
      <bookPublishYear>2002</bookPublishYear>
    </book>
    <book ID="4">
      <bookName>Fishing tips</bookName>
      <bookPublishYear>1999</bookPublishYear>
    </book>
  </books>
</author>
```

Locating text

The text() method returns all of the text nodes in an element. Note that these must be children of the specific element, rather than descendants. Here is an example of using this method:

```
trace(authorsXML.author[0].books.book.bookName.text());
```

If you test the expression, you will see the text nodes under all <bookName> elements for the first author:

```
Shopping for profit and pleasureFishing tips
```

It's possible to specify a single node by adding an index, as in this expression:

```
trace(authorsXML.author[0].books.book[1].bookName.text());
```

In this case, the output would display as follows:

```
Fishing tips
```

You can also combine the text() method with other methods, such as children(), as in this example:

```
trace (authorsXML.author[0].books.book.children().text());
```

Testing this expression produces the following output:

```
Shopping for profit and pleasure2002Fishing tips1999
```

You see all of the text inside the child elements of this author's <book> elements.

You can find all of the expressions discussed in this section in the resource files xmlObjectLocatingContent.fla and xmlObjectLocatingContent.mxml. Uncomment the expressions you wish to test. Run the file by pressing Ctrl/Cmd+Enter in Flash, or by clicking Debug or pressing F11 in Flex Builder.

79

Finding information about XML content

Other methods of the XML class provide information about the content in an XML object. Table 3-3 summarizes these methods.

Table 3-3. Methods of the XML class that provide information about XML content

Method	Description
childIndex()	Identifies the position of the child within its parent node, starting from zero.
hasComplexContent()	Determines whether an XML object contains complex content.
hasSimpleContent()	Determines whether an XML object contains simple content.
length()	Determines the number of nodes in the object. For an XML object, it always returns 1.
localName()	Returns the local name portion of a qualified name of an XML object, without the namespace reference.
name(prefix)	Returns the qualified name of the XML object.
namespace()	Returns the namespace associated with a qualified name.
nodeKind()	Returns the node kind: text, attribute, comment, processing-instruction, or element.
toString()	For complex content, returns XML content as a string containing all tags. It returns text only for simple content.
toXMLString()	Returns all XML content as a string including all tags, regardless of whether the content is simple or complex.
XML ()	Constructor method that creates a new XML object.

Most of these methods are self-explanatory—they return information about the specified XML element. Let's see how some of these methods work in Flash and Flex. Follow the instructions in the "Instructions for the code samples" section earlier in this chapter to set up the examples.

Finding an object's position within its parent

You can find the position of an object within its parent by using the childIndex() method, as in this example:

```
trace(authorsXML.author[3].books.childIndex());
```

Testing this line in the Flash document will produce the output 2. Because this value is zero-based, it indicates that the <books> element is the third child element of the fourth <author> element.

Determining content type

You can determine what type of content an XML object contains using the methods hasComplexContent()
and hasSimpleContent(). Simple content contains only text; complex content contains child nodes.
Both methods return a Boolean value.

The following example returns a value of true because the first <author> element has child nodes:

```
trace(authorsXML.author[0].hasComplexContent());
```

The next example returns a value of true because the <bookName> element contains only text.

```
trace(authorsXML.author[0].books.book[0].bookName.
➥hasSimpleContent());
```

Determining the number of elements

The length() method determines the number of elements in an XML object or XMLList. In the case
of an XML object, the method will always return a value of 1, because an XML object contains a single
item. This method returns the number of elements in an XMLList. It is typically used to loop through
all of the elements of the list, as shown in the following code sample:

```
for (var i:int=0; i < authorsXML.author.length();i++) {
  trace (authorsXML.author[i].authorLastName);
}
```

This loop displays each <authorLastName> from the authorsXML object. When you test your sample
file, this ActionScript block returns the following values:

```
Ambrose
Donaldson
Larcombe
Sorenson
```

Displaying the name of an element

Both the localName() and name() methods return the name of an element. The difference is that the
name() method returns the qualified name, which will occur if an element is part of a namespace.

The following shows the use of the name() method:

```
trace(authorsXML.author[0].children()[1].name());
```

In this case, testing the code will return the string authorLastName. Using the localName() method
would display the same output, as the element is not within a namespace.

Determining the type of node

You can determine the type of node within an XML object using the nodeKind() method. This method
will return one of the following values: text, comment, processing-instruction, attribute, or
element. Here is an example of using this method:

```
trace(authorsXML.author[0].books.nodeKind());
```

The expression returns the value element, indicating that <books> is an element.

81

Displaying a string representation of XML

The toString() and toXMLString() methods deserve some special attention. You can use both methods to return a string representation of an XML object. However, there is a slight difference. Consider the following XML object:

```
var simpleXML:XML = <contact>Sas Jacobs</contact>;
```

If you're working in Flash, add the XML object to the Actions layer. For Flex, add the following <mx:XML> element:

```
<mx:XML id="simpleXML">
  <contact>Sas Jacobs</contact>
</mx:XML>
```

Call both the toString() and toXMLString() methods on this XML object, as follows:

```
trace(simpleXML.toString());
trace(simpleXML.toXMLString());
```

When you apply the expression simpleXML.toString(), it returns the text Sas Jacobs. The expression simpleXML.toXMLString() returns <contact>Sas Jacobs</contact>. In this case, the XML object contains only simple content; that is, it is a single node containing text. It means that the toString() method will return only the text content inside the <contact> element. The toXMLString() method returns the full element, including the opening and closing tags.

If the XML object contained child elements or complex content, both the toString() and toXMLString() methods would return the same content. It would include all elements and text.

If you use the trace() method to display an XML or XMLList object without using either toString() or toXMLString(), the data will display using the toString() method.

You can find the examples in this section within the resource file xmlObjectFindingInformation.fla.

In addition to the methods mentioned previously, there are a number of methods that allow you to manipulate the content in XML and XMLList objects.

Modifying XML content

Several methods of the XML class can be used to modify an existing XML object. These are listed in Table 3-4.

You can use these methods to manipulate content within an XML object. For example, you may want to do the following:

- Change the values of nodes and attributes
- Add new nodes
- Duplicate nodes
- Delete nodes

You'll see how to carry out these tasks later in the book, in Chapter 8.

Table 3-4. Methods of the XML class for modifying XML content

Method	Description
appendChild(child)	Inserts a child node at the end of the child nodes collection of the specified node
copy()	Creates a copy of a node
insertChildAfter(child1, child2)	Inserts a child node after a specified child node
insertChildBefore(child1, child2)	Inserts a child node before a specified child node
prependChild(value)	Inserts a child node at the beginning of the child nodes of the specified node
replace(propertyName, value)	Replaces a specified property with a value
setChildren(value)	Replaces children of an XML object with specified content

Working with the XMLList class

An XMLList object is an ordered list of XML objects. It could be part of an XML document or a collection of XML objects. The XMLList class is useful because, being ordered, you can loop through the content. In fact, you saw an example of this a little earlier in the chapter. An XML object is the same as an XMLList that contains a single XML object.

If you're working with an XMLList containing a single XML object, you can use any of the methods of the XML class. Methods such as childIndex() wouldn't make sense if you were working with more than one XML object in the XMLList. You can also apply XML class methods on single elements of an XMLList.

If you try to use XML class methods on an XMLList containing more than one XML object, you'll cause an error. Instead, you'll need to loop through the XMLList and apply the methods on each individual XMLList element. For example, you can't find out if an entire XMLList contains simple content. Instead you need to apply the isSimpleContent() method on each XMLList element individually.

You can loop through an XMLList in several different ways. Here, I'll show you examples of each type of loop. Again, follow the instructions in the "Instructions for the code samples" section earlier in this chapter to set up the examples.

The first code example shows a simple for loop using a counter variable called i.

```
for (var i:int=0; i < authorsXML.author.length();i++) {
  trace (authorsXML.author[i].authorFirstName + " " +  authorsXML.
    ➥author[i].authorLastName);
}
```

The expression authorsXML.author returns an XMLList of all <author> elements. You can use the length() method to return the number of items in this XMLList. In this type of loop, you refer to each item in the list using its position, a zero-based number. The first item in the list is at position 0.

Testing the loop produces the following output:

```
Alison Ambrose
Douglas Donaldson
Lucinda Larcombe
Saul Sorenson
```

You can also use a for in loop to work through the XMLList. The following code block produces the same output as the previous example when tested:

```
for (var node:String in authorsXML.author) {
  trace(authorsXML.author[node].authorFirstName + " " + authorsXML.
    ➥author[node].authorLastName);
}
```

You declare node as a String variable because you're using it as a placeholder for the name of the node. This time, you pass the variable to the path authorsXML.author to locate each separate element.

A third alternative is to use a for each loop, as shown here:

```
for each(var aXML:XML in authorsXML.author) {
  trace(aXML.authorFirstName + " " + aXML.authorLastName);
}
```

This example produces the same output as the previous two examples. You define a placeholder variable called aXML to refer to each authorsXML.author element in the XMLList. You can then use the placeholder in a path with the child node values, as in aXML.authorFirstName.

You can find examples of all of these loop types in the resource files xmlListObjectLoops.fla and xmlListObjectLoops.mxml.

Working with the XMLListCollection class in Flex

If you're working with Flex, you can access the XMLListCollection class. This class is a wrapper for working with the XMLList class. It adds extra collection functionality to an XMLList. For example, you can access methods like removeItemAt() and removeAll(), which aren't available to the XMLList.

You would use the XMLListCollection object if you wanted to use the content as a data provider, because the collection will update when the XML content changes. In fact, Adobe recommends that you use the XMLListCollection object each time you assign an XMLList as a data provider. If you bind an XMLList object directly, the binding isn't monitored for changes.

To work with an XMLListCollection object in ActionScript code, you'll need to import the class first:

```
import mx.collections.XMLListCollection;
```

You can create an XMLListCollection object by passing an XMLList object when you call the constructor method, XMLListCollection():

```
var myXML_LC:XMLListCollection = new XMLListCollection(myXMLList);
```

You can also create the object without passing the XMLList as an argument. You do this by setting the source property of the XMLList after it is created, as follows:

```
var myXML_LC:XMLListCollection = new XMLListCollection();
myXML_LC.source = myXMLList;
```

Table 3-5 shows some of the additional properties that the XMLListCollection class makes available to an XMLList.

Table 3-5. Some of the properties of the XMLListCollection

Property	Type	Description
filterFunction	Function	A function that filters items in the list
length	int	The number of items in the list
sort	Sort	Specifies the order for the list
source	XMLList	The underlying XMLList

Two important tasks for developers are filtering and sorting content, so let's see how the filterFunction and sort properties work with an XMLListCollection.

Setting up the Flex application

Follow these steps to create the new Flex application that you'll use to test these examples:

1. Create a new Flex application in the project you set up earlier. You normally would have only one application file per project, but for simplicity, you can keep the files together in the same project.

2. Add the following interface elements:

```
<?xml version="1.0" encoding="utf-8"?>
<mx:Application xmlns:mx="http://www.adobe.com/2006/mxml"
  layout="absolute"  creationComplete="initApp(event)">
  <mx:XML id="authorsXML" source="assets/authors.xml"/>
  <mx:VBox x="10" y="10">
    <mx:TextArea id="txtAuthorsXML" width="400" height="100"/>
    <mx:Button id="btnClick" label="Click Me!"
      click="clickHandler(event)"/>
  </mx:VBox>
</mx:Application>
```

The interface contains a VBox that holds TextArea and Button components. The TextArea will display a string representation of the XML object. Clicking the button will apply a filter and a sort.

85

3. Add the following ActionScript code block to the file:

```
<mx:Script>
  <![CDATA[
    import mx.events.FlexEvent;
    import mx.collections.XMLListCollection;
    private var myXMLListCollection:XMLListCollection
    private function initApp(e:FlexEvent):void{
      myXMLListCollection = new XMLListCollection();
      myXMLListCollection.source = authorsXML.child("author")[0].
        ➥child("books").child("book");
      txtAuthorsXML.text = myXMLListCollection.toXMLString();
    }
    private function clickHandler(e:MouseEvent):void {
    }
  ]]>
</mx:Script>
```

The initApp() function sets up the object myXMLListCollection, which is of the type XMLListCollection. The application calls this function after the interface has been created. The function sets the source of the XMLListCollection object to an XMLList of all <book> elements inside the first <author> element.

```
authorsXML.child("author")[0].child("books").child("book")
```

The function then displays a string representation of the list in the txtAuthorsXML <mx:TextArea> element. You'll use the clickHandler function to demonstrate the filterFunction and sort properties of the XMLListCollection object.

4. Run the application, and you should see something like the output shown in Figure 3-4.

Figure 3-4. Displaying an XMLListCollection object

The TextArea displays an XMLListCollection containing books associated with the first author.

Next, you'll use the filterFunction property to apply a filter to this list.

Using a function to filter an XMLListCollection

The filterFunction property property creates a function that filters the items in an XMLListCollection. Calling the refresh() method of the XMLListCollection applies the filter.

The filterFunction determines whether a data item matches a filter expression and returns either true or false. If it returns true, the item appears in the filtered list.

You'll add a filter function that filters the XMLListCollection to display the book with an ID of 4. The application will call the function when a user clicks the Click Me! button.

1. Modify the clickHandler() function as shown here. The new lines appear in bold.

```
private function clickHandler(e:MouseEvent):void {
   myXMLListCollection.filterFunction = filterBooks;
   myXMLListCollection.refresh();
   txtAuthorsXML.text = myXMLListCollection.toXMLString();
}
```

The function sets the filterFunction property of the XMLListCollection object to the filterBooks function. It then calls the refresh() method to apply the filter, and finishes by displaying the filtered XMLListCollection in the <mx:TextArea> element.

2. The filterBooks() function needs to be added to the <mx:Script> block, as follows:

```
private function filterBooks(item:Object):Boolean {
 var booMatch:Boolean = false;
   if(item.attribute("bookID")== 4){
     booMatch = true;
   }
    return booMatch;
}
```

This function works through all items in the XMLListCollection. It uses a Boolean variable booMatch to determine whether the list item should appear in the filtered list. It compares the bookID attribute with the value 4. If there is a match, it sets the booMatch variable to true; otherwise, the variable contains the default value false.

> *It's a common naming convention to prefix the name of a variable with its data type. This example uses a Boolean variable, so I've used the name booMatch.*

The function returns the value of the booMatch variable. Items with a return value of true remain in the XMLListCollection when the refresh() method is called.

3. Run this application. The TextArea initially displays the entire XMLListCollection object.

4. Click the Click Me! button. The TextArea will display only the book with the bookID value of 4, as shown in Figure 3-5.

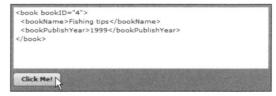

Figure 3-5. Filtering an XMLListCollection object

You can remove the filterFunction from an XMLListCollection by setting the value to null and applying the refresh() method.

Sorting an XMLListCollection

Another useful feature of the XMLListCollection class is the ability to sort content. We'll work through an example that changes the clickHandler() function to sort the XMLListCollection in order of the <bookName> element.

1. Before you add the ActionScript, you need to import the Sort and SortField classes. Add the following lines under the other import statements:

```
import mx.collections.Sort;
import mx.collections.SortField;
```

2. You'll create a Sort object and use the SortField class to specify the sort order. Modify the clickHandler() function as shown here. The changed lines appear in bold.

```
private function clickHandler(e:MouseEvent):void {
  var mySort:Sort = new Sort();
  mySort.fields = [new SortField("bookName", true)];
  myXMLListCollection.sort = mySort;
  myXMLListCollection.refresh();
  txtAuthorsXML.text = myXMLListCollection.toXMLString();
}
```

The function starts by declaring a new Sort object called mySort. It then sets the fields property of the sort, using a SortField that specifies the <bookName> element. The true parameter indicates that the sort is not case-sensitive. Note that if you had only one field to sort in the XMLListCollection, you would pass null instead of the element name.

The function sets the sort property of the XMLListCollection to the Sort object and calls the refresh() method. It finishes by displaying a string representation of the sorted list in the TextArea.

3. Run the application. Figure 3-6 shows the application in a web browser. The order of the <book> elements has changed so that they appear in alphabetical order of <bookName>.

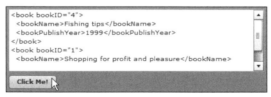

Figure 3-6. Applying a sort to the XMLListCollection

The XMLListCollection class also makes a number of additional methods available to an XMLList object. These methods are listed in Table 3-6.

Table 3-6. Some methods of the XMLListCollection

Method	Description
addItem(item)	Adds an item at the end of the list
addItemAt(item, index)	Adds an item at a specified position
getItemAt(index, prefetch)	Gets the item at the specified position
getItemIndex(item)	Gets the index of the item
removeAll()	Removes all items from the list
removeItemAt(index)	Removes the item at the specified position
setItemAt(item, index)	Places an item at a specified position

These methods add, move, and delete content from the XMLListCollection. The methods work in the same way as with an ArrayCollection object.

Next, let's look at working with the Namespace class.

Understanding the Namespace class

The Namespace class defines or references namespaces that are included in an XML object. It also has other uses in ActionScript 3.0 that we won't touch on here.

Namespace objects aren't usually required when you're working with simple XML content in your SWF applications. You need to work with namespaces only when you have XML content that refers to a namespace, perhaps because there's more than one element of the same name. This can happen when you refer to XML content from more than one source in the same XML object. The namespace provides the context for each element so it can be uniquely identified.

The following example shows an XML object containing two namespaces in the root element. The namespace attribute appears in bold.

```
var phoneBookXML:XML = <phoneBook
  xmlns:foe="http://www.foe.com/ns/"
  xmlns="http://www.sasjacobs.com/">
  <contact id="1">
    <foe:name>Sas Jacobs</name>
    <address>123 Red Street, Redland, Australia</address>
    <phone>123 456</phone>
  </contact>
</phoneBook>
```

The first namespace in the root element has the prefix foe. Any elements that start with this prefix fall within the http://www.foe.com/ns/ namespace. The code identifies that they are associated with that source.

The second namespace doesn't have a prefix. It is the default namespace for all elements inside the <phoneBook> element. The <contact>, <address>, and <phone> elements all fall within the default namespace.

To refer to any of the elements in this XML object, you need to qualify them with their namespace. In order to do that, you need to define a Namespace object for each namespace. You can define a Namespace object by referring to its URI, as shown in the following code:

```
var myNS:Namespace = new Namespace("http://www.foe.com/ns/");
var defaultNS:Namespace = new Namespace(http://www.sasjacobs.com/);
```

This code creates two Namespace objects, which I will refer to using the prefixes myNS and defaultNS.

As I mentioned previously, the URI that you use in a Namespace object doesn't actually need to house a document. The only requirement is that the location is unique among all of the namespaces in your SWF application.

The <name> element in the phoneBookXML object is prefixed by the text foe. This element has a local name of <name> and a qualified name of <foe:name>. If you had other <name> elements, you would need to work with the qualified name to distinguish them from this one.

Because the other elements are within the default namespace, they aren't written with a prefix. However, when you want to work with them in ActionScript, you'll need to qualify them with the default namespace.

You can access an element within a namespace by using the scoping operator ::. The scoping operator indicates that the local name is qualified by that namespace. XML documents use a colon to indicate the namespace. As the colon is reserved in ActionScript, you use the next best thing—two colons.

```
phoneBookXML.myNS::name
```

In this example, the <name> element, is qualified by the myNS Namespace object, which was declared earlier.

The next example shows an element in the default namespace.

```
phoneBookXML..defaultNS::contact
```

Even though the element doesn't display with a prefix in the XML object, you still need to work with the default Namespace object.

If all XML objects are within the same namespace, you can set a default namespace by using the statement's default xml namespace, as shown here:

```
var myNS:Namespace = Namespace("http://www.foe.com/ns/");
default xml namespace = myNS;
```

Let's look at an example so you can see where the Namespace class might come in handy. We'll work with a simple document that describes an XHTML <table> element as well as a furniture <table> element. I'll show this example in Flash; feel free to try to re-create it in Flex.

1. Create a new Flash document. Add the contents of the `sample.xml` document to an XML object called sampleXML, as follows:

```
var sampleXML:XML = <sample
  xmlns:html="http://www.w3.org/1999/xhtml">
  <table>Wood with four legs</table>
  <html:table>Text for an XHTML table</html:table>
</sample>;
```

2. Set a reference to the html namespace in the constructor of the Namespace class, as shown here:

```
var htmlNS:Namespace = new Namespace("http://www.w3.org/1999/xhtml");
```

3. Add the following `trace()` statements to view the contents of the XML object. You need to use the scoping operator to reference the htmlNS namespace.

```
trace(sampleXML.table);
trace(sampleXML.htmlNS::table);
```

4. Test the application. It should produce the following output:

```
Wood with four legs
Text for an XHTML table
```

In this example, you can see that the XML object contains two elements of the same name, `<table>`, one within the namespace prefixed with html. Tracing the local name table shows the contents of the `<table>` element that has no namespace assigned. If you had defined a default namespace, the second `<table>` element would be associated with it.

Using the scoping operator to add the htmlNS namespace to the `<table>` element produces a different result. It displays the contents of the `<table>` element associated with the http://www.w3.org/1999/xhtml namespace.

You'll need to understand this technique if you're working with elements that fall within declared namespaces. You can find the example used here saved in the resource file namespaceObject.fla.

Namespace objects are also used with the QName class.

Understanding the QName class

The QName class is really an abbreviation for the term *qualified name*. This class provides a mechanism for identifying qualified names for elements and attributes in an XML object. Qualified names are necessary when you are working with elements that fall in namespaces.

A QName has two parts: the local name for the element or attribute and a namespace URI to associate the element with a namespace. The namespace URI is optional, and you can omit it. If you do this, you'll map the element or attribute to the default global namespace for the XML object.

A QName object has two properties:

- localName: Returns the local (unqualified) name of the object.
- uri: Returns the URI of the namespace associated with the QName object.

You can create a QName object using the QName() constructor method. If you're using a namespace in your QName, you can either create a Namespace object or pass a string representing the namespace. The following example shows the use of a namespace in creating the QName object:

```
var myNS:Namespace = new Namespace("http://www.foe.com/ns/");
var myQName:QName = new QName(myNS, "localName");
```

This example is equivalent to the following line, which uses a string representation of the namespace:

```
var myQName:QName = new QName("http://www.foe.com/ns/", "localName");
```

The following steps demonstrate how to create QName objects and access their properties. We'll do this with a Flash file. Again, you might want to re-create this example yourself in Flex.

1. Create a new file and add the authorsShort.xml file contents to an XML object called authorsXML, as shown here:

```
var authorsXML:XML = <foe:allAuthors xmlns:foe=
➥"http://www.friendsofed.com/ns/"
➥xmlns="http://www.sasjacobs.com/ns/">
<author authorID="1">
  <authorFirstName>Alison</authorFirstName>
  <authorLastName>Ambrose</authorLastName>
  <books>
    <foe:book bookID="1">
      <bookName>Shopping for profit and pleasure</bookName>
      <bookPublishYear>2002</bookPublishYear>
    </foe:book>
    <book ID="4">
      <bookName>Fishing tips</bookName>
      <bookPublishYear>1999</bookPublishYear>
    </book>
  </books>
</author>
</foe:allAuthors>;
```

The XML document contains two namespaces in the root element. One is the default namespace, http://www.sasjacobs.com/ns/ and the other is the namespace foe, which has the URI http://www.friendsofed.com/ns/. The default namespace has no prefix. The first <book> element is within the foe namespace. The second is within the default namespace. You will create QName objects from these elements.

2. You need to map the two namespaces in the XML object. Use the following code to create two Namespace objects:

```
var foeNS:Namespace = new Namespace("foe",
  "http://www.friendsofed.com/ns/");
var defaultNS:Namespace = new Namespace("sas",
  "http://www.sasjacobs.com/ns/");
```

3. Create two QName objects to reference the `<book>` elements, as follows:

```
var foeBookQName:QName = new QName(foeNS, "book");
var defaultBookQName:QName = new QName(defaultNS, "book");
```

Using a QName object allows you to provide a unique reference for each of the qualified element names.

4. Add the following `trace()` actions to view the URI associated with each QName:

```
trace(foeBookQName.uri);
trace(defaultBookQName.uri);
```

5. Test the code. You should see this output:

```
http://www.friendsofed.com/ns/
http://www.sasjacobs.com/ns/
```

This example is simplistic, but it shows that you've mapped two different elements of the same name to different namespaces, and you have two different QName objects that you can use to reference the two `<book>` elements. You can find this example saved in the file `qNameObject.fla`.

Incidentally, if you were trying to locate elements in this XML object, you would need to use both Namespace objects with the scoping operator. For example, to get to the `<foe:book>` object, you would need to use this E4X expression:

```
trace (authorsXML.defaultNS::author[0].defaultNS::books.foeNS::book);
```

It could get very confusing if you didn't understand that the default namespace qualifies the `<author>` and `<books>` elements so it must be included in the expression. This issue is particularly important when working with web services and RSS feeds. You'll see this later, in Chapter 10.

As you've seen, the new E4X classes provide a more streamlined approach to working with XML content in SWF applications. However, you need to be aware of their limitations.

Limitations of working with the XML class

While the XML and XMLList classes are great additions to the ActionScript language, there are a couple limitations to their use. The first is within the ActionScript parser itself. The second relates to the relationship of the XML class to external XML documents.

The ActionScript 3.0 parser is nonvalidating, which means that if the XML content refers to an XML schema or DTD, the parser is not able to check that the content is valid. If you need to check that your XML content conforms to the rules of its vocabulary, you must do this outside your SWF application. This could prove cumbersome when using dynamically generated content from a database.

The second issue relates to the loading of external, dynamically generated XML documents into SWF applications. In order to load external content into a SWF application, the application must first request the XML document. If the external content changes, the SWF application must request the document again in order to access the changed content.

When working with the XML class, the only solution is for the SWF application to poll the server continually, in case the content has changed. It's simply not possible for the external XML data source to push content into an XML object in a SWF application. I'm sure you'll agree that this is not a very practical approach. An alternative is to use the XMLSocket class. We won't cover that approach in the book, as it's an advanced topic.

Summary

This chapter introduced the ActionScript 3.0 classes that fall within the E4X specification. You learned how to work with the XML object as a data type, and you saw examples of the XML class properties and methods. You also learned how to work with the XMLList, XMLListCollection, Namespace, and QName classes.

In the next chapter, we'll look at some other types of E4X expressions and see how they can be used to locate content in an XML object.

Chapter 4

USING E4X EXPRESSIONS

E4X is a new recommendation for working with XML documents. ActionScript 3.0 bases all of its XML functionality on this recommendation. E4X is short for the ECMAScript for XML specification, ECMA-357. This is a standard managed by the European Computer Manufacturers Association (ECMA). You can find a copy of the standard at http://www.ecma-international.org/publications/standards/ Ecma-357.htm.

In the previous chapter, you saw the classes that form part of the new E4X functionality. We worked through the methods of the XML class that you can use to locate content in an XML document. E4X expressions provide an alternative to the XML class methods for navigating through XML content. As with the XML class methods, in addition to retrieving values, E4X expressions can assign values to both attributes and elements.

E4X expressions provide a type of shorthand that's similar to XPath, which is a W3C recommendation that explains how to address content in different parts of an XML document. You can read more about this recommendation at http://www.w3.org/ TR/xpath, if you're interested.

E4X expressions allow you to navigate through an XML document using node names in paths separated by dots. Instead of complicated and not very descriptive ActionScript 2.0 paths, E4X expressions describe a path to the data using the names of nodes and attributes to create expressions. These expressions can also apply filters and insert new content.

In this chapter, you'll work through some examples of E4X expressions and see how to use them to locate content in an XML object. You can find the resources for this chapter at http://www.friendsofed.com.

Understanding E4X expressions

Like XML class methods, E4X expressions specify a path through element and node names starting with the root element. A dot separates each name, and the expression reads from left to right. Here is an example of an E4X expression:

```
authorsXML.author[0].books.book[0];
```

This expression lists each of the node names in order, ending with the <book> element. It also includes index numbers, to identify the location of the item in its list. It's much easier to understand this expression compared with an ActionScript 2.0 path, which might look like the following:

```
authorsXML.firstChild.childNodes[0].childNodes[0];
```

In the second example, you can't easily determine which content you're targeting. The use of childNodes bears no relationship to the name of any element in the XML document.

In addition, because you don't use names in ActionScript 2.0 paths, you need to loop through collections of child elements, testing the element name until you locate the correct content. Not only does this require more code, but it also takes longer to process an XML document than in ActionScript 3.0, where you can write an expression that targets a precise location.

Using dot notation to locate content is familiar to Flash and Flex developers used to working in object-oriented environments. They frequently use this type of expression when working with objects, methods, and classes.

As I mentioned earlier, if you've worked with XPath, using dot notation to target XML content will be an approach familiar to you. In fact, compatibility with XPath was one of the aims of E4X. You'll find that the syntax for expressions matches exactly, although E4X expressions provide somewhat less functionality than XPath.

In broad terms, you can use the following constructs in an E4X expression:

- A dot operator (.) to specify a path through child elements
- An attribute operator (@) to identify an attribute name
- The descendants operator (..) to specify descendant elements
- Filter expressions to provide an expression to match

We'll cover each of these areas in turn by working through some examples. We'll also compare the E4X expressions with the equivalent expressions using XML class methods. If you want to work through the examples yourself, you can use either Flash or Flex Builder, and I've provided instructions for both environments.

Working through the examples

To explore E4X expressions, we'll work with the following XML document, saved as authorDetails.
xml with your chapter resources.

```
<allAuthors>
  <publisher>Friendly Books</publisher>
  <publishYear>2008</publishYear>
  <author authorID="1">
    <authorFirstName>Alison</authorFirstName>
    <authorLastName>Ambrose</authorLastName>
    <books>
      <book ID="1">
        <bookName>Shopping for profit and pleasure</bookName>
        <bookPublishYear>2002</bookPublishYear>
        <bookCost>14.99</bookCost>
      </book>
      <book ID="4">
        <bookName>Fishing tips</bookName>
        <bookPublishYear>1999</bookPublishYear>
        <bookCost>23.50</bookCost>
      </book>
    </books>
  </author>
  <author authorID="2">
    <authorFirstName>Douglas</authorFirstName>
    <authorLastName>Donaldson</authorLastName>
    <books>
      <book ID="5">
        <bookName>Outstanding dinner parties</bookName>
        <bookPublishYear>2003</bookPublishYear>
        <bookCost>35.99</bookCost>
      </book>
      <book ID="9">
        <bookName>Cooking for fun and profit</bookName>
        <bookPublishYear>2007</bookPublishYear>
        <bookCost>24.75</bookCost>
      </book>
    </books>
  </author>
</allAuthors>
```

This XML document describes a list of authors and their books. It includes several elements of each type so that the examples can demonstrate many different types of expressions.

We'll load this content into an XML object and write a series of E4X expressions. In our expressions, the name of the XML object will be equivalent to the root element <allAuthors>, so we won't need to include that element in the paths that we create.

Before starting, you need to set up the working environment for the examples. Feel free to use either Flash or Flex.

Working with Flash

You can work through with the examples in this chapter using Flash by setting up a file according to the following instructions:

1. Create a new Flash document and add a new layer called actions.

2. Open the actions layer in the Actions panel using the F9 shortcut key, and add the following code:

```
initApp();
function initApp():void {
}
```

3. Add an XML object called authorsXML to the initApp() function. Copy the content from the authorDetails.xml document and assign it to an XML object. The following block shows the first two lines to get you started:

```
var authorsXML:XML = <allAuthors>
  <publisher>Friendly Books</publisher>
```

You'll add the sample expressions that you want to test inside the initApp() function, underneath the authorsXML object. We'll use trace() and the toXMLString() method of the XML class to display the results of each expression in the Output panel. Obviously, in the future, you won't need these methods if you're identifying content that you don't need to display in the Output panel.

Working with Flex

Here are the instructions for the Flex examples:

1. Create a new project and application file with the name of your choosing.

2. Create a new folder in the src folder of the project called assets and copy the authorDetails.xml file to that folder.

3. Enter the following <mx:XML> element after the opening <mx:Application> element:

```
<mx:XML id="authorsXML" source="assets/authorDetails.xml"/>
```

This line assigns the contents from the authorDetails.xml document in the assets folder to the authorsXML object.

4. Modify the <mx:Application> element to add a creationComplete attribute as shown here:

```
<mx:Application xmlns:mx="http://www.adobe.com/2006/mxml"
layout="absolute" creationComplete="initApp(event)">
```

When the creation of the interface completes, the application will call the initApp() function, passing a FlexEvent object.

5. Add the following <mx:Script> block below the opening <mx:Application> element:

```
<mx:Script>
  <![CDATA[
    import mx.events.FlexEvent;
    private function initApp(e:FlexEvent):void {
    }
  ]]>
</mx:Script>
```

This script block includes the initApp() function. You need to import the FlexEvent class, as that object is passed within the initApp() function.

You'll add the expressions that you want to test inside the initApp() function. These expressions will include trace() so that you can see the results in the Console view. You won't need to include this method normally. You must remember to debug the application instead of running it, so you can view the output. To do so, choose Run ➤ Debug and select the application to run.

Let's start by looking at how to use the dot operator to specify paths.

Using the dot operator to specify a path

E4X expressions specify their paths in the same way as the XML class methods that you saw in the previous chapter. They start with the root element, and use element and attribute names in order until they reach the ending point. The most important thing to remember is that the name of the XML object provides the starting point or root node for the path. In our example, all expressions will start with the name authorsXML, which equates to the root node and is the name of the XML object.

E4X expressions can target elements and attributes within an XML object using their names, and sometimes their position in the list. Some expressions will return text information; others will return an XMLList object. We'll start with the simplest of E4X expressions—one that returns text.

Returning text

Very simple E4X expressions appear to return only text. This is the case when you're targeting the content that contains only a text node. Here is an example:

```
authorsXML.publisher;
```

Technically, this expression returns an XMLList object with a single element, <publisher>.

To see the results of this expression, wrap it in the trace() method, as shown here:

```
trace(authorsXML.publisher);
```

When tested, the expression displays the output Friendly Books. This is the text stored in the <publisher> element, a child of the root element. Because this example doesn't specify the toString() or toXMLString() method to display the information, the toString() method is used. If you're not sure about the difference between these two methods, refer to the "Displaying a string representation of XML" section in the previous chapter.

You can also use the text() method to return the text content inside the element, as shown in this example:

```
trace (authorsXML.publisher.text());
```

This expression returns an XMLList of all text nodes within the <publisher> element. In this case, there is only one text node: the content Friendly Books.

Although the second expression appears to return the same content as the first, it's actually a little different. The first expression returns an XMLList object, whereas the second example returns the text inside the XMLList object.

Another way to access content is to use the child() method of the XML class to retrieve the <publisher> element, as shown here:

```
trace (authorsXML.child("publisher"));
```

This expression returns the element itself, rather than just the text. You might use this approach inside a function. It's useful if you need to pass a String argument representing the name of the element to locate. You can't do that using dot notation.

I think you'll agree that using the shorthand E4X expression is probably a little easier. It certainly takes less code, and it is easier to read. When you start to work with more complicated paths, you'll see that it's easier to use the dot notation.

Returning an XMLList

E4X expressions usually return XMLList objects. For example, the following expression returns an XMLList of all <author> elements:

```
authorsXML.author;
```

This expression retrieves all <author> child elements within the root node and returns an XMLList object.

Wrap the expression inside a trace() action with the toXMLString() method, as shown here:

```
trace(authorsXML.author.toXMLString());
```

Test or debug the application, and you'll see the following output:

```
<author authorID="1">
  <authorFirstName>Alison</authorFirstName>
  <authorLastName>Ambrose</authorLastName>
  <books>
    <book bookID="1">
      <bookName>Shopping for profit and pleasure</bookName>
      <bookPublishYear>2002</bookPublishYear>
      <bookCost>14.99</bookCost>
    </book>
    <book ID="4">
      <bookName>Fishing tips</bookName>
      <bookPublishYear>1999</bookPublishYear>
      <bookCost>23.50</bookCost>
    </book>
  </books>
</author>
```

```
<author authorID="2">
  <authorFirstName>Douglas</authorFirstName>
  <authorLastName>Donaldson</authorLastName>
  <books>
    <book ID="5">
      <bookName>Outstanding dinner parties</bookName>
      <bookPublishYear>2003</bookPublishYear>
      <bookCost>35.99</bookCost>
    </book>
    <book ID="9">
      <bookName>Cooking for fun and profit</bookName>
      <bookPublishYear>2007</bookPublishYear>
      <bookCost>24.75</bookCost>
    </book>
  </books>
</author>
```

The example locates a complete list of <author> elements, including all of their children.

This expression is equivalent to the following XML class method:

```
trace (authorsXML.child("author"));
```

You'll see the same output if you test this equivalent expression.

When an E4X expression returns an XMLList containing more than one element, you may need to loop through the elements to work with each in turn. The following code block demonstrates how to loop through this XMLList returned by the previous example and identify the name of each author:

```
for each(var aXML:XML in authorsXML.author) {
  trace(aXML.authorFirstName + " " + aXML.authorLastName);
}
```

This type of loop is new to ActionScript 3.0. There are alternative methods for looping. The "Working with the XMLList class" section in the previous chapter shows three different approaches to looping through XMLList objects.

You can check that what the E4X expression returns is actually an XMLList object by using is XMLList, as follows:

```
trace(authorsXML.author is XMLList);
```

> Note that there is a space between the word is and XMLList in this expression. Do not try to use isXMLList, as that will throw an error.

Testing the output displays the value true because the expression produces an XMLList object.

Specifying an index

You might want to work with a specific item from the XMLList returned by the E4X expression. For this reason, E4X expressions can target a specific element by using its index number in the XMLList. Each element has a position in the list, starting at 0 for the first element. You identify the index number using square brackets: [ ]. This approach is very similar to working with arrays in ActionScript.

You can target the first <author> element in the collection of all <author> elements with the following expression:

```
trace(authorsXML.author[0].toXMLString());
```

This expression produces the following output:

```
<author authorID="1">
  <authorFirstName>Alison</authorFirstName>
  <authorLastName>Ambrose</authorLastName>
  <books>
    <book bookID="1">
      <bookName>Shopping for profit and pleasure</bookName>
      <bookPublishYear>2002</bookPublishYear>
      <bookCost>14.99</bookCost>
    </book>
    <book ID="4">
      <bookName>Fishing tips</bookName>
      <bookPublishYear>1999</bookPublishYear>
      <bookCost>23.50</bookCost>
    </book>
  </books>
</author>
```

The details of the first author, Alison Ambrose, display.

This shorthand E4X expression is equivalent to the following line, which uses XML class methods.

```
trace(authorsXML.child("author")[0].toXMLString());
```

The item index does not need to appear as the last point in the path. You can also include the item index at other positions, as shown here:

```
trace(authorsXML.author[0].books.book[1].toXMLString());
```

This expression includes two indexes and targets the second book of the first author. Testing the expression produces the following output:

```
<book ID="4">
  <bookName>Fishing tips</bookName>
  <bookPublishYear>1999</bookPublishYear>
  <bookCost>23.50</bookCost>
</book>
```

Another way to find this information is as follows:

```
trace(authorsXML.child("author")[0].child("books").child("book")[1]
➥.toXMLString());
```

Again, using XML class methods creates a much longer expression.

> If XML *class methods create longer expressions, do you still need to use them? The answer is definitely!* XML *class methods help out where the name of an element is a reserved word in ActionScript. For example, if the element were called <result>, in some situations you would see an error when including the element in an E4X expression. The solution would be to use* `child("result")` *instead.*
>
> *You also use* XML *class methods when you want to pass a dynamic element name to an expression. By using a string value, you are able to substitute a variable name, for example, when passing an element name to a public method of a class file.*

Finding the last element

You can find the last element in an XMLList object by using the length() method in the expression. This method returns a number equal to the number of items in the XMLList. This will be one more than the last item in the XMLList, because the index is a zero-based number.

The following lines show how to use this approach to find the last element in an XMLList.

```
var lastIndex:int = authorsXML.author[0].books.book.length() - 1;
trace(authorsXML.author[0].books.book[lastIndex].toXMLString());
```

This expression displays the second book of the first author, which also happens to be the last book, as in the previous example.

Casting returned content

It's important to note that ActionScript treats all nodes and attribute values as strings, so you may need to cast values of a different data type; for example, if you want to use a number in a calculation.

The following lines provide a good illustration:

```
trace(authorsXML.author[0].books.book[1].bookCost);
trace (authorsXML.author[0].books.book[1].bookCost + 10);
trace (Number(authorsXML.author[0].books.book[1].bookCost) + 10);
```

Testing the first line displays 23.50 in the Output panel or Console view. You can tell that this value is a string by the expression in the second line, which adds 10. Testing that expression produces the output 23.5010—the two values are concatenated. If you cast the value as a number first and add 10, you'll create an addition, as shown in the third line. Testing this line produces the sum 33.5.

> *Working with dates can be even more problematic, as it's much harder to cast XML date types directly as ActionScript date types. The two formats just don't translate easily. I've found that in most cases, it's better to use string manipulation to separate out the date parts and create a new ActionScript date from those parts.*

Using the wildcard operator (*)

You can use the wildcard operator * to match any name in the XML object. You can use this operator in the following way:

```
trace(authorsXML.*.toXMLString());
```

This expression finds all children of the root element, regardless of their name, and produces the following output:

```
<publisher>Friendly Books</publisher>
<publishYear>2008</publishYear>
<author authorID="1">
  <authorFirstName>Alison</authorFirstName>
  <authorLastName>Ambrose</authorLastName>
  <books>
    <book bookID="1">
      <bookName>Shopping for profit and pleasure</bookName>
      <bookPublishYear>2002</bookPublishYear>
      <bookCost>14.99</bookCost>
    </book>
    <book ID="4">
      <bookName>Fishing tips</bookName>
      <bookPublishYear>1999</bookPublishYear>
      <bookCost>23.50</bookCost>
    </book>
  </books>
</author>
<author authorID="2">
  <authorFirstName>Douglas</authorFirstName>
  <authorLastName>Donaldson</authorLastName>
  <books>
    <book ID="5">
      <bookName>Outstanding dinner parties</bookName>
      <bookPublishYear>2003</bookPublishYear>
      <bookCost>35.99</bookCost>
    </book>
    <book ID="9">
      <bookName>Cooking for fun and profit</bookName>
      <bookPublishYear>2007</bookPublishYear>
      <bookCost>24.75</bookCost>
    </book>
  </books>
</author>
```

You can see that the expression returns all of the content from the XML object, except the root element. This expression is equivalent to the following, which uses XML class methods:

```
trace(authorsXML.children().toXMLString());
```

You can also include the wildcard in a longer expression, as shown here:

```
trace(authorsXML.author[1].*.toXMLString());
```

This expression finds all children of the second author. You would see the following output when testing the expression:

```
<authorFirstName>Douglas</authorFirstName>
<authorLastName>Donaldson</authorLastName>
<books>
  <book ID="5">
    <bookName>Outstanding dinner parties</bookName>
    <bookPublishYear>2003</bookPublishYear>
    <bookCost>35.99</bookCost>
  </book>
  <book ID="9">
    <bookName>Cooking for fun and profit</bookName>
    <bookPublishYear>2007</bookPublishYear>
    <bookCost>24.75</bookCost>
  </book>
</books>
```

Notice that the expression provides all content as elements and attributes. The text nodes aren't provided separately.

The equivalent expression with XML class methods follows:

```
trace(authorsXML.child("author")[1].children().toXMLString());
```

You can also use a wildcard in this way:

```
trace(authorsXML.*[1].toXMLString()));
```

This expression retrieves the second child from the list of all child elements of the root node. You would see the following output upon testing:

```
<publishYear>2008</publishYear>
```

And here is the equivalent expression using XML methods:

```
trace(authorsXML.children()[1].toXMLString());
```

You can find all the examples referred to in this section saved in the resource files e4xDotNotationExamples.fla and E4xDotNotationExamples.mxml. If you didn't work through the examples yourself, uncomment the lines you wish to test.

Using the attribute operator (@)

It's possible to target attributes within an element by using the shorthand attribute operator, @. This operator is identical to the one used in XPath.

Consider the following example:

```
trace(authorsXML.author.@authorID.toXMLString());
```

This expression returns a list of all of the authorID attributes of every `<author>` element in the XML object. You see the following output after testing:

```
1
2
```

This expression is equivalent to the following XML class attribute() method:

```
trace(authorsXML.child("author").attribute("authorID")
➥.toXMLString());
```

You can use the following expression to find the ID attribute of the first `<book>` element of the second `<author>`:

```
trace(authorsXML.author[1].books.book[0].@ID.toXMLString());
```

You would see 5 when you tested the expression.

The equivalent XML class methods expression follows:

```
trace(authorsXML.child("author")[1].child("books").child("book")[0]
➥.attribute("ID").toXMLString());
```

I know which expression is easier to read!

You can also include a wildcard in the expression with the attribute operator to get a list of all attribute values within an element, as in the following example:

```
trace(authorsXML.author[0].@*.toXMLString());
```

This expression finds all attribute values of the first author. In this case, it displays a value of 1, because we have only a single attribute in the `<author>` element. The expression is equivalent to the following:

```
trace(authorsXML.child("author")[0].attributes().toXMLString());
```

Looping through attributes

The new ActionScript 3.0 for each loop allows you to loop through all attributes of an element using the following approach:

```
for each(var att:XML in authorsXML.author[0].attributes()) {
  trace(authorsXML.author[0].@[att.name()].toXMLString());
}
```

This example iterates through all of the attributes of the first <author> element. It uses the name() method with the shorthand operator @ to identify each attribute and displays the value. Again, in our example, the <author> element has only a single attribute, so you'll see the value 1 when you test the code.

You can also loop through the authorID attributes of each author using the following code:

```
for each(var aXML:XML in authorsXML.author) {
   trace(aXML.@authorID.toString());
}
```

This produces the following output:

```
1
2
```

The following code block is equivalent:

```
for each(var aXML:XML in authorsXML.child("author")) {
   trace(aXML.attribute("authorID").toString());
}
```

You can find these examples in the resource files e4xAttributesExamples.fla and E4xAttributesExamples.mxml. You'll need to uncomment the relevant lines to test them.

Using the descendants operator (..)

The descendants operator (..) retrieves all descendants that exist within the XML object, regardless of their position. It works in the same way as the XML class method descendants().

The following expression locates all <book> elements within the authorsXML object, regardless of their position:

```
trace(authorsXML..book.toXMLString());
```

Testing this expression produces the following output:

```
<book bookID="1">
  <bookName>Shopping for profit and pleasure</bookName>
  <bookPublishYear>2002</bookPublishYear>
  <bookCost>14.99</bookCost>
</book>
<book ID="4">
  <bookName>Fishing tips</bookName>
  <bookPublishYear>1999</bookPublishYear>
  <bookCost>23.50</bookCost>
</book>
<book ID="5">
  <bookName>Outstanding dinner parties</bookName>
  <bookPublishYear>2003</bookPublishYear>
  <bookCost>35.99</bookCost>
</book>
```

```
<book ID="9">
  <bookName>Cooking for fun and profit</bookName>
  <bookPublishYear>2007</bookPublishYear>
  <bookCost>24.75</bookCost>
</book>
```

The expression returns all <book> elements as an XMLList. It is equivalent to using the following method of the XML class:

```
trace(authorsXML.descendants("book").toXMLString());
```

You can return all descendants of a specific element by using the wildcard *, as follows:

```
trace (authorsXML.author[0].books..*);
```

This expression finds all descendants of the <books> element of the first author. Testing produces the following output:

```
<book bookID="1">
  <bookName>Shopping for profit and pleasure</bookName>
  <bookPublishYear>2002</bookPublishYear>
  <bookCost>14.99</bookCost>
</book>
<bookName>Shopping for profit and pleasure</bookName>
Shopping for profit and pleasure
<bookPublishYear>2002</bookPublishYear>
2002
<bookCost>14.99</bookCost>
14.99
<book ID="4">
  <bookName>Fishing tips</bookName>
  <bookPublishYear>1999</bookPublishYear>
  <bookCost>23.50</bookCost>
</book>
<bookName>Fishing tips</bookName>
Fishing tips
<bookPublishYear>1999</bookPublishYear>
1999
<bookCost>23.50</bookCost>
23.50
```

Notice that the output includes the elements and text nodes. Compare this with the expression that finds all child elements that you saw earlier. It didn't return the text nodes.

The equivalent expression using XML class methods follows:

```
trace (authorsXML.child("author")[0].child("books")
➥.descendants("*"));
```

You can find these examples in the resource files e4xDescendantsExamples.fla and E4xDescendantsExamples.mxml.

Table 4-1 provides a summary of E4X expressions and their equivalent XML class methods.

Table 4-1. Summary of E4X expressions and equivalent XML class methods

E4X expression	XML class expression
authorsXML.publisher	authorsXML.child("publisher")
authorsXML.author	authorsXML.child("author")
authorsXML.author[0]	authorsXML.child("author")[0]
authorsXML.author[0].books.book[1]	authorsXML.child("author")[0].child("books").child("book")[1]
authorsXML.*	authorsXML.children()
authorsXML.author[1].*	authorsXML.child("author")[1].children()
authorsXML.*[1]	authorsXML.children()[1]
authorsXML.author.@authorID	authorsXML.child("author").attribute("authorID")
authorsXML.author[1].books.book[0].@ID	authorsXML.child("author")[1].child("books").child("book")[0].attribute("ID")
authorsXML.author[0].@*	authorsXML.child("author")[0].attributes()
authorsXML..book	authorsXML.descendants("book")
authorsXML.author[0].books..*	authorsXML.child("author")[0].child("books").descendants("*")

Working with filter expressions

As with XPath, you can use filters in E4X expressions by writing a predicate or condition inside parentheses. The filters work in much the same way as XPath. However, unlike XPath, E4X expressions cannot be used to search for ancestors. When you apply a filter, you're essentially looping through the entire collection of elements and returning only those that match the specified condition or conditions.

You can use the == and != comparison operators to identify specific elements. You can also use AND (&&) and OR (||) expressions. You can even use the additive operator (+) for either mathematical expressions or concatenation.

Let's see how each type of filter works.

111

Working with equality

You can apply a filter that tests for equality using ==. This operator is the same one used in ActionScript expressions.

You need to specify the element or attribute to compare and the comparison value, as shown here:

```
authorFirstName =="Douglas"
```

The following example finds the details of the `<authorFirstName>` element that has the value equal to Douglas:

```
trace(authorsXML.author.(authorFirstName =="Douglas").toXMLString());
```

The predicate `authorFirstName == "Douglas"` works just like an `if` statement. It locates only authors with a first name of Douglas. Filters can be a great way to avoid using conditional statements such as `if` in your ActionScript code. They save you from using the ActionScript 2.0 approach of having to loop through all elements and attributes to test for a condition.

The filter expression produces the following output when tested:

```
<author authorID="2">
  <authorFirstName>Douglas</authorFirstName>
  <authorLastName>Donaldson</authorLastName>
  <books>
    <book ID="5">
      <bookName>Outstanding dinner parties</bookName>
      <bookPublishYear>2003</bookPublishYear>
      <bookCost>35.99</bookCost>
    </book>
    <book ID="9">
      <bookName>Cooking for fun and profit</bookName>
      <bookPublishYear>2007</bookPublishYear>
      <bookCost>24.75</bookCost>
    </book>
  </books>
</author>
```

This expression is equivalent to the following:

```
trace(authorsXML.child("author").(authorFirstName =="Douglas")
➥.toXMLString());
```

It returns the entire `<author>` node for this first name. It's important to note that, even though you applied the filter to a child of the `<author>` element, `<authorFirstName>`, you didn't retrieve elements from that point onward. It doesn't matter which element or attribute has the filter applied; the expression returns content from the point prior to the filter. In this case, it still returns the `<author>` element.

A filter doesn't need to appear last in the E4X expression. You can include the filter partway through an expression, as shown here:

```
trace(authorsXML.author.(authorFirstName =="Douglas").books.book
➥.toXMLString());
```

In this case, the filter still applies to the <authorFirstName> element, but it returns only the <book> elements. The expression produces the following output:

```
<book ID="5">
  <bookName>Outstanding dinner parties</bookName>
  <bookPublishYear>2003</bookPublishYear>
  <bookCost>35.99</bookCost>
</book>
<book ID="9">
  <bookName>Cooking for fun and profit</bookName>
  <bookPublishYear>2007</bookPublishYear>
  <bookCost>24.75</bookCost>
</book>
```

The following expression is equivalent:

```
trace(authorsXML.child("author").(child("authorFirstName")
➥=="Douglas").child("books").child("book").toXMLString());
```

Applying a filter to an attribute is similar.

```
trace(authorsXML.author.(authorFirstName =="Douglas")
➥books.book.(@ID=="9").toXMLString());
```

This expression returns the entire <book> element for the author with the last name Douglas where the ID attribute is equal to 9, as follows:

```
<book ID="9">
  <bookName>Cooking for fun and profit</bookName>
  <bookPublishYear>2007</bookPublishYear>
  <bookCost>24.75</bookCost>
</book>
```

You can see that it's possible to apply more than one filter in an expression. The equivalent expression using XML class methods follows:

```
trace (authorsXML.child("author").(child("authorFirstName")
➥== "Douglas").child("books").child("book")
➥.(attribute("ID") == "9").toXMLString());
```

Finding inequality

To find elements or attributes that don't match, you can use the inequality operator (!=). This works in the same way as in ActionScript expressions.

The following example shows how to use this operator to find authors with a first name that isn't Douglas.

```
trace(authorsXML.author.(authorFirstName !="Douglas").toXMLString());
```

When you test the expression, you'll see the following output:

```
<author authorID="1">
  <authorFirstName>Alison</authorFirstName>
  <authorLastName>Ambrose</authorLastName>
  <books>
    <book bookID="1">
      <bookName>Shopping for profit and pleasure</bookName>
      <bookPublishYear>2002</bookPublishYear>
      <bookCost>14.99</bookCost>
    </book>
    <book ID="4">
      <bookName>Fishing tips</bookName>
      <bookPublishYear>1999</bookPublishYear>
      <bookCost>23.50</bookCost>
    </book>
  </books>
</author>
```

The expression shows all other <author> elements. In this case, it produces details of the author Alison Ambrose. The equivalent XML class expression follows:

```
trace(authorsXML.child("author").
➥(child("authorFirstName") !="Douglas").toXMLString());
```

Other comparisons

In your comparisons, you can also use the > and < operators, as well as the <= and >= operators. The following example finds the name of all books where the cost is below 20:

```
trace(authorsXML..book.(bookCost < 20).bookName.toString());
```

Notice that this example uses the descendants operator (..) to locate all <book> child elements. This expression produces the following book, which has a cost of less than 20:

```
Shopping for profit and pleasure
```

Here is an equivalent expression:

```
trace(authorsXML.descendants("book").
➥(child("bookCost") < 20).child("bookName").toString());
```

Using AND and OR in conditions

You can write more complicated filtering expressions by using the && (AND) and || (OR) operators. Again, these are the same operators used in ActionScript. An example follows:

```
trace(authorsXML..book.(@ID=="9" || @ID=="5").toXMLString());
```

This expression looks for <book> elements with the ID of 9 or 5. It uses the descendants operator (..) as well as the OR operator. Testing the expression produces the following output:

```
<book ID="5">
  <bookName>Outstanding dinner parties</bookName>
  <bookPublishYear>2003</bookPublishYear>
  <bookCost>35.99</bookCost>
</book>
<book ID="9">
  <bookName>Cooking for fun and profit</bookName>
  <bookPublishYear>2007</bookPublishYear>
  <bookCost>24.75</bookCost>
</book>
```

This expression is equivalent to the following:

```
trace(authorsXML.descendants("book").(attribute("ID")=="9" ||
➥attribute("ID")=="5").toXMLString());
```

An AND example follows:

```
trace(authorsXML.author.(authorFirstName=="Alison" &&
➥authorLastName=="Ambrose").toXMLString());
```

This expression finds an author with the first name of Alison and the last name of Ambrose. You see the following output after testing the expression:

```
<author authorID="1">
  <authorFirstName>Alison</authorFirstName>
  <authorLastName>Ambrose</authorLastName>
  <books>
    <book ID="1">
      <bookName>Shopping for profit and pleasure</bookName>
      <bookPublishYear>2002</bookPublishYear>
      <bookCost>14.99</bookCost>
    </book>
    <book ID="4">
      <bookName>Fishing tips</bookName>
      <bookPublishYear>1999</bookPublishYear>
      <bookCost>23.50</bookCost>
    </book>
  </books>
</author>
```

You would get the same result with the following expression:

```
trace(authorsXML.child("author").(child("authorFirstName")=="Alison"
➥&& child("authorLastName")=="Ambrose").toXMLString());
```

You could also use the AND and OR operators to find different elements, as follows:

```
trace(authorsXML..*.(name() == "bookName"
➥|| name() == "bookCost").toXMLString());
```

This expression uses the name() XML class method with the wildcard operator (*) to apply the filter to an element name. It finds all descendants where the name of the element is either bookName or bookCost. Testing produces the following output:

```
<bookName>Shopping for profit and pleasure</bookName>
<bookCost>14.99</bookCost>
<bookName>Fishing tips</bookName>
<bookCost>23.50</bookCost>
<bookName>Outstanding dinner parties</bookName>
<bookCost>35.99</bookCost>
<bookName>Cooking for fun and profit</bookName>
<bookCost>24.75</bookCost>
```

Using the additive operator (+)

You can use E4X expressions in numeric calculations so long as the returned values produce numbers rather than XMLList or XML objects. For example, you can use the additive operator (+) to either add or concatenate element or attribute values. Bear in mind that all values are treated as strings, so you will need to cast any numeric types appropriately before you carry out the calculation. I'll illustrate what I mean with some examples.

The following expression uses the additive operator with two <bookCost> elements:

```
trace(authorsXML.author[0].books.book[0].bookCost.text() +
➥authorsXML.author[0].books.book[1].bookCost.text());
```

Testing it produces the following:

```
14.9923.50
```

The expression concatenates the values 14.99 and 23.50. This occurs because the returned values are of the String data type.

Instead, you can cast the values as numbers before adding them by using the following expression:

```
trace(Number(authorsXML.author[0].books.book[0].bookCost.text()) +
➥Number(authorsXML.author[0].books.book[1].bookCost.text()));
```

In this case, you'll see the numeric value 38.49, which is a result of adding the two book costs.

You can use a returned number in any other mathematical expression, as long as you cast it appropriately first, as shown here:

```
trace(Number(authorsXML.author[0].books.book[0].bookCost.text())
➥*1.5);
```

In this case, the expression multiplies the numeric value of the book cost by 1.5.

Including other ActionScript expressions

You can include other ActionScript expressions inside parentheses. The following example shows how you could add a trace() statement instead of a filter, tracing the <address> element:

```
authorsXML.author[1].(trace(authorFirstName.toXMLString()));
```

The example would return the following content:

```
<authorFirstName>Douglas</authorFirstName>
```

You might also want to find elements with a specific number of child nodes. The following expression uses the length() method of the XML class to identify the last name of any authors with exactly two <book> elements:

```
trace (authorsXML.author.(books.book.length() == 2).authorLastName
➥.toXMLString());
```

In this case, both authors have exactly two <book> elements, so the expression returns the following output:

```
<authorLastName>Ambrose</authorLastName>
<authorLastName>Donaldson</authorLastName>
```

I'll leave you to work out the equivalent expression using XML class methods!

These examples all appear in the resource files e4xFilterExamples.fla and E4xFilterExamples.mxml.

So far, you've seen how to retrieve content from an XML object by using E4X expressions. It's also possible to assign values to elements and attributes with these expressions.

Assigning values

You can use an equal sign (=) to assign a new value to an element or an attribute. We'll look at how this works using a simpler XML object than in the previous example:

```
var phoneBookXML:XML = <phoneBook>
  <contact id="1">
    <name>Sas Jacobs</name>
    <address>123 Red Street, Redland, Australia</address>
    <phone>123 456</phone>
  </contact>
</phoneBook>
```

Simple assignment with =

Consider the following expressions:

```
trace(phoneBookXML..phone[0]);
phoneBookXML..phone[0] = "999 9999";
trace(phoneBookXML..phone[0]);
```

In this example, the initial `trace()` statement displays the value of the first `<phone>` element. There is only one `<phone>` element, but I've assigned the index so I can be sure that I'm working with the first element, rather than with a collection of `<phone>` elements. The code then assigns a new value 999 9999 to the element and displays the value again in the Output panel using `trace()`.

Testing the example shows the following:

```
123 456
999 9999
```

You can see that the value of the first `<phone>` element has been changed.

You can also change the value of attributes in the same way. Here is another example that uses `trace()` to display the before and after values:

```
trace(phoneBookXML.contact[0].@id);
phoneBookXML.contact[0].@id = "10";
trace(phoneBookXML.contact[0].@id);
```

Testing these lines displays the following results:

```
1
10
```

The expression changed the value of the id attribute from 1 to 10.

Note that this change will affect only the XML object inside the SWF application. It doesn't do any updating of the external XML content. You would need to use server-side language to make an external change, and I'll address that topic in Chapter 9.

Compound assignment with +=

ActionScript 3.0 also supports the use of the compound assignment operator (+=) in XML objects. You might use this operator to insert an element or attribute. The following example shows how to add a new element:

```
phoneBookXML.contact.phone +=  <email>sas@email.com</email>;
trace(phoneBookXML.toXMLString());
```

In this case, the expression adds an <email> element after the <phone> element. Testing the expression produces the following output:

```
<phoneBook>
  <contact id="1">
    <name>Sas Jacobs</name>
    <address>123 Red Street, Redland, Australia</address>
    <phone>123 456</phone>
    <email>sas@email.com</email>
  </contact>
</phoneBook>
```

The <email> element has been added and appears after the <phone> element as the last child of <contact>. I'll cover the use of XML methods that change content in Chapter 8.

You can find the examples in this section within the resource files e4xAssigningValues.fla and E4xAssigningValues.mxml.

Deleting content

The delete keyword deletes content based on E4X expressions. The following example deletes the <phone> element from the phoneBookXML object you saw in the previous section:

```
delete phoneBookXML.contact[0].phone;
```

Tracing the resulting XML object shows the following:

```
<phoneBook>
  <contact id="1">
    <name>Sas Jacobs</name>
    <address>123 Red Street, Redland, Australia</address>
  </contact>
</phoneBook>
```

The <phone> element has been removed from the XML object.

You can delete all <contact> elements using the following expression:

```
delete phoneBookXML.contact;
```

The resulting output shows that only the root element remains:

```
<phoneBook/>
```

You can also delete an attribute using the following E4X expression:

```
delete phoneBookXML.contact.@id;
```

Testing the expression shows the <contact> element without an attribute:

```
<phoneBook>
  <contact>
    <name>Sas Jacobs</name>
    <address>123 Red Street, Redland, Australia</address>
    <phone>123 456</phone>
  </contact>
</phoneBook>
```

You can't use delete with a filter in the expression, as in this example:

```
delete phoneBookXML.contact[0].(@id="1");
```

If you do so, you'll see the following error message:

```
Delete operator is not supported with operand of type XMLList.
```

The error occurs because the E4X expression returns an XMLList. If you wanted to delete attributes or elements based on a filter, you would need to loop through the <contact> elements, testing the attribute value of each. When the code locates the relevant element, it should then call the delete statement. This is true even if the returned XMLList contains only a single item.

You can find these examples in the files e4xDeletingValues.fla and E4xDeletingValues.mxml. As with the other examples, uncomment the lines you need.

Let's see how to put some of these expressions into practice.

E4X in action

We'll finish the chapter by working through examples that demonstrate how to use E4X expressions with ComboBox and List components. We'll go through examples in both Flash and Flex—a simple, procedure-based example in Flash and a class-based example in Flex.

Both examples will show a list of author names in a ComboBox control. When a name is selected, the books by that author will display in a List control. All content comes from the XML document authorMoreDetails.xml. We'll start with the Flash example.

Flash example

Here are the instructions to set up the Flash example:

1. Create a new ActionScript 3.0 Flash file in Flash. I called the file authorExample.fla and sized it to 420 × 450 pixels. If you change the interface shown in the next step, you may need to choose a different size.

2. Create an interface that includes ComboBox, List, and TextArea components, as shown in Figure 4-1. Add the prompt Choose author for the ComboBox in the Parameters panel. Feel free to change the interface to something more interesting than that shown in the screenshot!

Figure 4-1. The Flash interface

3. Give the ComboBox component the instance name author_cbo. Give the List component the instance name books_list. Use XML_txt as the instance name for the TextArea component.

4. Name the current layer interface. Add a new layer and name it actions.

5. Select the actions layer and open the Actions panel by pressing the F9 shortcut key. Add the following lines at the top:

```
import fl.data.DataProvider;
var authorsXML:XML;
var authorList:XML;
var bookList:XML;
initApp();
stop();
```

The code starts by importing the fl.data.DataProvider class. You'll need this class to create a data provider from the XML content for both the ComboBox and the List.

The code also declares a number of variables. It creates an XML object called authorsXML. This object stores the XML content for the interface. The code also creates two XML objects that you'll use as data providers for the ComboBox and List controls. These are called authorList and bookList, respectively.

The code block finishes by calling the initApp() function to set up the application. The final line is a stop() action. You'll create the initApp() function next.

You might be wondering why the example uses XML *objects for the component data providers. When you work with XML content, you frequently use E4X expressions that return* XMLList *objects. It seems reasonable to expect that an* XMLList *object would be suitable as a data provider.*

If you look in the Flash help file, you'll find that the DataProvider *class can use only a list, XML instance, or an array of data objects as a data source. There is no mention of an* XMLList. *You also don't have access to the* XMLListCollection *class, which is available for use as a data provider in Flex.*

Because your only choice here is an XML *object, you'll need to make sure that your E4X expressions return an* XMLList *with a single item. You can then cast the* XMLList *object as an* XML *object, because there is effectively a single root element. Using this approach allows you to set an E4X expression as the data source for any* DataProvider *object you create.*

6. Add the `initApp()` function signature shown here below the `stop()` action:

```
function initApp():void {
}
```

7. Now you need to populate the authorsXML object. Normally, you would do this by loading content from an external XML file, and I'll cover that topic in the next chapter. For this example, however, you'll just use a static approach by assigning the content directly to the XML object.

Open the file authorMoreDetails.xml and copy the content to the clipboard. Assign the content to the authorsXML object by pasting the content as shown here. I've shown only the first and last lines because the XML document contains a lot of content.

```
function initApp():void {
  authorsXML = <allAuthors>
//the remaining lines follow
  </allAuthors>;
}
```

8. You'll display the XML object in the TextArea component using the `toXMLString()` method so you can check the structure. Add the following line before the closing brace in the `initApp()` function:

```
XML_txt.text = authorsXML.toXMLString();
```

9. Before moving on, you should check that you've created the authorsXML object correctly. Test the movie using the Ctrl+Enter (Cmd+Enter) shortcut. You should see the output shown in Figure 4-2.

Figure 4-2. The TextArea displays the contents of the authorsXML object.

10. If you look at the XML structure, you'll see that all authors appear inside the <authors> element. You want to display the author's first and last names in the ComboBox, so you need to set the <authors> element as the data provider for this control. Add the following lines before the closing brace of the initApp() function:

```
authorList = new XML(authorsXML.authors);
author_cbo.dataProvider = new DataProvider(authorList);
```

The first new line populates the authorList object using the E4X expression authorsXML. authors. This expression returns an XMLList of all <authors> elements. There is only one of these elements, so you're able to cast it to the type of an XML object using the XML() constructor method.

You can then create a DataProvider object from the authorList XML object and set it as the dataProvider property for the author_cbo instance. Because you're working with an XML object, the data provider has access to all of the child elements of the <authors> root element.

11. Because there are multiple child elements, you need to specify which to use for the ComboBox label. You could assign a single element or use the labelFunction property of the ComboBox. Because you want to display both the author's first and last name, you'll need to create a labelFunction that joins these values and adds a space in between. Name this function getFullName().

Add the following line underneath the data provider assignment line. It sets the labelFunction property of the ComboBox.

```
author_cbo.labelFunction = getFullName;
```

123

12. You now need to create the `getFullName()` function. Add the new function, shown here, to the bottom of the actions layer:

```
function getFullName(item:Object):String{
  return item.authorFirstName + " " + item.authorLastName;
}
```

The label function receives an `Object` called `item` as a parameter. This `Object` contains the data item from the data provider. The `getFullName()` function finds the `authorFirstName` and `authorLastName` properties of this `Object` and concatenates them with a space in between to create the full name.

13. Test the movie again. Figure 4-3 shows how the ComboBox should appear, with the names of four authors. If you can see all of the names, continue with the next steps. If not, you'll need to recheck your steps to this point to make sure that you've carried them out correctly.

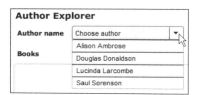

Figure 4-3. Populating the ComboBox control

14. When the author selection changes, the List control should show all books associated with that author. The ComboBox needs a change handler to deal with this action, so add the following line to the `initApp()` function:

```
author_cbo.addEventListener(Event.CHANGE, changeHandler);
```

This line assigns a change handler function called changeHandler. It's common practice to name the handler functions in this way so it's easy to determine which event they manage.

15. Now you need to create the function that will be called when the ComboBox selection changes. Add the following changeHandler() function at the bottom of the actions layer:

```
function changeHandler(e:Event):void {
showBooks(e.currentTarget.selectedIndex);
}
```

The function calls the showBooks() function, which you haven't created yet, passing the selectedIndex property of the ComboBox. The number is zero-based, so it will tell you exactly which <author> element has been selected from the data provider.

You find the ComboBox control using the currentTarget property of the event passed with the changeHandler() function. You could also use the ActionScript expression author_cbo.selectedIndex to achieve the same result.

16. The next step is to create the showBooks() function. Remember that it receives the selected index in the ComboBox from the changeHandler() function. Add the showBooks() function to the bottom of the actions layer.

```
function showBooks(authorIndex:int):void{
  bookList = new XML(authorsXML..author[authorIndex].books);
  books_list.dataProvider = new DataProvider(bookList);
  XML_txt.text = bookList.toXMLString();
}
```

The showBooks() function starts by identifying the list of all of the selected author's books using the E4X expression authorsXML..author[authorIndex].books. In other words, find any <author> descendants with the same index as the selected index of the ComboBox and return all of that author's books.

The function creates a new XML object and populates it with the XMLList returned from the E4X expression. You can assign the value in this way because the E4X expression returns an XMLList containing a single element, <author>, which becomes the root element of the new XML object.

The showBooks() function sets the new XML object as the dataProvider property for the List component, by creating a new DataProvider object. It finishes by displaying the XML object in the TextArea so you can check what has been returned.

17. The last task is to display the name of the book in the List control. If you tested the movie now, you would see the correct number of items in the List control, but there wouldn't be any associated labels—only blank lines would appear.

You need to add a label function for the List to the initApp() function, at the bottom of the actions layer, as follows:

```
books_list.labelFunction = getBookName;
```

This label function is named getBookName(). It works in the same way as the getFullName() function described earlier.

```
    function getBookName(item:Object):String {
      return item.bookName;
    }
```

I've included the complete code from the actions layer next. I've removed the XML content except for the first and last lines for brevity. In your version, you should see the entire XML object.

```
    import fl.data.DataProvider;
    var authorsXML:XML;
    var authorList:XML;
    var bookList:XML;
    initApp();
    stop();
    function initApp():void {
      authorsXML = <allAuthors>
    //remaining XML content appears between these lines
      </allAuthors>;
```

```
      XML_txt.text = authorsXML.toXMLString();
      authorList = new XML(authorsXML.authors);
      author_cbo.dataProvider = new DataProvider(authorList);
      author_cbo.labelFunction = getFullName;
      author_cbo.addEventListener(Event.CHANGE, changeHandler);
      books_list.labelFunction = getBookName;
   }
   function getFullName(item:Object):String{
      return item.authorFirstName + " " + item.authorLastName;
   }
   function getBookName(item:Object):String {
      return item.bookName;
   }
   function changeHandler(e:Event):void {
      showBooks(e.currentTarget.selectedIndex);
   }
   function showBooks(authorIndex:int):void{
      bookList = new XML(authorsXML..author[authorIndex].books);
      books_list.dataProvider = new DataProvider(bookList);
      XML_txt.text = bookList.toXMLString();
   }
```

Test the SWF file now. Choose an author from the ComboBox, and you should see the List component populate with the book titles from that author, as shown in Figure 4-4.

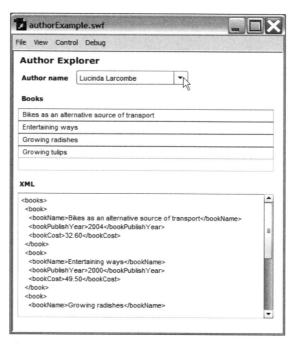

Figure 4-4. The completed Flash application

In this example, you used a static XML object to populate a ComboBox control and a List control. As I mentioned earlier, you would normally load this content from an external file, and I'll show you that approach in the next chapter.

You can find the completed file saved as authorExample.fla with the other chapter resources. If you're feeling adventurous, you may want to extend the example by displaying the year of publication and book cost as well. You may also wish to add some styling to improve the appearance of the interface!

Let's see how we might approach the same application in Flex.

Flex example

For the Flex version of this example, some useful tools are available. You can use data binding with E4X expressions to update the content of your controls automatically. You have access to the XMLListCollection class for use in your bindings. It's also possible to set the external XML document as the source for the <mx:XML> element, instead of including all of the content within the application file.

This example uses a class-based approach. Creating custom classes allows you to create reusable code that you can access in other applications. Again, you'll display the author names in a ComboBox and show their book titles in a List control.

1. Create a new Flex project with a single application file. I called the application file AuthorExample.mxml. Add an assets folder and copy the authorMoreDetails.xml file there.

2. Create the interface shown in Figure 4-5.

Figure 4-5. The Flex application interface

The interface includes the same elements as in the Flash example. The declarative code follows. Even if you choose a different layout for the interface, use the same component id properties to ensure that the code works correctly.

```
<?xml version="1.0" encoding="utf-8"?>
<mx:Application xmlns:mx="http://www.adobe.com/2006/mxml"
  layout="absolute">
  <mx:VBox x="10" y="10">
    <mx:Label text="Author explorer" fontWeight="bold"
      fontSize="14"/>
    <mx:HBox>
      <mx:Label text="Author name" width="100" fontWeight="bold"/>
      <mx:ComboBox id="author_cbo" prompt="Choose author"
        width="175"/>
    </mx:HBox>
    <mx:Label text="Books" fontWeight="bold"/>
    <mx:List width="400" height="100"  id="books_list"/>
    <mx:Label text="XML" fontWeight="bold"/>
      <mx:TextArea id="XML_txt" width="400" height="200"/>
  </mx:VBox>
</mx:Application>
```

3. You need to add the XML content to the application. Add an `<mx:XML>` element above the interface elements with the source property set to the `assets/authorMoreDetails.xml` file, as follows:

```
<mx:XML id="authorsXML" source="assets/authorMoreDetails.xml"/>
```

> *Remember that the application doesn't reference this XML document at runtime. The content is added to the compiled SWF file, which means that you can't update the XML document and expect the application interface to update as well. You'll need to recompile the SWF application each time you change the external document. As I mentioned previously, we'll look at more dynamic approaches in the next chapter.*

4. Add a class to process the content coming from the XML document. To do this, create a new class called XMLExplorer using the command File ➤ New ➤ ActionScript Class. Create this class file in the package XMLUtilities, as shown in Figure 4-6.

Once created, the file will automatically contain the following ActionScript:

```
package XMLUtilities {
  public class XMLExplorer {
    public function XMLExplorer() {
    }
  }
}
```

Don't worry if the arrangement of curly braces is slightly different in your class file.

Figure 4-6. Creating the new ActionScript class

5. You need to add some private variables to the class file. Start by adding the following variables after the second line, inside the class definition line:

```
private var XMLContent:XML;
private var currXMLString:String;
private var authorXML:XMLList;
private var authorList:XMLListCollection;
```

The XMLContent object will reference the entire XML document referred to in the authorsXML element. The currXMLString variable will provide the content for display in the TextArea. The authorXML object will contain the XMLList of all authors, and the authorsList is the XMLListCollection associated with these authors. You'll bind to the XMLListCollection object, rather than to the XMLList object, because the XMLList object doesn't support binding.

6. The constructor method XMLExplorer() must be modified. The method will receive the XML content as a parameter and will set the initial values of two of the variables you created in the previous step.

```
public function XMLExplorer(xmlDoc:XML) {
  XMLContent = xmlDoc;
  currXMLString = XMLContent.toXMLString();
}
```

The constructor method assigns the passed-in XML object to the XMLContent object. It uses the toXMLString() method of the XML object to store the string representation in the variable currXMLString.

129

7. The class will need two public methods: currentXML(), which returns the current XMLString variable for debugging purposes, and allAuthors(), which returns an XMLListCollection of all <author> elements. Add these methods now.

```
public function currentXML():String {
  return currXMLString;
}
public function allAuthors():XMLListCollection {
  authorXML = XMLContent..author;
  authorList = new XMLListCollection(authorXML);
  currXMLString = authorXML.toXMLString();
  return authorList;
}
```

The currentXML() method is self-explanatory. It returns the value of the currXMLString variable for debugging purposes.

The allAuthors() method starts by locating the <author> descendants of the XMLContent object using the E4X expression XMLContent..author. The method assigns the returned XMLList to the object authorXML. The next line uses this XMLList to create the authorList XMLListCollection object. The method also sets the currXMLString variable to the string representation of all <author> elements.

Adding the reference to the XMLListCollection object should add an import statement for that class, but if it doesn't, you may need to add the following line yourself:

```
import mx.collections.XMLListCollection;
```

The complete class file follows:

```
package XMLUtilities {
  import mx.collections.XMLListCollection;
  public class XMLExplorer {
    private var XMLContent:XML;
    private var currXMLString:String;
    private var authorXML:XMLList;
    private var authorList:XMLListCollection;
    public function XMLExplorer(xmlDoc:XML) {
      XMLContent = xmlDoc;
      currXMLString = XMLContent.toXMLString();
    }
    public function currentXML():String {
      return currXMLString;
    }
    public function allAuthors():XMLListCollection {
      authorXML = XMLContent..author;
      authorList = new XMLListCollection(authorXML);
      currXMLString = authorXML.toXMLString();
      return authorList;
    }
  }
}
```

8. Switch back to the MXML application and add an `<mx:Script>` block underneath the opening `<mx:Application>` element. Add the following code:

```
<mx:Script>
  <![CDATA[
    import mx.events.FlexEvent;
    import XMLUtilities.XMLExplorer;
    [Bindable]
    private var myXMLExplorer:XMLExplorer;
    private function initApp(e:FlexEvent):void {
      myXMLExplorer = new XMLExplorer(authorsXML);
    }
  ]]>
</mx:Script>
```

This code block starts by importing the `FlexEvent` class, which you'll need because the code calls the `initApp()` function in the `creationComplete` event of the application. The code also imports the custom class you just created, `XMLUtilities.XMLExplorer`.

The code declares a bindable variable called `myXMLExplorer`, which is of the type `XMLExplorer`. It also creates the `initApp()` function. This function creates the new `XMLExplorer` object, passing the `authorsXML` object as an argument.

9. You need to call the `initApp()` function when the application finishes creating the interface. Add the following attribute, shown in bold, to the opening `<mx:Application>` element:

```
<mx:Application xmlns:mx="http://www.adobe.com/2006/mxml"
  layout="absolute" creationComplete="initApp(event)">
```

When the application finishes creating the interface, it calls the `initApp()` function, passing a `FlexEvent`. You won't use this `FlexEvent` in the `initApp()` function, but it is good practice to recognize that the object is passed with the function call.

10. Bind the ComboBox control to the `XMLListCollection` created by the class file. You can access the object with a call to the public method `allAuthors()`. The code handles this by setting the `dataProvider` attribute for the ComboBox to the bound expression `{myXMLExplorer.allAuthors()}`. The data provider will provide access to all child elements of each `<author>` element.

You also need to specify a label function so you can determine what to display as the label for the ComboBox. Call this function `getFullName()`, as in the previous example. Modify the `<mx:ComboBox>` element as shown here in bold:

```
<mx:ComboBox id="author_cbo" prompt="Choose author" width="175"
  dataProvider="{myXMLExplorer.allAuthors()}"
  labelFunction="getFullName"/>
```

11. Before testing this application, you need to add the `getFullName()` function to the `<mx:Script>` block. The function follows:

```
private function getFullName(item:Object):String{
  return item.authorFirstName + " " + item.authorLastName;
}
```

131

This function receives an item object as an argument. This object represents the data item from the dataProvider behind the current row in the ComboBox. This data item is one of the XMLListCollection entries, and it contains the <authorFirstName> and <authorLastName> elements. The function returns a String made up of the <authorFirstName> element, a space, and the <authorLastName> element.

12. You'll bind the TextArea to the value of the currXMLString in the class file by calling the currentXML() method. I've included this in the example so you can see what's going on with the XML content from the authorsXML object. Modify the <mx:TextArea> element as shown here in bold:

```
<mx:TextArea id="XML_txt" width="400" height="200"
  text="{myXMLExplorer.currentXML()}"/>
```

13. Test the application. Figure 4-7 shows how the interface should appear. The ComboBox is populated with author names, and the TextArea shows the complete XML content from the <mx:XML> element.

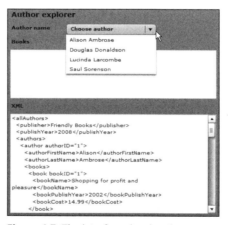

Figure 4-7. The interface showing the populated ComboBox component

14. At the moment, nothing happens when you choose an author from the ComboBox. The application needs to respond when the selected item changes in the ComboBox control. It must find the books associated with the selected author.

To achieve this outcome, you'll bind the data provider for the List control to an E4X expression that finds the <bookName> element from the ComboBox data provider. Remember that the ComboBox provides access to all child elements, including the <bookName> element.

Modify the List control as shown here in bold:

```
<mx:List width="400" height="100"  id="books_list"
  dataProvider="{author_cbo.selectedItem..book.bookName}"/>
```

The E4X expression author_cbo.selectedItem..book.bookName returns an XMLList of all <bookName> elements. The expression author_cbo.selectedItem references the XMLList item associated with the chosen author <element>. From there, the E4X expression finds the <book> descendant and returns the <bookName> element. You'll be able to follow this path more easily once you display the XML content in the TextArea control.

15. The final step is to display the XML details of the author in the TextArea. Modify the <mx:ComboBox> as shown here in bold:

```
<mx:ComboBox id="author_cbo" prompt="Choose author" width="175"
  dataProvider="{myXMLExplorer.allAuthors()}"
  labelFunction="getFullName"
  change="XML_txt.text=author_cbo.selectedItem.toXMLString()"/>
```

The change attribute sets the text property of the XML_txt control to the value of the selectedItem from the ComboBox. You'll be able to see the XMLList associated with the selected <author> element in the TextArea.

16. Test the application again. You should be able to select an author to see the list of books written by that author. Figure 4-8 shows the finished result.

Figure 4-8. The completed application

In this example, you used an <mx:XML> object with an external file to populate a ComboBox and List control. You were able to display the correct data by using data binding with E4X expressions. This Flex example provides the same functionality as the Flash example you saw earlier. You can find the completed resource files for this example saved as AuthorExample.mxml and XMLExplorer.as.

Summary

In this chapter, you've seen how to use a variety of E4X expressions to locate content in an XML object. You saw how to use the dot (.), attribute (@), descendants (..), and wildcard (*) operators. You also learned about the many different ways to filter the XML content, as well as how to assign and add values. We finished the chapter by looking at an example in both Flash and Flex.

So far in this book, we've used XML content loaded directly into an application. That's not a very flexible approach. In the next chapter, you'll see how to load an external XML document into both Flash and Flex.

Chapter 5

USING THE URLLOADER CLASS WITH XML DOCUMENTS

So far in the book, I've shown you how to work with the new XML and XMLList classes in ActionScript 3.0. You can create a new XML object declaratively, in the same way that you would create any other type of variable. While it can be useful to create XML variables with ActionScript, it's much more flexible to load XML content from an external data source, and that's the topic of this chapter.

You can load external XML content either by accessing a static XML document or by requesting data from a database. If you choose the second option, you'll need some type of server-side page to generate an XML information stream from the database. You can use a language like ASP.NET, PHP, or ColdFusion to create the content for you. As long as the resulting XML document is well-formed, you can consume it in a SWF application.

Both Flash and Flex offer several different ways to request external XML content. Both software packages can use the URLLoader and related classes in ActionScript 3.0. In addition, Flex can use the HTTPService class, which can either be scripted or added as an MXML element. If you create a Flash ActionScript 2.0 document, you can also use the version 2 data components with minimal scripting.

This chapter concentrates on using the URLLoader class to load external XML files. The URLLoader class can load plain-text files, text in name/value pairs, and well-formed XML documents. The URLLoader class is available to SWF files created in both Flash and Flex. You'll see methods specific to each software package in the next two chapters.

When you use the URLLoader class to load an external XML document, you can traverse the loaded content with methods of the XML class or E4X expressions. You will need to cast the loaded content into XML format before you can apply E4X expressions or call XML class methods.

You need to remember that the URLLoader class uses a request-response approach. The class needs to request the content from the server, and the server responds by providing the relevant XML document. The process can't be initiated by the server. If the XML content changes externally—for example, in the database—the application needs to request the data again. If you are working with external content that changes regularly, you'll need to poll the server continually in order to detect changed content. I'm sure you can see that this solution is not very practical.

The XMLSocket class allows you to create a real-time connection to XML content so that the server automatically pushes any changes to the application automatically. When an external document or database changes, the XMLSocket class can provide the information to the SWF application, which can respond appropriately. The XMLSocket class requires that the application runs on a socket server. As the subject can be a little difficult, we're not going to cover XML sockets in this book.

In this chapter, I will show you code samples illustrating how the URLLoader class works in both Flash and Flex, and take you through examples using the XML document that we have used in the past two chapters. I'll also cover the security implications of working with external content using the URLLoader object in Flash Player.

You can download the resources for this chapter from http://www.friendsofed.com. This download includes the XML documents used for the examples, as well as the completed files.

Using the URLLoader class

The URLLoader class makes server requests and handles responses. You can use it to load information from external files. The information can be formatted as raw text, text containing name/value variable pairs, or as a well-formed XML document. The URLLoader class is one of the classes in the flash.net package, along with the URLRequest and URLVariables classes.

When you work with a URLLoader object, all information must finish loading before it becomes available to the SWF application. So, the application should respond only when it detects that loading has completed.

Let's look at the properties, methods, and events of the URLLoader class.

Properties of the URLLoader class

The URLLoader class has four properties, as shown in Table 5-1.

The first two properties, bytesLoaded and bytesTotal, are useful in determining how much of an external document has been loaded. You can compare the two values to see how much of the content has loaded, perhaps if you're working with a preloader.

The data property contains all of the content requested from the external document. This property is available only after loading has finished.

Table 5-1. Properties of the URLLoader class

Property	Data type	Description
bytesLoaded	uint	The number of bytes loaded so far
bytesTotal	uint	The total number of bytes to be downloaded, populated when the operation is complete
data	Multiple	The data received when the load() method completes
dataFormat	String	The format expected for received data; choose from URLLoaderDataFormat.TEXT, URLLoaderDataFormat.BINARY, or URLLoaderDataFormat.VARIABLES

The dataFormat property determines the format for the contents inside the data property. You can choose from three formats: URLLoaderDataFormat.TEXT, URLLoaderDataFormat.BINARY, or URLLoaderDataFormat.VARIABLES.

If the dataFormat is set to the default value URLLoaderDataFormat.TEXT, the data property is a string containing all of the text from the loaded document. Where the format is set to URLLoaderDataFormat.BINARY, the data property is a ByteArray object that contains the raw binary information. Finally, URLLoaderDataFormat.VARIABLES loads the data property with name/value variable pairs.

In the case of XML content, the default format URLLoaderDataFormat.TEXT is appropriate, as XML-formatted information is just text. However, in order to apply E4X expressions to the data property, it needs to be cast as an XML object first.

You'll see some examples of how to use these properties soon, in the "Putting it all together" section. Next, we will look at the methods of the URLLoader class.

Methods of the URLLoader class

There are three methods of the URLLoader class, as summarized in Table 5-2.

Table 5-2. Methods of the URLLoader class

Method	Parameters	Description	Returns
close()		Closes the current load operation	Nothing
load()	request: URLRequest	Sends and loads data to the specified URLRequest.	Nothing
URLLoader()	request: URLRequest	Constructor method	Nothing

The constructor method URLLoader() instantiates a URLLoader object. It can take an optional URLRequest object as an argument. If so, the URLRequest object specifies the URL to access, providing it as a string value. The URL could be an external static XML document or a server-side file that creates a stream of XML information. You'll see how the URLRequest object interacts with the URLLoader object shortly, in the "Putting it all together" section.

If the constructor method includes a URLRequest object, the URLLoader object starts to load the URL immediately using the load() method. If no URLRequest object is passed, you can call the load() method at a later stage, again passing a URLRequest object. It's probably more common to choose the second method and load the external content in response to an event such as a button click.

The load() method sends and loads data from the URL that you specify in the URLRequest object. You can send information to the URL within the URLRequest object by setting its data property. This process might be useful to send variables or a parameter to a server-side page. Again, you'll see how this works in practice in the "Putting it all together" section later in the chapter.

The close() method closes any load() method call that is currently in progress. The call immediately ends the load() operation. If there isn't a load() operation in progress, calling the close() method throws an invalid stream error.

Let's move on to look at the events of the URLLoader class.

Events of the URLLoader class

The URLLoader class dispatches a number of events to help with tracking the progress of the call to the URL. Table 5-3 summarizes these events.

Table 5-3. The events dispatched by the URLLoader class

Event	Type	Description
complete	Event	Dispatched after all received data is decoded and placed in the data property
httpStatus	HTTPStatusEvent	Dispatched if the load() method attempts to access data over HTTP, and Flash Player can detect and return the status code for the request
ioError	IOErrorEvent	Dispatched if the load() method results in a fatal error that terminates the download
open	Event	Dispatched when downloading commences after a call to the load() method
progress	ProgressEvent	Dispatched as downloaded data is received; this event occurs before all data is received and decoded
securityError	SecurityErrorEvent	Dispatched if the load() method attempts to load data from outside the security sandbox

You can see that the URLLoader class dispatches a number of different events, which make it easy to respond to errors and to determine the progress of the request. To respond to any one of these events, add an event listener to the URLLoader object with a corresponding handler function.

The open event is dispatched when the request starts and downloading begins. While the downloaded data is received, the progress event is dispatched. Once all data is successfully loaded, the complete event is dispatched.

If there is a security error, for example, the securityError event will be dispatched. A security error occurs if there's an unsuccessful attempt to load content from outside the current security sandbox. You can find out more about security sandboxes in the "Understanding Flash Player security" section later in this chapter.

If the load() operation can't be completed because of an error that forces it to terminate, the URLLoader object dispatches an ioError event.

You can find out the progress of any calls made over HTTP through the httpStatus event. The httpStatus event doesn't necessarily provide error codes; it just provides any HTTP status code sent when the SWF application requests a document. However, to access the relevant status codes, Flash Player must be able to receive status codes. In other words, Flash Player must be embedded within a web page that can communicate using HTTP.

Limits of the URLLoader class

The operation of the URLLoader class is restricted to use of the GET and POST methods when calling the load() method. You can't use the class to perform any operations that use PUT and DELETE.

Putting it all together

Let's see how these properties, methods, and events fit together to allow you to load an external XML document.

Creating a URLLoader object

The first step in loading external XML content is to create a URLLoader object with the constructor method. The following ActionScript shows how to create this object, without passing a URLRequest object as an argument.

```
var loader:URLLoader = new URLLoader();
```

Although you can make the request at the same time as instantiating the object, it's more flexible to do this at a later stage with the load() method.

You can also specify the type of data that you expect to receive by setting the dataFormat property. If you're loading an XML document, you don't need to do this, because you'll be using the default dataFormat, URLLoaderDataFormat.TEXT. The following line shows how you could set this dataFormat explicitly:

```
loader.dataFormat = URLLoaderDataFormat.TEXT;
```

Making the request

To request the URL, you call the load() method of the URLLoader object and pass a URLRequest object as an argument. The URLRequest object specifies the URL to load as well as the loading method: GET or POST. It can also specify header information and MIME type.

The following code shows how to request a physical XML file from the server:

```
var request:URLRequest = new URLRequest("myFile.xml");
var loader:URLLoader = new URLLoader();
loader.load(request);
```

The default loading method is GET, and the property is not set here. However, you can set the method property of the URLRequest object before you pass it to the URLLoader object, as shown here:

```
var request:URLRequest = new URLRequest("myFile.xml");
request.method = URLRequestMethod.POST;
var loader:URLLoader = new URLLoader();
loader.load(request);
```

If you want to request an XML stream generated by a server-side file, you'll need to include the full HTTP path in the request, as shown here:

```
var strURL:String = "http:/localhost/xmlStream.aspx";
var request:URLRequest = new URLRequest(strURL);
```

Of course, you could also rewrite this code in a single line, as follows:

```
var request:URLRequest = new URLRequest(
    ➡"http:/localhost/xmlStream.aspx");
```

Including the full path allows the content within the server-side file to be parsed by the web server before it is delivered to the SWF application. If you don't include the full path, the SWF application will treat the server-side code as literal content.

Sending variables with the request

You can send variables with a request by using the data property of the relevant URLRequest object. The data property needs to reference a URLVariables object. You'll need to create this object first and set the variables as properties of the object, as shown in the following code:

```
var strURL:String = "http://localhost/xmlStream.aspx";
var request:URLRequest = new URLRequest(strURL);
var params:URLVariables = new URLVariables();
params.continent = "Europe";
params.timeStamp = new Date().getTime();
request.data = params;
```

In this code snippet, the URLRequest object sends the variable continent with a value of Europe and a variable named timeStamp containing the current time.

Sending variables with a request can be very useful to filter the data returned from the server. You can request the same server-side page each time, but use variables from the SWF file to specify which results to return.

In the preceding example, imagine that you are requesting an XML document that provides information about sales staff for a global company. By sending the parameter Europe with the request, you can filter the returned information to see only sales staff that service the Europe area. You could request the same page, xmlStream.aspx, but filter the results by passing a variable so that you show only North American or Australasian staff.

You'll also need to send variables with a request when you want to update an external data source. A SWF application can modify the content in an XML object, but it doesn't have permission to update a static file or database. To carry out such an update, the SWF application needs to send the updated values to a server-side file for processing. In the preceding example, you could be logging requests for information. You might be updating the database to tell it that a request for information on Europe was received at the time indicated by the timestamp. You'll find out more about communicating with the server in Chapter 9.

> When you pass variables with a URLVariables object, the method uses an ampersand character (&) as a delimiter for the name/value variable pairs. If you're using this method, you'll need to use %26 to encode any & characters that you send as variable values. If you don't, you'll get an error message.

Tracking the progress of a request

You can track the progress of a request by adding a progress event listener. You can also assign event listeners for errors and other events. For example, the following code assigns event listeners for the open and progress events to the request URLLoader object:

```
var request:URLRequest = new URLRequest("myFile.xml");
var loader:URLLoader = new URLLoader();
loader.addEventListener(Event.OPEN, openHandler);
loader.addEventListener(ProgressEvent.PROGRESS, progressHandler);
loader.load(request);
```

After assigning the relevant event listeners, you'll then need to create the functions that deal with each event.

> You'll notice that I used the names openHandler and progressHandler for these functions. There is no requirement to use this naming convention and you could choose any name that seems appropriate to you. However, using this approach makes it easy to determine which functions handle each event.

The following functions show some simple responses for each of the events listed in the previous code block. The code handles the open and progress events, and each function call receives a different event object as an argument. The open event passes an Event object; the progress event passes a progressEvent object.

```
    private function openHandler(e:Event):void {
      trace("openHandler: started loading");
    }
    private function progressHandler(e:ProgressEvent):void {
      trace("progressHandler loaded:" + event.bytesLoaded
      ➥ + " total: " + event.bytesTotal);
    }
```

Receiving a response

When a successful response is received from the server, the complete event is dispatched by the URLLoader. You can add an event handler to respond to this event, as shown here:

```
    var request:URLRequest = new URLRequest("myFile.xml");
    var loader:URLLoader = new URLLoader();
    loader.addEventListener(Event.COMPLETE, completeHandler);
    loader.load(request);
```

You can use the completeHandler() function to capture the returned data in the data property of the URLLoader.

```
    function completeHandler(e:Event):void {
      var loadedXML:XML= XML(e.target.data);
      trace("loaded: " + loadedXML.toXMLString());
    }
```

The code finds the data property of the URLLoader object using e.target.data. By default, the response from the URLLoader is treated as a string. Notice that I have used the constructor method XML() to cast the response as an XML object. If I didn't do this, the loaded content would be treated as a string.

Detecting errors

You can use the ioError and securityError events to respond to errors. You can also use the httpStatus event to determine the status of the request if you're working over HTTP. Assign the handlers as shown in the following code block:

```
    var request:URLRequest = new URLRequest("myFile.xml");
    var loader:URLLoader = new URLLoader();
    loader.addEventListener(IOErrorEvent.IO_ERROR, ioErrorHandler);
    loader.addEventListener(SecurityErrorEvent.SECURITY_ERROR,
      ➥securityErrorHandler);
    loader.addEventListener(HttpStatusEvent.HTTP_STATUS,
      ➥httpStatusHandler);
    loader.load(request);
```

You would use the relevant event handler functions to respond, as shown here:

```
function ioErrorHandler(e:IOErrorEvent):void {
  trace("ioErrorHandler: " + e);
}
function httpStatusHandler(e:HTTPStatusEvent):void {
  trace("httpStatusHandler: " + e);
  trace("status: " + e.status);
}
function securityErrorHandler(e:SecurityErrorEvent):void {
  trace("securityErrorHandler: " + e);
}
```

The preceding code samples will make much more sense when you work through some examples in both Flash and Flex.

Working through examples

In this section, the examples will use the resource file authorsAndBooks.xml, which is essentially the same file that you saw in the last example in the previous chapter. You'll load the XML file with a URLLoader object and use it to populate a ComboBox component, as in the previous chapter. The Flash example is a simple version that uses procedural code. The Flex version uses class files.

Working in Flash

Here are the instructions to set up the Flash example:

1. Start by creating a new Flash document with two layers: one for the interface and one called actions for the ActionScript code.

2. Add a ComboBox component and a TextArea component, and set up the stage as shown in Figure 5-1. You'll use the author names from the XML document to populate the ComboBox. The TextArea control will display messages and the loaded XML so you can keep track of the current content.

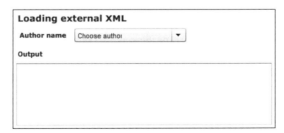

Figure 5-1. The Flash example interface

3. Use the instance name author_cbo for the ComboBox and the instance name output_txt for the TextArea.

4. Open the actions layer in the Actions panel with the F9 shortcut key and add the following declarations:

```
import fl.data.DataProvider;
var authorsXML:XML;
var authorList:XML;
var request:URLRequest = new URLRequest("authorsAndBooks.xml");
var loader:URLLoader = new URLLoader();
```

The first line imports the DataProvider class, which you'll need so that you can use a DataProvider object to populate the ComboBox component. The next two lines create the XML objects that you'll use: authorsXML for the loaded content and authorList, which will be the data provider for the ComboBox.

The last two lines create a URLRequest object, which handles the XML document authorsAndBooks.xml. The code also declares a new URLLoader object.

5. You'll use the initApp() function to set up the event listeners and load the XML document. Call the function at the bottom of the actions layer with the following code. The code block finishes with a stop() action.

```
initApp();
stop();
```

6. The code calls the initApp() function, but it doesn't yet exist. Add the initApp() function that follows:

```
function initApp():void {
  loader.addEventListener(ProgressEvent.PROGRESS, progressHandler);
  loader.addEventListener(Event.COMPLETE, completeHandler);
  author_cbo.labelFunction = getFullName;
  loader.load(request);
}
```

The initApp() function adds event listeners to the URLLoader object. The application listens for the progress event, to track the progress of the download. It also listens for the complete event. You'll add the event handler functions progressHandler() and completeHandler() shortly.

The initApp() function also sets the labelFunction property of the ComboBox. It needs to do this to determine which values from the loaded XML document should display as the label for the control.

The function finishes by calling the load() method of the URLLoader object. This line requests and loads the XML document. The completeHandler() function will deal with the parsing of the loaded content once the load() operation finishes.

7. Add the following progressHandler() function to track the downloading of the authorsAndBooks.xml document:

```
function progressHandler(e:ProgressEvent):void {
  output_txt.text +="progressHandler loaded: " +
    ➥e.bytesLoaded + " total: " + e.bytesTotal + "\n";
}
```

This function receives a ProgressEvent object as an argument. It shows output in the output_txt TextArea control. The function tracks the loaded property and the bytesTotal property of the ProgressEvent object.

When the document finishes loading, the values of bytesLoaded and bytesTotal will be the same. For large XML documents, you could compare these two properties when displaying a preloader.

8. You need to deal with the loaded XML content, so add the completeHandler() function to the Actions panel, as follows:

```
function completeHandler(e:Event):void {
  authorsXML = XML(e.target.data);
  authorList = new XML(authorsXML.authors);
  output_txt.text += authorList.toXMLString();
  author_cbo.dataProvider = new DataProvider(authorList);
}
```

The completeHandler() function receives an Event object as an argument, and uses the data property of the target of this object to access the loaded content. The function assigns the loaded content to the authorsXML object. It uses the XML() constructor method to cast the loaded content appropriately.

The function then uses the E4X expression authorsXML to locate the <authors> element in the loaded document. Because this expression returns an XMLList with a single item, the code can cast it as an XML object called authorList, ready for use as a data provider. You need to do this because the ComboBox data provider cannot be an XMLList object.

So you can check what data is being accessed, the code displays a text representation of the authorList object in the output_txt control. The function finishes by setting the authorList XML object as the data provider for the ComboBox control. It passes the authorList object as an argument to the DataProvider constructor.

9. The last step is to add the getFullName() function to the application. When you created the initApp() function, it set the getFullName() function as the labelFunction property of the ComboBox. The getFullName() function locates the authorFirstName and authorLastName properties of each item in the data provider and joins them with a space in between.

Add the following function to the actions layer:

```
function getFullName(item:Object):String{
  return item.authorFirstName + " " + item.authorLastName;
}
```

10. Test the application using the shortcut Ctrl/Cmd+Enter. Figure 5-2 shows an example of the finished application with an author name selected.

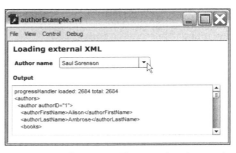

Figure 5-2. The completed example

The first line of the TextArea should show the loaded and total bytes for the external XML document. The remaining lines show the <authors> element and child elements. This element is the data provider for the ComboBox control. You should be able to open the ComboBox and see a list of all author names.

I've saved this simple example as authorsAndBooksExample.fla with the chapter resource files. The complete code from the file follows:

```
import fl.data.DataProvider;
var authorsXML:XML;
var authorList:XML;
var request:URLRequest = new URLRequest("authorsAndBooks.xml");
var loader:URLLoader = new URLLoader();
initApp();
stop();
function initApp():void {
  loader.addEventListener(ProgressEvent.PROGRESS, progressHandler);
  loader.addEventListener(Event.COMPLETE, completeHandler);
  author_cbo.labelFunction = getFullName;
  loader.load(request);
}
function progressHandler(e:ProgressEvent):void {
  output_txt.text +="progressHandler loaded: " + e.bytesLoaded +
    ➥" total: " + e.bytesTotal + "\n";
}
function completeHandler(e:Event):void {
  authorsXML = XML(e.target.data);
  authorList = new XML(authorsXML.authors);
  output_txt.text += authorList.toXMLString();
  author_cbo.dataProvider = new DataProvider(authorList);
}
function getFullName(item:Object):String{
  return item.authorFirstName + " " + item.authorLastName;
}
```

Let's move on to the Flex example, created with Flex Builder.

Working in Flex

In this example, you'll create a custom ActionScript class that uses the URLLoader class to load an external XML document. You'll use XML class methods to locate the required content so you can pass the element name as an argument when assigning the data provider. This approach will make the class file much more flexible than if you hard-code the element name in an E4X expression. You'll see what I mean when you create the custom class file.

This example uses a slightly different version of the XML content, called authorsAndBooksFlex.xml. In this document, the <author> element is a child of the root element, instead of being enclosed in an <authors> element. This structure is more suited to the points I want to make in this Flex example.

1. Start by creating a new Flex project. I called mine Chapter05FlexProject; you can use any name you prefer. I called the main application file authorsAndBooks.mxml. Add an assets folder to the project and copy the authorsAndBooksFlex.xml file there.

2. Create a new ActionScript class file using File ➤ New ➤ ActionScript Class. This class file will handle the loading and parsing of the external XML content. Figure 5-3 shows the settings for this class.

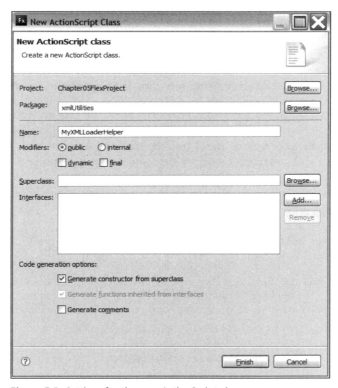

Figure 5-3. Settings for the new ActionScript class

I've set the package as xmlUtilities and the class file name as MyXMLLoaderHelper. The class file contains the following code, which was automatically generated by Flex Builder. Don't worry if Flex Builder arranges the curly braces a little differently than you see in this example.

```
package xmlUtilities {
  public class MyXMLLoaderHelper{
    public function MyXMLLoaderHelper () {
    }
  }
}
```

3. Modify the class file to make it bindable. This makes all public methods available for use in binding expressions. Add the following line above the class declaration:

```
[Bindable]
```

147

4. Add the following import statements below the first line package declaration. These statements reference the class files that you'll need to use.

```
import flash.net.URLLoader;
import flash.net.URLRequest;
import mx.collections.XMLListCollection;
```

5. Add the following private variable declarations beneath the class file declaration:

```
private var xmlAllContent:XML;
private var xmlLoader:URLLoader;
private var childElements:XMLList;
private var childElements:XMLListCollection;
```

The first variable, xmlAllContent, refers to the content loaded from the external XML document. The code uses the name xmlLoader for the URLLoader object. The childElements object refers to the XMLList of child elements that will be returned from the loaded content.

This content will ultimately populate the data provider of the ComboBox. However, it will do so via an intermediate class. The application will use the XMLListCollection object allElementsCollection as a wrapper class when assigning the data provider.

6. Modify the constructor method to create the URLLoader object and add an event listener to handle the complete event. The new lines appear in bold in the following code block:

```
public function MyXMLLoaderHelper() {
  xmlLoader = new URLLoader();
  xmlLoader.addEventListener(Event.COMPLETE, completeHandler);
}
```

7. The code will call the load() method of the URLLoader object in a public method called loadXML(). The application can then control when to call this method. The loadXML() method will receive the name of the external document to load as an argument.

```
public function loadXML(xmlFile:String):void {
  try {
    xmlLoader.load(new URLRequest(xmlFile));
  }
  catch (e:Error) {
    trace ("Can't load external XML document");
  }
}
```

You'll notice that the function includes a try/catch statement to provide some very basic error handling. In the case of an error, debugging the application will display a message in the Console view. This could be a little more robust, but the code will suffice for this simple example.

8. When the external document finishes loading, the completeHandler() method will be called. You specified this handler in the constructor method, but didn't add the private method to the class file. Add this method now, as shown in the following code block:

```
private function completeHandler(e:Event):void {
  xmlAllContent = XML(e.target.data);
  trace (xmlAllContent.toXMLString());
  dispatchEvent(new Event(Event.COMPLETE));
}
```

This method is private because it doesn't need to be accessed by the SWF application. The method includes a debugging line to display the loaded content in the Console view. Tracing loaded data is a useful tool, as it helps to check that you're loading the content that you expect.

The completeHandler() method also dispatches a complete event to the SWF application. The application can listen for this event and respond appropriately.

9. The custom class also needs to provide a method to locate the elements that will populate the data provider for the ComboBox. This method, getChildElements(), will receive the name of the specific child element to locate in the loaded content as an argument. In this case, the <author> elements are a direct child of the root element in the XML document, so you can use the child() XML class method.

Add the following method to the class file:

```
public function getChildElements(elementName:String):
 ➡XMLListCollection {
    childElements = xmlAllContent.child(elementName);
    trace(childElements.toXMLString());
    childElementsCollection = new XMLListCollection(childElements);
    return childElementsCollection;
}
```

The getChildElements() method finds all child elements with the specified name using the child() method of the XML class. You need to use this approach, rather than an E4X expression, because getChildElements() receives a String value for the child element name. This method returns an XMLList of the matching elements.

The code block includes a trace() action to display the returned elements so you can check that the XMLList contains the correct information. Again, this action is included only for debugging purposes, and you would probably comment it out when moving the application to production.

The method finishes by assigning the XMLList to the childElementsCollection object. The method then returns this XMLListCollection object. You can call this method to provide a data source for any data-aware component. In our case, that will be the ComboBox control.

The complete class file follows so you can check to make sure your code is correct so far.

```
package xmlUtilities {
  import flash.net.URLLoader;
  import flash.net.URLRequest;
  import mx.collections.XMLListCollection;
  [Bindable]
  public class MyXMLLoaderHelper {
    private var xmlAllContent:XML;
    private var xmlLoader:URLLoader;
    private var childElements :XMLList;
    private var childElementsCollection: XMLListCollection;
    public function MyXMLLoaderHelper() {
      xmlLoader = new URLLoader();
      xmlLoader.addEventListener(Event.COMPLETE, completeHandler);
    }
```

```
public function loadXML(xmlFile:String):void {
  try {
    xmlLoader.load(new URLRequest(xmlFile));
  }
  catch (e:Error) {
    trace ("Can't load external XML document");
  }
}
public function getChildElements(elementName:String):
  ➥XMLListCollection {
  childElements = xmlAllContent.child(elementName);
  trace(childElements.toXMLString());
  childElementsCollection = new XMLListCollection(childElements);
  return childElementsCollection;
}
private function completeHandler(e:Event):void {
  xmlAllContent = XML(e.target.data);
  trace (xmlAllContent.toXMLString());
  dispatchEvent(new Event(Event.COMPLETE));
}
  }
}
```

10. Switch back to the application file for your project. You'll create an interface similar to that used in the Flash example. The interface contains Label controls and a ComboBox component. Create the interface for the Flex application using the following code:

```xml
<?xml version="1.0" encoding="utf-8"?>
<mx:Application xmlns:mx="http://www.adobe.com/2006/mxml"
  layout="absolute">
  <mx:VBox x="10" y="10">
    <mx:Label text="Loading external XML" fontSize="14"
      fontWeight="bold"/>
    <mx:HBox>
      <mx:Label text="Author name" fontWeight="bold"/>
      <mx:ComboBox id="author_cbo" prompt="Choose author"/>
    </mx:HBox>
  </mx:VBox>
</mx:Application>
```

Figure 5-4 shows how the interface should appear. The ComboBox has the ID author_cbo.

Figure 5-4. The Flex interface

11. Add a creationComplete attribute to the <mx:Application> element, as shown here in bold:

```
<mx:Application xmlns:mx="http://www.adobe.com/2006/mxml"
  layout="absolute" creationComplete="initApp(event)">
```

When the creation of the interface completes, the application will call the initApp() function.

12. Add the following script block to the application:

```
<mx:Script>
  <![CDATA[
    import mx.events.FlexEvent;
    import xmlUtilities.MyXMLLoaderHelper;
    import mx.collections.XMLListCollection;
    private var myXMLLoader:MyXMLLoaderHelper;
    private var authorsXMLLC:XMLListCollection;
    private function initApp(e:FlexEvent):void {
      myXMLLoader = new MyXMLLoaderHelper();
      myXMLLoader.addEventListener(Event.COMPLETE, completeHandler);
      myXMLLoader.loadXML("assets/authorsAndBooksFlex.xml");
    }
    private function completeHandler(e:Event):void {
    }
  ]]>
</mx:Script>
```

The code starts by importing the classes needed for the application. This includes FlexEvent, passed by the initApp() function; the custom class MyXMLLoaderHelper; and the XMLListCollection class, required for the ComboBox data provider.

The code block declares a private variable for the MyXMLLoaderHelper object, called myXMLLoader. It also creates a variable called authorsXMLLC, which will be used as the data provider for the ComboBox control.

The <mx:Script> element includes the initApp() function, called when the interface has finished creating. This function creates a new MyXMLLoaderHelper object, assigns a complete event listener, and calls the loadXML() method of this object, passing the name of the file to load. You'll also see an empty completeHandler() function, which will be populated a little later.

13. Now it's time to do some testing. Debug the application to check that the class file is able to load the XML document correctly. You should see the loaded XML content in the Console view, as shown in Figure 5-5.

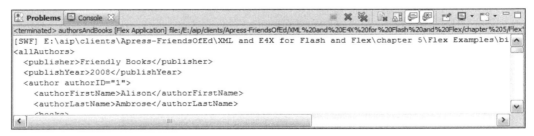

Figure 5-5. Testing the Flex application

14. The next task is to assign the `<author>` elements as the data provider for the ComboBox. Then you'll be able to see the author name in the control.

You'll need to modify the completeHandler() function as shown in bold here:

```
private function completeHandler(e:Event):void {
  author_cbo.dataProvider = myXMLLoader.getChildElements("author");
}
```

The new line calls the getChildElements() method of the myXMLLoader object, passing the author name as an argument. Because you're passing a child element name, you use this method to locate any child element within the loaded XML content.

15. The dataProvider property is set to an XMLListCollection object containing all of the child nodes of each `<author>` element. Without a label function, the control won't be able to determine what to display as the label. You need to create a labelFunction for the ComboBox so you can specify which values to display in the control. Add the following label function to the code block:

```
private function getFullName(item:Object):String {
  return item.authorFirstName + " " + item.authorLastName;
}
```

The getFullName() function locates the authorFirstName and authorLastName properties from each item in the XMLListCollection. It joins these values with a space between to create the author's full name.

16. Assign the getFullName() function as the labelFunction property by modifying the initApp() function. Add the bold line shown in the following block:

```
private function initApp(e:FlexEvent):void {
  myXMLLoader = new MyXMLLoaderHelper();
  myXMLLoader.addEventListener(Event.COMPLETE, completeHandler);
  myXMLLoader.loadXML("assets/authorsAndBooksFlex.xml");
  author_cbo.labelFunction = getFullName;
}
```

17. Debug the application again. You should see the list of `<author>` elements in the Console view. You should also see that the ComboBox in the application is populated with a list of author names, as shown in Figure 5-6.

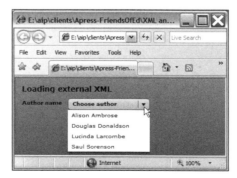

Figure 5-6. Testing the Flex application

Congratulations, you have finished this simple Flex application. The complete code listing for the application file follows:

```
<?xml version="1.0" encoding="utf-8"?>
<mx:Application xmlns:mx="http://www.adobe.com/2006/mxml"
  layout="absolute" creationComplete="initApp(event)">
  <mx:Script>
    <![CDATA[
      import mx.events.FlexEvent;
      import xmlUtilities.MyXMLLoaderHelper;
      import mx.collections.XMLListCollection;
      private var myXMLLoader:MyXMLLoaderHelper;
      private var authorsXMLLC:XMLListCollection;
      private function initApp(e:FlexEvent):void {
        myXMLLoader = new MyXMLLoaderHelper();
        myXMLLoader.addEventListener(Event.COMPLETE,
          ➥completeHandler);
        myXMLLoader.loadXML("assets/authorsAndBooksFlex.xml");
        author_cbo.labelFunction = getFullName;
      }
      private function completeHandler(e:Event):void {
        author_cbo.dataProvider = myXMLLoader.
          ➥getChildElements("author");
      }
      private function getFullName(item:Object):String {
        return item.authorFirstName + " " + item.authorLastName;
      }
    ]]>
  </mx:Script>
    <mx:VBox x="10" y="10">
      <mx:Label text="Loading external XML" fontSize="14"
        fontWeight="bold"/>
      <mx:HBox>
        <mx:Label text="Author name" fontWeight="bold"/>
        <mx:ComboBox id="author_cbo" prompt="Choose author"/>
      </mx:HBox>
    </mx:VBox>
</mx:Application>
```

You can find the files authorsAndBooks.mxml and MyXMLLoaderHelper.as saved with the other chapter resources.

These examples didn't pass variables to the requested page. That's the topic of the next section.

Updating content with the URLLoader class

As you saw earlier, you can pass variables to the requested page with the URLLoader object. You might use this approach to send a parameter to a server-side file so that you can filter the content returned to the object. You could also use the approach to send values for updating by the server-side page. Whatever your reason, you will need to work with a URLVariables object.

Earlier in the chapter, we covered how to create a URLVariables object and set variables and values. The following code provides a quick refresher:

```
var params:URLVariables = new URLVariables();
params.continent = "Europe";
params.timeStamp = new Date().getTime();
```

Once you've created the URLVariables object, you need to set it as the data property of the URLRequest object that you'll pass to the URLLoader. You can see how to do this in the following lines:

```
var request:URLRequest = new URLRequest(strURL);
request.data = params;
```

The next example demonstrates how to send values from a SWF file, using the URLVariables object. We'll work through both Flash and Flex versions that demonstrate sending login details with the request. This practice is common when users needs to log in to an application before they can access any details. The interface in both cases will consist of text fields that allow a user to enter a username and password, as well as a button to submit the details. The application will also display a message from the requested file.

In this case, you will work with a static XML document, so it won't matter which values you pass. In Chapter 9, you'll see how to integrate this approach with server-side pages to retrieve a response. For now, these simple examples will get you started.

We'll begin with the Flash example. Like the previous Flash examples, it uses procedural code to keep the example simple. You can see a class-based solution in the Flex example that follows the Flash example.

Sending variables in a Flash application

Here are the instructions to set up the Flash example:

1. Create a new ActionScript 3.0 document and add the interface elements shown in Figure 5-7.

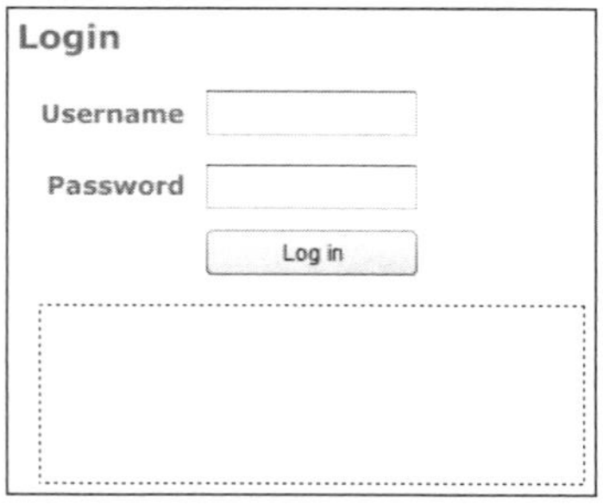

The interface consists of some static text, two TextInput controls, a Button component, and a dynamic text field. The TextInput controls have the instance names username_ txt and password_txt, respectively. The Button is called login_btn and has the label Log in. The dynamic text field has the instance name message_txt. In the Parameters tab, set the displayAsPassword field to true for the password_ txt instance.

Figure 5-7. The Flash login example interface

2. Add a new layer called actions and open it in the Actions panel with the F9 shortcut key. Add the following ActionScript code to set up the application:

```
var sender:URLLoader;
var sendPage:URLRequest;
var sendVars:URLVariables;
initApp();
```

The first three lines declare the variables that the application needs. First, the sender variable is a URLLoader object that will send the request. The second variable, sendPage, is a URLRequest object that details the page that the application will request. sendVars, the last variable, is a URLVariables object that will pass the username and password. The final line calls the initApp() function, which you'll create in the next step.

3. The initApp() function will need to create the URLLoader, URLRequest, and URLVariables objects. The URLRequest object will need to specify the page to be requested.

Add the following function underneath the function call from step 2:

```
function initApp():void {
  sender = new URLLoader();
  sendPage = new URLRequest("message.xml");
  sendPage.method = URLRequestMethod.POST;
  sendVars = new URLVariables();
}
```

In this example, instead of working with a server-side page, the application calls a simple XML document. Because it sends values to a static XML document, you need to use the POST method; otherwise, the application will throw an error. There won't actually be any processing of the username or password values.

4. The application will send the variable names and values to the XML document in response to the login_btn button click. You'll need to add an event listener to the Button that listens for the click event. I've called this function clickHandler().

Modify the initApp() function as show here, to include the line shown in bold:

```
function initApp():void {
  sender = new URLLoader();
  sendPage = new URLRequest("message.xml");
  sendPage.method = URLRequestMethod.POST;
  sendVars = new URLVariables();
  login_btn.addEventListener(MouseEvent.CLICK, clickHandler);
}
```

5. Add the clickHandler() function that follows. At this stage, the code includes a simple trace() statement so you can test your code, but you'll add something more useful shortly.

```
function clickHandler(e:MouseEvent):void {
  trace ("I'm clicked");
}
```

6. Test the application with the Ctrl/Cmd+Enter shortcut. You should be able to click the button and see the message I'm clicked in the Output panel.

7. You now need to modify the clickHandler() function so it actually performs a task. First, it will check that values have been entered for both the username and password. If not, an error message will display. If the user enters both values, the function will add them to the sendVars URLVariables object and request the external document with the URLLoader object. It will also need to clear any existing value from the message_txt text field.

Add the following function to the actions layer:

```
function clickHandler(e:MouseEvent):void {
  if (username_txt.text.length && password_txt.text.length > 0) {
    message_txt.text = "";
    sendVars.username = username_txt.text;
    sendVars.password = password_txt.text;
    sendPage.data = sendVars;
    sender.load(sendPage);
  }
  else {
    message_txt.text = "You must enter both a username and password
      ➥before clicking the button."
  }
}
```

8. You don't yet have a function to respond to the requested page, so you need to add an event listener that responds to the complete event of the URLLoader. Add the following line to the initApp() function:

```
sender.addEventListener(Event.COMPLETE, completeHandler);
```

9. Now you need the function that responds when this event is dispatched. Add the following completeHandler() function:

```
function completeHandler(e:Event):void {
  message_txt.text = XML(e.target.data).toString();
}
```

The completeHandler() function finds the loaded content using e.target.data, and casts it as an XML object using the XML() constructor method. The function displays a string representation of the returned content in the dynamic text field using the toString() method.

The external XML document contains a single element: <message>Login successful </message>. Because this is a simple element, without children, the toString() method returns only the text inside the <message> element.

Figure 5-8. Testing the Flash application

10. You can't test this example until you copy the message.xml document from the chapter resources to the same folder as your Flash application. Once you've done so, test the file and click the Log in button. You should see the message Login successful displayed in the dynamic text field, as shown in Figure 5-8.

> *In this example, you can't tell whether the variables have been sent successfully to the XML document, because no processing occurs in that page. You'll see some more sophisticated examples of sending variables with a URLLoader object in Chapter 9, where the variables that you send will elicit a response from the requested page.*

The complete code from the actions layer follows. Check it against your own code to make sure that you don't have any errors.

```
var sender:URLLoader;
var sendPage:URLRequest;
var sendVars:URLVariables;
initApp();
function initApp():void {
  sender = new URLLoader();
  sendPage = new URLRequest("message.xml");
  sendPage.method = URLRequestMethod.POST;
  sendVars = new URLVariables();
  login_btn.addEventListener(MouseEvent.CLICK, clickHandler);
  sender.addEventListener(Event.COMPLETE, completeHandler);
}
function clickHandler(e:MouseEvent):void {
  if (username_txt.text.length && password_txt.text.length > 0) {
      message_txt.text = "";
    sendVars.username = username_txt.text;
    sendVars.password = password_txt.text;
    sendPage.data = sendVars;
    sender.load(sendPage);
  }
  else {
    message_txt.text = "You must enter both a username and password
       ➥before clicking the button."
  }
}
function completeHandler(e:Event):void {
  message_txt.text = XML(e.target.data).toString();
}
```

You can find the files for this example saved as loginExample.fla and message.xml with the other chapter resources.

If you want to see another event in action, try removing the sendPage.method property and add an event handler listening for an IOError. Removing the method property will make the example use the GET method. This method will cause an IOError when you try to request the static XML document. You can see a sample of this error-handling function in the resource file.

157

Sending variables in a Flex application

Let's re-create the previous example using Flex Builder. In this case, the example uses a custom class file to work with the content.

1. Create a new Flex project and application file with the name of your choosing. Add an assets folder and copy the message.xml file there.

2. Use the File ➤ New ➤ ActionScript Class command to create a new ActionScript class. Add the class to the xmlUtilities package and call it XMLLoaderWithVariables.

3. Add the following import statements beneath the package declaration. These statements reference the classes that the application needs to use. Note that these statements will also be added automatically when you declare the variables in step 4.

```
import flash.net.URLLoader;
import flash.net.URLRequest;
import flash.net.URLVariables;
import flash.net.URLRequestMethod;
```

> You could replace these import statements with one that imports all classes in the flash.net package at the same time: import flash.net.*. Even though that statement is valid and much shorter than my approach, my preference is still to import classes individually so that I can see which I'm using in the current application. Feel free to use the wildcard instead if you prefer.

4. Add a bindable declaration above the class declaration. This declaration makes all public methods and properties bindable in the application file.

```
[Bindable]
```

5. Declare the following private variables below the class declaration:

```
private var xmlMessage:XML;
private var xmlLoader:URLLoader;
private var xmlRequest:URLRequest;
```

The first variable, xmlMessage, will store the returned XML content from the document. The second variable, xmlLoader, refers to the URLLoader object that will make the request. The third variable, xmlRequest, refers to the URLRequest object that will handle the page request and passed variables.

6. Modify the constructor method as shown here:

```
public function XMLLoaderWithVariables() {
  xmlLoader = new URLLoader();
  xmlLoader.addEventListener(Event.COMPLETE, completeHandler);
}
```

The XMLLoaderWithVariables() method creates the URLLoader object and adds an event listener that responds when the operation is complete. When the external file finishes loading, the handler completeHandler will execute.

7. Add the completeHandler() method now as shown here:

```
private function completeHandler(e:Event):void {
  xmlMessage = XML(e.target.data);
  dispatchEvent(new Event(Event.COMPLETE));
}
```

This method assigns the loaded XML content from the external file to the object xmlMessage, casting it to the type XML with the XML() constructor method. The method then dispatches the complete event to the application so it will know that the request has finished and the loaded data is available.

8. You'll need a public method that handles the request for the external file. This method, loadXML(), will receive two arguments: the name of the file to request and the variables to send with that request. When the Flex application calls the loadXML() method, it will pass a URLVariables object as the second argument.

```
public function loadXML(xmlFile:String, vars:URLVariables):void {
  try {
    xmlRequest = new URLRequest(xmlFile);
    xmlRequest.data = vars;
    xmlRequest.method = URLRequestMethod.POST;
    xmlLoader.load(xmlRequest);
  }
  catch (e:Error) {
    trace ("Can't load external XML document");
  }
}
```

This method encloses the content in a try/catch block to provide some simple error handling. In the case of an error, the application will display the message Can't load external XML document in the Console view. You would probably make the error handling a little more robust in a real-world application, so feel free to modify the code at this point if you want.

The loadXML() method creates a new URLRequest object, using the URL passed in as the first argument. The method assigns the variables argument to the data property of the URLRequest object and sets the method property to POST the variables to the requested page. It finishes by calling the load() method to make the request.

9. The XMLLoaderWithVariables class will need one public method to return the content from the external document. The external document will send back a single simple element, <message>. Applying the toString() method will result in only the text from the element being identified.

Add the following public message() method to the class file:

```
public function message():String {
  return xmlMessage.toString();
}
```

That's it for the class file. Check your contents against the complete code block that follows:

```
package xmlUtilities {
  import flash.net.URLLoader;
  import flash.net.URLRequest;
  import flash.net.URLVariables;
  import flash.net.URLRequestMethod;
  [Bindable]
  public class XMLLoaderWithVariables {
    private var xmlMessage:XML;
    private var xmlLoader:URLLoader;
    private var xmlRequest:URLRequest;
    public function XMLLoaderWithVariables() {
      xmlLoader = new URLLoader();
      xmlLoader.addEventListener(Event.COMPLETE, completeHandler);
    }
    public function loadXML(xmlFile:String, vars:URLVariables):void {
      try {
        xmlRequest = new URLRequest(xmlFile);
        xmlRequest.data = vars;
        xmlRequest.method = URLRequestMethod.POST;
        xmlLoader.load(xmlRequest);
      }
      catch (e:Error) {
        trace ("Can't load external XML document");
      }
    }
    public function message():String {
      return xmlMessage.toString();
    }
    private function completeHandler(e:Event):void {
      xmlMessage = XML(e.target.data);
      dispatchEvent(new Event(Event.COMPLETE));
    }
  }
}
```

10. Switch back to the Flex application file. Create the interface shown in Figure 5-9.

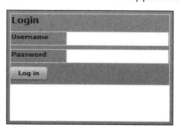

Figure 5-9. The Flex login application interface

The interface consists of some Label controls, as well as two TextInput components for collecting the username and password. The second component has its displayAsPasword setting set to true.

There is also a Log in button, which will trigger the URLLoader request, as well as a TextArea, which displays messages. If you change this interface, make sure that you use the same ID settings for all components.

The declarative code to create the interface follows:

```
<?xml version="1.0" encoding="utf-8"?>
<mx:Application xmlns:mx="http://www.adobe.com/2006/mxml"
  layout="absolute">
  <mx:VBox x="10" y="10">
    <mx:Label text="Login" fontSize="14" fontWeight="bold"/>
    <mx:HBox>
      <mx:Label text="Username" fontWeight="bold" width="80"/>
      <mx:TextInput id="username_txt"/>
    </mx:HBox>
    <mx:HBox>
      <mx:Label text="Password" fontWeight="bold" width="80"/>
      <mx:TextInput id="password_txt" displayAsPassword="true"/>
    </mx:HBox>
    <mx:Button id="login_btn" label="Log in" />
    <mx:TextArea width="250" height="60" id="message_txt"/>
  </mx:VBox>
</mx:Application>
```

11. You'll set up the application by calling a function in the creationComplete attribute of the `<mx:Application>` element. This function is called initApp(), and it will set up the variables you'll need, including a new XMLLoaderWithVariables object.

Modify the `<mx:Application>` element as shown here in bold:

```
<mx:Application xmlns:mx="http://www.adobe.com/2006/mxml"
  layout="absolute" creationComplete="initApp(event)">
```

12. Add the following `<mx:Script>`, including the initApp() function. I'll explain it after the code block.

```
<mx:Script>
  <![CDATA[
    import mx.events.FlexEvent;
    import xmlUtilities.XMLLoaderWithVariables;
    private var myXMLLoaderVars:XMLLoaderWithVariables;
    private function initApp(e:FlexEvent):void {
      myXMLLoaderVars = new XMLLoaderWithVariables();
      myXMLLoaderVars.addEventListener(Event.COMPLETE,
        ➥completeHandler);
      login_btn.addEventListener(MouseEvent.CLICK, clickHandler);
    }
    private function completeHandler(e:Event):void {
    }
    private function clickHandler(e:MouseEvent):void {
    }
  ]]>
</mx:Script>
```

161

This `<mx:Script>` element starts by importing the relevant classes. The application needs the FlexEvent class, as this type of event is dispatched when the interface finishes creating. It also needs to import the custom class that you just created, XMLLoaderWithVariables, and to create an object of this type called myXMLLoaderVars.

The initApp() function receives a FlexEvent as an argument. It starts by creating a new instance of the XMLLoaderWithVariables class and then assigns the completeHandler() function to be called when the URLLoader finishes loading the external document. At the moment, this function doesn't contain any code.

The function also assigns an event listener to the login_btn instance. This listener responds to the click event of the button with the clickHandler() function. The `<mx:Script>` block also contains an empty clickHandler() function.

13. When the Log in button is clicked, the application needs to check that the username and password are filled in before calling the loadXML() method of the XMLLoaderWithVariables object. When the loadXML() method is called, the method call will pass the URL of the document to load, as well as a URLVariables object containing the entered username and password.

Modify the clickHandler() function as shown here in bold:

```
private function clickHandler(e:MouseEvent):void {
  if (username_txt.text.length > 0 && password_txt.text.length > 0) {
    var myVars:URLVariables = new URLVariables();
    myVars.username = username_txt.text;
    myVars.password = password_txt.text;
    myXMLLoaderVars.loadXML("assets/message.xml", myVars);
  }
  else {
    message_txt.text = "You must enter both a username and password
      ➥before clicking the button";
  }
}
```

The clickHandler() function starts by testing that the length of both the username and password entries is greater than 0. If this is the case, the function creates a new URLVariables object and assigns the username and password properties from the entries in the TextInput controls. It then calls the loadXML() method, passing the name of the document to request and the URLVariables object.

If either of the TextInput controls do not contain any text, the message You must enter both a username and password before clicking the button displays in the TextArea at the bottom of the interface.

14. The last step in building this application is to respond when a reply is received from the messages.xml file. The application will display the reply in the TextArea control. It does this in the completeHandler() function, so modify it as shown in bold here:

```
private function completeHandler(e:Event):void {
  message_txt.text = myXMLLoaderVars.message();
}
```

15. Now you're ready to test the application. Run it and enter values for a username and password. When you click the button, you should see the TextArea update, as shown in Figure 5-10.

Figure 5-10. The completed Flex login application example

The complete code for the application file follows:

```
<?xml version="1.0" encoding="utf-8"?>
<mx:Application xmlns:mx="http://www.adobe.com/2006/mxml"
  layout="absolute" creationComplete="initApp(event)">
  <mx:Script>
    <![CDATA[
      import mx.events.FlexEvent;
      import xmlUtilities.XMLLoaderWithVariables;
      private var myXMLLoaderVars:XMLLoaderWithVariables;
      private function initApp(e:FlexEvent):void {
        myXMLLoaderVars = new XMLLoaderWithVariables();
        myXMLLoaderVars.addEventListener(Event.COMPLETE, completeHandler);
        login_btn.addEventListener(MouseEvent.CLICK, clickHandler);
      }
      private function completeHandler(e:Event):void {
        message_txt.text = myXMLLoaderVars.message();
      }
      private function clickHandler(e:MouseEvent):void {
        if (username_txt.text.length > 0 && password_txt.text.length
          ➡ > 0) {
          var myVars:URLVariables = new URLVariables();
          myVars.username = username_txt.text;
          myVars.password = password_txt.text;
          myXMLLoaderVars.loadXML("assets/message.xml", myVars);
        }
        else {
          message_txt.text = "You must enter both a username and
          ➡password before clicking the button";
        }
      }
    ]]>
  </mx:Script>
```

```
      <mx:VBox x="10" y="10">
        <mx:Label text="Login" fontSize="14" fontWeight="bold"/>
        <mx:HBox>
          <mx:Label text="Username" fontWeight="bold" width="80"/>
          <mx:TextInput id="username_txt"/>
        </mx:HBox>
        <mx:HBox>
          <mx:Label text="Password" fontWeight="bold" width="80"/>
          <mx:TextInput id="password_txt" displayAsPassword="true"/>
        </mx:HBox>
        <mx:Button id="login_btn" label="Log in" />
        <mx:TextArea width="250" height="60" id="message_txt"/>
      </mx:VBox>
    </mx:Application>
```

You can find the resource files for this example with the other chapter resources, saved as LoginExample.mxml and XMLLoaderWithVariables.as.

You've seen several examples of loading external content using the URLLoader class. When you request external data, you're subject to Flash Player security restrictions, so it's important to understand these and the limitations that apply.

Understanding Flash Player security

When accessing external documents, the security model in Flash Player 9 and 10 is based on the relative locations of the SWF file loading the data and the source of the data. The rules discussed in this section also apply to Flash Player 8, although Flash Players 9 and 10 have some extra restrictions discussed in the section entitled "Finding problems with the cross-domain policy file." Note that earlier versions of Flash Player have different approaches to security. I'll refer only to Flash Player 10 here, as it is the most recent player at the time of writing, but the same rules apply to Flash Player 9, too.

The basic rule is that a SWF file can access any data from the same subdomain as its own location. By default, it's not possible for the SWF file to load content from a different domain or subdomain. This restriction also applies between local and network domains. SWF files on the network cannot access local data, and local SWF files cannot access network data, because they're in different domains.

Understanding security sandboxes

Flash Player 10 allocates SWF files to their own security sandbox, which equates to their exact domain. For example, SWF files located in the following domains are considered to be in separate sandboxes:

- http://www.friendsofed.com
- http://friendsofed.com
- http://examples.friendsofed.com
- http://65.19.150.101

Even though the IP address 65.19.150.101 may resolve to the first domain in this list, it is still considered to be in a separate security sandbox.

If you need to load data from another domain into your Flex application, you can choose from the following two alternatives:

- Specifically allow access by using a cross-domain policy file on the server hosting the data source
- Use a server-side proxy file to access the remote data and locate it within the local domain

Creating a cross-domain policy file

A cross-domain policy file is an XML file called crossdomain.xml, which lives in the root of the web server that hosts the external data. The file does *not* live in the same domain as the requesting SWF application. The cross-domain policy file grants permissions to specific domains to access the data stored there.

If the crossdomain.xml file does not reside in the root directory of the server, the SWF file can request it from a different location using the Security.loadPolicyFile method. The cross-domain policy file will apply only to the directory from which it is loaded and any child directories. For example, you might use this method to restrict access to content in the _data folder and any child folders.

Writing a cross-domain policy file

The cross-domain policy file needs to have the following structure. For Flash Player 10, this structure must be exact.

```
<?xml version="1.0"?>
<cross-domain-policy>
  <allow-access-from domain="www.friendsofed.com" />
  <allow-access-from domain="*.friendsofed.com" />
  <allow-access-from domain="65.19.150.101" />
</cross-domain-policy>
```

This cross-domain policy file allows access to the data by www.friendsofed.com, any subdomain of friendsofed.com, and the IP address 65.19.150.101. Note that you can use the wildcard * to specify any subdomain.

You can also use a wildcard to grant access to all domains:

```
<?xml version="1.0"?>
<cross-domain-policy>
  <allow-access-from domain="*" />
</cross-domain-policy>
```

If the SWF requesting the data appears in any of the domains listed in the cross-domain policy file, it will be granted access to the content by Flash Player 10. If not, the SWF won't be granted permission to load the data, and the application will generate a securityError.

If you're working with secure domains, it's possible to include the secure attribute within an <allow-access-from> tag. This attribute has a default value of true, which restricts data on a secure HTTPS server from being accessed by anything other than another HTTPS server. You can set this value to false if you want a secure server to be able to be accessed by both secure and insecure servers.

Issues with the cross-domain policy file

Be aware that Flash Player 10 has tightened up some of the requirements for cross-domain policy files. First, Flash Player 10 will recognize cross-domain policy files only where the content type is set to any text type (text/*), or to application/xml or application/xhtml+xml. The content type is set by the response headers provided by the HTTP server, so you may need to check that the server settings are correct if you're having difficulties with the policy file.

In addition, Flash Player 10 will reject any policy file with contents that are not well-formed or that are invalidly formatted. The root element of the file *must* be <cross-domain-policy>, and none of the elements in the file can contain text children. In addition, if the cross-domain policy file contains characters before or after the opening and closing <cross-domain-policy> tag, with the exception of legal declarations, Flash Player 10 will reject the file.

If the HTTP server redirects a cross-domain policy file to a location within the same domain, Flash Player 10 will treat the redirected location as the final destination, *not* the initially requested URL. Earlier versions of Flash Player did the opposite, treating the initial location as the final destination and ignoring the location of the redirect.

Because the final destination dictates which domain and subdomain will be accessible to Flash Player 10, any HTTP server redirects could potentially cause problems. If the policy file doesn't reference the redirected location, Flash Player 10 will not access the external data.

If you don't have access to a cross-domain policy file on the remote server, you can proxy the external data locally.

Proxying data locally

If you can't add a cross-domain policy file to a remote server, you can use a server-side file to request the external content and provide it to your SWF application. This is likely to be particularly useful where you're requesting an XML-formatted stream from an external source, perhaps as a web service.

As long as the server-side file is in the same domain as the SWF application, you'll be able to load the proxied content. The application will think that the data is local and therefore in the same security sandbox.

You can write the simple server-side proxy file in the language of your choice. You can find out more about the topic at http://kb.adobe.com/selfservice/viewContent.do?externalId=tn_16520&sliceId=1. At the time of writing, the article had examples of proxy files written in ColdFusion, PHP, ASP, and using a Java Servlet. LiveCycle Data Services ES also provides a complete proxy management system for Flex applications.

Summary

This chapter covered the URLLoader class and discussed its properties, methods, and events. We worked through Flash and Flex examples to demonstrate how to use this class and related classes to request external content. We finished by looking at some of the security issues surrounding Flash Player.

The next chapter covers some of the loading methods that are specific to Flex.

Chapter 6

LOADING METHODS SPECIFIC TO FLEX

In the previous chapter, I showed you how to load external XML content into both Flash and Flex using the URLLoader class. You saw that you can load content from a static XML file or from a server-side page that generates an XML stream. Both Flash and Flex can use the URLLoader class. The advantage of loading external content is that your applications will be more flexible than if you store the content within the application itself.

While Flex can use the URLLoader class, it can also use the HTTPService class to access many types of external content, including XML-formatted content. It's possible to either use a tag-based approach with the <HTTPService> MXML element or to write ActionScript 3.0 code to work with the HTTPService class. In this chapter, I'll cover both options and show you how to use them to load external XML files.

As with the URLLoader class, when you use the HTTPService class or <mx:HTTPService> element to load external XML content, you can access the loaded XML tree using methods of the XML class or by writing E4X expressions. Unlike the URLLoader class, in which all content arrives as text, with the HTTPService class and <mx:HTTPService> element, you can specify the format for the loaded content in advance, so there's no need to cast the loaded content as an XML data type.

The HTTPService class and <mx:HTTPService> element both use a request-response approach. This means that any application using them needs to request the content from the server first, before the XML content is provided to the Flex application.

If the external data changes, the server cannot initiate the process and inform the Flex application that something has changed. So, if you are working with external content that changes regularly, you'll need to poll the server at regular intervals in order to detect if the content has changed. This process is likely to be unwieldy, so you may wish to look at an approach involving the XMLSocket class. You can use the XMLSocket class to create a real-time connection to XML content. When the content changes, the server can notify the Flex application of any changes, causing the application to update without first making a request. The XMLSocket class requires that the application runs on a socket server. That topic is beyond the scope of this book.

In this chapter, we'll focus on the <mx:HTTPService> element and HTTPService class. I'll explain the properties, methods, and events of both, and show you how they differ. The code samples will illustrate how to use MXML tags and also demonstrate a class-based approach.

Remember that the loading of external content is subject to the security restrictions of Flash Player. Each version of the Flash Player has slightly different security considerations. At the time of writing, the latest version was Flash Player 10. You can find out information about Flash Player 10 security in Chapter 5 of this book.

As usual, you can download all of the resources for this chapter from http://www.friendsofed.com. This download includes the XML documents used for the examples, as well as my completed files.

Let's begin!

Loading external content

Both the <mx:HTTPService> tag and HTTPService class allow you to request content from a URL and to receive a response. You can optionally send parameters with the request, perhaps if you need to filter the content. The <mx:HTTPService> tag exists in the mx.rpc.http.mxml package; the HTTPService class is in the mx.rpc.http package. Both work in much the same way, although there are some subtle differences between the two.

As with the URLLoader class, when using either the <mx:HTTPService> tag or HTTPService class, processing of the loaded content should wait until the request has successfully completed. The application is notified either when it receives the results of the request or a fault is generated.

I'll deal with the <mx:HTTPService> tag and HTTPService class separately. We'll start by looking at the <mx:HTTPService> tag.

Using the <mx:HTTPService> tag

The <mx:HTTPService> MXML element provides a tag-based approach that developers can use to request an external document and access its content. The element works with only the Flex framework and has no equivalent in Flash.

The <mx:HTTPService> element is useful for developers who don't wish to adopt a scripted approach in their applications. Thanks to data binding, it's possible to request a document, access the contents, and display them in a Flex interface without writing a single line of ActionScript 3.0.

Before we see this element in action, let's start by looking at the properties, methods, and events of the <mx:HTTPService> tag.

Properties of the <mx:HTTPService> tag

The properties of the HTTPService tag are shown in Table 6-1.

Table 6-1. Properties of the <mx:HTTPService> tag

Property	Data type	Description	Default value
channelSet	ChannelSet	Provides access to the ChannelSet used by the service. These are the channels used to send messages to the destination.	
concurrency	String	Indicates how to handle multiple calls to the same service. The choices are multiple, single, and last.	multiple
contentType	String	Specifies the type of content for the request. The choices are application/x-www-form-urlencoded and application/xml.	application/x-www-form-urlencoded
destination	String	Indicates the HTTPService destination name specified in the services-config.xml file. This file is used with LiveCycle Data Services ES.	
headers	Object	Custom headers to send with the HTTPService.	
lastResult	Object	The result of the last request made to the service.	
makeObjectsBindable	Boolean	Determines whether returned anonymous objects are forced to bindable objects.	
method	String	The HTTP method used to send the request. Choose from GET, POST, HEAD, OPTIONS, PUT, TRACE, and DELETE. Chapter 9 explains more about the GET and POST methods.	GET
request	Object	An object containing name/value pairs that are parameters for the requested URL.	
requestTimeout	int	Sets the timeout for the request in seconds.	

Continued

171

Table 6-1. Continued

Property	Data type	Description	Default value
resultFormat	String	Indicates the expected format for returned content from the request. Choose from object, array, xml, flashvars, text, and e4x.	object
rootURL	String	The URL to use as the basis for calculating relative URLs. Used only when useProxy is set to true.	
url	String	The URL or location for the service.	
showBusyCursor	Boolean	Determines whether to display a busy cursor while the request is loading.	false
useProxy	Boolean	Determines whether to use the Flex proxy service.	false
xmlDecode	Function	Sets the function to use to decode XML returned with the resultFormat of object.	
xmlEncode	Function	Sets the function to use to encode a service request as XML.	

Some of these properties need a little more explanation:

- concurrency: The concurrency property dictates how the application should deal with multiple calls made to the same service. The default value of multiple indicates that multiple requests to the same service are allowed. With this setting, the developer would need to manage the response from each request separately to make sure that the results don't get mixed up. A concurrency value of single allows the application to make only a single request at a time. If the application makes more than one request, these additional requests will generate a fault. Setting the value of the concurrency property to last means that when the application makes a request, any preexisting requests to that service are canceled. You might use this value if you provide the functionality for canceling requests in your application.

- contentType: You can set the contentType property to indicate what type of content the request sends to the target URL. The default value of application/x-www-form-urlencoded sends the request as name/value pairs. You can override this default value and specify that the content sends the request in XML format by using the application/xml setting.

- headers: The headers property allows you to set custom headers that will be passed with the request. At the time of writing, there is a known bug that prevents custom headers from being sent when the HTTP GET method is selected. The bug is documented at https://bugs.adobe.com/jira/browse/SDK-12505. The work-around is to use the POST method instead.

- method: You can set the method property to indicate which HTTP method should be used to send the request. If you don't set a value, the request will be made using GET. As detailed in the previous paragraph, you may need to set the method to POST in order to pass custom headers. Unless you go through the server-based proxy service, you can use only HTTP GET or POST methods with the request. However, the other methods become available if you set the useProxy property to true and use the server-based proxy service. This topic is beyond the scope of this book; consult the Flex help for more information.

- request: If you need to send parameters or variables with the request, the request property passes an Object of name/value pairs. However, you would need to pass an XML object instead if the contentType property is set to application/xml.

- requestTimeout: You can set a timeout for the request with the requestTimeout property. The property uses a value in seconds. You can bypass this property and consequently allow no timeout by using a value of zero or less. You might set a timeout so you can prevent the user from waiting if there is no response from the web server in a reasonable amount of time. If you don't set a timeout, the request might fail without the user being aware that there is a problem.

- resultFormat: The resultFormat property indicates the expected format for the returned results. The default value, object, expects a returned XML value and parses it as a tree of ActionScript objects. A resultFormat value of array expects an XML value, which is parsed as a tree of ActionScript objects. The difference from the first value, object, is that if the top-level object is not an Array, a new Array is created, and the result is set as the first item.

  When loading XML content, you need to set the value of the resultFormat to e4x if you want to take advantage of the new XML class and traverse the content using E4X expressions. The e4x value returns the content as literal XML.

  It's confusing but you shouldn't use the resultFormat of xml when you work with ActionScript 3.0. You should use this value only if you want to work with the ActionScript 2.0 XML class. This book addresses mainly ActionScript 3.0, so we won't look at the legacy XML class at all.

  The other two values for the resultFormat property are flashvars and text. flashvars returns text containing name/value pairs separated by ampersands. If you've worked with the LoadVars class in ActionScript 2.0, you'll be familiar with this format. The text value returns the content as raw text.

- url: The url property determines the URL or page used in the request.

- showBusyCursor: The showBusyCursor property does exactly as its name suggests: it displays an hourglass busy cursor while the application makes a request. This property is available only to the MXML tag and it can't be scripted (which I think is a great pity).

I'll show you how these properties work shortly, in the "Putting it all together" section. Next, let's look at the methods of the <mx:HTTPService> tag.

Methods of the <mx:HTTPService> tag

Table 6-2 summarizes the main methods of the HTTPService tag.

Table 6-2. Methods of the HTTPService tag

Method	Parameters	Description	Returns
cancel()		Overrides the most recent request	AsyncToken
disconnect()		Disconnects the network connection of the service without waiting for the request to complete	Nothing
HTTPService()	rootURL:String, destination: String	Constructor method	Nothing
send()	parameters: Object	Executes the HTTPService request	AsyncToken

The disconnect() method is straightforward. The other methods work as follows:

- cancel(): The cancel() method cancels the most recent HTTPService request. It returns an AsyncToken object, which provides a way to set token-level data for remote procedure calls so you can identify each one individually.

- HTTPService(): The constructor method HTTPService() instantiates an HTTPService object. It can take an optional rootURL value as an argument, which specifies the root to use when calculating relative URLs. The method can also take an optional destination argument, which corresponds to an HTTPService destination name in the services-config.xml file. That topic is a little beyond the scope of this book, so I won't go into it here, other than to say you might use this approach if you're working with Flex Data Services or making a non-HTTP request.

- send(): The send() method is probably the most important method of all. It actually sends the request, optionally with an Object containing name/value parameters for the request. If the contentType property is set to application/xml, the application would need to pass an XML object with the request.

Let's move on to events next.

Events of the <mx:HTTPService> tag

The HTTPService tag dispatches a number of events, as summarized in Table 6-3. Unlike the progress and httpStatus events dispatched by the URLLoader, there aren't any events here to determine the progress of the request.

Table 6-3. The events dispatched by the HTTPService class

Event	Type	Description
fault	FaultEvent	Dispatched when an HTTPService call fails
invoke	InvokeEvent	Dispatched when the HTTPService call is invoked, providing an error isn't encountered first
result	ResultEvent	Dispatched when an HTTPService call returns successfully

Of these, you're most likely to use the fault and result events.

Putting it all together

Let's see how these properties, methods, and events work together to create an HTTPService request using a tag-based approach. A little later, you'll see how to accomplish the same tasks using the HTTPService class.

We'll start with creating the initial request.

Creating an HTTPService request

To create an HTTPService request using an MXML tag, you need to use the <mx:HTTPService> element. In order to use it within your applications, you should specify an id attribute and a url for the component, as shown here:

```
<mx:HTTPService id="xmlService" url="myfile.xml" />
```

This example creates an <mx:HTTPService> element with an id of xmlService that requests the external file myfile.xml.

The url property will need to include the full path for any server-side files so that the server-side code can be processed correctly. For example, if you are generating XML content using the file myfile.aspx running in the xmlTest folder on localhost, use the following MXML tag:

```
<mx:HTTPService id="xmlService"
  url="http://localhost/xmlTest/myfile.aspx" />
```

Making the request

You need to make the request for the URL specified in the tag by using the send() method of the <mx:HTTPService> element. You call this method and refer to the element using the id property from its tag. You can optionally send variables inside this method call; you'll see that approach in the next section.

To make the data available when the application first loads, it's common to call this method in the initialize or creationComplete event of the <mx:Application> tag, as shown in the example here:

```
<mx:Application xmlns:mx="http://www.adobe.com/2006/mxml"
  layout="absolute" creationComplete="xmlService.send()">
```

175

If the content doesn't need to be available when the application first loads, you could also call the send() method in response to a button click or some other event. In this case, you would add the method call inside the click handler for the button. You can see an example of this approach in the following simple event-handler function:

```
function clickHandler(e:MouseEvent):void{
  xmlService.send();
}
```

The request won't be made until the button is clicked.

Sending variables with the request

You can send variables or parameters with the HTTPService request. For example, if you're requesting database content through a server-side file that collates the XML content, you might send one or more parameters to filter the results returned in the response. This approach allows you to be more flexible by using the same server-side page in different situations.

There are several ways to send variables with the request. First, you can send variables at the same time that you call the send() method. If you choose this approach, you can specify an Object containing the name/value variable pairs inside the method call, as shown here:

```
<mx:Application xmlns:mx="http://www.adobe.com/2006/mxml"
  layout="absolute"
  creationComplete="xmlService.send({lastname:'Ambrose'})">
```

Here, the use of the curly braces indicates that you've created an Object containing a property with the name lastname and the value Ambrose.

You can also can use the <mx:request> tag inside the <mx:HTTPService> tag to list the parameters. In the next code block, the <mx:HTTPService> tag sends the same parameter, lastname, as in the previous example:

```
<mx:HTTPService id="xmlService"
  url="http://localhost/FlexApp/getAuthors.aspx">
  <mx:request>
    <lastname>Ambrose</lastname>
  </mx:request>
</mx:HTTPService>
```

In this example, notice that the <mx:request> property is written as a tag within the <mx:HTTPService> element. Notice also that the tag uses a lowercase initial letter <mx:request>, unlike the uppercase letter in most other elements. The <mx:request> tag is a container for the parameters, rather than a class in its own right.

The format for the parameters is determined by the contentType property. The default value of this property is application/x-www-form-urlencoded, which equates to name/value variable pairs. You can also use the setting application/xml if the URL that you request expects to receive raw XML data. You could set this value as shown in bold in the following code block:

```
<mx:HTTPService id="xmlService" url="myfile.xml"
  result="resultHandler(event)" fault="faultHandler(event)"
  resultFormat="e4x" method="POST" contentType="application/xml"/>
```

In this case, you would need to send the variables in XML format. The following block shows how you might do this inside the creationComplete event of the application:

```
<mx:Application xmlns:mx="http://www.adobe.com/2006/mxml"
  layout="absolute"
  creationComplete="xmlService.send(<lastname>Ambrose</lastname>)">
```

Specifying a return type

Remember that there are several different return types that you can specify for the <mx:HTTPService> element. These are object, array, xml, flashvars, text, and e4x. When you're working with external XML content in ActionScript 3.0, you'll use the e4x value in most cases, as this return type will allow you to interrogate the loaded content using E4X expressions.

You set the returnType property for the <mx:HTTPService> element as shown in bold in the following code block:

```
<mx:HTTPService id="xmlService" url="myfile.xml"
  result="resultHandler(event)" fault="faultHandler(event)"
  resultFormat="e4x"/>
```

In this case, the code sets the resultFormat property to e4x so that you can use E4X methods with the loaded content.

Specifying a request method

Parameters are always sent using HTTP GET, unless you specify something else with the method property. In most cases, you would add this property to the <mx:HTTPService> tag to use the POST method for the request, as you can see in the following example:

```
<mx:HTTPService id="xmlService" url="myfile.xml"
  result="resultHandler(event)" fault="faultHandler(event)"
  resultFormat="e4x" method="POST"/>
```

You can also specify HEAD, OPTIONS, PUT, TRACE, or DELETE, but only if you set the useProxy property to true and use the server-based proxy service. As I mentioned earlier, I'm not going to cover this topic because it is beyond the scope of the book.

Receiving a response

When the <mx:HTTPService> element receives a response, it dispatches a result event to the application to notify the application that the server response is available. If the request fails, a fault event is dispatched to the application.

You can specify handlers for each of these events in the `<mx:HTTPService>` element, as shown in the following example.

```
<mx:HTTPService id="xmlService" url="myfile.xml"
    result="resultHandler(event)"
    fault="faultHandler(event)"/>
```

Both of these handler functions receive an event object as a parameter; however, they are different event types.

The role of the `result` event handler function is to process the loaded content and add it to the application interface appropriately. This handler function will receive an event that is of the type `ResultEvent`.

The `fault` event handler should process the passed `FaultEvent`. Its role is to respond so that the request for the service doesn't fail silently without the user knowing what has gone wrong. The `fault` event handler would normally notify the user that the call has failed and provide a reason for the failure wherever possible.

> *It's not necessary to name the handler functions as I've done here, using the names* `resultHandler` *and* `faultHandler`. *In fact, you can use any name that seems logical to you for these functions. However, it's a handy convention to name the handler functions according to the event that they handle, because it is easier to follow the logic within the application code. If you want to see which method deals with the* `result` *event, you can immediately look for the* `resultHandler` *function.*

The final task is to access the loaded content, However, I'll deal with this topic separately, after I cover the HTTPService class.

Using the HTTPService class

The HTTPService class exists within the `mx.rpc.http` package. Although it operates in a similar way to the `<mx:HTTPService>` tag, there are some minor differences, which I'll highlight next.

Properties, methods, and events of the HTTPService class

The HTTPService class has most of the same properties as the `<mx:HTTPService>` element. However, the concurrency and showBusyCursor properties from the `<mx:HTTPService>` element are not available to the HTTPService class.

The only difference between the methods of the `<mx:HTTPService>` tag and class is the constructor method. The HTTPService class constructor method, HTTPService(), takes only a single optional parameter, the rootURL, which is a String value used when calculating relative references. It does not allow destination as an optional parameter.

The events of the `<mx:HTTPService>` tag and the HTTPService class are identical.

Putting it all together

This section describes how to use a scripted approach with the HTTPService class properties, methods, and events. I'll show you the same tasks that we covered when looking at a tag-based approach. Again, we'll start with making the request for the service.

Creating an HTTPService request

You can create an HTTPService request with the following ActionScript code:

```
var xmlService:HTTPService = new HTTPService();
xmlService.url = "myfile.xml";
```

The code starts by calling the constructor method without passing a rootURL parameter to create the HTTPService object. It then sets the url property for the service to call the external file myfile.xml.

This example is equivalent to the tag-based code that you saw earlier.

Making the request

To make the request, you need to use the send() method of the HTTPService class and refer it using the id assigned to the object. If the data needs to be available to the application when it first loads, it's common to call the send() method in an initializing function, as shown here:

```
<mx:Application xmlns:mx="http://www.adobe.com/2006/mxml"
  layout="absolute" creationComplete="initApp(event)">
```

The initApp() function would set any properties for the HTTPService object, including event handlers. It will usually finish by calling the send() method of the HTTPService object.

You might see code similar to the following in the initApp() function:

```
var xmlService:HTTPServer = new HTTPService();
function initApp(e:FlexEvent):void{
  xmlService.url = "myfile.xml";
  xmlService.addEventListener(ResultEvent.RESULT, resultHandler);
  xmlService.send();
}
```

As I discussed earlier, if the content doesn't need to be available when the application first loads, you might call the send() method in response to some other event. For example, you could add the call inside the click handler for a button, as you can see in the following example:

```
function clickHandler(e:MouseEvent):void{
  xmlService.send();
}
```

In this case, clicking the button calls the send() method.

Sending variables with the request

You can send parameters or variables to the request using ActionScript 3.0. As I mentioned before, you might use these parameters to filter the results returned by the request.

The first approach is to add an Object containing the name/value pairs inside the call to the send() method, as you can see in the following line:

```
xmlService.send({lastname: 'Ambrose'};
```

This line sends the parameter lastname and its value Ambrose with the request.

Another approach is to add the parameters to an Object first. You can then assign the Object to the request property of the HTTPService class.

```
var params:Object = new Object();
params.lastname = "Ambrose";
xmlService.request = params;
```

You can also set the contentType property for the parameters, as shown here:

```
xmlService.contentType= "application/xml";
```

You would do this if you were sending an XML object containing the parameters for the request.

Specifying a return type

You can set the return type for the results of the request when scripting the HTTPService class, as shown here:

```
xmlService.resultFormat = "e4x";
```

In this case, the results will be treated as an XML document that you will be able to interrogate with E4X expressions.

Specifying a request method

As I've mentioned previously, parameters are always sent using HTTP GET, unless you specify something else with the method property. You can set this value in ActionScript, as shown here:

```
xmlService.method = "POST";
```

This line sets the method to POST. You can find a discussion about using GET and POST in Chapter 9.

Receiving a response

As you saw earlier, when the HTTPService receives a response, it dispatches a result event. It dispatches a fault event if the call fails.

You can specify handlers for each of these events, as shown in the following example using the ActionScript addEventListener() method. You would probably include these method calls in a function that initializes the application, as in the example shown earlier.

```
xmlService.addEventListener(ResultEvent.RESULT, resultHandler);
xmlService.addEventListener(FaultEvent.FAULT, faultHandler);
```

These lines of code assign two event handlers that listen for the `result` and `fault` events. Don't forget that you don't need to use the function names `resultHandler` and `faultHandler`. You could use any other name that seems appropriate.

Whichever approach you choose—either tag-based or using ActionScript 3.0—you'll need to access the content loaded by the request, and that's the topic of the next section.

Accessing loaded content

Once a request has been successfully processed, you can access the response in the `lastResult` property of the `HTTPService` object.

You can work with this property in the `result` event handler function, or you can bind the content directly to another component.

Accessing the lastResult property directly

The following lines show how you might use a `result` event handler function to access the loaded content:

```
function resultHandler(e:ResultEvent):void {
  //do something with e.target.lastResult
}
```

Notice that the function uses the `ResultEvent` object passed to the handler function. It addresses the `target` property of this event, the `HTTPService` object, and accesses the `lastResult` property.

If you've specified a `resultFormat` of e4x, you can use E4X expressions to target the content within the loaded XML document. Treat the expression `e.target.lastResult` as the root node of the XML document and build the expression from that point. You'll see this expression in the examples that follow.

You can also use the `lastResult` property in binding expressions to components.

Binding the lastResult property

Binding expressions with curly braces allows you to bind a property of a control directly to a value or property from a loaded XML document. You can use an E4X expression to identify which part of the document should be bound to the property of the target component.

The following example shows how you might bind a property within the `lastResult` property directly to a target component property. The relevant binding expression appears in bold.

```
<mx:Text text="{txtLoader.lastResult.publisher}"/>
```

181

This example binds the publisher property from the response to the text property of a Text control using curly braces notation. The <publisher> element is a child of the root element, which is equivalent to txtLoader.lastResult. Whenever you work with a resultFormat of e4x, the lastResult property is equivalent to the root element in the loaded XML content.

You can use much more complicated E4X expressions to target specific content. This might include longer paths and even filters. You can find out more about E4X expressions in Chapter 4 of the book.

If you assign the loaded XML content to an ActionScript XML object first, you can still use curly braces binding with properties of other controls. Before you do this, though, you need to make sure that the XML object is a bindable variable by adding the [Bindable] metatag above its declaration.

The following example creates an XML object called loadedXML, which could be used in binding expressions:

```
[Bindable]
private var loadedXML:XML;
```

You can then populate this variable with XML content as part of the result event handler function.

```
function resultHandler(e:ResultEvent):void{
  loadedXML = e.target.lastResult;
}
```

The XML object can then be bound to the target property with an E4X expression within curly braces, as shown here:

```
<mx:ComboBox id="cboAuthor"
  dataProvider="{loadedXML.author.authorLastName}"/>
```

The previous example would bind the <authorLastName> XMLList within the <author> nodes directly to the dataProvider property of the cboAuthor component.

Working through an <mx:HTTPService> tag example

Let's work through a simple example. You'll create an application that uses the content from an XML document to populate a ComboBox control. This example won't use any scripting at all.

1. Create a new Flex project for the chapter. Add a new folder called assets to the src folder. Copy the resource file authorsAndBooks.xml to this folder.

2. In the MXML application file, create an application with the following interface. Figure 6-1 shows how the application will appear when you switch to Design view in Flex Builder.

```
<mx:VBox x="10" y="10">
  <mx:HBox>
    <mx:Label id="author_txt" text="Author name" fontWeight="bold"/>
    <mx:ComboBox id="author_cbo" prompt="Choose author"/>
  </mx:HBox>
```

```
    <mx:Label text="Output" fontWeight="bold"/>
    <mx:TextArea id="output_txt" width="350" height="100"/>
</mx:VBox>
```

Figure 6-1. The <mx:HTTPService> tag example application interface

This is a very simple application that contains two Label controls, a ComboBox control, and a TextArea control. You'll populate the ComboBox with the author names, and use the TextArea to display messages and the loaded XML so you can keep track of the current content.

3. Add an <mx:HTTPService> tag above the <mx:VBox> element, as follows:

```
<mx:HTTPService id="xmlService" url="assets/authorsAndBooks.xml"
    resultFormat="e4x"/>
```

The code specifies the resultFormat of e4x so you can use E4X expressions to target the content in the XML file. Feel free to open this XML document if you want to see its structure. This file is the same one we used for the Flex examples in the previous chapter.

4. The application will load the external document by calling the send() method of the <mx:HTTPService> element. It will do so in the creationComplete event of the application. Modify the <mx:Application> tag, as shown here in bold:

```
<mx:Application xmlns:mx="http://www.adobe.com/2006/mxml"
    layout="absolute" creationComplete="xmlService.send()">
```

After the application is created, the send() method will request the authorsAndBooks.xml document. The contents will be returned as an ActionScript 3.0 XML object, capable of being accessed with E4X expressions.

5. You'll bind the results returned from the xmlService to the TextArea control so you can see what's loaded. Modify the <mx:TextArea> tag as shown here in bold:

```
<mx:TextArea id="output_txt" width="350" height="100"
    text="{xmlService.lastResult}"/>
```

The text property of the TextArea control is bound to the lastResult property of the xmlService object. When the <mx:HTTPService> element receives a result, it will display in the TextArea.

6. The example will also use a binding expression to populate the ComboBox control. Modify the element as shown here in bold:

```
<mx:ComboBox id="author_cbo" prompt="Choose author"
    dataProvider="{xmlService.lastResult.author.authorLastName}"/>
```

The code sets the dataProvider property of the ComboBox to an E4X expression. The element targets the loaded content using the expression xmlService.lastResult. This expression is equivalent to the root element of the loaded XML document. The application can then target the <authorLastName> elements in the loaded content using the expression author.authorLastName.

7. Run the application from Flex Builder. Figure 6-2 shows how the completed application will appear in a web browser. The loaded content appears in the TextArea, while the ComboBox displays a list of all author last names.

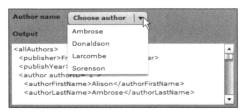

Figure 6-2. The <mx:HTTPService> tag example completed application

In this example, you populated the ComboBox control without using any scripting at all. You bound the dataProvider property of the ComboBox control directly to the loaded content from the <mx:HTTPService> tag using an E4X expression.

The expression xmlService.lastResult.author.authorLastName returns an XMLList object made up of the author last names. Notice that you didn't need to specify the root node <allAuthors>, as that is equivalent to the lastResult property of the <mx:HTTPService> tag.

You can find my finished file saved as ComboTagExample.mxml with the other resources for the chapter. This simple example shows how easy it is to bind loaded external content directly to UI components without the need for any scripting.

An alternative approach is to script the HTTPService class.

Working through an HTTPService class example

The following exercise shows how you would script the same example as in the previous exercise. In this approach, you'll use a custom class to handle the loading. The advantage of a custom class is that if you make it generic, you'll be able to use the same class in different circumstances.

1. Start by creating the class file that will handle the loading and parsing of the external XML content. Create a new ActionScript class file using File ➤ New ➤ ActionScript Class. Figure 6-3 shows the settings for this class.

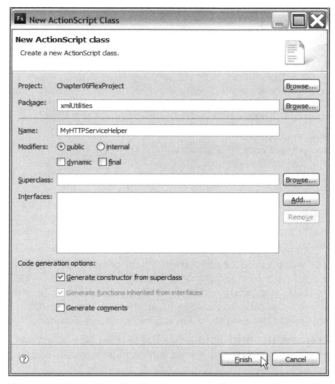

Figure 6-3. The settings for the custom class file used in the exercise

I've set the package as xmlUtilities and the class file name as MyHTTPServiceHelper. Flex Builder will create the folder xmlUtilities as the location for this file.

The class file contains the following code automatically generated by Flex Builder:

```
package xmlUtilities {
  public class MyHTTPServiceHelper{
    public function MyHTTPServiceHelper() {
    }
  }
}
```

Don't worry if Flex Builder has used a slightly different arrangement for the opening curly braces.

2. Modify the class file to make it bindable by adding a [Bindable] metatag. This change makes all public methods of the class file available for use in binding expressions in the application file. Add the following line, shown in bold, above the class declaration:

```
[Bindable]
public class MyHTTPServiceHelper{
```

3. Add the following import statements below the first line package declaration. These statements reference the class files that you'll need to use. They will also be added automatically as you complete the class file.

```
import mx.collections.XMLListCollection;
import mx.rpc.http.HTTPService;
import mx.rpc.events.ResultEvent;
```

4. Add the following private variable declarations underneath the class file declaration:

```
private var xmlAllContent:XML;
private var xmlService:HTTPService;
private var childElements:XMLList;
private var childElementsLC:XMLListCollection;
```

The first variable, xmlAllContent, refers to the content loaded from the external XML document. The code uses the name xmlService for the HTTPService object. The childElements object refers to the XMLList of child elements that will be returned from the loaded content.

The XMLList will be used to populate the data provider of the ComboBox. However, it will do so via an intermediate class. The application will use the XMLListCollection object childElementsLC as a wrapper class when assigning the data provider. This class adds extra functionality for applications working with an XMLList. Unlike an XMLList, it also tracks changes made to any bound data, which makes it a better choice as a data provider.

5. Modify the constructor method to create the HTTPService object and add an event listener to handle the result event. The new lines appear in bold in the following code block:

```
public function MyHTTPServiceHelper () {
    xmlService = new HTTPService();
    xmlService.addEventListener(ResultEvent.RESULT, resultHandler);
}
```

6. The application will call the send() method of the HTTPService object in a public method called sendRequest(). The application can then determine when to call this method, based on when it is notified of the result event. The sendRequest() method will receive the URL to use in the request as an argument.

```
public function sendRequest(xmlURL:String):void {
    xmlService.url = xmlURL;
    xmlService.resultFormat = "e4x";
    xmlService.send();
}
```

This public method starts by assigning the passed in URL as the url property of the HTTPService object. It also sets the result format to e4x. I've hard-coded the property in this case for simplicity, although I could also have sent it in as an additional parameter. The function finishes by calling the send() method of the HTTPService class.

7. When a response is received from the request, the resultHandler() method will be called. The listener was added in the constructor method, but we haven't yet created the corresponding function. Add this method now, as shown in the following code block:

```
private function resultHandler(e:ResultEvent):void {
  trace (e.target.lastResult.author.toXMLString());
  childElements = e.target.lastResult.author;
  dispatchEvent(new ResultEvent(ResultEvent.RESULT));
}
```

The function is private because it will be used only by the class file. It starts by tracing the loaded content, which acts as a debugging tool so you can check what has loaded. You should remove this action before moving the application to its production environment.

The function assigns the <author> elements XMLList to the childElements XMLList object. The application will use this to create an XMLListCollection when the user wants to populate the ComboBox. The final line dispatches a result event indicating that the request has completed. The application can listen for this event and respond accordingly.

8. The custom class also needs to provide a public method that will supply the content to populate the dataProvider for the ComboBox component. I'll call this method getAuthorNames(), and it will provide the names of all authors as an XMLListCollection object. Add the following public method to the class file.

```
public function getChildElements():XMLListCollection {
  childElementsLC = new XMLListCollection(childElements);
  return childElementsLC;
}
```

The getChildElements() method returns an XMLListCollection of all of the <author> elements that were identified in the resultHandler() function. The application can call this method to provide a data source for any data-aware component. In this application, that will be the dataProvider property of the ComboBox control.

The complete class file follows so that you can check your code to make sure that everything is correct so far. The file exists in the xmlUtilities folder in the src folder of your project.

```
package xmlUtilities {
import mx.collections.XMLListCollection;
import mx.rpc.http.HTTPService;
import mx.rpc.events.ResultEvent;
  [Bindable]
  public class MyHTTPServiceHelper {
    private var xmlAllContent:XML;
    private var xmlService:HTTPService;
    private var childElements:XMLList;
    private var childElementsLC:XMLListCollection;
    public function MyHTTPServiceHelper() {
      xmlService = new HTTPService();
      xmlService.addEventListener(ResultEvent.RESULT, resultHandler);
    }
    public function sendRequest(xmlURL:String):void {
      xmlService.url = xmlURL;
      xmlService.resultFormat = "e4x";
      xmlService.send();
    }
```

187

```
      public function getChildElements():XMLListCollection {
        childElementsLC = new XMLListCollection(childElements);
        return childElementsLC;
      }
      private function resultHandler(e:ResultEvent):void {
        trace (e.target.lastResult.author.toXMLString());
        childElements = e.target.lastResult.author;
        dispatchEvent(new ResultEvent(ResultEvent.RESULT));
      }
    }
  }
}
```

9. Create a new application file for your project. Create an interface that contains a Label control and a ComboBox component using the following code:

```
<?xml version="1.0" encoding="utf-8"?>
<mx:Application xmlns:mx="http://www.adobe.com/2006/mxml"
  layout="absolute">
  <mx:HBox x="10" y="10">
    <mx:Label text="Author name" fontWeight="bold"/>
    <mx:ComboBox id="author_cbo" prompt="Choose author"/>
  </mx:HBox>
</mx:Application>
```

Figure 6-4. The scripted example application interface

This interface is a simplified version of the one that appeared in the previous example. Figure 6-4 shows how the interface used in this example should appear when viewed in a web browser.

10. Add a creationComplete attribute to the <mx:Application> element, as shown here in bold:

```
<mx:Application xmlns:mx="http://www.adobe.com/2006/mxml"
  layout="absolute" creationComplete="initApp(event)">
```

You'll call the initApp() function when the interface has finished creating. This function will set up the MyHTTPServiceHelper object within the application and request the content from the external XML document.

11. Add the following script block to the application:

```
<mx:Script>
  <![CDATA[
    import mx.events.FlexEvent;
    import mx.rpc.events.ResultEvent;
    import xmlUtilities.MyHTTPServiceHelper
    import mx.collections.XMLListCollection;
    private var myXMLService:MyHTTPServiceHelper;
    private var authorsXMLLC:XMLListCollection;
    private function initApp(e:FlexEvent):void {
      myXMLService = new MyHTTPServiceHelper();
      myXMLService.addEventListener(ResultEvent.RESULT, resultHandler);
      myXMLService.sendRequest("assets/authorsAndBooks.xml");
    }
```

```
      private function resultHandler(e:ResultEvent):void {
      } ]]>
</mx:Script>
```

The code starts by importing the classes needed for the application. This includes FlexEvent, passed by the initApp() function; ResultEvent, to determine when the request has finished; the custom class MyHTTPServiceHelper; and the XMLListCollection class, required for the ComboBox data provider.

The code block declares a private variable for the MyHTTPServiceHelper object, called myXMLService. It also creates a variable called authorsXMLLC, which will be used as the dataProvider for the ComboBox control.

The <mx:Script> element includes the initApp() function, called when the interface has finished creating. This function creates a new MyHTTPServiceHelper object and assigns a result event listener. It also calls the sendRequest() method of this object, passing the name of the file to load. You'll see an empty resultHandler() function below this one, which you'll populate a little later.

12. You're now at the stage where you can debug the application to check that you're correctly loading the external XML document. Click the Debug button on the Flex Builder toolbar and switch back to Flex Builder from the web browser. You should see the XMLList of all <author> elements in the Console view, as shown in Figure 6-5.

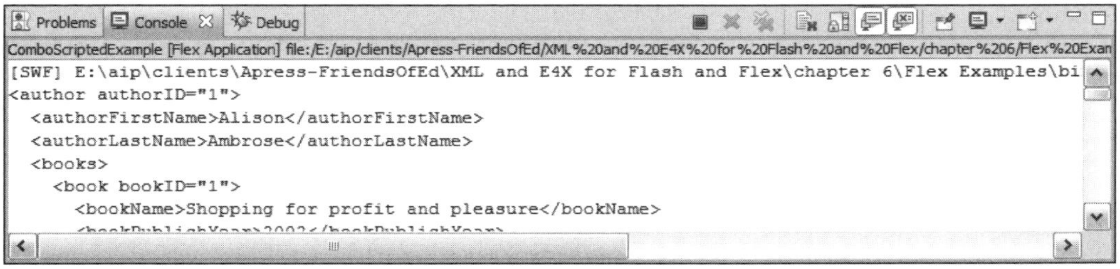

Figure 6-5. Debugging the scripted example application

13. Assuming everything is working so far, it's time to populate the ComboBox control from the loaded content. You'll need to modify the resultHandler() function as shown in bold here:

```
private function resultHandler(e:Event):void {
   author_cbo.dataProvider = myXMLService.getChildElements();
}
```

The new line calls the getChildElements() public method of the myXMLService object. The dataProvider property is set to an XMLListCollection object containing all of the child nodes of each <author> element.

14. Without a label function, the ComboBox control won't be able to determine what to display as the label. You need to create a labelFunction for the ComboBox to specify which values to display in the control and how they should appear. Add the following label function to the code block:

```
private function getFullName(item:Object):String {
   return item.authorFirstName + " " + item.authorLastName;
}
```

The getFullName() function locates the authorFirstName and authorLastName properties from each item in the XMLListCollection. It joins these values with a space between to create the author's full name, which will display as the label for the ComboBox control.

15. Assign the getFullName() function as the labelFunction property of the ComboBox by modifying the initApp() function. Add the bold line shown in the following block:

```
private function initApp(e:FlexEvent):void {
  myXMLService = new MyHTTPServiceHelper();
  myXMLService.addEventListener(ResultEvent.RESULT, resultHandler);
  myXMLService.sendRequest("assets/authorsAndBooks.xml");
  author_cbo.labelFunction = getFullName;
}
```

16. That's it for the application and class file. Run it from Flex Builder, and you should see the same result as shown in Figure 6-6.

Figure 6-6. The scripted example completed application

The ComboBox is populated with the first and last names of each author.

The complete application file follows if you want to check your code:

```
<?xml version="1.0" encoding="utf-8"?>
<mx:Application xmlns:mx="http://www.adobe.com/2006/mxml"
  layout="absolute" creationComplete="initApp(event)">
  <mx:Script>
    <![CDATA[
      import mx.events.FlexEvent;
      import mx.rpc.events.ResultEvent;
      import xmlUtilities.MyHTTPServiceHelper
      import mx.collections.XMLListCollection;
      private var myXMLService:MyHTTPServiceHelper;
      private var authorsXMLLC:XMLListCollection;
      private function initApp(e:FlexEvent):void {
        myXMLService = new MyHTTPServiceHelper();
        myXMLService.addEventListener(ResultEvent.RESULT,
          ➥resultHandler);
        myXMLService.sendRequest("assets/authorsAndBooks.xml");
        author_cbo.labelFunction = getFullName;
      }
      private function resultHandler(e:ResultEvent):void {
        author_cbo.dataProvider = myXMLService.getChildElements();
      }
```

```
        private function getFullName(item:Object):String {
          return item.authorFirstName + " " + item.authorLastName;
        }
      ]]>
    </mx:Script>
    <mx:HBox x="10" y="10">
      <mx:Label text="Author name" fontWeight="bold"/>
      <mx:ComboBox id="author_cbo" prompt="Choose author"/>
    </mx:HBox>
  </mx:Application>
```

You can find the completed application files saved as `ComboScriptedExample.mxml` and `MyHTTPServiceHelper.as` with the chapter resource files.

In the previous examples, you didn't send any variables with the request. We'll remedy that in the final two examples.

Passing variables with the request

Earlier in the chapter, I showed you how to pass variables to the requested URL with the `<mx:HTTPService>` tag and `HTTPService` class. One use might be to send a parameter to a server-side file so that you can filter the content returned to the Flex application. You can also pass variables that will be used for updating the external data source.

We'll work through a simple example that sends a username and password to a server-side page. I'll show how to do this with both the `<mx:HTTPService>` element and the `HTTPService` class. The interface in both examples will include text fields that allow the users to enter their username and password, as well as a button to submit the details. You'll also display a message from the requested file.

In this case, you're going to work with a static XML document. This means that no matter what values you pass with the request, you'll see the same message from the XML document. In Chapter 9, you'll see how to integrate this approach with server-side pages. For now, these simple examples will get you started.

Let's begin by working with the `<mx:HTTPService>` tag.

Using <mx:request> to send variables

Earlier in the chapter, I showed you how to use the `<mx:request>` tag to send variables with an HTTPService request. The following code provides a quick refresher:

```
<mx:HTTPService id="xmlService"
  url="http://localhost/FlexApp/getAuthors.aspx">
  <mx:request>
    <lastname>Ambrose</lastname>
  </mx:request>
</mx:HTTPService>
```

The `<mx:request>` element is nested inside the `<mx:HTTPService>` element and contains tags that use the variable name to surround the variable value.

You'll use this approach in the first of the final two examples, so let's get started.

1. Create a new application file and name it anything that you like.

2. Create the following interface. Figure 6-7 shows how the interface should appear in the Design view of Flex Builder.

```
<?xml version="1.0" encoding="utf-8"?>
<mx:Application xmlns:mx="http://www.adobe.com/2006/mxml"
  layout="absolute">
  <mx:VBox x="10" y="10">
    <mx:Label text="Login" fontSize="14" fontWeight="bold"/>
    <mx:HBox>
      <mx:Label text="Username" fontWeight="bold" width="80"/>
      <mx:TextInput id="username_txt"/>
    </mx:HBox>
    <mx:HBox>
      <mx:Label text="Password" fontWeight="bold" width="80"/>
      <mx:TextInput id="password_txt" displayAsPassword="true"/>
    </mx:HBox>
    <mx:Button id="login_btn" label="Log in" />
    <mx:TextArea width="250" height="60" id="txtMessage"/>
  </mx:VBox>
</mx:Application>
```

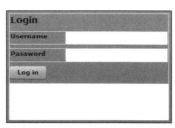

Figure 6-7. The <mx:request> example application interface

The interface consists of some labels, two TextInput controls, a Button component, and a dynamic text field. The TextInput controls have the instance names username_txt and password_txt, respectively. The Button is called login_btn and has the label Log in. The dynamic text field has the instance name message_txt. The password_txt instance has its displayAsPassword property set to true.

3. Add the following `<mx:HTTPService>` tag above the opening `<mx:VBox>` component:

```
<mx:HTTPService id="xmlService" url="assets/message.xml"
  resultFormat="e4x">
</mx:HTTPService>
```

Notice that the code includes a closing tag, as you will add an <mx:request> element between the opening and closing tags. The element specifies e4x as the resultFormat because the application expects an XML format for the response. You will be able to extract the message from this response using an E4X expression.

4. The entries from the user in the TextField controls will provide the variables that will be passed in the <mx:request> element. Modify the <mx:HTTPService> tag as shown in bold here:

```
<mx:HTTPService id="xmlService" url="assets/message.xml" resultFormat="e4x">
  <mx:request>
    <username>{username_txt.text}</username>
    <password>{password_txt.text}</password>
  </mx:request>
</mx:HTTPService>
```

The change adds an <mx:request> element containing two variables: username and password. The variables are bound to the text property of the username_txt and password_txt controls using curly braces notation.

5. The application will send the variables with the request when the Log in button is clicked. The next step is to add a click attribute to the Button to call the send() method of the xmlService object. Modify the Button as shown in bold in the following line:

```
<mx:Button id="login_btn" label="Log in" click="xmlService.send()"/>
```

6. The final step is to display the message in the TextArea component. The message.xml file contains a single element, <message>Login successful</message>. The example will bind the text inside this element to the TextArea. Modify the element as shown here in bold:

```
<mx:TextArea width="250" height="60" id="message_txt"
  text="{xmlService.lastResult}"/>
```

7. Run the application. Enter a username and password and click the Log in button. Figure 6-8 shows how the application should appear in a web browser. Notice that the message Login successful appears in the TextArea.

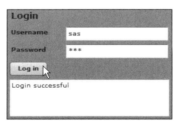

Figure 6-8. The completed
<mx:request> example application

The complete code for the application follows in case you want to check your file:

```
<?xml version="1.0" encoding="utf-8"?>
<mx:Application xmlns:mx="http://www.adobe.com/2006/mxml"
  layout="absolute">
  <mx:HTTPService id="xmlService" url="assets/message.xml"
    resultFormat="e4x">
```

193

```
        <mx:request>
          <username>{username_txt.text}</username>
          <password>{password_txt.text}</password>
        </mx:request>
      </mx:HTTPService>
      <mx:VBox x="10" y="10">
        <mx:Label text="Login" fontSize="14" fontWeight="bold"/>
        <mx:HBox>
          <mx:Label text="Username" fontWeight="bold" width="80"/>
          <mx:TextInput id="username_txt"/>
        </mx:HBox>
        <mx:HBox>
          <mx:Label text="Password" fontWeight="bold" width="80"/>
          <mx:TextInput id="password_txt" displayAsPassword="true"/>
        </mx:HBox>
        <mx:Button id="login_btn" label="Log in"
          click="xmlService.send()"/>
        <mx:TextArea width="250" height="60" id="message_txt"
          text="{xmlService.lastResult}"/>
      </mx:VBox>
    </mx:Application>
```

You can find my example saved as LoginTagExample.mxml with the chapter resource files.

You can also take a scripted approach to sending variables by using the HTTPService class.

Sending variables with the HTTPService class

In this final example for the chapter, you'll achieve the same outcome as in the last example, but using the HTTPService class with a custom ActionScript class.

1. Use the File ➤ New ➤ ActionScript Class command to create a new ActionScript class. Add the class to the xmlUtilities package and call it HTTPServiceWithVariables. The file should contain the following code:

```
package xmlUtilities {
  public class HTTPServiceWithVariables {
    public function HTTPServiceWithVariables() {
    }
  }
}
```

2. Add the following import statements underneath the package declaration. These statements reference the classes that you'll need to use. Note that these statements will also be added automatically when you declare the variables and write additional code a little later.

```
import mx.rpc.http.HTTPService;
import mx.rpc.events.ResultEvent;
```

3. Add a [Bindable] declaration above the class declaration. This declaration makes all public methods and properties bindable in the application file.

```
[Bindable]
```

194

4. Declare the following private variables below the class declaration:

```
private var xmlMessage:String;
private var xmlService:HTTPService;
```

The first variable, xmlMessage, will store the returned message from the document as String data. The second variable, xmlService, refers to the HTTPService object that will make the request.

5. Modify the constructor method HTTPServiceWithVariables() as shown here:

```
public function HTTPServiceWithVariables() {
    xmlService = new HTTPService();
    xmlService.addEventListener(ResultEvent.RESULT, resultHandler);
}
```

The HTTPServiceWithVariables() method creates the HTTPService object and adds an event listener that responds when the object receives a result event. When this occurs, the resultHandler will execute, processing the response.

6. Add the resultHandler() method shown here:

```
private function resultHandler(e:ResultEvent):void {
    xmlMessage = String(xmlService.lastResult);
    dispatchEvent(new ResultEvent(ResultEvent.RESULT));
}
```

The resultHandler() method is private because it will be called only by the class file. The method locates the message text by using the expression xmlService.lastResult. As this expression is equivalent to the root element of the loaded XML content, it will return the text inside the root element <message>.

The method assigns the loaded content to the variable xmlMessage, casting it as a String. It then dispatches the result event to the application so that it will know that the request has finished and that a result has been received.

7. The class file will need a public method that handles the request for the external file. I'll call the method sendRequest(). This method will receive two arguments: the name of the file to request as well as the variables to send with that request.

```
public function sendRequest(xmlURL:String, vars:Object):void {
    xmlService.url = xmlURL;
    xmlService.resultFormat = "e4x";
    xmlService.request = vars;
    xmlService.method = "POST";
    xmlService.send();
}
```

The sendRequest() method creates a new HTTPService object, using the URL passed in as the first argument. The method assigns the vars argument to the request property of the xmlService object and sets the method property to POST the variables to the requested page. It finishes by calling the send() method to make the request.

8. The HTTPServiceWithVariables class will need one public method to return the content from the external document, which is stored in the String variable xmlMessage.

Add the following public message() method to the class file:

```
public function message():String {
  return xmlMessage;
}
```

That's it for the class file. Check your contents against the complete code block that follows.

```
package xmlUtilities {
  import mx.rpc.http.HTTPService;
  import mx.rpc.events.ResultEvent;
  [Bindable]
  public class HTTPServiceWithVariables {
    private var xmlMessage:String;
    private var xmlService:HTTPService;
    public function HTTPServiceWithVariables() {
      xmlService = new HTTPService();
      xmlService.addEventListener(ResultEvent.RESULT, resultHandler);
    }
    public function sendRequest(xmlURL:String, vars:Object):void {
      xmlService.url = xmlURL;
      xmlService.resultFormat = "e4x";
      xmlService.request = vars;
      xmlService.method = "POST";
      xmlService.send();
    }
    public function message():String {
      return xmlMessage;
    }
    private function resultHandler(e:ResultEvent):void {
      xmlMessage = String(xmlService.lastResult);
      dispatchEvent(new ResultEvent(ResultEvent.RESULT));
    }
  }
}
```

9. Now you need to create a Flex application file containing the following interface. It is the same interface as the one shown earlier in Figure 6-7.

```
<?xml version="1.0" encoding="utf-8"?>
<mx:Application xmlns:mx="http://www.adobe.com/2006/mxml"
  layout="absolute">
  <mx:VBox x="10" y="10">
    <mx:Label text="Login" fontSize="14" fontWeight="bold"/>
    <mx:HBox>
      <mx:Label text="Username" fontWeight="bold" width="80"/>
      <mx:TextInput id="username_txt"/>
    </mx:HBox>
    <mx:HBox>
      <mx:Label text="Password" fontWeight="bold" width="80"/>
      <mx:TextInput id="password_txt" displayAsPassword="true"/>
    </mx:HBox>
```

```
    <mx:Button id="login_btn" label="Log in" />
    <mx:TextArea width="250" height="60" id="message_txt"/>
  </mx:VBox>
</mx:Application>
```

10. The example will set up the application by calling a function in the creationComplete attribute of the <mx:Application> element. This function is called initApp(), and it will set up the variables you'll need, including a new HTTPServiceWithVariables object.

    Modify the <mx:Application> element as shown here in bold:

```
<mx:Application xmlns:mx="http://www.adobe.com/2006/mxml"
  layout="absolute" creationComplete="initApp(event)">
```

11. Add the following <mx:Script> block, which includes the initApp() function:

```
<mx:Script>
  <![CDATA[
    import mx.events.FlexEvent;
    import mx.rpc.events.ResultEvent;
    import xmlUtilities.HTTPServiceWithVariables;
    private var myHTTPServiceVars:HTTPServiceWithVariables;
    private function initApp(e:FlexEvent):void {
      myHTTPServiceVars = new HTTPServiceWithVariables();
      myHTTPServiceVars.addEventListener(ResultEvent.RESULT,
        ➥resultHandler);
      login_btn.addEventListener(MouseEvent.CLICK, clickHandler);
    }
    private function resultHandler(e:Event):void {
    }
    private function clickHandler(e:MouseEvent):void {
    }
  ]]>
</mx:Script>
```

This <mx:Script> block starts by importing the relevant classes. If you forget to add these classes, the import statements should be added automatically when you enter the remaining code.

The application needs the FlexEvent class, as this is the event type dispatched when the interface finishes creating. It also imports the ResultEvent class to deal with the result event dispatched by the HTTPService element. The last import statement deals with the custom class that you just created, HTTPServiceWithVariables.

The code then creates an HTTPServiceWithVariables object called myHTTPServiceVars. Next, it declares the initApp() function, which receives a FlexEvent as an argument. This function starts by creating a new instance of the HTTPServiceWithVariables class and then assigns the resultHandler() function to be called when the HTTPServiceWithVariables class finishes requesting the external document and receives a result. At the moment, this function doesn't contain any code.

The function assigns an event listener to the login_btn instance. This listener responds to the click event of the button with the clickHandler() function. The <mx:Script> block also contains an empty clickHandler() function.

12. When the Log in button is clicked, the function needs to check that the username and password are filled in before calling the sendRequest() method of the HTTPServiceWithVariables object. It does this by testing that the entries have a length greater than zero.

When the sendRequest() public method is called, the method call will pass the URL of the document to load as well as an object containing the entered username and password.

Modify the clickHandler() function as shown here in bold:

```
private function clickHandler(e:MouseEvent):void {
  if (username_txt.text.length > 0 && password_txt.text.length > 0) {
    var myVars:Object = new Object();
    myVars.username = username_txt.text;
    myVars.password = password_txt.text;
    myHTTPServiceVars.sendRequest("assets/message.xml", myVars);
  }
  else {
    message_txt.text = "You must enter both a username and password
      ➥before clicking the button"
  }
}
```

The clickHandler() function starts by testing that the length of both the username and password entries is greater than 0. If this is the case, the function creates a new Object and assigns the username and password properties from the entries in the TextInput controls. It then calls the sendRequest() method of the HTTPServiceWithVariables object, passing the URL to request, message.xml, as well as the Object containing the variables.

If either of the TextInput controls has no text, the message You must enter both a username and password before clicking the button displays in the TextArea at the bottom of the interface.

13. The last step in building this application is to respond when a reply is received from the messages.xml file. The application will display the reply in the TextArea control in the resultHandler() function. Modify it as shown in bold here:

```
private function resultHandler(e:Event):void {
  message_txt.text = myHTTPServiceVars.message();
}
```

14. Now you're ready to test the application. Run it and enter values for a username and password. When you click the button, you should see the TextArea update, as shown earlier in Figure 6-8.

The complete code for the application file follows:

```xml
<?xml version="1.0" encoding="utf-8"?>
<mx:Application xmlns:mx="http://www.adobe.com/2006/mxml"
  layout="absolute" creationComplete="initApp(event)">
  <mx:Script>
    <![CDATA[
      import mx.events.FlexEvent;
      import mx.rpc.events.ResultEvent;
      import xmlUtilities.HTTPServiceWithVariables;
      private var myHTTPServiceVars:HTTPServiceWithVariables;
      private function initApp(e:FlexEvent):void {
        myHTTPServiceVars = new HTTPServiceWithVariables();
        myHTTPServiceVars.addEventListener(ResultEvent.RESULT,
          ➥resultHandler);
        login_btn.addEventListener(MouseEvent.CLICK, clickHandler);
      }
      private function resultHandler(e:Event):void {
        message_txt.text = myHTTPServiceVars.message();
      }
      private function clickHandler(e:MouseEvent):void {
        if (username_txt.text.length > 0 &&
          ➥password_txt.text.length > 0) {
          var myVars:Object = new Object();
          myVars.username = username_txt.text;
          myVars.password = password_txt.text;
          myHTTPServiceVars.sendRequest("assets/message.xml", myVars);
        }
        else {
          message_txt.text = "You must enter both a username and
            ➥password before clicking the button"
        }
      }
    ]]>
  </mx:Script>
  <mx:VBox x="10" y="10">
    <mx:Label text="Login" fontSize="14" fontWeight="bold"/>
    <mx:HBox>
      <mx:Label text="Username" fontWeight="bold" width="80"/>
      <mx:TextInput id="username_txt"/>
    </mx:HBox>
    <mx:HBox>
      <mx:Label text="Password" fontWeight="bold" width="80"/>
      <mx:TextInput id="password_txt" displayAsPassword="true"/>
    </mx:HBox>
    <mx:Button id="login_btn" label="Log in" />
    <mx:TextArea width="250" height="60" id="message_txt"/>
  </mx:VBox>
</mx:Application>
```

199

You can find the resource files for this example with the other chapter resources, saved as `LoginScriptedExample.mxml` and `HTTPServiceWithVariables.as`.

> *You could have modified the first class file that you created to achieve the same outcome, instead of creating two separate custom classes. That approach provides much more flexibility and allows you to create a useful class that you can reuse in different situations. Why don't you try to do that as an additional exercise? You could also see what other changes you might make to increase the flexibility of this approach. Don't forget that you may also want to add some additional error handling to make the class more robust.*

Summary

This chapter covered the `<mx:HTTPService>` tag and the `HTTPService` class and discussed their properties, methods, and events. We worked through both tag-based and scripted Flex examples to demonstrate how to request and access external content. In the second pair of examples, we sent variables with the request.

The next chapter covers some of the loading methods that are specific to Flash. We'll be working with the Flash data components, which are written in ActionScript 2.0. At the time of writing, these components haven't been rewritten in ActionScript 3.0, but it's still useful to be aware of them and the functionality they offer.

Chapter 7

LOADING METHODS SPECIFIC TO FLASH

In the previous chapter, I showed you some methods that you can use to load external XML content in Flex. Specifically, we looked at the HTTPService class and <mx:HTTPService> element. You saw how to work with both a tag-based and scripted approach.

In this chapter, we will look at loading methods that are unique to Flash Professional, which involve using the data components. Instead of writing ActionScript to work with XML content, you can use the data components supplied with Flash Professional. These components allow you to work visually with a minimum of ActionScript. You drag the components into your movies and configure them using the Component Inspector panel. This can speed up your development process, since you can include XML content without needing to write a single line of ActionScript.

When working with the data components, you can use data binding to connect the XML content from the XMLConnector directly to user interface (UI) components. You configure the bindings visually through the Component Inspector, and Flash does the hard work.

The data components were first released for ActionScript 2.0 and were never upgraded to ActionScript 3.0. This means if you want to use the data components, you'll need to create an ActionScript 2.0 document.

In addition to configuring the components with the Component Inspector, you can also script them. Again, because the components are built for ActionScript 2.0, you'll need to use that version of the language.

You can use ActionScript 2.0 to set all of the properties that are available through the Component Inspector. This may be useful if you're adding components to the Stage dynamically. However, scripting data binding between components can be a tricky proposition. You'll probably find it much easier to work with the Component Inspector—so much easier that I'm not going to cover scripting at all.

There are some disadvantages to using the data components. First, you can use these components only in Flash Player 7 and above. Another disadvantage is the size of the components. Adding data components increases the size of your FLA files, often by 400KB to 500KB. Luckily, this size reduces again when you compile your SWF file. In my experience, the components tend to add around 30KB to 50KB to the size of the compiled SWF file.

In this chapter, I'll show you how to use the XMLConnector component to load XML data into Flash. We'll load the same document that we've worked with in the past two chapters so you can compare the approach. Note that Flash can't update external data, so you would still need to use a server-side file to update the external XML document. We'll finish with a new example, creating a complete application that allows you to add, edit, and delete XML data.

As with the techniques covered in the previous two chapters, the XMLConnector component uses a request-response approach to load external content. The application must issue a request before it can access the external content. If the external data changes, the server cannot initiate the process and inform the application that something has changed.

If your application requires up-to-the-minute data, to avoid polling the server at regular intervals, you may wish to use the XMLSocket class to create a real-time connection to XML content. When the content changes, the server can notify the application, causing the content to refresh. This topic is beyond the scope of the book.

You need to be aware that the data components are written for ActionScript 2.0, so you won't be able to use them with an ActionScript 3.0 document. For all the examples in this chapter, you'll need to create an ActionScript 2.0 Flash document first.

As with all loading of external content, you need to be mindful of the security restrictions of Flash Player. At the time of writing, the latest version was Flash Player 10, and you can find out information about Flash Player 10 security in Chapter 5 of this book.

You can download all of the resources for this chapter from http://www.friendsofed.com. This download includes the XML documents used for the examples as well as my completed files.

Understanding the AS 2.0 data components

Flash Professional includes a number of data components suitable for ActionScript 2.0 documents. The advantage of these data components is that they simplify the process of loading and updating external content. You don't need to script them. Instead, you can use the Flash interface to configure these components.

The components become available only after you create an ActionScript 2.0 Flash file in Flash Professional. You can then find the data component in the Components panel, under the Data section, as shown in Figure 7-1.

Figure 7-1. The Components panel showing the Data section

You can see that there are several components and that some of them have strange names. Table 7-1 summarizes each of these components and explains their purpose.

Table 7-1. The AS 2.0 data components available with Flash Professional

Component	Purpose
DataHolder	Stores data and can be used to share information between other components. Unlike the DataSet, it doesn't track changes made by other components.
DataSet	Stores data that you can share with other components. The DataSet allows you to keep track of modifications that you make using other components. You can then notify external applications of the changes made within Flash.
RDBMSResolver	Sends changes in data to an external data source. It works with database content.
WebServiceConnector	Consumes SOAP web services. You'll find out more about this component in Chapter 11.
XMLConnector	Connects to external XML documents. You can use the component to read and write XML data. You can use the component with the DataSet and XUpdateResolver components when you need to change external data using a server-side page.
XUpdateResolver	Creates XUpdate statements that describe changes made to your XML data within Flash. You use this component with the DataSet component.

We'll start by looking at the XMLConnector component.

Understanding the XMLConnector

The XMLConnector component is an ActionScript 2.0 alternative to working with the XML class in either ActionScript 2.0 or ActionScript 3.0. Instead of writing ActionScript to work with XML data, you can use the XMLConnector. The component can send and/or receive XML content, in the same way as the URLLoader class. The most common use for the XMLConnector is to load an external XML document and bind the data to other components.

You can use the XMLConnector component to bind data directly to other components. Instead of writing ActionScript 3.0, you can configure the Component Inspector panel so that Flash automatically adds information from the external XML document to the relevant components. You can even add formatting during the binding process to control how the content displays in your movie.

If you choose to bind content directly to components, a user of your application won't be able to update the data in Flash. If the user needs to be able to update the content, you can track updates to the XML content by including a DataSet component and an XUpdateResolver component. I'll show you this process in the final example in this chapter.

Displaying read-only XML content

If you are using Flash to display data from an external XML document, the process is simple. You load the XML document into Flash using an XMLConnector component. You then bind the XML content directly to one or more UI components. You can also bind the data through the DataHolder or DataSet component, although this is less common. Figure 7-2 shows the process for displaying read-only XML content in Flash.

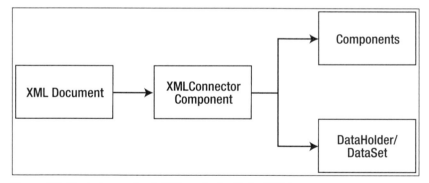

Figure 7-2. Displaying read-only XML content with the XMLConnector component

Things become more complicated if you need Flash to track the changes made by users. The data components can monitor these changes, but because Flash can't modify external content, you'll need to send this content to a server-side page before you can update the external data source.

Displaying updatable XML data

If you want to be able to update the XML content, you'll still use the XMLConnector to load the external XML document. However, you'll need to bind the XML data to a DataSet component first, and then bind the DataSet to the other components.

The DataSet monitors changes made to the data within the other components. The DataSet can then generate a list of all changes for an XUpdateResolver component. The role of the XUpdateResolver is to convert the changes into statements for processing by a server-side file. Figure 7-3 shows this process.

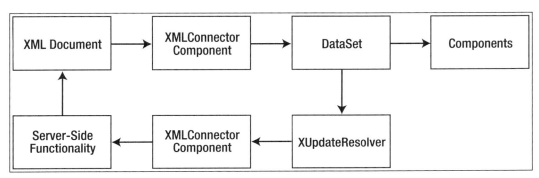

Figure 7-3. Displaying updatable XML content with the data components

Whichever process you use, you'll need to start by adding an XMLConnector component and configuring it with the Component Inspector. You should note that all of the security restrictions on external data still apply to the XMLConnector component.

Configuring the XMLConnector

You can add an XMLConnector to your Flash movie by dragging it from the Components panel. You would normally give it an instance name at this point. You can place data components anywhere you like, as they have no visual appearance in compiled Flash movies. Once you've added the component, you'll see the icon shown in Figure 7-4.

Figure 7-4. The XMLConnector component icon

You can configure the settings for the XMLConnector in the Component Inspector. This panel allows you to specify the location of the external XML document and configure other settings, such as how to deal with whitespace.

Using the Component Inspector

Once you've added an XMLConnector to your Flash movie, you'll need to configure it with the Component Inspector. Figure 7-5 shows the Component Inspector panel.

Figure 7-5. The Component Inspector panel

The Component Inspector has three tabs that you'll use to work with the XMLConnector. To start with, you'll need to configure the Parameters tab so that you can set the connection properties. Table 7-2 shows a summary of the parameters in this tab and their purpose.

Table 7-2. The properties listed in the Parameters tab of the Component Inspector

Parameter	Purpose
URL	The path to an external XML document. This setting does not need to refer to a file ending with .xml. You can enter the path to a server-side file that results in an XML document. If you do this, you must remember to include the full server path, as in http://localhost/XML/generateXML.aspx.
direction	Determines whether you are sending, sending/receiving, or receiving the XML data. These values correspond to the send, load, and sendAndLoad methods of the ActionScript 2.0 XML class.
ignoreWhite	Determines whether whitespace is included in the XML document. Note that this is set to true by default.
multipleSimultaneousAllowed	Specifies whether to allow multiple connections. If you set this property to false, when you are triggering one XMLConnector, further triggers are not possible.
suppressInvalidCall	Sets the behavior for invalid data parameters. If you set the value to true, the component won't be triggered if you have any invalid parameters.

Most of the time, you'll need to configure only the first two settings: URL and direction.

After you've configured the parameters for the XMLConnector, you can import a sample XML document into Flash so you can view the XML element and attribute structures. This gives you a visual representation of the XML document structure and lists the names and data types of attributes and elements. Flash refers to this representation as a *schema*. Bear in mind that this is not the same as an XML schema.

Let's see how to import an XML structure into Flash.

Creating a schema from an XML document

The Schema tab in the Component Inspector allows you to generate a schema from an existing XML document. You choose a document with an .xml extension, and Flash will find the names and data types of each element and attribute.

If you're using a static XML file instead of a server-side file that generates an XML stream, you can generate a schema from the document that you're loading into Flash. You can also use a trimmed-down version of the XML file, as long as it contains at least two data elements. Flash needs at least two elements to determine the structure of the XML document correctly. Note that you can't load a schema from a server-side file that results in an XML document; this time you need a static XML document.

Flash allows you to generate two different types of schemas from external XML documents: one called params:XML and the other results:XML. The params type represents the structure of data being sent out of Flash, while you use results for the structure of incoming XML data. Figure 7-6 shows both options.

Figure 7-6. The Schema tab in the Component Inspector panel

You can see the schema direction by looking at its arrow. The right arrow to the left of params indicates that XML data is outgoing; the left arrow indicates incoming data for results.

To create a schema, select either params or results, click the Import a schema button at the right side of the Schema tab, and navigate to the XML document. Once you've imported the document, Flash will display the structure within the Schema tab.

I've used the resource file authorsAndBooks.xml to generate the structure shown in Figure 7-7. Open the file if you want to see this structure.

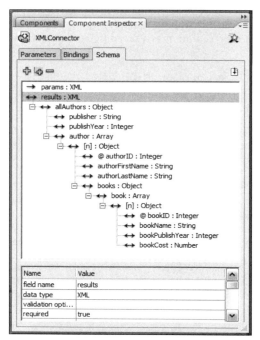

Figure 7-7. The schema resulting from the authorsAndBooks.xml file

The panel lists the name and data type of each element. In Figure 7-7, the root element shown is allAuthors. It has an Object data type. It contains several child elements, including publisher and publishYear. It also contains an array of author elements. The author element contains a number of other elements. Attributes appear with an @ sign to the left.

Flash doesn't maintain a link back to the XML document used to generate the results schema. If you change the XML document, you'll need to import the XML document again and regenerate the schema. You may also need to change your data bindings. It's not a good idea to use the XMLConnector component if the structure of your XML document is likely to change regularly.

If you don't have a sample XML document, you can create a schema in Flash manually.

Creating a schema by adding fields

While the usual method is to generate a schema by importing an existing XML document, it is possible for you to create the schema yourself. Select the parent element for your schema field and click the Add a field button, as shown in Figure 7-8. If you're adding the root element, you'll need to select either params or results first. For each subsequent element, you'll need to click the parent and add another field.

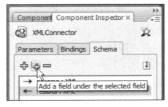

Figure 7-8. Click the Add a field
button to create a schema manually.

Flash will add a new field underneath the selected element. You can configure the field using the settings at the bottom of the Schema tab. Of most importance are fields like the field name, data type, required, and storage type. However, this option is far more difficult than importing a schema from a sample XML document.

You can also use the Schema tab with other components. For example, if you're binding the XML data to a DataGrid component, you'll use the Schema tab to set the details for each column of the DataGrid. I'll show you an example of this later in this chapter, in the "Putting it all together" section.

Understanding schema settings

Once you've created a schema for your XML document, you can configure the settings in the panel at the bottom of the Schema tab. The panel will display the settings for whatever you've currently selected. Figure 7-9 shows the settings for an Array item called author.

Name	Value
field name	author
data type	Array
validation opti...	
required	true
read only	false
kind	none
kind options	
formatter	none
formatter opti...	
encoder	none
encoder options	
default value	
path	
storage type	array

Figure 7-9. The settings
for an Array field

You won't often need to change the field properties within the Schema tab. However, in case you do, Table 7-3 summarizes each setting and its purpose.

Table 7-3. Schema element settings

Setting	Description
field name	Lists the name of the field.
data type	Sets the data type for the field. You can choose from Array , Boolean, Custom, DataProvider, Date, DeltaPacket, Integer, Number, Object, PhoneNumber, SocialSecurity, String, XML, or ZipCode.
validation options	Specifies the validation for the field contents; for example, the number of characters within a String field. This option is available only for the following data types: Custom, Integer, Number, String, and XML.
required	Specifies whether the field is required.
read only	Specifies whether the content can be updated through data binding.
kind	Sets the kind of data at runtime. Select from none, AutoTrigger, Calculated, or Data. You could use a Calculated kind to create a calculation based on other field values.
kind options	Specifies any additional settings associated with the kind setting.
formatter	Details the name of a formatter to use when converting the field to a String type. Choose from Boolean, Compose String, Custom Formatter, Date, Rearrange Fields, or Number Formatter.
formatter options	Specifies any additional settings associated with the selected formatter.
encoder	Sets the encoding for the data at runtime. Select from Boolean, DataSetDeltaToXUpdateDelta, Date, DateToNumber, or Number.
encoder options	Specifies any additional settings associated with the encoder.
default value	Specifies the default setting when the data is undefined or when you add a new item in Flash.
path	An optional setting specifying a path expression for the data.
storage type	The way data is stored. This setting relates to the data type chosen and is one of the following values: simple, attribute, array, or complex. You shouldn't need to change this setting.

Once you've configured the parameters and added a schema, you need to trigger the XMLConnector component to load the content. After you've done that, you can bind the XML data to other components in your application.

Triggering the XMLConnector component

The code must trigger the XMLConnector component before it sends or loads an XML document. One option is to trigger the XMLConnector in response to a button click. You can also trigger the component when the Flash movie first loads.

Triggering requires a single line of ActionScript that you can either write yourself or generate by adding a behavior. Whichever method you choose, you should give the XMLConnector an instance name first. If you forget this step, Flash will prompt you for an instance name.

I'll start by showing you how you can trigger the component with a behavior. First, you'll need to display the Behaviors panel by using the Shift+F3 shortcut. Select frame 1 of the layer that will contain the ActionScript. You can also select a button instance. Click the plus sign in the Behaviors panel, choose the Data category, and select Trigger Data Source, as shown in Figure 7-10.

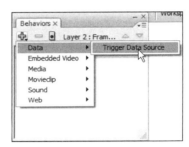

Figure 7-10. Using a behavior to trigger the XMLConnector

Flash will prompt you to select the component instance to trigger, as shown in Figure 7-11. Choose the instance and select whether you want a Relative or Absolute path. I normally leave the default Relative option selected. Click OK, and Flash will create a new behavior to trigger the XMLConnector.

Flash adds the ActionScript that triggers the XMLConnector. You'll also be able to see the new behavior in the panel. You can view the Actions panel to see the code that Flash generates. The following code block shows what was added:

```
// Trigger Data Source Behavior
// Macromedia 2003
this.my_xc.trigger();
```

The code to trigger the component is very simple. It consists of the instance name of the XMLConnector and the `trigger()` method. It also includes the word this. If you're working on the main timeline, you can remove this without affecting the `trigger()` method.

The `trigger()` method creates a call to the XML document specified in the Component Inspector. When it completes the call, it broadcasts the result event. You can write ActionScript that responds to this event to access the results from the loaded XML document.

Figure 7-11. Selecting the XMLConnector component instance

Testing for a loaded XML document

To test whether an XML document has loaded, you'll need to write ActionScript that accesses the contents from the XMLConnector. You can use an event listener to listen for the result event. The results property of the XMLConnector contains the XML document, and you can use a trace() action to see the contents. Be careful not to mix up result and results—they mean very different things. This code snippet shows an example of listening for the result event:

```
var xmlListener:Object = new Object();
xmlListener.result = function(e:Object):Void {
  trace (e.target.results);
};
my_xc.addEventListener("result", xmlListener);
my_xc.trigger();
```

This ActionScript 2.0 block creates a new object and sets the result property to an anonymous function. If you've been working with ActionScript 3.0, you'll notice that the ActionScript 2.0 method for assigning event listeners is a little different.

The listener function traces the results of the event target. The code assigns a listener for the result event using the addEventListener() method. Finally, it triggers the XMLConnector. Notice that I needed to assign the event listener before triggering the component.

If you tested this code, you would see the XML document contents displayed in the Output panel. The event listener passes the event object to the event handler function. The expression e.target. results accesses the complete XML document tree.

Working through a loading example

Let's work through an exercise that uses the XMLConnector to load an external XML document into Flash. In this example, you'll load the file authorsAndBooks.xml into Flash using the XMLConnector component. You'll add some ActionScript to display the XML content within the Output panel.

1. Open Flash and create a new ActionScript 2.0 Flash File.

2. Rename Layer 1 as interface and add another layer called actions.

3. Drag an XMLConnector component to the interface layer. Position it off the Stage and give it the instance name authors_xc.

4. Save the file as loadAuthors.fla in the same folder as the XML document.

5. Select the XMLConnector and configure the Parameters tab in the Component Inspector as shown in Figure 7-12. These settings will load the file authorsAndBooks.xml.

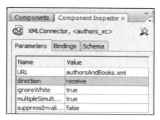

Figure 7-12. The settings for the Parameters tab

6. Click the Schema tab and import the file authorsAndBooks.xml to create a schema. You should see the structure of the document displayed in the tab. It's quite complicated!

7. Click in frame 1 of the actions layer. If necessary, open the Behaviors panel using the Shift+F3 shortcut.

8. Add a new behavior to trigger the authors_xc component. Click the plus sign in the Behaviors panel, choose the Data category, and select Trigger Data Source.

9. Open the Actions panel with the F9 shortcut key and modify the code as shown here (the new lines appear in bold):

```
var xmlListener:Object = new Object();
xmlListener.result = function(e:Object):Void {
  trace(e.target.results);
};
authors_xc.addEventListener("result", xmlListener);
this. authors_xc.trigger();
```

The lines create a new listener called xmlListener. The listener responds to the result event and displays the results of the XMLConnector component called authors_xc.

10. Test the movie, and you should see the Output panel displaying the contents of authorsAndBooks.xml, as shown in Figure 7-13. You can also see my completed resource file loadContacts.fla.

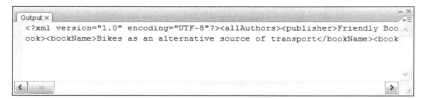

Figure 7-13. Tracing the results property of the XMLConnector

This simple exercise used the XMLConnector component to load XML content from the external file authorsAndBooks.xml. The application included ActionScript to display the XML tree so you could test that the XML document loaded successfully.

After you load an XML document, you'll probably bind the content to other components. You can bind the XML directly to one or more components, or you can bind to a DataSet component first. In the next section, I'll show you how to bind directly to UI components.

Binding XML data directly to UI components

You use data binding to add the data from your XML document to one or more UI components. This is done visually, through the Component Inspector. Visual data binding is much easier than writing ActionScript 2.0 to populate the other components.

If you've worked with XML in ActionScript 2.0, you'll be aware of how convoluted the code can become when it comes to accessing content. Instead of looping through childNodes, you can configure the bindings in the Bindings tab of the Component Inspector. For example, you can bind XML directly to the dataProvider of a ComboBox or List component.

215

The Bindings tab of the Component Inspector determines how data is bound to another component. You'll need to bind *from* the XMLConnector *to* a data-aware component, such as a List, DataGrid, or ComboBox.

You'll need to set the direction for the binding. Bindings are often one way: the data will come out of one component—the source—and go into another—the target. This is the case where you want to display external data within Flash, without tracking updates. For example, the data could come out of the XMLConnector component into a List or TextInput component.

Sometimes you'll have a two-way binding between your components, especially where you want to be able to update your content within Flash. In this case, the content in both components is synchronized, regardless of which component makes the change. You'll see an example of this later, when we bind a DataSet component using two-way bindings in the "Putting it all together section."

You need to add your bindings in the first frame of your Flash movie. They won't work on components that you add later in the timeline. The other restriction is that you can't bind components in multiple scenes in a Flash movie.

Data binding is a huge topic, and I won't give it full coverage here, as that's beyond the scope of this book. Instead, I will show you some of the most important aspects so that you can create bindings using the XMLConnector component.

Adding a binding

Figure 7-14. Selecting a property of the XMLConnector results for binding

Figure 7-15. A binding in the Bindings tab

To add a binding, first select the component on the Stage and display the Bindings tab in the Component Inspector. Click the Add Binding button, which appears as a blue plus sign.

You'll need to identify which property of the XMLConnector results you want to bind. If you're binding multiple values to a data-aware component, you'll usually choose an Array. You might choose a String property if you were binding directly to the text property of a TextInput component.

Select the relevant element from your schema and click OK. Make sure that you've chosen the parent of any items that you want to include within your data-aware component. Figure 7-14 shows the selection of the author Array. Choosing this element means I can access the authorFirstName and authorLastName elements.

As I've selected an Array element, I can bind the data to the dataProvider of a data-aware component such as a List, ComboBox, or DataGrid.

Once you've added the binding, you'll see it displayed within the Bindings tab, as shown in Figure 7-15. Notice that the path for the binding uses a dot notation to drill down through the elements in the structure, starting with results, which is equivalent to the root node of the XML document.

The example in Figure 7-15 demonstrates binding to the author element in the allAuthors element. This element is part of the results property of the XMLConnector component.

After you've added a binding, you'll need to configure the other component involved in the binding, or the *target* for the bound data.

Configuring the binding

You can use the Component Inspector to select a direction and a second component for the binding. The direction—in or out—specifies whether the data is sent out of a component or received by a component. You can also change the way that the bound data displays in the target component.

Table 7-4 summarizes each of the settings in the Bindings tab and explains their purpose.

Table 7-4. Settings for each binding

Setting	Purpose
direction	Specifies whether the binding sends data, receives it, or does both. Choose in, out, or in/out.
bound to	Specifies the other component or target for the binding.
formatter	A formatter to change the display within the target component. The choices are None, Boolean, Compose String, Custom Formatter, Date, Rearrange Fields, and Number Formatter.
formatter options	Lists the options available for the chosen formatter.

You'll learn more about formatters in the next examples.

If you're directly binding from an XMLConnector component to another component, you would set the direction to out and select the target component instance. If you've chosen an Array element from the results, you'll need to select a component capable of displaying more than one value, perhaps a ComboBox component. You can then set the Array as the dataProvider for the target component. You could also bind to the selectedIndex property. You'll see how both of these bindings work in the upcoming examples in this chapter.

When you click in the bound to setting, a magnifying glass icon appears at the right of the field. Click the icon to select the target component. Make sure that you have set an instance name for the target first.

Figure 7-16 shows the Bound To dialog box. In Figure 7-16, I've selected a List component. Because the List component has a dataProvider property, I can select this property from the Schema location section of the dialog box. A dataProvider is an Array, so you can assign the Array from the XMLConnector results.

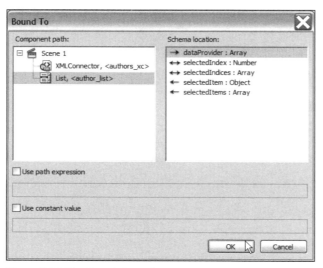

Figure 7-16. The Bound To settings

The arrows in the Bound To dialog box indicate which directions are available to each binding. In Figure 7-16, the right arrow indicates that the XMLConnector can send data to the dataProvider of the author_list component. Because the binding is one way, the List can't add a new item to the authors_xc component.

The selectedIndex location allows you to add a two-way binding. This means that selecting an item in the component selects the same item in the XML data. You would use the selectedIndices item if you were selecting multiple items in the UI component.

Click OK to set the binding. If you select the target component on the Stage, you'll see that Flash has added an equivalent binding in the Bindings tab.

If the data has more than one child element, you'll assign all the children to the bound component. For example, if you've bound an Array directly to the dataProvider of a component, it will display a list of all values from the Array, separated by commas. This is shown in a List component in Figure 7-17.

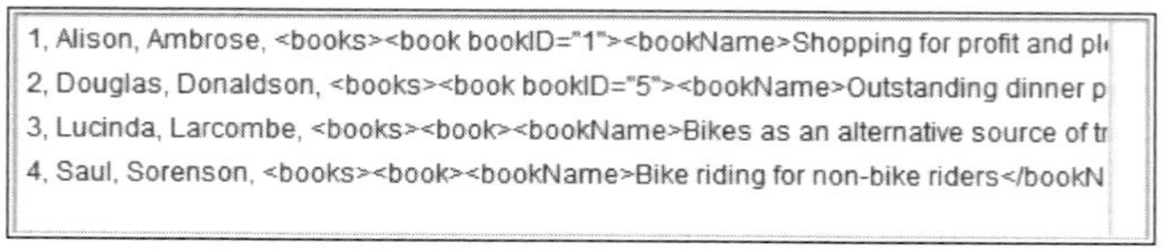

```
1, Alison, Ambrose, <books><book bookID="1"><bookName>Shopping for profit and pl
2, Douglas, Donaldson, <books><book bookID="5"><bookName>Outstanding dinner p
3, Lucinda, Larcombe, <books><book><bookName>Bikes as an alternative source of tr
4, Saul, Sorenson, <books><book><bookName>Bike riding for non-bike riders</bookN
```

Figure 7-17. Without a formatter, the complete element displays in the component.

You can add a formatter to the binding to choose which element displays in the target component. For example, for the data in Figure 7-17, you could use a Rearrange Fields formatter to assign values to the label and data properties of the List component. This would allow the List to display only the name.

To make this clearer, let's work through an example that binds the contents of the authorsAndBooks.xml file directly to a List component. The example will use a formatter to display the full name of each author.

Working through a binding example

You'll use the file from the first exercise and bind the authorFirstName and authorLastName elements to a List component. If you didn't complete the first exercise, you can use the starter file loadAuthors.fla.

1. Open either the starter file loadAuthors.fla or your completed file from the first exercise. Make sure the file is in the same folder as the authorsAndBooks.xml file.

2. Drag a List component to the interface layer and size it appropriately in the Properties panel. Give it the instance name author_list.

3. Select the XMLConnector component, display the Bindings tab in the Component Inspector, and click the Add Binding button.

4. Select the author array from the XMLConnector schema and click OK.

5. Select the binding and click the magnifying glass icon in the bound to setting and add a binding to the dataProvider of the author_list component. Click OK to create the binding.

6. Change the binding direction to out.

7. Test the movie, and you'll see the complete contact element displayed in the List component. Your application should look like the image shown in Figure 7-17. You'll need to add a formatter to display only the name.

8. Select the binding and choose the Rearrange Fields formatter. This formatter will allow the application to select the authorFirstName and authorLastName elements for the label within the list. It can also add a data value at the same time.

9. Click the formatter options setting to show the magnifying glass icon. Click the icon and enter the following settings. When you've finished, click OK to apply the settings.

   ```
   label='<authorFirstName> <authorLastName>';data=authorID;
   ```

   The code sets the label property of the List items to the author's full name and the data property to the authorID attribute. The code creates the full name by joining the <authorFirstName> and <authorLastName> elements with a space between. Notice that for the label property, you need to use angle brackets and place the expression between single quotes. You can just use the field name when assigning the data property.

10. Test the movie. You should see something similar to the screenshot in Figure 7-18. You can see the completed file saved as loadAddress_Binding.fla in your resource files.

Figure 7-18. The List component showing the author's full name from the XML document

In this exercise, you bound the data from an XMLConnector component directly to a List component. The example used a Rearrange Fields formatter to display the author's full name from two elements within the loaded XML tree. It also assigned the authorID attribute to the data property.

> The Rearrange Fields formatter transforms the content from the XMLConnector before it displays in the target component, the List. Because it creates a new Array of objects from the original Array in the XML tree, you can use it only with fields that are arrays—in this example, the <author> elements.
>
> You create the new Array by using a template. You can refer to the original field by using its name or, as you did in this example, by creating a string entry containing a mix of text and fields. In this case, you had to write the field names as XML elements with opening and closing angle brackets.
>
> Your code needs to assign the template to a property on the bound component. In the example, the code assigned the template to the label property. It also assigned the authorID attribute to the data property of the List component.

You can extend the example so that when you click the name, the author's details will display in other components. You'll do this by adding more bindings.

Extending the binding example

In this exercise, you'll add multiple bindings so that when you choose an item from the List, the details display in TextInput and TextArea components. If you didn't complete the previous exercise, you can use the starter file loadAddress_Binding.fla from the resources.

1. Open either the starter file loadAddress_Binding.fla or your completed file from the previous exercise. Again, the file should be in the same folder as authorsAndBooks.xml.

2. Set up the interface as shown in Figure 7-19. I've called the books List component books_list. The year TextInput component has the instance name year_txt. The cost TextInput component is named cost_txt.

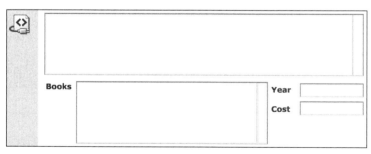

Figure 7-19. The Flash interface

3. Select the XMLConnector component and add a new binding to the books element. Set the direction to out and bind it to the dataProvider property of the books_list component. You'll see an additional setting at the bottom of the Bindings tab called Index for 'author' with a value of 0. This setting shows which value from the array to display in the List component. The application will bind this to the selectedIndex from the author_list component.

4. Click the magnifying glass icon in the Index for 'author' setting to bring up the Bound Index dialog box. Uncheck the Use constant value check box. Select the author_list component and choose the selectedIndex property. This tells the application that the values in the books_list component depend on the item chosen from the author_list component. Figure 7-20 shows the settings for the Bound Index dialog box.

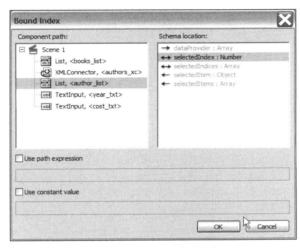

Figure 7-20. The settings for the books binding

5. Test the movie and check that the books_list component populates when you select an author name from the List component. You'll notice that the entire <books> element displays, so the example will need to use another formatter.

6. Add the Rearrange Fields formatter for this binding and add the following formatter option:

```
label=bookName;data=bookID;
```

7. Test the movie again. You should see the book name in the books_list component when you select an item from the author_list component.

8. You might notice that when the application first appears, the word undefined shows in the books_list component. This entry occurs because no index is selected in the author_list component. You can fix this problem by removing the item after the XMLConnector finishes loading. Modify the xmlListener.result function on the actions layer as shown in bold here:

```
xmlListener.result = function(e:Object):Void {
  trace(e.target.results);
  books_list.removeAll();
};
```

When you test the movie, you'll see nothing in the books_list component until you select an item from the author_list component.

221

9. Add another binding to the book year as follows:

    a. Select the XMLConnector component and add a binding to the bookPublishYear element.

    b. Set the direction to out and bind the data to the year_txt component.

    c. You'll see two Index settings, one for each List component. Set the Index for 'author' to the selectedIndex property of the author_list component. Set the Index for 'book' to the selectedIndex property of the book_list component. Figure 7-21 shows the settings.

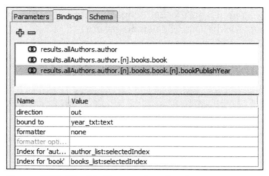

Figure 7-21. The Bindings settings for the bookPublishYear binding

10. Add a similar binding for the bookCost element. In order to display the cost to two decimal places, you'll need to add a Number Formatter with a precision of 2 decimal places. Figure 7-22 shows the settings for this binding.

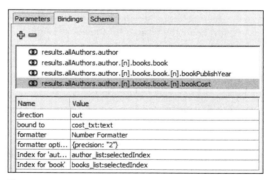

Figure 7-22. The Bindings settings for the bookCost binding

11. Test the movie. You should be able to select an author and book, and see the publish year and cost, as shown in Figure 7-23.

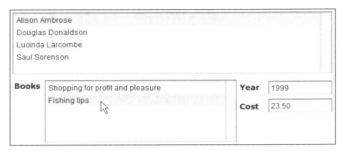

Figure 7-23. The completed application interface

You can find my completed example saved as loadAuthors_multipleBinding.fla with the chapter resources.

In the previous examples, you've seen how easy it is to load XML content into an XMLConnector component and bind it directly to one or more components. You created a very simple application that displays details of an author's books, without writing much ActionScript at all.

However, if you need to update the XML content, things become a lot more complex, as you need to introduce other data components into the mix.

Using the DataSet component

You've seen how to bind XML data directly to other components. This approach works well if you have data that you don't need to update. However, if you want to make changes in Flash, you'll need to work with DataSet and XUpdateResolver components to keep track of your updates. Like the XMLConnector, the DataSet has no visual appearance, which means you can place it anywhere in your Flash movie.

You use the DataSet component to store and organize the data before you bind it to other components. You can also use the DataSet to track changes that you make in the other components. Remember that Flash can't alter external content and requires server interaction for any updates, so you'll also need to send these updates to a server-side file for processing.

Once the updates are complete, the DataSet sends information about the updated data to an XUpdateResolver component in a deltaPacket. The XUpdateResolver processes the deltaPacket and generates an xupdatePacket for use by server-side files.

223

Creating bindings with a DataSet component

You'll bind data from an XMLConnector component to a DataSet component. This is necessary so that the DataSet can keep track of any changes made by other components.

The process is as follows:

1. Configure the XMLConnector.
2. Bind the XMLConnector to a DataSet.
3. Apply two-way bindings from the DataSet to the other components. The two-way bindings ensure that the DataSet always contains the latest data.
4. Add bindings between the DataSet and XUpdateResolver.

You normally bind an Array property of the XMLConnector to the dataProvider of the DataSet. There are other properties that you can use for binding. In addition, you can bind to the deltaPacket—an XML packet describing changes to the data. This binding tracks updates. You can also bind to the items in the component or to the selectedIndex.

When you add bindings from the DataSet to other components, you must select an in/out direction so that the components will inform the DataSet of any changes that a user makes. For list-based components, you'll need to bind both the dataProvider and selectedIndex properties to synchronize the DataSet and component.

You should also create fields in the schema of the DataSet so that the schema matches the exact structure of the results from the XMLConnector component. If you don't do this, the two components won't be identical, and you may have difficulty generating updates later on. Make sure that when you specify the name and data type of the field they are the same as in the XMLConnector schema; that way, you ensure that the two components contain exactly the same content. This is necessary so that you'll be able to update the data correctly.

To capture any changes made to the data, you'll need to add an XUpdateResolver component that binds to the DataSet component. This component keeps the data in Flash consistent with an external data source. The resolver translates information about changes from a DataSet component into a format that the external data source understands.

The relationship between the DataSet and XUpdateResolver is a little complicated. The DataSet monitors any user changes in the components and stores them in a deltaPacket. When you're ready to process these changes, the DataSet sends the deltaPacket to the XUpdateResolver. The resolver converts the deltaPacket into an xupdatePacket that you can send to an XMLConnector. This XMLConnector sends the xupdatePacket to a server-side file where the updates are processed. The server-side file returns an updateResults packet to the XMLConnector. This packet may contain updated values for components, such as those from ID fields. Figure 7-24 shows the process, reading from left to right.

The XUpdateResolver uses XUpdate statements to describe changes that you've made to the data. At the time of writing, XUpdate was a working draft from the XML: DB Working Group. You can find out more about XUpdate at http://xmldb-org.sourceforge.net/xupdate/.

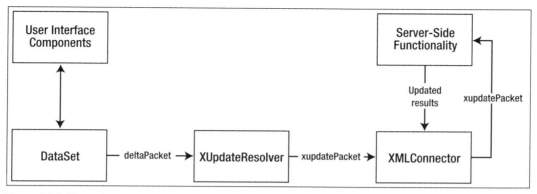

Figure 7-24. The update process using a DataSet and XUpdateResolver

To make sure that you track all of the changes to your data, you'll need to add two bindings: one for the deltaPacket and one for the xupdatePacket. The first binding occurs between the deltaPacket of the DataSet and the deltaPacket of the XUpdateResolver. The deltaPacket is generated by the DataSet component to summarize changes made to the XML content. You'll need to set the direction to out for the DataSet and in for the XUpdateResolver. In other words, the DataSet sends the changes in the deltaPacket to the XUpdateResolver component.

You'll need to add another binding to the XUpdateResolver so that the xupdatePacket is sent out to a second XMLConnector. This XMLConnector sends the xupdatePacket to a server-side file for processing. The XMLConnector will also receive an updateResults packet from the server-side file after processing. The server-side page can use the updateResults packet to send additional data to Flash, such as the primary key values of new entries.

One crucial step in the process is setting the encoder for the XUpdateResolver deltaPacket in the Schema tab of the Component Inspector. You'll need to choose the DatasetDeltaToXUpdateDelta encoder and specify the rowNodeKey in the encoder options. The rowNodeKey is an XPath statement that identifies the path to the rows of data. It's a little like the primary key for a database. The XPath statement also contains a predicate that links the path to the relevant data in the DataSet.

The following code shows the structure of this setting:

```
XPathStatement/rowNode[keyFieldName='?DSKeyFieldName']
```

The setting includes an XPath expression that identifies the path directly to the row node of the data. The predicate, within square brackets, includes the key field from the schema, an equal sign, and the key field from the DataSet, prefaced by a question mark. The DataSet key field name is usually the same as the schema key field. The text to the right of the equal sign is surrounded by single quotes. When Flash creates the xupdatePacket, it will convert the single quotes to the entity '.

It's critical that you write this path correctly; otherwise, you won't be able to generate the correct XUpdate statements in your xupdatePacket.

You need to trigger the DataSet to create the deltaPacket by calling the applyUpdates method. The DataSet then generates the deltaPacket containing the changes to the data. The DataSet sends the deltaPacket to the XUpdateResolver, where the contents are converted into XUpdate statements and added to an xupdatePacket.

The following code shows the structure of an xupdatePacket:

```
<?xml version="1.0"?>
<xupdate:modifications version="1.0"
xmlns:xupdate="http://www.xmldb.org/xupdate">
  <xupdate:update select="XPath statement">
  Updated value </xupdate:update>
  <xupdate:remove select="XPath statement "/>
  <xupdate:append select="XPath statement">
    <xupdate:element name="parentEName">
      <child1Element>Updated value</child1Element>
    </xupdate:element>
  </xupdate:append>
</xupdate:modifications>
```

The packet contains three different sections: one each for updates, deletions, and additions to the data. These are the <xupdate:update>, <xupdate:remove>, and <xupdate:append> nodes. You can repeat each of these elements in the xupdatePacket to reflect the multiple additions, updates, or deletions from Flash.

As you can see, things get a lot more complicated when you include DataSet and XUpdateComponents in your Flash movies. We'll work through a detailed example so that you can see this process for yourself.

Putting it all together

This section will put together everything this chapter has covered so far. You'll create a simple application to add, edit, and delete records in an address book. The application will use the XML document address.xml, and you'll use Flash to manage changes to the data. You'll use a DataGrid component and create multiple component bindings, and you'll track the changes in a DataSet component.

The XML document is very simple and contains three records using the following structure:

```
<phoneBook>
  <contact>
    <contactID></contactID>
    <contactName></contactName>
    <contactPhone></contactPhone>
  </contact>
</phoneBook>
```

This exercise won't include the external updating of content, but you will see the XML content that Flash provides to the server-side file. If you want to add server-side functionality, you'll need to build it yourself using a language like ColdFusion, PHP, or ASP.NET.

1. Open the starter file addressBook.fla and add an XMLConnector component. It's best to keep the Flash file in the same folder as the address.xml file; otherwise, you'll need to include folder names in the path listed at step 2.

    Figure 7-25 shows the interface. It consists of a DataGrid component, two TextInput components, a TextArea, and three buttons.

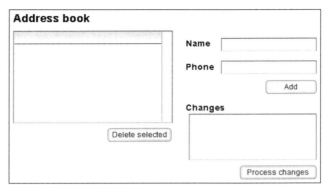

Figure 7-25. The Flash interface for the address book application

I've set the editable property for the DataGrid component to true, so you can modify the data within each cell. You'll use the TextInput components to add new entries, and click the Delete selected button to delete the selected row from the DataGrid. You can process the changes by clicking the Process changes button. The TextArea component will display the XUpdate statements generated.

2. Drag an XMLConnector component into the Flash movie and configure it as shown in Figure 7-26. Give it the instance name address_xc.

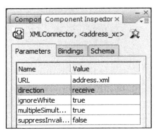

Figure 7-26. Configuring the XMLConnector component

3. In the Schema tab of the Component Inspector, import a schema from the file address.xml. Make sure you select results : XML first. Figure 7-27 shows the imported schema. It replicates the structure from the XML document.

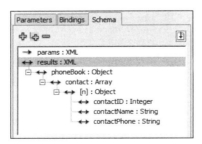

Figure 7-27. The schema created from the file address_simple.xml

227

4. Drag a DataSet component into your movie and give it the instance name address_ds.

5. Add a binding from the XMLConnector to the DataSet. Select the contact Array and bind it to the dataProvider of the DataSet. Make sure the direction is set to out.

6. Create a new layer called actions and add the following code line on frame 1:

```
address_xc.trigger();
```

The line triggers the XMLConnector to load the external XML document. If you test the movie at this point, nothing will happen, because the DataSet isn't yet bound to the DataGrid component.

7. Add two bindings between the DataSet and DataGrid components. Both are in/out bindings. The first should bind the dataProvider, and the second should bind the selectedIndex. These bindings will keep the DataSet and DataGrid synchronized. You should have three bindings now for the DataSet.

8. The application will need to include component properties in the schema for the DataSet. This will create the correct columns in the DataGrid component. Select the DataSet on the Stage and click the Schema tab in the Component Inspector. Click the Add a component property button, which is the plus sign on the far left.

9. Enter the field name contactID and make sure that you select the data type Integer. Repeat the process to add the contactName and contactPhone fields. These have String data types. Make sure that the names you use match the names of the elements in the schema. Figure 7-28 shows the completed Schema tab for the DataSet with the new component properties.

Figure 7-28. The Schema tab showing the new component properties

10. Test the movie. You should see the DataGrid populated with data from the XML document. Figure 7-29 shows the interface at this point. The order of the component properties dictates the order of the columns in the DataGrid.

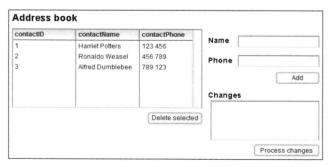

Figure 7-29. The Flash interface showing the populated DataGrid component

At this point, the application has bound data from the XMLConnector to a DataSet, and then to the dataProvider of a DataGrid component. It also bound the selectedIndex of the DataSet and DataGrid, so that both components always contain the same data. It's critical that you don't forget to add the second binding.

11. Now you need to modify the DataGrid so that you can add new contacts, as well as edit and delete existing entries. Add the following code to the actions layer. This code specifies what happens when you click the Add button, which has the instance name update_btn.

```
update_btn.onRelease = function():Void {
  var newName:String = name_txt.text;
  var newPhone:String = phone_txt.text;
  if (newName.length >0 && newPhone.length>0) {
    address_dg.dataProvider.
      ➥addItem({contactName:newName, contactPhone:newPhone});
  }
}
```

The code block finds the new name and phone number from the data-input fields and adds them to the dataProvider of the DataGrid. This function will display the new entry in the DataGrid. The dataProvider of the DataGrid is bound to the dataProvider of the DataSet, so the DataSet will be updated with the new information.

12. Add the following block of code to the actions layer to configure the Delete button. When you click this button, Flash will remove the selected row from the dataProvider of the DataGrid. Again, the binding to the DataSet ensures that Flash also updates the dataProvider for the DataSet.

```
delete_btn.onRelease = function():Void {
  var selRow:Number = address_dg.focusedCell.itemIndex;
  address_dg.dataProvider.removeItemAt(selRow);
}
```

13. Test the movie and check that you can add, edit, and delete data in the DataGrid. The contactID column will be blank for new entries. This is because your server-side pages would normally generate the contactID or primary key field.

14. In order to track the changes to the data, the application needs to generate a deltaPacket from the DataSet component. You'll add an XUpdateResolver component to interpret the deltaPacket from the DataSet component and create XUpdate statements. Drag an XUpdateResolver component into your movie and name it address_rs.

15. Bind the deltaPacket from the XUpdateResolver to the deltaPacket of the DataSet component. Set the direction to in so that the XUpdateResolver receives the delta packet from the DataSet.

16. Display the Schema tab and select the deltaPacket from the XUpdateResolver component. Change the encoder setting to DatasetDeltaToXUpdateDelta and enter the following path in the encoder options field:

```
phoneBook/contact[contactID='?contactID']
```

Figure 7-30 shows the settings.

229

Name	Value
field name	deltaPacket
data type	DeltaPacket
validation opti...	{}
required	true
read only	false
kind	none
kind options	
formatter	none
formatter opti...	
encoder	DatasetDeltaToXUpdateDelta
encoder options	{rowNodeKey: "phoneBook/contact[contactID='?contactID']"}
default value	
path	
storage type	complex

Figure 7-30. The Schema tab settings for the deltaPacket

This is a critical step. If you don't add the correct path, you won't generate the correct XUpdate statements in the xupdatePacket. The XPath statement identifies the contact child element of the phoneBook element and sets the child contactID element to the value from the contactID field in the DataSet.

17. Add a second XMLConnector to your movie and name it sendChanges_xc. You will use this XMLConnector to send the changes from Flash to server-side pages for updating. This example doesn't include configuration of this XMLConnector, since we don't have any server-side pages prepared. You may want to complete these pages yourself.

18. Add another binding to the XUpdateResolver. This time, the binding should send the xupdatePacket from the XUpdateResolver to the sendChanges_xc component. You'll notice that you must select params when you add the binding, because the data will be sent out of Flash.

19. The application still needs to generate the deltaPacket from the DataSet. It will need to configure the Process changes button to call the applyUpdates() method of the DataSet component. Add the following code to your actions layer:

```
change_btn.onRelease = function():Void {
  address_ds.applyUpdates();
}
```

When you click the Process changes button, the DataSet will prepare the deltaPacket. Because the DataSet is bound to the XUpdateResolver, that component will receive the deltaPacket and generate an xupdatePacket.

If you test the movie at this point, nothing will appear to happen, because you haven't configured the sendChanges_xc component. Normally, you would link this to a server-side file to process the XUpdate statements. This exercise won't do so, but you will set up another binding to view the contents of the xupdatePacket in the TextArea.

20. Add another binding to the XUpdateResolver component. The binding should send the xupdatePacket to the text property of the xupdate_txt component. Set the direction to out. By binding the xupdatePacket to the text property of the TextArea component, you'll be able to display the XUpdate statements in the TextArea.

21. Test the movie and make some additions, edits, and deletions to the data. Click the Process changes button and check the contents of the TextArea. Here is some sample XUpdate content that I generated:

```
<?xml version="1.0"?>
<xupdate:modifications version="1.0"
  xmlns:xupdate="http://www.xmldb.org/xupdate">
  <xupdate:remove
    select="/phoneBook/contact[contactID=&apos;2&apos;]" />
  <xupdate:append select="/phoneBook">
    <xupdate:element name="contact"><contactID />
      <contactPhone>987 654</contactPhone>
      <contactName>Sas Jacobs</contactName>
    </xupdate:element>
  </xupdate:append>
</xupdate:modifications>
```

In the XML packet shown here, I removed the contact with a contactID of 2 and added another entry.

That's it for this exercise. You can see the completed application addressBook_completed.fla with your chapter resource files. Apologies for the complexity of this final exercise, but as you can see, the process of tracking changes with the data components is quite difficult.

In this chapter, we've used the Component Inspector to configure the data components in all of the examples. It's also possible to achieve the same functionality using ActionScript 2.0, but that's beyond the scope of this chapter. You may wish to look at this area yourself.

Data components can be a very useful way to include XML content in an application. If you're writing an application that works with an XML source, using the XMLConnector component with data binding provides a very quick way to populate the interface without writing much ActionScript at all. Unfortunately, the ActionScript that you do write will be version 2.0. The only other alternative in Flash is to write ActionScript 3.0 to load and parse the external XML source with the URLLoader class, as discussed in Chapter 5.

If you're loading simple XML content and working with straightforward bindings, the data components provide an excellent solution. However, if you need to monitor changes or write ActionScript to parse the content manually, you're better off sticking with an ActionScript 3.0 approach and avoiding the data components altogether.

Summary

In this chapter, you've seen how to use the XMLConnector component to load an external XML document into Flash. You've also learned how to bind XML data to other components. Binding data allows you to associate part of a loaded XML document directly with a UI component. By using visual data binding, you can avoid writing ActionScript 2.0 code to display the XML data in your movie.

We've completed exercises in this chapter that bind the data from the XMLConnector component directly to one or more other components. I've also shown you how to bind the XMLConnector to DataSet and XUpdateResolver components to keep track of changes and send them to a server-side file for external processing.

In the next chapter, we'll look at how you can modify XML content in both Flash and Flex.

Chapter 8

MODIFYING XML CONTENT WITH ACTIONSCRIPT 3.0

Congratulations for making it this far. As you worked your way through the book, you've seen many different ways to load and access content inside Flash and Flex applications. In the previous chapter, you even saw how to work with XML data using data components and ActionScript 2.0 in Flash Professional.

This chapter describes how to update XML content in SWF applications by using ActionScript 3.0. You'll see how to change the values of elements as well as the structure of loaded XML content.

Earlier in the book, in Chapter 3, you learned about the properties, methods, and events of the XML class. You saw that some of the methods can modify the structure of an XML object. In this chapter, we will look more closely at those methods. Specifically, this chapter covers changing the values of nodes and attributes; adding, duplicating, and deleting nodes; modifying namespaces; and changing element and attribute names.

As with the other chapters, you can download the resource files from http://www.friendsofed.com.

Note that the XML structure changes made in the examples in this chapter won't affect any external data source. Within this chapter, the changes will occur only within the SWF application that you create. In order to send modified content to the server, you'll need to use the approaches shown in the next chapter.

I think it helps you to work through the explanations in this chapter in Flash or Flex. Before we get started, you might find it useful to set up your testing files.

Setting up the examples

Before we dive into the content of this chapter, let's take a moment to set up the Flash and Flex applications for testing the code samples in the next few sections. As in previous chapters, I've used simple procedural code for the Flash examples and class-based code for the Flex examples.

We're using the file authors.xml for these examples. It contains information about several authors and the books that they've published.

Setting up the Flash examples

For the Flash examples, create a new Flash ActionScript 3.0 document and load the authors.xml document into an XML object called authorsXML. You can use the following code to load the external content into Flash:

```
var authorsXML:XML;
var request:URLRequest = new URLRequest("authors.xml");
var loader:URLLoader = new URLLoader();
initApp();
stop();
function initApp():void {
  loader.addEventListener(Event.COMPLETE, completeHandler);
  loader.load(request);
}
function completeHandler(e:Event):void {
  authorsXML = XML(e.target.data);
  trace(authorsXML);
}
```

You'll replace the trace() action in the completeHandler() function with the ActionScript lines shown in the following examples.

Setting up the Flex examples

You can also work through the code samples with Flex Builder. Create a new Flex project and application file with the names of your choosing. Create an assets folder in the src folder of your Flex project. Add the XML document authors.xml to this folder.

For simplicity, use an <mx:XML> element to load the XML content. Add this element to your application file and set the source property to the authors.xml file as shown here:

```
<mx:XML id="authorsXML" source="assets/authors.xml" />
```

Add the following creationComplete attribute to the <mx:Application> element:

```
creationComplete="initApp(event)"
```

Add the following code block:

```
<mx:Script>
  <![CDATA[
    import mx.events.FlexEvent;
    private function initApp(e:FlexEvent):void {
      //add testing lines here
    }
  ]]>
</mx:Script>
```

You'll add the code examples inside the initApp() function. Replace the //add testing lines here comment with the code that you want to test. Because we'll be using trace() statements, you'll need to debug rather than run the Flex application.

Let's start by seeing how to change the values of elements and attributes.

Changing element and attribute values

You can change the values of elements and attributes easily. Bear in mind that when you make these changes, you'll be changing only the values within the SWF application. The changes won't affect the XML data source, so you won't be updating an external XML document or database at the same time.

You update element and attribute values by first locating the relevant node or attribute and then assigning the new value with an equal sign (=). You can use E4X expressions, XML methods, or a mix of both to create the path to the target element or attribute.

The process of assigning values is straightforward. However, you must remember that any expressions that you construct *must* return a single XML element. You can't assign a value to an expression that returns an XMLList. In that case, you would be trying to assign a single value to more than one XML element at the same time, and you would get an error.

To see how this approach works, we'll change the name of the first author in the XML object from Alison Ambrose to Alan Amberson. These values appear in the first <author> element in the <authorFirstName> and <authorLastName> elements. We can assign the new values to these elements by using the following lines of code:

```
authorsXML.author[0].authorFirstName = "Alan";
authorsXML.author[0].authorLastName = "Amberson";
```

If we use a trace() action to view the value of the first <author> element, we should see the following author name values:

```
<authorFirstName>Alan</authorFirstName>
<authorLastName>Amberson</authorLastName>
```

We've successfully updated the text inside these two elements.

It's also possible to use the `replace()` method to assign a new value to an element, as shown here:

```
authorsXML.author[0].replace("authorFirstName",
  ➥"<authorFirstName>Alan</authorFirstName>");
```

The first argument to the method indicates what you're replacing. Here, it's the `<authorFirstName>` element. The second argument provides the replacement content—in this case, `<authorFirstName>Alan </authorFirstName>`. You'll notice that the second argument requires the opening and closing tags to be included.

Using the `replace()` method is obviously more cumbersome than adding a simple assignment that uses an equal sign. However, this method allows you to specify a different element structure to use as a replacement. It would be possible to replace the `<authorFirstName>` element with a completely different set of elements.

> You can also use the `replace()` method to change an element name or completely modify the XML structure of the specified element. This use of `replace()` is covered in the "Editing content" section later in the chapter.

Modifying attribute values is just as easy. For example, we can change the value of the `authorID` attribute of the first author using the following line:

```
authorsXML.author[0].@authorID="99";
```

Tracing the value of the first `<author>` element shows the following content:

```
<author authorID="99">
```

We've successfully changed the value of the attribute.

It is possible to change more than one value at a time by working through the entire collection. For example, you could modify more than one element or attribute by looping through the collection and treating each item individually.

For example, to add the number 10 before each of the current `authorID` attribute values, you could use the following code:

```
for each(var aXML:XML in authorsXML.author) {
  aXML.@authorID = "10" + aXML.@authorID;
}
```

This example uses a for each statement to iterate through all of the `<author>` elements in the XML object. You can then treat each `<author>` individually. Because the code treats the elements separately, each `<author>` element is an XML object in its own right.

Tracing the XML tree for this example shows the following values for each of the <author> elements:

```
<author authorID="101">
<author authorID="102">
<author authorID="103">
<author authorID="104">
```

The code changes all attributes to include the number 10 at the start. Note that, unlike what is shown in the preceding code block, the opening elements won't all appear next to each other when you run the example.

You can find all of these examples saved in the file changingValues.fla and ChangingValues.mxml with your other chapter resources.

Unfortunately, it's not quite as easy to modify XML element and attribute structures. In the next section, you'll see how to use methods of the XML class to make changes to XML structures.

Adding, editing, and deleting XML content

Chapter 3 demonstrated how to use several of the methods of the XML class to modify the structure of an existing XML object. I've summarized these methods in Table 8-1.

Table 8-1. Methods of the XML class for modifying XML content

Method	Description
appendChild(child)	Adds the specified child node at the end of the child nodes collection of the identified node
copy()	Makes a copy of an existing node
insertChildAfter(child1, child2)	Inserts a new child node after the identified child node
insertChildBefore(child1, child2)	Inserts a new child node before the specified child node
prependChild(value)	Adds the specified child node at the beginning of the child nodes of the identified node
replace(propertyName, value)	Replaces a specified property, perhaps an element or attribute, with the provided value
setChildren(value)	Replaces children of an XML object with specified content

We'll now work through each of these methods in a little more detail so you can see how they work. A little later in the chapter, in the "Working through a modification example" section, you will use some of the methods in a practical application.

We'll start by examining the appendChild() method.

Using appendChild()

The appendChild() method adds a new child node at the end of the current collection of child nodes. It takes a single argument—the child to append—and adds it as the last child element. Here is an example:

```
var newAuthor:XML =
  <author id="5">
    <authorFirstName>Sas</authorFirstName>
    <authorLastName>Jacobs</authorLastName>
  </author>
authorsXML.appendChild(newAuthor);
```

The code starts by creating a new XML object called newAuthor. It then assigns the details of the new node to this object, including the structure and values of elements and attributes. The last line of the code calls the appendChild() method from the root element authorsXML. It passes the new XML object to the method. Tracing the authorsXML object shows that the new element is added as the last child of the <allAuthors> element. The end of the XML object follows:

```
<author id="5">
  <authorFirstName>Sas</authorFirstName>
  <authorLastName>Jacobs</authorLastName>
</author>
```

The appendChild() method can add the new child element at any point in the XML object. It doesn't need to refer to the root element. The following code block shows how to add a new child book to the second <author> element:

```
var newBook:XML = <book bookID="10">
  <bookName>Hearty Soups</bookName>
  <bookPublishYear>2008</bookPublishYear>
  </book>;
authorsXML.author[1].books.appendChild(newBook);
```

After running this code, the list of books by this author includes the following:

```
<books>
  <book bookID="5">
    <bookName>Outstanding dinner parties</bookName>
    <bookPublishYear>2003</bookPublishYear>
  </book>
  <book bookID="9">
    <bookName>Cooking for fun and profit</bookName>
    <bookPublishYear>2007</bookPublishYear>
  </book>
  <book bookID="10">
    <bookName>Hearty Soups</bookName>
    <bookPublishYear>2008</bookPublishYear>
  </book>
</books>
```

The new book appears last in the list of all books by this author.

Instead of creating the new element separately, you can also add it directly as an argument to the appendChild() method. In the following example, the new XML element appears inside the call to the appendChild() method.

```
authorsXML.appendChild(<author id="5">
    ➥<authorFirstName>Sas</authorFirstName>
    ➥<authorLastName>Jacobs</authorLastName></author>);
```

You can see that this approach produces some unwieldy code. My preference is to create the child element separately, as it makes the code easier to read.

It's also possible to set the child elements of the new XML object as properties using dot notation. You can see this approach in the following example:

```
var newAuthor:XML = <author id="5"></author>;
newAuthor.authorFirstName = "Sas";
newAuthor.authorLastName = "Jacobs";
```

Instead of using XML structures, the code defines the child elements as properties. This approach creates the same result, and you'll use it in examples later in the chapter.

Using prependChild()

The prependChild() method works in much the same way as appendChild(), except that it adds the new child element as the first child of the selected parent. Using this method moves all of the existing child elements to a position one ahead of their original position.

We could use the same new <author> element and add it as the first child with the following code:

```
var newAuthor:XML = <author id="5">
    <authorFirstName>Sas</authorFirstName>
    <authorLastName>Jacobs</authorLastName>
  </author>;
authorsXML.prependChild(newAuthor);
```

If you add this example and trace the authorsXML object, you'll see the new element appearing as the first child of the <allAuthors> element. The existing elements appear afterward.

Copying a node

In the previous examples, we created the new node by assigning its value directly to an XML object. You also saw that it's possible to add the children with dot notation instead of writing them to the XML object.

Another approach is to use the copy() method to duplicate an existing node. Once you've replicated the structure, you can change the values and then insert the copied element using the appendChild() or prependChild() method. Here's an example of this approach:

```
var cookbookXML:XML = authorsXML.author[0].books.book[0].copy();
cookbookXML.@bookID = "10";
cookbookXML.bookName = "Hearty Soups";
cookbookXML.bookPublishYear = "2008";
authorsXML.author[1].books.prependChild(cookbookXML);
```

This example creates a new XML object by calling the copy() method on the first book of the first author. Any <book> element would do here; it's only the structure that interests us.

The next three lines assign the new values to the copied <book> element structure. The final line calls the prependChild() method to add the new <book> element as the first child of the <books> element for the second author. Running the code sample produces the same output that you saw earlier.

If you want to add a new element that has a complex structure, you'll probably find that using the copy() method will be quicker than the previous approaches. It is likely to take more work to create the element structure and insert it with appendChild() or prependChild() than it is to copy the structure and modify the values.

Inserting a child node

Both the insertChildAfter() and insertChildBefore() methods insert a new child node at a specific place in the XML object. You could use these methods to add a new child node at a position other than as the first or last child. The difference between the two methods is obvious from their names.

The insertChildAfter() and insertChildBefore() methods take the same two arguments. The first argument is the position at which to insert the new element. The second argument is the new child element to insert. Here's an example showing the insertChildAfter() method:

```
var newAuthor:XML = <author id="5">
  <authorFirstName>Sas</authorFirstName>
  <authorLastName>Jacobs</authorLastName>
  </author>;
authorsXML.insertChildAfter(authorsXML.author[1], newAuthor);
```

In this example, the code adds the new <author> element after the second author. If you add the code to the sample files, the new author will appear after Douglas Donaldson and before Lucinda Larcombe.

We could achieve the same result using the following insertChildBefore() method, as follows:

```
authorsXML.insertChildBefore(authorsXML.author[2], newAuthor);
```

This example inserts a new <author> element before the current third author. It will move the existing third and later <author> elements one position forward, so that the current third element becomes the fourth and so on.

Using the insertChildBefore() method with any element at index 0 is equivalent to using the prependChild() method. It adds the new element as the first child.

Similarly, using the insertChildAfter() method and specifying the index of the last child element is equivalent to using appendChild(). It adds the new element as the last child.

Editing content

The replace() method works a little differently from the other methods. It allows you to change the structure of the XML content by replacing one XML element with entirely different content. It's up to you whether you preserve the existing XML structure.

The replace() method takes two arguments. The first is the property to replace. You can express this argument as the String name of an element or attribute. It can also be provided as the index of a child element. The second argument is the replacement content. You need to provide this argument as an XML object.

You could use the replace() method to replace the first <author> element with a <publisherName> element, as shown here:

```
authorsXML.replace(0, "<publisherName>FOE</publisherName>");
```

Here, we've specified the first child of the authorsXML object by providing the index 0. This number equates to the first <author> element in the XML object. Its replacement is an entirely new element name.

The following example shows how to use a String value for the element that will be replaced.

```
authorsXML.author[0].replace("books", "<nobooks/>");
```

Here, the code replaces the first author's <books> element with an empty <nobooks> element. Running the code and tracing the output produces the following change to the first author:

```
<author authorID="1">
  <authorFirstName>Alison</authorFirstName>
  <authorLastName>Ambrose</authorLastName>
  <nobooks/>
</author>
```

We could also replace the entire contents of the first <author> element, as shown here:

```
authorsXML.author[0].replace("*",
 ➡"<authorFirstName>Alan</authorFirstName>");
```

The code uses the wildcard operator * to specify that all children of the first <author> element are to be replaced. Running this example produces the following result, where there is a single child element for this <author> element:

```
<author authorID="1">
  <authorFirstName>Alan</authorFirstName>
</author>
```

However, you couldn't use the following code to provide a replacement value:

```
authorsXML.author[0].replace("*",
 ➡"<authorFirstName>Alan</authorFirstName>
 ➡<authorLastName>Amberson</authorLastName>");
```

241

If you tried to use this code, you would get an error message indicating that the document markup was not well-formed. This code is invalid because the replacement value is *not* a valid XML object. Instead, it contains two elements that aren't inside a single root element.

If the objective were to replace the <authorFirstName> and <authorLastName> elements in the first <author> element, you would need to use the following approach:

```
authorsXML.replace(0,
   ➥"<author><authorFirstName>Alan</authorFirstName>
   ➥<authorLastName>Amberson</authorLastName></author>");
```

You could also add the first child only using the replace() method, and then call the appendChild() method to add the second element afterward.

Using setChildren()

The setChildren() method replaces all of the children of the specified element with the content passed to the method. You can pass either an XML or XMLList object to the method.

This previous example:

```
authorsXML.author[0].replace("*",
   ➥"<authorFirstName>Alan</authorFirstName>")
```

is equivalent to the following line:

```
authorsXML.author[0].setChildren(
➥<authorFirstName>Alan</authorFirstName>);
```

In the previous section's example, you couldn't pass an XMLList argument to the replace() method. That invalid example could be replaced with the following valid example:

```
authorsXML.author[0].setChildren
   ➥(<author><authorFirstName>Alan</authorFirstName>
   <authorLastName>Amberson</authorLastName></author>);
```

Deleting an element

You can delete content by using the delete() ActionScript operator. The following example removes the first <author> element from the authorsXML object:

```
delete(authorsXML.author[0]);
```

If you test this line, the first author in the XML tree becomes Douglas Donaldson. All <author> elements move down one position.

> *Note that* delete() *is not specifically a method of the XML object. Rather, it is an ActionScript 3.0 operator that can be used in circumstances other than working with XML content.*

You can find the Flash and Flex examples saved as modifyingStructure.fla and ModifyingStructure.mxml respectively with the chapter resources. Don't forget that you will need to debug the Flex application to view the results of the trace() actions in the examples.

Modifying element names and namespaces

One area that we haven't yet touched on in any detail is how to make modifications to the names of elements and attributes. We also haven't looked at how you can make changes to namespaces. Remember that a namespace associates an element with a particular URI. It allows you to ensure that each element and attribute name in an XML document can be uniquely identified, even if you have more than one with the same name.

Let's start by looking at namespaces. The examples in this section use a slightly different XML document, authorsNS.xml. Make sure you modify your code to load this file instead of authors.xml. For the Flex example, make sure you add the file to the assets folder in your Flex project as well.

Adding a namespace

You can add a namespace to an XML object using the addNamespace() method. The method receives the namespace that you want to add as an argument. You provide the namespace either as a Namespace object or as a QName object.

When you load the new XML file, you'll see that the root element of the new authorsXML object contains two namespaces.

```
<allAuthors xmlns:sj="http://www.sasjacobs.com/ns/"
  xmlns:aa="http://www.alisonambrose.com/ns/">
```

The following example shows how to add a third namespace to the root element:

```
var ns:Namespace = new Namespace("foe", "http://www.foe.com/ns/");
authorsXML.addNamespace(ns);
```

The code starts by creating a new Namespace object with the prefix foe that references the URI http://www.foe.com/ns/. It then uses the addNamespace() method to add the namespace attribute to the root element.

After running this example, you should see the following root element:

```
<allAuthors xmlns:sj="http://www.sasjacobs.com/ns/"
  xmlns:aa="http://www.alisonambrose.com/ns/"
  xmlns:foe="http://www.foe.com/ns/">
```

The code adds the third namespace listed in this root element.

Adding a namespace to the root element means that it's available to all other child elements. However, you don't need to add the namespace to the root element. You can add it anywhere in the XML document tree, as shown here:

```
authorsXML.author[0].books.addNamespace(ns);
```

This line of code would add the namespace to the <books> element of the first author, indicating that it is within that namespace:

```
<books xmlns:foe="http://www.foe.com/ns/">
```

It's also possible to determine the namespace from an existing element and apply it to another element. The author Saul Sorenson has the namespace http://www.saulsorenson.com/ns/ in his <author> element. You can see it in the following line:

```
<author authorID="4" xmlns:ss="http://www.saulsorenson.com/ns/">
```

In the next example, we'll refer to this namespace and add it to the second <author> element as well.

```
var ss:Namespace = authorsXML.author[3].namespace("ss");
authorsXML.author[1].addNamespace(ss);
```

In this example, the object ss refers to the namespace prefixed with ss in the third <author> element. The code adds this namespace to the second <author> element using the addNamespace() method. Tracing the XML content shows the following opening element for the second author:

```
<author authorID="2" xmlns:ss="http://www.saulsorenson.com/ns/">
```

The ss namespace appears as a new namespace for this <author> element.

Removing a namespace

You can remove a namespace from an existing element with the removeNamespace() method. Let's see an example.

The root element of the authorsNS.xml file contains two namespaces, as shown here:

```
<allAuthors xmlns:sj="http://www.sasjacobs.com/ns/"
    xmlns:aa="http://www.alisonambrose.com/ns/">
```

These elements have the prefixes sj and aa. We'll remove the namespace prefixed with aa with the following code:

```
authorsXML.removeNamespace(aa);
```

Running the example and displaying the XML object shows only one namespace remaining in the root element.

```
<allAuthors xmlns:sj="http://www.sasjacobs.com/ns/">
```

Again, you can remove the namespace from elements other than the root element. We can remove the namespace declaration from the last <author> element using the following code:

```
var ss:Namespace = authorsXML.author[3].namespace("ss");
authorsXML.author[3].removeNamespace(ss);
```

If you used this code and traced the XML object, this <author> element would appear as follows:

```
<author authorID="4">
```

The element doesn't contain any namespaces.

Setting the namespace

The setNamespace() method sets the namespace associated with an XML object. You could use this to apply the namespace from one XML object to another and set it as the default namespace. Consider the following code block:

```
var myXML:XML = <greeting>Hello world</greeting>;
var aa:Namespace = authorsXML.namespace("aa");
myXML.setNamespace(aa);
trace(myXML.toXMLString());
```

This block of code creates a new XML object called myXML with some simple content. The second line determines the namespace associated with the aa prefix in the authorsXML XML object and stores it in a Namespace object called aa. The third line calls the setNamespace() method of the myXML object, passing the aa namespace as an argument. When you view the modified XML tree for the myXML object, you see the following element:

```
<aa:greeting xmlns:aa="http://www.alisonambrose.com/ns/">
  Hello world</aa:greeting>
```

The setNamespace() method adds the aa namespace to this XML object. It also sets aa as the default namespace by adding the prefix aa to the root element <greeting>.

> Note that I had to use the toXMLString() method here to display the XML content, as the myXML object contains only simple content. If I used toString() instead, I would have seen only the text Hello world.

You can find all of these examples saved in the modifyingNamespaces.fla and ModifyingNamespaces.mxml files.

As well as working with namespaces, you can also change the names of elements and attributes. We'll continue working with the authorsNS.xml file for the next set of examples.

Changing the local element name

You can change a local element name or attribute using the setLocalName() method of the XML object. You need to pass the new element name when calling this method. The method doesn't change the prefix in a qualified name.

We could use the following line of code to change the name of the root element of the authorsXML object to authorList:

```
authorsXML.setLocalName("authorList");
```

Applying this code results in the following newly named root element:

```
<authorList xmlns:sj="http://www.sasjacobs.com/ns/"
  xmlns:aa="http://www.alisonambrose.com/ns/">
```

In addition to the root element, you can also change the names of other elements farther down the document tree. The following example changes the first author element name from <author> to <myAuthor>:

```
authorsXML.author[0].setLocalName("myAuthor");
```

Viewing the XML document tree shows that the element is renamed to <myAuthor>, as shown in the following line:

```
<myAuthor authorID="1">
```

The setLocalName() method also works to change the name of attributes, as shown in the following example:

```
authorsXML.author[0].@authorID.setLocalName("myID");
```

Introducing this change rewrites the first author element, as shown here:

```
<author myID="1">
```

Changing the qualified element name

You can also change the qualified name of an element or attribute using the setName() method. Again, the method receives a String argument indicating the new name to use for the element. If you apply this method to an unqualified element, the result is the same as applying the setLocalName() method.

For example, the following line produces the same output as calling the setLocalName() method:

```
authorsXML.author[0].setName("myAuthor");
```

In both cases, you end up with the element <myAuthor>, as shown here:

```
<myAuthor authorID="1">
```

The difference between the setLocalName() and setName() methods will be apparent with an example that includes a namespace. The third author in the XML document, Lucinda Larcombe, has the following opening <author> element:

```
<ll:author authorID="3"
  xmlns:ll="http://www.lucindalarcombe.com/ns/">
```

Notice that the element name author is qualified with the prefix ll, which refers to the namespace http://www.lucindalarcombe.com/ns/. We can change *only* the author portion of the element name with the setLocalName() method, as shown in these lines of code:

```
    var ll:Namespace =
    ➥new Namespace("http://www.lucindalarcombe.com/ns/");
    authorsXML.ll::author[0].setLocalName("myAuthor");
```

Notice that we needed to prefix the element with the namespace ll, as shown in the XML document. We also needed to use the :: operator to indicate that the prefix belonged to the author element. Because this is the only <author> element with the ll prefix, we referred to it using an index value of 0: ll::author[0].

Running this example produces the following element for this author:

```
    <ll:myAuthor authorID="3"
       xmlns:ll="http://www.lucindalarcombe.com/ns/">
```

The prefix ll remains in the element, but the local name of the element is changed from author to myAuthor.

If we use the setName() method instead, we'll see a different result. The following line of code uses the setName() method on the same element. Again, the element name is qualified with the prefix ll.

```
    authorsXML.ll::author[0].setName("myAuthor");
```

Applying this code, you should see the following change to the element:

```
    <myAuthor authorID="3"
       xmlns:ll="http://www.lucindalarcombe.com/ns/">
```

The element is no longer qualified by the prefix ll. However, the namespace declaration remains.

These examples demonstrate that you should be very careful with the setName() and setLocalName() methods when working with qualified element names!

You can find all the examples referred to in this section saved in the files modifyingNames.fla and ModifyingNames.mxml.

Now that we've covered the ways that you can modify an XML document, let's work through an example so you can see some of these concepts in action.

Working through a modification example

We'll work through an example that demonstrates how to modify an XML tree structure. We'll use the resource file authorsAndBooks.xml, which you've seen in other chapters.

In this example, we'll load the contents of the document and display a list of authors in a ComboBox and their books in an editable DataGrid. We'll use the application to add, modify, and delete book details for the selected author. We'll use XML class methods to modify the XML object to keep it consistent with the changes made in the interface.

In the Flash example, I'll show a simplistic version, using procedural code. The Flex version uses class files.

247

Working in Flash

Here are the instructions to set up the Flash example:

1. Open the starter file authorBookEditor.fla in Flash. Figure 8-1 shows the interface. The application will populate the ComboBox with authors from the loaded XML object. It will show the books for each author in an editable DataGrid below the author name. A TextArea control will show the contents of the XML object.

A user can add details of a new book, modify a row in the DataGrid, or select a row in the DataGrid to delete a book.

Figure 8-1. The application interface

2. Create a new layer called actions. Open the Actions panel using the F9 shortcut and add the following code to load the external XML document. If you've worked through the previous exercises, there's nothing new in this code, but I'll explain it after the listing.

```
import fl.data.DataProvider;
var authorsXML:XML;
var authorList:XML;
var booksList:XML;
var request:URLRequest = new URLRequest("authorsAndBooks.xml");
var loader:URLLoader = new URLLoader();
initApp();
stop();
```

This script block starts by importing the DataProvider class, which the application will use to populate both the ComboBox and DataGrid controls. The code creates three XML objects. The first is authorsXML, which will store the complete XML tree from the loaded content. The second XML object, authorList, will populate the ComboBox. The third XML object, booksList, will store the books for each author and populate the DataGrid.

The code then creates a URLRequest object called request and a URLLoader object called loader. The URLRequest requests the authorsAndBooks.xml file and assumes that the XML document is in the same folder as the Flash application.

The second-to-last line calls a function named initApp() to set up the application. You'll create this function in the next step. The code block finishes with a stop() action.

3. The initApp() function sets up the application and loads the external XML document. Add the following code at the bottom of the Actions panel. It contains two other functions, which I'll explain after the listing.

```
function initApp():void {
  loader.addEventListener(Event.COMPLETE, completeHandler);
  authors_cbo.labelFunction = getFullName;
  loader.load(request);
}
function completeHandler(e:Event):void {
  authorsXML = XML(e.target.data);
  authorList = new XML(authorsXML.authors);
  authors_cbo.dataProvider = new DataProvider(authorList);
  tree_txt.text = authorsXML.toXMLString();
}
function getFullName(item:Object):String{
  return item.authorFirstName + " " + item.authorLastName;
}
```

First, the initApp() function adds an event listener to the loader object. The listener will respond when the loader dispatches the complete event by calling the function completeHandler(). In other words, this handler function will process the loaded content to make it available to the application.

The initApp() function also sets the labelFunction property for the authors_cbo control so that it can display the full name of each author. The function finishes by calling the load() method of the loader object to request the external XML document.

The completeHandler() function receives an Event as an argument and uses the target. data property of this Event object to locate the loaded data. The first line casts this data as an XML object, assigning it to the authorsXML object. You need to do this because the content is loaded as String data.

The function creates an XML object containing the list of authors by targeting the <authors> element in the XML document with the E4X expression authorsXML.authors. The third line of the completeHandler() function sets the dataProvider property for the ComboBox control to this XML object. The labelFunction for the ComboBox will format the appearance of the data in the ComboBox. The final line displays a String representation of the loaded XML content in the TextArea component called tree_txt.

The getFullName() label function should be familiar to you from the earlier examples. It creates the full name by locating the first and last names of the author in the <authorFirstName> and <authorLastName> elements. It joins these elements with a space in between.

4. At this point, the application has loaded the XML document and populated the ComboBox control. Test the movie and check that the external XML document loads successfully. Figure 8-2 shows how the interface should appear at this point. You should see the TextArea populated with the loaded XML document and the ComboBox displaying the first author name, Alison Ambrose.

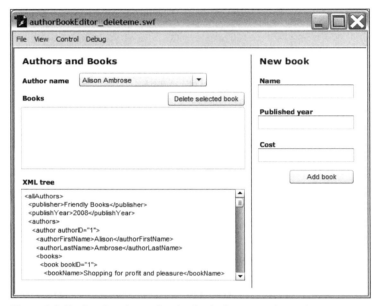

Figure 8-2. Testing that the application loads the external XML document

5. The application now needs to load the books for the author displayed in the ComboBox. When the application first starts, it will display the first author's books in the DataGrid to match the value initially shown in the ComboBox. When the user selects a different author, the books shown will change. To accomplish this, the application needs to detect when the selection in the ComboBox changes, and then locate the <books> element for the selected author.

Add the following line to the initApp() function to detect a change in the ComboBox component:

```
authors_cbo.addEventListener(Event.CHANGE, changeHandler);
```

Each change in the selected value in the ComboBox calls the changeHandler() function. Add the following changeHandler() function at the bottom of the Actions panel:

```
function changeHandler(e:Event):void {
  var authorIndex:int = e.target.selectedIndex;
  loadBooks(authorIndex);
}
```

The changeHandler() function receives an Event as an argument. You can determine the selectedIndex from the target of this event, which is the ComboBox control.

The function assigns the selectedIndex value of the ComboBox to the authorIndex variable. The number will be the same as the author index from the XML object, as both are zero-based.

The function finishes by calling another function, loadBooks(), passing the value of the selectedIndex property. The loadBooks() function will populate the DataGrid component.

6. Add the loadBooks() function shown here to the actions layer:

```
function loadBooks(authorIndex:int):void {
  var booksDP:DataProvider;
  booksList = new XML(authorsXML.authors.author[authorIndex].books);
  booksDP = new DataProvider(booksList);
  books_dg.dataProvider = booksDP;
}
```

Each time the user selects a new author, the loadBooks() function will locate that author's books and use them to populate the DataGrid.

This function starts by declaring a DataProvider object called booksDP, which the application will use to populate the DataGrid. It then locates the <books> element using the E4X expression authorsXML.authors.author[authorIndex].books. Notice that the E4X expression includes the authorIndex passed from the changeHandler() function.

The loadBooks() function sets the returned XMLList as the source for the booksList XML object. It then assigns the booksList object to the DataProvider object. Finally, the bookDP object is assigned as the dataProvider for the DataGrid.

7. If you tested the application now, you wouldn't see any books populated initially. That's because you need to add another call to the loadBooks() function, which runs when the XML content first loads. This call will allow you to see the first author's books.

Add the line shown in bold to the completeHandler() function:

```
function completeHandler(e:Event):void {
  authorsXML = XML(e.target.data);
  authorList = new XML(authorsXML.authors);
  authors_cbo.dataProvider = new DataProvider(authorList);
  loadBooks(0);
  tree_txt.text = authorsXML.toXMLString();
}
```

Once the content is loaded, the application will call the loadBooks() function, passing the first author's index of 0 as an argument.

8. Test the application again and check that the books for the first author appear when the application first loads. You also need to test that you can see other authors' books when you change the selection in the ComboBox.

Figure 8-3 shows the interface when the application first loads.

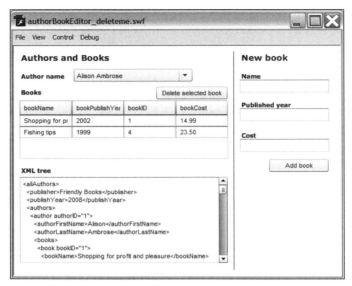

Figure 8-3. Loading the DataGrid

9. The DataGrid doesn't look too good. The column headings are the default field names, and the book titles are cut off. You can fix the way it looks by calling another function, setupDataGrid(), which formats the DataGrid's appearance.

Add the following function call to the end of the completeHandler() function. The new line appears in bold.

```
function completeHandler(e:Event):void {
  authorsXML = XML(e.target.data);
  authorList = new XML(authorsXML.authors);
  authors_cbo.dataProvider = new DataProvider(authorList);
  loadBooks(0);
  setupDataGrid();
  tree_txt.text = authorsXML.toXMLString();
}
```

You also need to add the setupDataGrid() function to your actions layer.

```
function setupDataGrid():void {
  books_dg.columns = ["ID", "Name", "Publish year", "Cost"];
  books_dg.columns[0].width = 50;
  books_dg.columns[1].width = 200;
  books_dg.columns[2].width = 50;
  books_dg.columns[3].width = 50;
  books_dg.columns[0].dataField = "bookID";
  books_dg.columns[1].dataField = "bookName";
  books_dg.columns[2].dataField = "bookPublishYear";
  books_dg.columns[3].dataField = "bookCost";
  books_dg.columns[0].editable = false;
}
```

The role of this function is to set column headings, widths, and assign which data field to display. This function starts by declaring the column headings for the DataGrid. It refers to each column using its position in the columns collection.

The function then sets the width and dataField properties for each column. Feel free to modify the width settings to display more or less of each column.

The function finishes by making the first column read-only. The application needs to do this because the users should not be able to change the bookID field. Normally, that field would be the primary key and would be allocated externally.

10. Test the application again. The DataGrid looks much better, as shown in Figure 8-4.

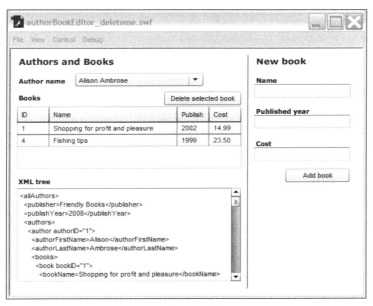

Figure 8-4. The DataGrid has been formatted.

11. The application has now set up the interface to display the data. The next step is to allow the users to modify the books for each author. They will be able to add, edit, and delete book information.

Let's start by providing the functionality to add a new book. You'll need to add a handler function that responds when the user clicks the Add book button.

Add the following line to the initApp() function:

```
addRow_btn.addEventListener(MouseEvent.CLICK, addClickHandler);
```

This line adds an event listener that responds when a user clicks the addRow_btn button. You also need to add the addClickHandler() function shown here:

```
function addClickHandler(e:MouseEvent):void {
  var newBookName:String = name_txt.text;
  var newPublishYear:String = year_txt.text;
  var newBookCost:String = cost_txt.text;
  var newBookXML:XML;
  if(newBookName.length > 0 && newPublishYear.length > 0 &&
    ➥newBookCost.length > 0) {
    books_dg.addItem({bookName: newBookName,
      ➥bookPublishYear: newPublishYear, bookCost: newBookCost});
    newBookXML = <book bookID=''></book>;
    newBookXML.bookName = newBookName;
    newBookXML.bookPublishYear = newPublishYear;
    newBookXML.bookCost = newBookCost;
    authorsXML.authors.author[authors_cbo.selectedIndex]
      ➥.books.appendChild(newBookXML);
    tree_txt.text = authorsXML.toXMLString();
  }
}
```

This function responds to the click of the Add book button and receives a MouseEvent as an argument. It starts by adding the user entries to three variables: newBookName, newPublishYear, and newBookCost. The function also declares an XML object that will store the new XML content.

The function checks that the user has entered values in each of the Name, Published year, and Cost TextInput controls. If so, it uses the addItem() method of the DataGrid to add the new entry. The code creates an object made up of name/value pairs and passes this object to the addItem() method. Notice that the code uses the field name from the XML object, rather than the column headings, to indicate where you want users to enter each new piece of information.

After adding the new row, the function then creates a <book> element for the newBookXML object. Notice that this element has one attribute that doesn't have a value. Normally, you would get the bookID value from the database.

The function then assigns the bookName, bookPublishYear, and bookCost properties to the newBookXML object. This approach provides a quick way to add the child elements to the <book> element.

The function finishes by using the appendChild() method to add the newBookXML object to the <books> element of the selected author. Notice that you pass the authors_cbo.selectedIndex as the author index. Finally, the function displays the updated XML object in the TextArea control.

Note that I haven't provided any processing in case the user clicks the button without filling in all of the TextInput controls. Feel free to add a text field and display a message to deal with this situation.

12. Test the application again. You should be able to enter details of a new book and add it to the DataGrid and XML object. Figure 8-5 shows an example of adding a new book to the author Douglas Donaldson. As I mentioned, we didn't create an ID for this book because that would most likely be managed by the database.

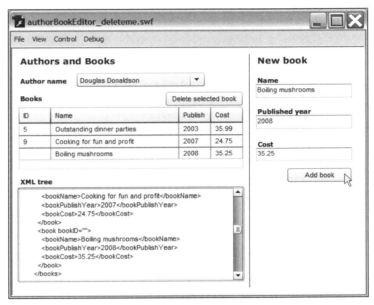

Figure 8-5. Adding a new book

You can see that the new book appears at the bottom of the list of books for Douglas Donaldson. It also appears as a new <book> element in his list of all books. Because the code uses the appendChild() method, the book appears as the last child of the <books> element.

13. Let's see how to delete a book from the DataGrid and the XML object. The user will select a row in the DataGrid and click the Delete selected book button. You'll need to add a listener for the click of this button.

Add the following line to the initApp() function:

```
delete_btn.addEventListener(MouseEvent.CLICK, deleteClickHandler);
```

This line adds an event listener that responds when the Delete selected book button is clicked. Add the deleteClickHandler() function now.

```
function deleteClickHandler(e:MouseEvent):void {
  var bookIndex:int = books_dg.selectedIndex;
  var authorIndex:int = authors_cbo.selectedIndex;
  if (bookIndex != -1) {
    books_dg.removeItemAt(bookIndex);
    delete(authorsXML.authors.author[authorIndex].books.book[bookIndex]);
    tree_txt.text = authorsXML.toXMLString();
  }
}
```

This function receives a MouseEvent as an argument. It starts by declaring two variables: one for the index of the selected book, called bookIndex, and one for the index of the selected author, called authorIndex. It populates these variables with the selectedIndex properties from each control.

The function checks to make sure that the user has selected a row in the DataGrid. In this case, the selectedIndex property of the DataGrid will have a value other than -1.

If a row is selected, the function finds the selected book and author indices and uses the removeItemAt() method of the DataGrid. It passes the index of the book to delete, which corresponds to the index of the <book> element in the DataProvider.

Finally, the function uses the delete() ActionScript 3.0 operator to remove the <book> element from the authorsXML object. The code locates the relevant book with an E4X expression that targets the relevant author and book indices. The function finishes by displaying a String representation of the XML object in the TextArea.

14. Test the application. You should be able to select a row in the DataGrid and click the Remove selected row button to remove the row. Check that the book has also been removed from the XML object by looking in the TextArea.

15. The last task is to allow users to modify the values in a row of the DataGrid. They can modify anything except for the bookID. In this case, the application is going to respond when the editing ends, which can be done with a DataGridEvent. You'll need to start by importing this class with the following statement at the top of the Actions panel:

```
import fl.events.DataGridEvent;
```

The application can now use a DataGridEvent in the addEventListener() call. You'll need to add an event listener that responds when the editing of a cell finishes.

Add the next line to the initApp() function:

```
books_dg.addEventListener(DataGridEvent.ITEM_EDIT_END,
  ➥itemEditEndHandler);
```

This line responds to ITEM_EDIT_END, which occurs when the user finishes editing an individual cell. The application will need to check if anything has changed, and if so, process the changes to that value.

Add the handler function itemEditEndHandler() to the actions layer:

```
function itemEditEndHandler(e:DataGridEvent):void {
  var dg:DataGrid = e.target as DataGrid;
  var field:String = e.dataField;
  var row:Number = Number(e.rowIndex);
  var col:int = e.columnIndex;
  var oldVal:String;
  var newVal:String;
  oldVal = e.itemRenderer.data[field];
  newVal = dg.itemEditorInstance[dg.columns[col].editorDataField];
  if (oldVal != newVal) {
    modifyXMLTree(dg.columns[col].dataField, row, newVal)
  }
}
```

This function starts by declaring dg as a DataGrid object and assigning the target of the DataGridEvent to this object. The target property refers to the DataGrid, but notice that the code needed to use an as statement to type it correctly.

The function identifies the dataField being changed using the property e.dataField and assigns it to the variable field. This value is a String. The function also locates the row and column of the edit using the rowIndex and columnIndex properties.

The itemEditHandler() declares variables for the old and changed values so the application can compare the two. It will treat them both as String variables, even if they contain numbers. A String data type is suitable, as all values will be treated as a String in the XML object.

The function finds the original value by looking at the itemRenderer property for the DataGridEvent. This property gets the item renderer for the item being displayed in the cell. The itemRenderer makes available a property called data, which the function can use to find the original value of the field. The function uses the expression e.itemRenderer.data[field]. The field variable created earlier determines the field name to use.

The itemEditEndHandler() function finds the changed value by looking at the itemEditorInstance property of the DataGrid. This property returns a reference to the active item editor after the user starts editing a cell. You can use it to locate changed values in edited cells, as you can see in the line that assigns a value to the newVal variable. The function passes the field name to the expression dg.itemEditorInstance[dg.columns[col]. editorDataField].

Finally, the function compares the original and changed values, and calls the modifyXMLTree() function if these values are different. The application doesn't need to respond if the values are the same, because that means the user hasn't made a change.

You have yet to create the modifyXMLTree() function, but it will receive the name of the dataField, the row being edited, and the newVal variable.

16. You can't test this functionality yet because no modifications are processed. Add the following modifyXMLTree() function:

```
function modifyXMLTree(fieldName:String, elementIndex:int,
    ➥newVal:String):void{
    var newXMLString:String = "<" + fieldName + ">" + newVal +
        ➥"</" + fieldName + ">";
    authorsXML.authors.author[authors_cbo.selectedIndex].
        ➥books.book[elementIndex].replace(fieldName, newXMLString);
    tree_txt.text = authorsXML.toXMLString();
}
```

This function processes the changes to the cell value in the XML object. It starts by creating a new variable that contains an XML String made up of the field name and the new value. The newXMLString variable will contain something in the form of *<fieldName>New value </fieldName>*. The field name can be taken from one of the three columns and can have only the values of bookName, bookPublishYear, or bookCost.

The function then locates the relevant book element, finding which author is selected in the ComboBox and using the row number as the <book> element index. It uses the replace() method to replace the entire existing element with the changed element, passing the String value that it created earlier.

This function finishes by displaying a string representation of the updated XML object in the TextArea.

17. Test the application again. You should be able to change the values in one of the DataGrid cells and see it immediately update in the TextArea. Notice that each time you edit a cell, the updates take place.

That's it for the finished application. If you want to check what you've done, the complete code from the actions layer follows:

```
import fl.data.DataProvider;
import fl.events.DataGridEvent;
var authorsXML:XML;
var authorList:XML;
var booksList:XML;
var request:URLRequest = new URLRequest("authorsAndBooks.xml");
var loader:URLLoader = new URLLoader();
initApp();
stop();
function initApp():void {
  loader.addEventListener(Event.COMPLETE, completeHandler);
  authors_cbo.addEventListener(Event.CHANGE, changeHandler);
  addRow_btn.addEventListener(MouseEvent.CLICK, addClickHandler);
  delete_btn.addEventListener(MouseEvent.CLICK, deleteClickHandler);
  books_dg.addEventListener(DataGridEvent.ITEM_EDIT_END,
    ➥itemEditEndHandler);
  authors_cbo.labelFunction = getFullName;
  loader.load(request);
}
function completeHandler(e:Event):void {
  authorsXML = XML(e.target.data);
  authorList = new XML(authorsXML.authors);
  authors_cbo.dataProvider = new DataProvider(authorList);
  loadBooks(0);
  setupDataGrid();
  tree_txt.text = authorsXML.toXMLString();
}
function itemEditEndHandler(e:DataGridEvent):void {
  var dg:DataGrid = e.target as DataGrid;
  var field:String = e.dataField;
  var row:Number = Number(e.rowIndex);
  var col:int = e.columnIndex;
  var oldVal:String;
  var newVal:String;
  oldVal = e.itemRenderer.data[field];
  newVal = dg.itemEditorInstance[dg.columns[col].editorDataField];
  if (oldVal != newVal) {
    modifyXMLTree(dg.columns[col].dataField, row, newVal);
  }
}
function changeHandler(e:Event):void {
  var authorIndex:int = e.target.selectedIndex;
  loadBooks(authorIndex);
}
```

```
function addClickHandler(e:MouseEvent):void {
  var newBookName:String = name_txt.text;
  var newPublishYear:String = year_txt.text;
  var newBookCost:String = cost_txt.text;
  var newBookXML:XML;
  if(newBookName.length > 0 && newPublishYear.length > 0 &&
    ➥newBookCost.length > 0) {
    books_dg.addItem({bookName: newBookName,
      ➥bookPublishYear: newPublishYear, bookCost: newBookCost});
    newBookXML = <book bookID=''></book>;
    newBookXML.bookName = newBookName;
    newBookXML.bookPublishYear = newPublishYear;
    newBookXML.bookCost = newBookCost;
    authorsXML.authors.author[authors_cbo.selectedIndex].
      ➥books.appendChild(newBookXML);
    tree_txt.text = authorsXML.toXMLString();
  }
}
function deleteClickHandler(e:MouseEvent):void {
  var bookIndex:int = books_dg.selectedIndex;
  var authorIndex:int = authors_cbo.selectedIndex;
  if (bookIndex != -1) {
    books_dg.removeItemAt(bookIndex);
    delete(authorsXML.authors.author[authorIndex].books.
      ➥book[bookIndex]);
    tree_txt.text = authorsXML.toXMLString();
  }
}
function getFullName(item:Object):String{
  return item.authorFirstName + " " + item.authorLastName;
}
function loadBooks(authorIndex:int):void {
  var booksDP:DataProvider;
  booksList = new XML(authorsXML.authors.author[authorIndex].books);
  booksDP = new DataProvider(booksList);
  books_dg.dataProvider = booksDP;
}
function setupDataGrid():void {
  books_dg.columns = ["ID", "Name", "Publish year", "Cost"];
  books_dg.columns[0].width = 50;
  books_dg.columns[1].width = 200;
  books_dg.columns[2].width = 50;
  books_dg.columns[3].width = 50;
  books_dg.columns[0].dataField = "bookID";
  books_dg.columns[1].dataField = "bookName";
  books_dg.columns[2].dataField = "bookPublishYear";
  books_dg.columns[3].dataField = "bookCost";
  books_dg.columns[0].editable = false;
}
```

```
function modifyXMLTree(fieldName:String, elementIndex:int,
    ➥newVal:String):void{
    var newXMLString:String = "<" + fieldName + ">" + newVal +
        ➥"</" + fieldName + ">";
    authorsXML.authors.author[authors_cbo.selectedIndex].
        ➥books.book[elementIndex].replace(fieldName, newXMLString);
    tree_txt.text = authorsXML.toXMLString();
}
```

You can find the completed file saved as authorBookEditor_completed.fla with the chapter resources.

Working in Flex

Let's see how you might work through the same example in Flex Builder. In this case, the application will use a class-based approach.

1. Open the starter file AuthorBookEditor.mxml in Flex Builder. You can copy the file and paste it into your existing Flex project. The interface for the application, shown in Design view of Flex Builder, appears in Figure 8-6.

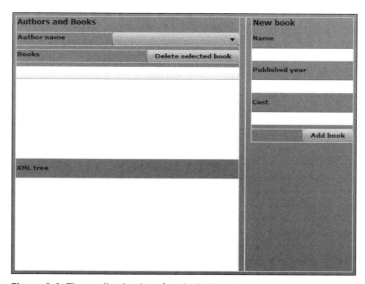

Figure 8-6. The application interface in Design view

As with the Flash version of this example, you'll populate the ComboBox with a list of authors from the external XML document. When an author is selected, the application will show the books for that author in the DataGrid component beneath the author name. It will show a String representation of the XML object in the TextArea at the bottom of the interface. To the right, TextInput controls allow a user to enter new book details.

2. If you're using a new Flex project, create an assets folder inside the src folder of the project. Copy the authorsAndBooks.xml file to this folder. The file contains the details of the authors and their books.

3. You'll load the XML document with the MyXMLLoaderHelper class that you created in Chapter 5. The class exists in the xmlUtilities package, so add a folder of that name to your Flex project. Copy the file MyXMLLoaderHelper.as from the chapter resources to the xmlUtilities folder. You can also use the version that you created yourself in Chapter 5.

This class file handles the loading of the external XML file. It also returns a specified child element from the XML object. However, you'll need to modify the class file to add a little more functionality for this example.

4. Because the XML file that you're loading is complicated, you're going to define the <authors> element from the external file as its own XML object. This approach will allow you to work with just that part of the XML document and make it easier to locate the <books> element for each author.

Add two new private variable declarations with the other declarations:

```
private var xmlRootString:String;
private var xmlRoot:XML;
```

The first variable will store the name of the element to use as the new XML object root. In this case, the new XML object xmlRoot will store the <authors> element information with all of its child elements.

The application will pass in an additional parameter to the loadXML() method to specify the child element to use for the new XML object root. Modify the function as shown in bold here. It will assign the new parameter to the xmlRootString variable.

```
public function loadXML(xmlFile:String, rootElement:String):void {
  xmlRootString = rootElement;
  try {
    xmlLoader.load(new URLRequest(xmlFile));
  }
  catch (e:Error) {
    trace ("Can't load external XML document");
  }
}
```

You also need to modify the completeHandler() private method as shown in bold:

```
private function completeHandler(e:Event):void {
  xmlAllContent = XML(e.target.data);
  xmlRoot = XML(xmlAllContent.child(xmlRootString));
  dispatchEvent(new Event(Event.COMPLETE));
}
```

The new line assigns the XML content from the specified child element to the xmlRoot object. Because the child() method actually returns an XMLList object, the code needs to cast it as an XML object so there isn't a type mismatch.

The class file needs a new public method to return the XML object to the calling application. Add the following getXML() method:

```
public function getXML():XML {
  return xmlAllContent;
}
```

The final change to the class file is to modify the getChildElements() public method to find a child of the xmlRoot object instead of the xmlAllContent element. Change the first line as shown here in bold:

```
childElements = xmlRoot.child(elementName);
```

The complete class file follows in case you want to check that you've included all of the changes correctly:

```
package xmlUtilities {
  import flash.net.URLLoader;
  import flash.net.URLRequest;
  import mx.collections.XMLListCollection;
  [Bindable]
  public class MyXMLLoaderHelper {
    private var xmlAllContent:XML;
    private var xmlLoader:URLLoader;
    private var xmlRootString:String;
    private var xmlRoot:XML;
    private var childElements:XMLList;
    private var childElementsCollection: XMLListCollection;
    public function MyXMLLoaderHelper() {
      xmlLoader = new URLLoader();
      xmlLoader.addEventListener(Event.COMPLETE, completeHandler);
    }
    public function loadXML(xmlFile:String,
      ➥rootElement:String):void {
      xmlRootString = rootElement;
      try {
        xmlLoader.load(new URLRequest(xmlFile));
      }
      catch (e:Error) {
        trace ("Can't load external XML document");
      }
    }
    public function getXML():XML {
      return xmlAllContent;
    }
    public function getChildElements(elementName:String):
      ➥XMLListCollection {
      childElements = xmlRoot.child(elementName);
      childElementsCollection = new XMLListCollection(childElements);
      return childElementsCollection;
    }
```

```
    private function completeHandler(e:Event):void {
      xmlAllContent = XML(e.target.data);
      xmlRoot = XML(xmlAllContent.child(xmlRootString));
      dispatchEvent(new Event(Event.COMPLETE));
    }
  }
}
```

You'll make further changes to this class as part of building this example, so leave the file open in Flex Builder.

5. You need to initialize the application and call the loadXML() method of our custom class to load the external document into the application. Switch to the AuthorBookEditor.mxml file and add the following code, including the initApp() function, to an <mx:Script> block at the top of the file:

```
import mx.collections.XMLListCollection;
import xmlUtilities.MyXMLLoaderHelper;
import mx.events.FlexEvent;
private var myXMLLoader:MyXMLLoaderHelper;
private function initApp(e:FlexEvent):void {
  myXMLLoader = new MyXMLLoaderHelper();
  myXMLLoader.addEventListener(Event.COMPLETE, completeHandler);
  myXMLLoader.loadXML("assets/authorsAndBooks.xml", "authors");
}
private function completeHandler(e:Event):void {
}
```

This code starts by importing the classes that the application needs, including the XMLListCollection, the custom class MyXMLLoaderHelper, and the FlexEvent class. The XMLListCollection wrapper class will work with XMLListCollection objects returned from the custom class. As you saw earlier in the book, this class provides additional functionality to an XMLList object and is suitable as a DataProvider for list-based components.

The code block then declares a private variable, myXMLLoader, which is an instance of the custom class. The code block includes the initApp() function, which creates a new instance of the MyXMLLoaderHelper class and assigns an event listener to respond to the complete event.

The function also calls the loadXML() method of the custom class, passing the external XML document file name and target element name.

I've included the function signature for the completeHandler() function without any code. You'll need to call this function in the creationComplete attribute of the <mx:Application> element as shown in bold in the following code, so make the change in your own file.

```
<mx:Application xmlns:mx="http://www.adobe.com/2006/mxml"
  layout="absolute" creationComplete="initApp(event)">
```

6. You'll modify the completeHandler() function to display the author names in the ComboBox control. The code will call the getChildElements() method of the custom class to return an XMLListCollection containing all of the <author> elements. It will assign this object as the dataProvider property for the ComboBox.

263

The completeHandler() function will also populate the TextArea with a String representation of the loaded XML object. The application will use this TextArea control to keep track of the current contents of the XML object.

Add the following lines to the completeHandler() function:

```
authors_cbo.dataProvider = myXMLLoader.getChildElements("author");
tree_txt.text = myXMLLoader.getXML().toXMLString();
```

The first line sets the dataProvider property of the ComboBox to the XMLListCollection returned by the getChildElements() method of the myXMLLoader class.

As the full name doesn't appear in a single element in the dataProvider, the application will need to use a labelFunction in the ComboBox control to display this value. You've seen this function earlier in the book. Add it to the <mx:Script> block.

```
private function getFullName(item:Object):String {
  return item.authorFirstName + " " + item.authorLastName;
}
```

The function joins the author's first and last names with a space in between to create a full name.

You also need to assign the getFullName() function to the ComboBox so it knows how to create the label. Modify the initApp() function as shown here in bold to assign it as the labelFunction property.

```
private function initApp(e:FlexEvent):void {
  myXMLLoader = new MyXMLLoaderHelper();
  myXMLLoader.addEventListener(Event.COMPLETE, completeHandler);
  authors_cbo.labelFunction = getFullName;
  myXMLLoader.loadXML("assets/authorsAndBooks.xml", "authors");
}
```

7. Test the movie and check that the ComboBox populates correctly with the full name of each author. Figure 8-7 shows how the interface should appear if you run the application and view it in a web browser.

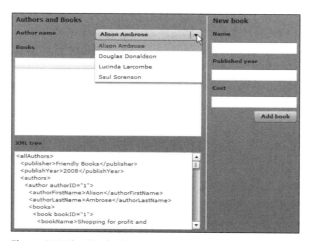

Figure 8-7. The ComboBox populates from the external XML document.

8. Now it's time to load the books for the author selected in the ComboBox. When the application first loads, it should show the books for the first author.

The class file needs a public method that returns the <books> element for the selected author. Switch to the custom class file and add the following getBooks() public method:

```
public function getBooks(authorIndex:int):XMLListCollection {
   bookElements = xmlAllContent.authors.author[authorIndex].books.book;
   bookElementsCollection = new XMLListCollection(bookElements);
   return bookElementsCollection;
}
```

This method takes as its only argument the selected author index from the ComboBox. This value equates to the index of the <author> element in the XML object.

The method creates an XMLList called bookElements from the list of all <book> elements for the current author. It does this using the E4X expression xmlAllContent.authors. author[authorIndex].books.book. The getBooks() method then creates an XMLListCollection from this XMLList object and returns it to be used as the dataProvider property for the DataGrid.

9. The application file calls this public method in two places. First, it calls the method after the ComboBox is loaded so the application can display the first author's books. It also calls the method in response to a change in the selectedIndex of the ComboBox so that the application can repopulate the DataGrid with the correct books.

Switch to the application file and add the following line to the completeHandler() function:

```
books_dg.dataProvider = myXMLLoader.getBooks(0);
```

This line calls the getBooks() public method when the application initializes, passing the first author index of 0. It sets the returned XMLListCollection as the dataProvider for the DataGrid, showing the books for the first author whose name displays in the ComboBox.

For the second method call, add the following line to the initApp() function:

```
authors_cbo.addEventListener(ListEvent.CHANGE, changeHandler);
```

Whenever the author chosen in the ComboBox changes, the application will call the changeHandler() function.

Now, you need to add the changeHandler() function. Add the following code block to your application file:

```
private function changeHandler(e:Event):void {
   books_dg.dataProvider = myXMLLoader.getBooks(e.target.
     ➥selectedIndex);
}
```

The changeHandler() function again sets the dataProvider property for the DataGrid by calling the getBooks() public method of the myXMLLoader object. This time, it passes the selectedIndex from the ComboBox to specify which <author> element to target. It finds the correct author using e.target.selectedIndex.

10. You need to set up the DataGrid to display the columns correctly before testing the application. If you tested the application now, you would see only the bookID displayed in the DataGrid; the remaining information wouldn't appear.

The easiest way to modify the setup of the DataGrid is within the MXML element itself. Modify the element as shown here. Notice that you need to rewrite the <mx:DataGrid> element with a closing tag.

```
<mx:DataGrid width="350" height="150" id="books_dg" editable="true">
  <mx:columns>
    <mx:DataGridColumn headerText="ID" dataField="@bookID"
      editable="false" width="50"/>
    <mx:DataGridColumn headerText="Name" dataField="bookName"
      width="200"/>
    <mx:DataGridColumn headerText="Publish year"
      dataField="bookPublishYear" width="50"/>
    <mx:DataGridColumn headerText="Cost" dataField="bookCost"
      width="50"/>
  </mx:columns>
</mx:DataGrid>
```

The <mx:DataGrid> element includes the list of all columns to display inside the <mx:columns> element. Each column contains a headerText, dataField, and width attribute. The dataField determines which element to display from the dataProvider, and the value equates to the name of a child element. Notice that the expression uses an @ sign to indicate that bookID is an attribute.

The first <mx:DataGridColum> element also sets the first column to be read-only so that the user can't edit the bookID value. Normally, this value would equate to the primary key in the data source and would be maintained externally. Because the <mx:DataGrid> element contains the attribute editable="true", it will be possible for a user to edit all other columns.

11. Test the application again. You should see the book information displaying correctly in the DataGrid, as shown in Figure 8-8.

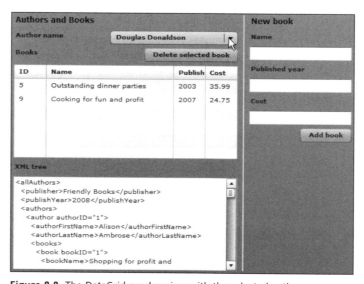

Figure 8-8. The DataGrid synchronizes with the selected author.

Now that the interface is set up, it's time to look at adding, editing, and deleting book information. Remember that the application will change only the XML object in the SWF application, and not in the external document, as Flex isn't capable of updating external content.

When you finish building this application, the class file will contain public methods that add, edit, and delete <book> elements from the XML object. The application file will call these methods to process the updates made in the interface. Before it continues, it will need to know that the updates have been completed. Each of the public methods must dispatch an event to the application, notifying it that this has occurred.

After the application receives this event, it can refresh the dataProvider for the DataGrid and display the updated XML object in the TextArea control. This process must occur with every type of modification made in the interface.

12. You'll create a new event in the class file to be dispatched when changes have been completed. This event is called xmlUpdated, and you'll create a handler function in the application file to respond when it is notified of the event.

Switch to the custom class file MyXMLLoaderHelper.as. Declare the event by adding the following [Event] metadata tag above the class declaration:

```
[Event(name="xmlUpdated", type="flash.events.Event")]
```

This is an event called xmlUpdated with an Event type. In this case, the application doesn't need a custom Event object, because you're not passing information with the event. The metadata tag needs to declare this event so that the application file will recognize it correctly.

13. Switch to the application file and add a handler for this new event in the initApp() function, as shown here:

```
myXMLLoader.addEventListener("xmlUpdated", xmlUpdatedHandler);
```

Whenever the application file is notified of the xmlUpdated event, it will call the xmlUpdatedHandler() function. Add the xmlUpdatedHandler() function that follows to the <mx:Script> block:

```
private function xmlUpdatedHandler(e:Event):void {
  books_dg.dataProvider = myXMLLoader.getBooks(
    ➡authors_cbo.selectedIndex);
  tree_txt.text = myXMLLoader.getXML().toXMLString();
}
```

This handler function sets the dataProvider property for the books_dg control, which effectively refreshes the content in the DataGrid. It also displays a String representation of the XML object in the TextArea component so that you can see the updated content. You'll want to repeat these steps every time a user changes book details.

14. Now it's time to add more functionality so that a user can make modifications to the books. You'll start by seeing how to add a new book to the currently selected author.

You need an event handler that responds when a user clicks the Add book button. Add the following line to the initApp() function:

```
addRow_btn.addEventListener(MouseEvent.CLICK, addClickHandler);
```

You also need to add the addClickHandler() function to the <mx:Script> block. The function follows. Note that it references a public method of a custom class, addBook(), that you have yet to create.

```
private function addClickHandler(e:MouseEvent):void {
  var newBookName:String = name_txt.text;
  var newPublishYear:String = year_txt.text;
  var newBookCost:String = cost_txt.text;
  var authorIndex:int = authors_cbo.selectedIndex;
  if(newBookName.length > 0 && newPublishYear.length > 0
    ➥&& newBookCost.length > 0) {
    myXMLLoader.addBook(authorIndex, newBookName, newPublishYear,
      ➥newBookCost);
  }
}
```

The addClickHandler() function receives a MouseEvent as an argument. The function declares variables for each of the user entries and checks that the user entered a value for each one. If this is the case, the function calls the addBook() method of the myXMLLoader instance, passing the selected author index as well as the new values. You'll set up this public method next.

I didn't add any functionality to deal with the situation where a user doesn't enter all of the information for a book and then clicks the button. Feel free to extend this example to display an error message in the interface when this occurs.

15. Switch to the MyXMLLoaderHelper class file. Add the following addBook() public method to process the new book details:

```
public function addBook(authorIndex:int, bookName:String,
  ➥bookPublishYear:String, bookCost:String):void {
  var newBookXML:XML;
  newBookXML = <book bookID=''></book>;
  newBookXML.bookName = bookName;
  newBookXML.bookPublishYear = bookPublishYear;
  newBookXML.bookCost = bookCost;
  xmlAllContent.authors.author[authorIndex].books.
    ➥appendChild(newBookXML);
  dispatchEvent(new Event("xmlUpdated"));
}
```

This method receives the selectedIndex from the ComboBox and the new book values as parameters. The selectedIndex is called authorIndex, and this value corresponds with the node index for the <author> element in the XML object.

The addBook() method declares a new local XML object called newBookXML and populates it with a <book> element containing an empty bookID attribute. It then adds the bookName, bookPublishYear, and bookCost properties to this object. Notice that, instead of using appendChild(), you've used dot notation to speed up the process.

This method finishes by using the appendChild() method to add the newly created <book> element as the last child of the current author's <books> element. In the last line, the method finishes by dispatching an xmlUpdated event to inform the application that the updating of the XML object is complete. The application will then respond by calling the xmlUpdatedHandler() function.

16. Test the application and enter a new book. The application should add the new book to the selected author, updating both the DataGrid and TextArea. Figure 8-9 shows a new book added to the author Douglas Donaldson. It appears in both the XML tree in the TextArea and as a new row at the bottom of the DataGrid.

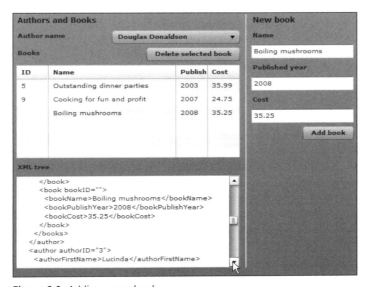

Figure 8-9. Adding a new book

17. You'll now add functionality so that a user can delete a book from the DataGrid and XML object. By selecting a row and clicking the Delete selected book button, a user can remove a book. Start by adding an event listener to respond when the Delete selected book button is clicked.

Add the following line to the initApp() function in the MXML file:

```
delete_btn.addEventListener(MouseEvent.CLICK, deleteClickHandler);
```

Add the following deleteClickHandler() function to the <mx:Script> block. This method calls a deleteBook() public method from the class file that you'll add shortly.

```
private function deleteClickHandler(e:MouseEvent):void {
  var bookIndex:int = books_dg.selectedIndex;
  var authorIndex:int = authors_cbo.selectedIndex;;
  if (books_dg.selectedIndex != -1) {
    myXMLLoader.deleteBook(authorIndex, bookIndex);
  }
}
```

The deleteClickHandler() function receives a MouseEvent as an argument and declares two variables: one for the selected DataGrid row index, called bookIndex, and one for the selected author index, called authorIndex. It assigns values for these variables.

The function then checks that the user has selected a row in the DataGrid. If no row is selected, the selectedIndex will have a value of -1.

The function finishes by calling the deleteBook() public method of the myXMLLoader object to carry out the deletion. It passes both the authorIndex and bookIndex so that the public method will be able to locate the correct element.

18. Switch to the MyXMLLoaderHelper class file. Add the following deleteBook() public method to handle the book deletion:

```
public function deleteBook(authorIndex:int, bookIndex:int):void {
  delete(xmlAllContent.authors.author[authorIndex].books.
    ➥book[bookIndex]);
  dispatchEvent(new Event("xmlUpdated"));
}
```

This public method uses the ActionScript 3.0 delete() operator to remove the relevant <book> element. It locates the correct element with the E4X expression xmlAllContent.authors. author[authorIndex].books.book[bookIndex]. The method then dispatches the xmlUpdated event to notify the application that the updates are finished.

19. Test the application and make sure that you can remove a row from the DataGrid. If you look at the TextArea control, you should see that the element has been removed from the XML object as well.

20. The final task is to allow the user to edit entries in the DataGrid. A user will be able to modify any value except for the bookID. As I've noted, that value is usually allocated by the external data source.

As with the Flash example, the application will handle when the editing of an individual cell ends by responding to a DataGridEvent. The updating will happen immediately after each cell has been edited.

Switch to the application file. Import the DataGridEvent class with the following import statement. Add it with the other import statements at the top of the <mx:Script> block.

```
import mx.events.DataGridEvent;
```

Add the following event listener to the initApp() function:

```
books_dg.addEventListener(DataGridEvent.ITEM_EDIT_END,
  ➥itemEditEndHandler);
```

The application responds when the user finishes editing a cell by referencing ITEM_EDIT_END. This value indicates that the editing of a cell is ending, and it will allow the application to capture both the starting and ending values.

Add the following itemEditEndHandler() function to process the changes to the cell value:

```
function itemEditEndHandler(e:DataGridEvent):void {
  var authorIndex:int = authors_cbo.selectedIndex;
  var dg:DataGrid = e.target as DataGrid;
  var field:String = e.dataField;
  var row:Number = Number(e.rowIndex);
  var col:int = e.columnIndex;
  var oldVal:String = e.itemRenderer.data[field];
  var newVal:String = dg.itemEditorInstance[dg.columns[col].
    ➥editorDataField];
  if (oldVal != newVal) {
    myXMLLoader.modifyXMLTree(authorIndex,
      ➥dg.columns[col].dataField, row, newVal);
  }
}
```

This function calls a public method, modifyXMLTree(), which you have yet to add to the class file. It starts by declaring an object for the DataGrid and locating it with the expression e.target. The code uses as to type the object correctly as a DataGrid.

The function identifies the dataField being modified as well as the row and column being changed. It also declares variables for the original and changed values so that they can be compared to see if a change actually took place.

If the values are not the same—that is, something has been modified—the itemEditEndHandler() function calls the modifyXMLTree() public method of the myXMLLoader object. It passes the name of the field being edited; the row number in the DataGrid, which will equate to the <book> node index; and the new value entered by the user.

21. Switch to the class file and add the modifyXMLTree() method shown here:

```
public function modifyXMLTree(authorIndex:int, fieldName:String,
  ➥elementIndex:int, newVal:String):void{
  var newXMLString:String = "<" + fieldName + ">" + newVal +
    ➥"</" + fieldName + ">";
  xmlAllContent.authors.author[authorIndex].books.book[elementIndex].
    ➥replace(fieldName, newXMLString);
  dispatchEvent(new Event("xmlUpdated"));
}
```

This public method creates a new String variable that contains the changed value, formatted as an XML element. It uses the fieldName value passed from the MXML file for the element name. It will produce a variable containing the structure *<fieldName>New value</fieldName>*.

The modifyXMLTree() method then uses an E4X expression to locate the relevant <book> element being edited. In the expression xmlAllContent.authors.author[authorIndex]. books.book[elementIndex], the authorIndex indicates which <author> element to target; the elementIndex indicates the <book> index to use. The function uses the replace() method to update the existing element and replace it with the provide String content. Finally, the function dispatches the xmlUpdated event so that the application can refresh the interface.

22. Test the application and check that you can edit the name, publish year, and cost of each item. Also make sure that the contents of the TextArea control are updated with each of your changes.

271

Congratulations! You've now completed the Flex application. The complete MyXMLLoaderHelper.as class file follows so you can check your work. The file is also included with the chapter resources.

```actionscript
package xmlUtilities {
  import flash.events.Event;
  import flash.net.URLLoader;
  import flash.net.URLRequest;
  import mx.collections.XMLListCollection;
  [Bindable]
  [Event(name="xmlUpdated", type="flash.events.Event")]
  public class MyXMLLoaderHelper {
    private var xmlAllContent:XML;
    private var xmlLoader:URLLoader;
    private var xmlRootString:String;
    private var xmlRoot:XML;
    private var childElements:XMLList;
    private var childElementsCollection: XMLListCollection;
    private var bookElements:XMLList;
    private var bookElementsCollection:XMLListCollection;
    public function MyXMLLoaderHelper() {
      xmlLoader = new URLLoader();
      xmlLoader.addEventListener(Event.COMPLETE, completeHandler);
    }
    public function loadXML(xmlFile:String, rootElement:String):void{
      xmlRootString = rootElement;
      try {
        xmlLoader.load(new URLRequest(xmlFile));
      }
      catch (e:Error) {
        trace ("Can't load external XML document");
      }
    }
    public function getXML():XML {
      return xmlAllContent;
    }
    public function getChildElements(elementName:String):
      ➡XMLListCollection {
      childElements = xmlRoot.child(elementName);
      childElementsCollection = new XMLListCollection(childElements);
      return childElementsCollection;
    }
    public function getBooks(authorIndex:int):XMLListCollection {
      bookElements = xmlAllContent.authors.author[authorIndex].
        ➡books.book;
      bookElementsCollection = new XMLListCollection(bookElements);
      return bookElementsCollection;
    }
```

```
      public function addBook(authorIndex:int, bookName:String,
        ➥bookPublishYear:String, bookCost:String):void {
        var newBookXML:XML;
        newBookXML = <book bookID=''></book>;
        newBookXML.bookName = bookName;
        newBookXML.bookPublishYear = bookPublishYear;
        newBookXML.bookCost = bookCost;
        xmlAllContent.authors.author[authorIndex].books.
          ➥appendChild(newBookXML);
        dispatchEvent(new Event("xmlUpdated"));
      }
      public function deleteBook(authorIndex:int, bookIndex:int):void {
        delete(xmlAllContent.authors.author[authorIndex].
          ➥books.book[bookIndex]);
        dispatchEvent(new Event("xmlUpdated"));
      }
      public function modifyXMLTree(authorIndex:int, fieldName:String,
        ➥elementIndex:int, newVal:String):void{
        var newXMLString:String = "<" + fieldName + ">" + newVal +
          ➥"</" + fieldName + ">";
        xmlAllContent.authors.author[authorIndex].books.
          ➥book[elementIndex].replace(fieldName, newXMLString);
        dispatchEvent(new Event("xmlUpdated"));
      }
    }
    private function completeHandler(e:Event):void {
      xmlAllContent = XML(e.target.data);
      xmlRoot = XML(xmlAllContent.child(xmlRootString));
      dispatchEvent(new Event(Event.COMPLETE));
    }
  }
}
```

The complete application file follows. It is also saved as AuthorBookEditor_completed.mxml with the chapter resources.

```
<?xml version="1.0" encoding="utf-8"?>
<mx:Application xmlns:mx="http://www.adobe.com/2006/mxml"
  layout="absolute" creationComplete="initApp(event)">
  <mx:Script>
    <![CDATA[
      import mx.events.ListEvent;
      import mx.collections.XMLListCollection;
      import xmlUtilities.MyXMLLoaderHelper;
      import mx.events.FlexEvent;
      import mx.events.DataGridEvent;
      private var myXMLLoader:MyXMLLoaderHelper;
```

```
                    private function initApp(e:FlexEvent):void {
                      myXMLLoader = new MyXMLLoaderHelper();
                      myXMLLoader.addEventListener(Event.COMPLETE,completeHandler);
                      myXMLLoader.addEventListener("xmlUpdated",xmlUpdatedHandler);
                      authors_cbo.addEventListener(ListEvent.CHANGE,changeHandler);
                      addRow_btn.addEventListener(MouseEvent.CLICK,
                        ➥addClickHandler);
                      delete_btn.addEventListener(MouseEvent.CLICK,
                        ➥deleteClickHandler);
                      books_dg.addEventListener(DataGridEvent.ITEM_EDIT_END,
                        ➥itemEditEndHandler);
                      authors_cbo.labelFunction = getFullName;
                      myXMLLoader.loadXML("assets/authorsAndBooks.xml", "authors");
                    }
                    private function completeHandler(e:Event):void {
                      authors_cbo.dataProvider =
                        ➥myXMLLoader.getChildElements("author");
                      tree_txt.text = myXMLLoader.getXML().toXMLString();
                      books_dg.dataProvider = myXMLLoader.getBooks(0);
                    }
                    private function getFullName(item:Object):String {
                      return item.authorFirstName + " " + item.authorLastName;
                    }
                    private function changeHandler(e:Event):void {
                      books_dg.dataProvider = myXMLLoader.getBooks(
                        ➥e.target.selectedIndex);
                    }
                    private function addClickHandler(e:MouseEvent):void {
                      var newBookName:String = name_txt.text;
                      var newPublishYear:String = year_txt.text;
                      var newBookCost:String = cost_txt.text;
                      var authorIndex:int = authors_cbo.selectedIndex;
                      if(newBookName.length > 0 && newPublishYear.length > 0
                        ➥&& newBookCost.length > 0) {
                        myXMLLoader.addBook(authorIndex, newBookName,
                          ➥newPublishYear, newBookCost);
                      }
                    }
                    private function deleteClickHandler(e:MouseEvent):void {
                      var bookIndex:int = books_dg.selectedIndex;
                      var authorIndex:int = authors_cbo.selectedIndex;;
                      if (books_dg.selectedIndex != -1) {
                        myXMLLoader.deleteBook(authorIndex, bookIndex);
                      }
                    }
```

```
    private function itemEditEndHandler(e:DataGridEvent):void {
      var authorIndex:int = authors_cbo.selectedIndex;
      var dg:DataGrid = e.target as DataGrid;
      var field:String = e.dataField;
      var row:int = e.rowIndex;
      var col:int = e.columnIndex;
      var oldVal:String = e.itemRenderer.data[field];
      var newVal:String = dg.itemEditorInstance[dg.columns[col].
        ➥editorDataField];
      if (oldVal != newVal) {
        myXMLLoader.modifyXMLTree(authorIndex, dg.columns[col].
          ➥dataField, row, newVal)
      }
    }
    private function xmlUpdatedHandler(e:Event):void {
      books_dg.dataProvider = myXMLLoader.getBooks(authors_cbo.
        ➥selectedIndex);
        tree_txt.text = myXMLLoader.getXML().toXMLString();
    }

  ]]>
</mx:Script>
<mx:HBox x="10" y="10">
  <mx:VBox>
    <mx:Label text="Authors and Books" fontWeight="bold"
      fontSize="12"/>
    <mx:HBox width="100%">
      <mx:Label fontWeight="bold" text="Author name"/>
      <mx:Spacer width="100%"/>
      <mx:ComboBox width="200" id="authors_cbo"/>
    </mx:HBox>
    <mx:HBox width="100%">
      <mx:Label fontWeight="bold" text="Books"/>
      <mx:Spacer width="100%"/>
      <mx:Button label="Delete selected book" id="delete_btn"/>
    </mx:HBox>
    <mx:DataGrid width="350" height="150" id="books_dg"
      editable="true">
      <mx:columns>
        <mx:DataGridColumn headerText="ID" dataField="@bookID"
          editable="false" width="50"/>
        <mx:DataGridColumn headerText="Name" dataField="bookName"
          width="200"/>
        <mx:DataGridColumn headerText="Publish year"
          dataField="bookPublishYear" width="50"/>
        <mx:DataGridColumn headerText="Cost" dataField="bookCost"
          width="50"/>
      </mx:columns>
    </mx:DataGrid>
```

275

```
      <mx:Label fontWeight="bold" text="XML tree"/>
      <mx:TextArea width="350" height="150" id="tree_txt"/>
    </mx:VBox>
    <mx:VRule height="100%"/>
    <mx:VBox>
      <mx:Label text="New book" fontWeight="bold" fontSize="12"/>
      <mx:Label text="Name" fontWeight="bold"/>
      <mx:TextInput id="name_txt"/>
      <mx:Label text="Published year" fontWeight="bold"/>
      <mx:TextInput id="year_txt"/>
      <mx:Label text="Cost" fontWeight="bold"/>
      <mx:TextInput id="cost_txt"/>
      <mx:HBox width="100%">
        <mx:Spacer width="100%"/>
        <mx:Button label="Add book" id="addRow_btn"/>
      </mx:HBox>
    </mx:VBox>
  </mx:HBox>
</mx:Application>
```

Before we finish, there are some points to consider from these examples.

Points to note about the example

There are several points to note about these exercises:

- The example changes only the structure and content of the XML object within the SWF application. It doesn't update the external file. Neither Flash nor Flex has the ability to update external content for obvious security reasons. You would need some server-side code to carry out the updates. You'll see how to communicate with the server in the next chapter.

- In both versions of the application, if a user clicked a button inappropriately, we didn't display an error message. As an exercise, you might want to add this functionality to the application.

- There is no validation of the new or changed entries made by the user. In a real-world application, you would handle the user entries a little more robustly. For example, you would check that the new value entered in the year field was an appropriate number. You would also check that the price was a numeric value, and format it to display as a String with two decimal places. I'll leave those niceties up to you as an area for self-study.

- There are other ways that you could have created the Flex application. Flex provides data binding opportunities that may have made it easier to keep the XML object synchronized with a DataGrid dataProvider and a TextArea control. However, the aim of this exercise was to show you how to modify XML content within Flex, so that's what we did! Feel free to tackle the job of modifying the example yourself if you wish.

Summary

In this chapter, I've shown you how to update the contents of an XML object. You've seen how to add, edit, and delete XML content, as well as how to modify element names and namespaces. We worked through an example that demonstrated how you might modify an XML tree with ActionScript 3.0. You saw how to do so in Flash and Flex, using both a procedural and class-based approach.

While it was possible to update the content within the SWF application, your updates didn't affect the external content. You would need the SWF application to communicate with the server where the updates would be processed. Communicating with the server is the topic of the next chapter.

Chapter 9

COMMUNICATING WITH THE SERVER

So far in this book, you've seen how to work with XML content in both Flash and Flex. We started by examining the new XML class. We've loaded external static XML documents and learned how to use a SWF application to make modifications to an XML object.

In this chapter, we'll focus on the interaction between the SWF and server-side files. The server-side logic is provided by an application server and a server-side language like PHP, VB .NET, or ColdFusion. The SWF application needs to request a page written in one of these languages and send variables for processing. The variables may be sent so that the server-side page can update the data source. They may also be sent so that the server-side page can do some processing and send a response.

The examples in this chapter won't use Flash or Flex to update an external source of data. Instead, you'll see how to send variables that are processed by a server-side page using the URLLoader class in Flash and Flex applications. You'll also see how a SWF application can receive a response and incorporate that in the Flash or Flex application. Additionally, we'll cover how to use the <mx:HTTPService> tag and HTTPService class in Flex applications to send variables to a server-side page and incorporate the server response in the application.

We'll work through several examples to demonstrate how you can achieve these aims. These examples use VB .NET, but I've provided alternative copies of the file written in PHP and ColdFusion, if you prefer working in those languages.

As always, you can find the examples for this chapter at http://www.friendsofed. com. You'll need to work with an application server to complete the examples. This could be the .NET Framework, or an Apache or ColdFusion server.

You can run the examples on your own computer or copy the finished code to a public web server. I won't go through how to set up an application server on your local machine, so you'll need to work through that process yourself.

Don't forget that loading external data in still governed by the Flash Player security rules. Basically, you can't load data from a different domain without some type of intervention. If you want to find out more about these rules, see the section about Flash Player 10 security in Chapter 5.

Let's get started with an overview of the process. This way, you will understand what's really happening when you exchange data between a web browser and application server.

Sending data to the server

For security reasons, you can't use Flex to carry out server-based tasks such as sending e-mail, deleting or modifying files, or updating databases. However, both a Flash and Flex application can send variables to an application server so that it can carry out the processing on behalf of the SWF application.

A SWF application might send variables to filter the results of a database query or have the variables processed by the server-side file in some way. Processing could include generating an e-mail from the values entered into the SWF file or saving them to a text file. The SWF application may also be sending values that need to be updated in a database or a static XML document.

The URLLoader class provides a mechanism for sending variables when the application requests a server-side page. This class is available to all SWF applications, whether they are created in Flash or Flex. The <mx:HTTPService> tag and HTTPService class achieve the same result and are both available to SWF applications created in Flex. In this chapter, you'll see how to use all of these approaches to send content from a SWF file to be processed by a server-side file.

Before we see the ActionScript code that you'll need to use, we need to cover the following areas:

- How to structure the path to the server-side file
- How to choose an HTTP method to use to send the variables
- How to choose a content type for the variables being sent

We'll cover each of these areas in turn, starting with creating the path to the server-side file.

Structuring the file path

One of the most important points to remember is that when you specify the URL for the <mx:HTTPService> element, HTTPService class, or URLLoader class, you must make sure that you include the full server path. Instead of writing just the file name, you need to include the address of the web server, starting with the http:// portion, as shown here:

```
http://localhost/FlexApp/login.apx
```

This path is necessary so that the application server knows that it is dealing with a file containing server-side code. Without the full path, the web server won't know to process server-side code in the page, and will treat it as a text file.

In the case of a `URLLoader` object, you might structure the code to work with the full path as follows:

```
var serverPage:String = "http://localhost/FlexApp/login.apx";
var request:URLRequest = new URLRequest(serverPage);
```

This example references the application server using `http://localhost`. This path is very common when working with an application server installed on a local desktop computer. The `FlexApp` part of the path in the code sample usually corresponds to the name of the folder containing your application files. In this example, the application files live in a folder called `FlexApp` on the local machine.

When you move the application to its production environment, the URL will usually change to the domain name associated with the site. You don't usually include the folder name for the files on the web server. A production URL might look like the following:

```
http://www.foe.com/login.apx
```

The code used by the `URLLoader` object in this case might look like this:

```
var serverPage:String = "http://www.foe.com/login.apx";
var request:URLRequest = new URLRequest(serverPage);
```

Because you need to switch the path when moving to a development environment, it's good practice to set a variable that specifies this path. You can then refer to this variable throughout your application. You can see how you might take this approach with the `URLLoader` class in the following code block:

```
var serverPath:String = "http://localhost/FlexApp/";
var serverPage:String = serverPath + "login.apx";
var request:URLRequest = new URLRequest(serverPage);
```

When you need to move the site to its production environment, you can change the value of the `serverPath` variable to update the application.

```
var serverPath:String = "http://www.friendsofed.com/";
var serverPage:String = serverPath + "login.apx";
var request:URLRequest = new URLRequest(serverPage);
```

Using this approach makes it much easier to manage the location of the server-side files in your application. When you set a variable for the server path, it means that you need to make a change in only one place to update the entire application.

Next, let's see how you can actually send the variables from a SWF application to a server-side file.

Sending the variables

You have choices about both the method and format to use when sending variables from a SWF application to an application server. The *method* refers to the HTTP method; the *format* refers to how the variables are structured.

Choosing a method

You send variables from one web page to another using the Hypertext Transfer Protocol (HTTP). This is the standard way to transfer variables from a web page to a web or application server. You'll notice that the address of all web pages starts with the letters http://, indicating that they use this protocol for communication.

HTTP provides for eight different ways to communicate: HEAD, GET, POST, PUT, DELETE, TRACE, OPTIONS, and CONNECT. GET and POST are the most common methods, and the URLLoader class allows you to work with both. The HTTPService class and <mx:HTTPService> element allow you to work with the POST, HEAD, OPTIONS, PUT, TRACE, and DELETE methods. We'll focus on GET and POST here, reviewing how they work and the difference between the two.

The GET method requests a resource from the web server. It is intended only for retrieving information from the web server. In itself, it doesn't cause changes to the web server. It's possible to send variables with the GET method when requesting data from the server, but any variables that you do send will be available in clear text to anyone viewing the page URL. The GET method isn't suitable for sending large amounts of data.

The POST method submits data that will be processed on the server. The variables that you send are included when you make the request. The POST method is usually used when you submit a form containing data to the server.

So, which method should you use when working with SWF applications? You should use the GET method when you want to send variables that filter the data returned by the application server. You should use the POST method when you are sending variables that will update the content through the application server.

You don't need to explicitly set the GET method for the URLLoader, <mx:HTTPService> element or HTTPService class, as it is the default value. You need to add the method property to your application only if you want to use the POST method.

The following code block shows how to set the method property when working with a URLLoader object:

```
var serverPath:String = "http://www.friendsofed.com/";
var serverPage:String = serverPath + "getCountries.apx";
var request:URLRequest = new URLRequest(serverPage);
request.method = URLRequestMethod.POST;
```

You can set the method attribute of an <mx:HTTPService> element to achieve the same effect, as shown here:

```
<mx:HTTPService id="xmlService"
  url="http://www.friendsofed.com/getCountries.aspx"
  resultFormat="e4x" method="POST" result="resultHandler(event)"
  fault="faultHandler(event)" />
```

You can set the method in the HTTPService class using ActionScript, as shown in the next lines:

```
xmlService = new HTTPService();
xmlService.method = "POST";
```

Choosing the format

You may also need to specify the format for the variables using the contentType property. This format indicates how the variables should be encoded before they're sent to the server. The contentType property equates to the MIME type on the web server.

The default value for SWF applications is application/x-www-form-urlencoded. When applications use this setting, the variables are sent as name/value pairs, just as you would see in an HTML form. The name of each variable is separated from the value with an equal sign (=). There is no limit to the number of variables that a SWF application can send. Each of the name/value pairs is separated from the others by the ampersand character (&).

In addition, the names and values are encoded before they are sent. This type of encoding is slightly different from the encoding that you'll sometimes see in a web address. Spaces are encoded as a plus (+) character. Other reserved characters—such as a question mark (?), colon (:), and equal sign (=)—use their own encoding. Nonalphanumeric characters are replaced by a percent sign (%), followed by two hexadecimal digits that represent the ASCII code of the character.

If the name/value variable pairs are sent to the web server in an HTTP GET request, the values are added to the address of the requested URL. They appear in the section starting with the question mark (?) after the page name, as shown in this example:

```
http://www.foe.com?var1=value1&var2=value2&var3=value3
```

So, if a web page sends values using the GET method, the name/value pairs are clearly visible to a user in the address bar of a web browser. When a SWF application sends variables using this method, the server-side page requested doesn't actually load into the browser window, so the name/value variable pairs are never visible.

If the application uses the POST method, name/value variable pairs appear in the body of the request, after the HTTP headers. They aren't included in the URL, so they aren't visible to the user. It's also possible to send more data with the POST method than with the GET method.

In addition to the default contentType setting in a SWF application, you can also use the application/xml setting. You would use this setting to send the variables as an XML document. The application/xml setting is often appropriate if you need to send raw XML data to the server-side page for processing.

When using the URLLoader class, you would change the contentType for the request with the following code:

```
var serverPath:String = "http://www.friendsofed.com/";
var serverPage:String = serverPath + "getCountries.apx";
var request:URLRequest = new URLRequest(serverPage);
request.contentType = "application/xml";
```

You would do the following with the <mx:HTTPService> element:

```
<mx:HTTPService id="xmlService"
  url="http:/www.friendsofed.com/getCountries.aspx"
  resultFormat="e4x" method="POST" contentType="application/xml"
  result="resultHandler(event)" />
```

The approach with the HTTPService is similar:

```
xmlService = new HTTPService();
xmlService.contentType = "application/xml";
```

Now that you understand some of the considerations for sending data to the server, let's see how to send variables with the URLLoader class.

Working with the URLLoader class

Both Flash and Flex can work with the URLLoader class. As you learned in Chapter 5, the URLLoader class is one of the classes in the flash.net package, along with the URLRequest and URLVariables classes. These classes work together to provide the functionality for requesting external content from a static or server-side page.

The URLLoader class requests a URL from the server and handles the response. You use it to load information from external files. As well as well-formed XML documents, the URLLoader class can also load raw text files and text files that contain name/value variable pairs.

We'll focus on dynamically generated XML documents here. These documents exist only as a stream of information sent by a server-side page. Of particular interest to us in this chapter is the URLLoader class's ability to send variables with a request.

Sending variables with the URLLoader class

The URLLoader class sends variables to a server-side page using a URLVariables object. You specify the name of the variable with dot notation, in the same way as you would specify a property of an object.

The following code block shows a URLVariables object named params. This example shows how to send username and password variables to the server using the HTTP POST method:

```
var serverPath:String = "http://localhost/FlexApp/";
var serverPage:String = serverPath + "login.apx";
var request:URLRequest = new URLRequest(serverPage);
var params:URLVariables = new URLVariables();
params.username = "sas";
params.password = "secret";
request.data = params;
request.method = URLRequestMethod.POST;
loader.load(request);
```

> As I mentioned in Chapter 5, make sure you encode any & characters in the variable values with %26. Because the SWF application uses this character as a delimiter for variable pairs, you'll get unintended variable names and values if the character is not encoded.

Receiving a response

When a SWF application sends variables to a server-side page, it needs to know that the response has been processed successfully. The server will usually send back a return value. In the case where the variables provide the filter, this will be the requested data. In other cases, it might be a notification of the success or failure of the processing request.

If you're working with the URLLoader class, a successful request that receives a response dispatches the complete event. In order to work with the response, you need to add an event handler for this event, as shown in the following code block. The relevant line appears in bold, and you can see it with the other code that you would need to make the request.

```
var serverPath:String = "http://localhost/FlexApp/";
var serverPage:String = serverPath + "login.apx";
var request:URLRequest = new URLRequest(serverPage);
var loader:URLLoader = new URLLoader();
var params:URLVariables = new URLVariables();
loader.addEventListener(Event.COMPLETE, completeHandler);
params.username = "sas";
params.password = "secret";
request.data = params;
request.method = URLRequestMethod.POST;
loader.load(request);
```

When the complete event is dispatched, the completeHandler() function deals with the processing of the reply from the server.

> You don't need to name the event handler function with the event name, as I have done here. It's simply a useful convention that indicates which event the function handles.

The response from the server is in the data property of the URLLoader object. You would construct a function something like the following code block:

```
function completeHandler(e:Event):void {
  var loadedXML:XML= XML(e.target.data);
  //do something with the loadedXML object
}
```

The expression e.target.data finds the data property of the URLLoader object, and therefore the response from the server. This response is treated as a String. If the response comes as an XML document, you'll need to use the constructor method XML() to cast the response appropriately, as you can see in the preceding example.

Handling errors

Two events respond to errors in the request:

- An ioError event is dispatched if the load() method results in a fatal error that ends the download.
- A securityError event occurs if the SWF application tries to load data that is outside the application's security sandbox.

You can add event handlers to respond in case either of these events is dispatched.

In addition, if you're working over HTTP, you can use the HTTPStatus event to determine the status of the request. You can use this event to determine the HTTP status code for the request.

The following code block shows how to assign handlers for these events. As with the other event listeners, you need to assign them before calling the load() method.

```
loader.addEventListener(IOErrorEvent.IO_ERROR, ioErrorHandler);
loader.addEventListener(SecurityErrorEvent.SECURITY_ERROR,
  ➡securityErrorHandler);
loader.addEventListener(HTTPStatusEvent.HTTP_STATUS,
  ➡HTTPStatusHandler);
loader.load(request);
```

Each of these events will call the appropriate event handler, and you would need to add them as well. The examples that follow show very simplistic error handling with a trace() statement. In a production application, your event handling is likely to be a little more robust, perhaps displaying an Alert control with a detailed error message.

```
function ioErrorHandler(e:IOErrorEvent):void {
  trace("ioErrorHandler: " + e);
}
function HTTPStatusHandler(e:HTTPStatusEvent):void {
  trace("HTTPStatusHandler: " + e);
  trace("status: " + e.status);
}
function securityErrorHandler(e:SecurityErrorEvent):void {
  trace("securityErrorHandler: " + e);
}
```

Let's work through an example to show how to send a username and password to a server-side page so that a user can log in. The server-side page will send back one of two values: true or false, indicating whether or not the user has successfully logged in.

Working through a URLLoader class example

We'll work through the login example using the URLLoader class in both a Flash and a Flex application. As with the other examples in the book, the Flash application will use procedural code, and the Flex version will use a custom class file.

This example will work with an ASP.NET page written in VB .NET. I've also provided PHP and ColdFusion versions of the same server-side functionality, if you would prefer to work with either of those languages.

Remember that to work through the examples, you'll need an application server capable of processing the server-side page. In my case, I'm using Microsoft's web server, IIS. You may also work with Apache or ColdFusion Server.

The server-side page is very simple. It will check that the passed-in username and password match variables hard-coded within the file. We're not concerned with connecting to a database in this example, although you would use the same general approach as shown here.

The server-side page will return a simple XML document containing one element: <loginResult>. This element will either contain the text true or false.

It's important to note that the server-side page receiving the request must know how it's going to receive the variables from the SWF application. Server-side pages use different approaches to access variables sent by the GET method from those that access variables sent by the POST method. In this example, we're using the POST method, although the GET method would suffice. I've chosen to use POST so that I can show you how to set the method property.

The server-side page must also know in which format the variables will appear. Accessing XML content sent from the SWF application works differently compared with accessing name/value pairs. In this example, we'll send the variables through in name/value pairs.

In the next section, I'll explain the server-side pages. I'm not providing a tutorial about how to write each server-side language, as you can find plenty of tutorials on the Web to help out. Rather, I'll walk through each of the server-side page examples so I can explain the code.

We'll start with the simple VB. NET page. This page is written in VB .NET 3.5.

Understanding the VB .NET page

The VB .NET page will check the variables sent from the user and generate a simple XML stream containing a response. In this section, I'll show you the declarative code for the page. I've actually used a code-behind page to keep the VB code separate from the interface. In my version, the VB code appears in the file login.aspx.vb. You can find this page with the chapter resources, along with the file login.aspx.

The login.aspx page contains only one line, as all of the processing code appears in the code-behind page login.aspx.vb. The single line in the login.aspx page follows:

```
<%@ Page Language="VB" AutoEventWireup="false"
  CodeFile="login.aspx.vb" Inherits="login" %>
```

This line declares that the page will be written in the VB language and that the events don't need to specify event handlers. It indicates that the code for the page exists in the login.aspx.vb page, and that page inherits the class login, created in the code-behind file.

The full code for the login.aspx.vb page follows. I'll explain it after the listing.

```vb
Imports System.IO
Imports System.Xml
Partial Class login
  Inherits System.Web.UI.Page
  Protected Sub Page_Load(ByVal sender As Object,
    ➡ByVal e As System.EventArgs) Handles Me.Load
    Dim strUsername As String = "sas"
    Dim strPassword As String = "secret"
    Dim strSuppliedUsername As String = Request.Form("username")
    Dim strSuppliedPassword As String = Request.Form("password")
    Dim strResponse As String = ""
    Dim loginResponse As XmlTextWriter = New XmlTextWriter(
      ➡Response.OutputStream, Encoding.UTF8)
    If StrComp(strUsername, strSuppliedUsername) = 0 Then
      If StrComp(strPassword, strSuppliedPassword) = 0 Then
        strResponse = "true"
      Else
        strResponse = "false"
      End If
    Else
      strResponse = "false"
    End If
    Response.ContentType = "text/xml"
    loginResponse.WriteStartDocument()
    loginResponse.WriteStartElement("loginResult")
    loginResponse.WriteValue(strResponse)
    loginResponse.WriteEndElement()
    loginResponse.Flush()
    loginResponse.Close()
  End Sub
End Class
```

The code appears in a Page_Load subroutine so that it is called after the page finishes loading. The subroutine starts with statements that reference the relevant namespaces for the file. In this case, the page needs the System.IO and System.Xml namespaces, so it can write an XML stream from this file.

When the page loads, it declares a number of variables, as follows:

- strUsername and strPassword: These variables store the master username and password. Normally, you would get this information from a database. In order to keep this example as simple as possible, the variables are declared within this file.

- strSuppliedUsername and strSuppliedPassword: These variables request the username and password details from the SWF application. The SWF application will POST the values to the server-side pages, so the pages must request the details as if the application had sent details from a form.

- strResponse: This variable will store either true or false, depending on whether the user has provided the correct username and password. Normally, you would make this a Boolean variable. However, the value will be treated as a String when the XML document loads the SWF application. It keeps things simple to treat the true or false values as String variables here as well.

- loginResponse: This variable will store the XML content that will be returned to the SWF application.

After declaring the variables, the subroutine compares the supplied username and password with the values in the strUsername and strPassword variables. If both sets of values match, the value of the strResponse variable will be set to true; otherwise, it will be set to false.

The page uses an XmlTextWriter object to create and structure the XML content. It specifies that the output will be an information stream, rather than a physical file, by using the Response.OutputStream setting. The XmlTextWriter also indicates that the XML document will use UTF-8 encoding.

The VB .NET page sets the ContentType for the page to text/xml to indicate that it is returning an XML document. It calls several methods of the XmlTextWriter object to create the XML document. This subroutine calls the WriteStartDocument() method to write the XML declaration for the file. It then writes the opening <loginResult> element using the WriteStartElement() method. It uses WriteValue() to write the value of the strResponse variable inside the <loginResult> element, and calls the WriteEndElement() method to write the closing tag.

Finally, the subroutine calls the Flush() method to write the content. It then calls the Close() method on the XmlTextWriter object. When it finishes, the page can return only one of the two following results to the SWF application:

```
<loginResult>true</loginResult>
<loginResult>false</loginResult>
```

Both are very simple, well-formed XML documents containing a single root element.

Figure 9-1 shows what appears in a web browser window when this page detects that the supplied and required values don't match. In fact, because of the way I've set up this file, if no values are supplied, the result will be a false value.

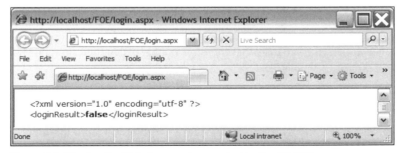

Figure 9-1. Viewing the XML document generated by the VB .NET page

Note the URL in the address bar of the web browser. It shows the address of the folder on my web server using an http:// path, rather than a path on the file system.

The PHP 5 example works in a similar way to the example you've just seen.

Understanding the PHP page

The PHP example is saved in the page login.php. The contents of this page follow:

```php
<?php
  header('Content-Type:text/xml');
  $strUsername = "sas";
  $strPassword = "secret";
  $strSuppliedUsername = '';
  $strSuppliedPassword = '';
  if (isset($_POST['username'])) {
    $strSuppliedUsername = $_POST['username'];
  }
  if (isset($_POST['password'])) {
    $strSuppliedPassword = $_POST['password'];
  }
  if (strcasecmp($strUsername, $strSuppliedUsername) == 0) {
    if (strcasecmp($strPassword, $strSuppliedPassword) == 0) {
      $strResponse = 'true';
    }
    else {
      $strResponse = 'false';
    }
  }
  else {
    $strResponse = 'false';
  }
  $loginResponse = new DomDocument("1.0", "UTF-8");
  $root = $loginResponse->createElement("loginResult", $strResponse);
  $root = $loginResponse->appendChild($root);
  echo $loginResponse->saveXML();
?>
```

This PHP example is also simple. It starts by declaring the content type for the document as text/xml. The next lines declare the variables that the page will need. I've used the same names for these variables as in the VB .NET example.

The $strUsername and $strPassword variables contain the values required for a successful login. Again, you would normally look these up in a database, but for simplicity, they are hard-coded here.

The $strSuppliedUsername and $strSuppliedPassword variables will store the supplied values from the user. The page starts by declaring them as empty strings. Then it tests each POST value using isset() to see if it has been sent from the SWF application. If so, the page assigns the values to the $strSuppliedUsername and $strSuppliedPassword variables.

The page compares the required and supplied values using the `strcasecmp()` function. If the user supplies the correct values, the $strResponse variable contains the value true; otherwise, it contains the value false.

The next line creates a new version 1.0 DomDocument object with UTF-8 encoding. This is the XML document that the page will return to the SWF application. The file creates a single element called <loginResult> using the `createElement()` and `appendChild()` methods.

The `createElement()` method requires the name of the element as the first argument and has an optional second argument that indicates the content for the element. In this case, the content is the $strResponse variable, so the text between the opening and closing <loginResult> tags will be either true or false.

Finally, the page finishes by writing the XML document to the browser window using saveXML(). You can find this page saved as login.php with the other chapter resources. Running it in a web browser will produce the same outcome that you saw in Figure 9-1.

The last server-side page we'll review is the ColdFusion example.

Understanding the ColdFusion page

I've saved the ColdFusion version of this processing file as login.cfm, and you can find this file with the chapter resources. The contents of this page follow:

```
<cfprocessingdirective suppresswhitespace="yes" pageencoding="utf-8">
  <cfset strUsername = "sas">
  <cfset strPassword = "secret">
  <cfparam name="FORM.username" default="">
  <cfparam name="FORM.password" default="">
  <cfset strSuppliedUsername = #FORM.username#>
  <cfset strSuppliedPassword = #FORM.password#>
  <cfxml variable="loginResponse">
    <?xml version="1.0" encoding="UTF-8"?>
    <loginResult
      <cfif compare(strUsername, strSuppliedUsername) EQ 0 >
        <cfif compare(strPassword, strSuppliedPassword) EQ 0 >
          <cfoutput>true</cfoutput>
        <cfelse>
        <cfoutput>false</cfoutput>
      </cfif>
      <cfelse>
        <cfoutput>false</cfoutput>
      </cfif>
    </loginResult>
  </cfxml>
  <cfset xmlString = ToString(loginResponse)>
  <cfcontent type="text/xml" reset="yes">
  <cfoutput>#xmlString#</cfoutput>
</cfprocessingdirective>
```

The page starts with a `<cfprocessingdirective>` tag, which provides the settings for the document. In this case, the page suppresses whitespace and uses `UTF-8` encoding.

As with the other examples, the page starts by declaring the variables it will use with `<cfset>` tags. The first two variables relate to the username and password that the user needs to provide to log in successfully. As in the other examples, these variables are hard-coded to keep things simple. Again, you don't need to set a data type for these variables in ColdFusion.

The page then sets default values to use for the username and password POST variables. The page finds these variables using `FORM.username` and `FORM.password`. The default values are empty strings. It's important to set the defaults, in case no variables are received from the SWF application.

After setting the defaults, the page then uses `<cfset>` to set the `strSuppliedUsername` and `strSuppliedPassword` variables to the value of the variables sent from the SWF application. The code will compare the supplied values when outputting the XML content.

The page generates the XML content within the `<cfxml>` block. The block has the variable name `loginReponse`, which the page will use to output the XML tree to the web browser window. The first part of the XML content is an XML declaration.

The block also includes the literal tags `<loginResult>` and `</loginResult>`. Inside these tags, the next lines use `<cfif>` and `<cfelse>` tags with the `comparenocase()` function to compare the values of the user-supplied variables with those required for a successfully login. The `<loginResult>` variable will contain either the text `true` or `false`.

The code converts the simple XML document to a `String` using the `ToString()` method. It then sets the content type of the document to `text/xml` and resets the buffer. Finally, it outputs the XML string using a `<cfoutput>` element.

You can use any one of the three server-side pages that I've covered here as you work through the example. You'll just need to remember to use the correct page name: `login.aspx`, `login.php`, or `login.cfm` and server path when you're entering the URL information.

Let's work through a Flash example that uses server-side processing to log in a user. The SWF application will have a simple interface that collects the username and password from the user. The Flash example will use procedural code, while the Flex example that appears later will use a custom class.

Working through the Flash example

In this example, the Flash application will collect the username and password from a user and send them to a server-side page for processing. The server-side page will check the user's credentials and inform the SWF application of the outcome in a simple XML document.

This example will use a single `URLLoader` object to pass variables and receive the response. Note that it is possible to use multiple `URLLoader` objects if you need to separate the loading of content from the updating of content.

1. Create a new folder in your web server for the application and give it the name of your choosing. I called my folder FOE. Copy the relevant server-side file to that folder. I'm using the file login.aspx in this example, so I needed to copy that file, as well as the bin folder containing the compiled VB .NET code.

2. Copy the file login.fla from the resources to the folder on the web server. This file contains the interface for the simple login application. Figure 9-2 shows how it appears when viewed in Flash.

Figure 9-2. The interface for the login application

The interface consists of two TextInput controls and a Button, along with a text field in which to display messages. The Password TextInput has the displayAsPassword field set to true.

3. Add a new layer and call it actions. You'll use this for all of the ActionScript code. Open the new layer in the Actions panel with the F9 shortcut key.

Add the following code at the top of the actions layer to set up the application:

```
var sender:URLLoader;
var sendPage:URLRequest;
var sendVars:URLVariables;
initApp
stop();
```

These lines declare the variables for the application. You've seen this code before. The first variable, sender, is a URLLoader object that will send the request. The sendPage variable is a URLRequest object that details the page that the application will request. The variable sendVars is a URLVariables object that will pass the username and password from the SWF application to the server-side file. The final line calls the initApp() function, which you'll create in the next step.

4. The SWF application will use the initApp() function to create the URLLoader, URLRequest, and URLVariables objects to make the request.

Add the following function to the actions layer, underneath the call to the initApp() function. I'll explain it after the code.

```
function initApp:void {
  var serverPath:String = "http://localhost/FOE/";
  var url:String = serverPath + "login.aspx";
  sender = new URLLoader();
  sendPage = new URLRequest(url);
  sendPage.method = URLRequestMethod.POST;
  sendVars = new URLVariables();
}
```

293

The first two lines set up the URL of the server-side page. The serverPath is separated from the page name. You may need to change the value of the serverPath variable and server-side file name to reflect your own settings.

As I discussed earlier, it's much easier if you set a variable for the path to the folder on the web server. You'll be able to change this value when you move the application to its production location. If you were going to use more than one URLLoader object, you would probably set this variable at the top of the actions layer, rather than as a local variable inside a function.

The application sets the method of the URLRequest to URLRequestMethod.POST, as the server-side files are expecting a POST request. If the server-side files weren't specific about how they expected the variables, you could omit the line, and the application would use the default method URLRequestMethod.GET.

5. The SWF application will request the server-side page after the user enters a username and password and clicks the Log in button. You'll need to add an event listener that responds when the user clicks the button to start the process.

Add the following line to the end of the initApp() function:

```
login_btn.addEventListener(MouseEvent.CLICK, clickHandler);
```

This line adds the handler function clickHandler() to the login_btn instance as an event listener. The function will respond to the click event. You'll add the clickHandler() function shortly.

6. The application also needs to react when it receives a response from the URLLoader object indicating that the request is complete and that it has received a response. You need to add an event listener that listens for the complete event.

Add the following line to the initApp() function, below the previous line of code:

```
sender.addEventListener(Event.COMPLETE, completeHandler);
```

Again, you'll add this handler function shortly.

7. The application should trap two more events: ioError and securityError. These event handlers will provide some basic error-handling capability and display error messages to the user.

Start by adding the following import statements at the top of the actions layer:

```
import flash.events.IOErrorEvent;
import flash.events.SecurityErrorEvent;
```

These statements import the two Event classes needed for the error handling.

8. Add the following event listeners in the initApp() function. You'll add the functions themselves in a later step.

```
sender.addEventListener(IOErrorEvent.IO_ERROR, ioErrorHandler);
sender.addEventListener(SecurityErrorEvent.SECURITY_ERROR,
    ➥securityErrorHandler);
```

9. Let's now move to the event handler functions, starting with the function to handle the Log in button click. Add the clickHandler() function below the initApp() function. This is the function that assembles the variables and makes the request for the server-side page, passing the variables.

```
function clickHandler(e:MouseEvent):void {
  var suppUsername:String = username_txt.text;
  var suppPassword:String = password_txt.text;
  if (suppUsername.length > 0 && suppPassword.length > 0) {
    message_txt.text = "";
    sendVars.username = suppUsername;
    sendVars.password = suppPassword;
    sendPage.data = sendVars;
    sender.load(sendPage);
  }
  else {
    message_txt.text = "You must enter both a username and password
      ➥before clicking the button."
  }
}
```

This function retrieves the user entries from the username_txt and password_txt fields. It then tests both entries to check that values have been supplied using the length property. If both entries have a length greater than 0, the code block inside the if portion of the code block executes. If not, the code in the else portion executes. In that case, the application displays the message You must enter both a username and password before clicking the button in the message_txt instance.

When the user provides both details, the function clears any existing messages in the message_txt text field. It then adds the username and password properties to the sendVars object, and assigns the relevant values from the user. These lines create the name/value pairs.

Once the function assigns the values, the URLVariables object is set as the data property of the URLRequest object. This portion of the code block finishes by calling the load() method of the URLLoader object to make the request for the supplied URLRequest object, sendPage.

10. Add the completeHandler() function to respond when the application receives the server response. Remember that the response is a simple XML document containing one element: <loginResult>. This element contains one of two values for the text: true or false.

Add the following completeHandler() function to the actions layer:

```
function completeHandler(e:Event):void {
  var xmlResponse:XML = XML(e.target.data);
  var userMessage:String;
  if (xmlResponse.text().toString() == "true") {
    userMessage = "Congratulations. You were successful";
  }
  else {
    userMessage = "Login failed. Please try again";
  }
  message_txt.text = userMessage;
}
```

The function receives an Event object, which it will use to locate the loaded data with the expression e.target.data. The function starts by assigning this property to the xmlResponse XML object. It uses the XML() constructor method to assign the value, because it needs to cast the loaded content as an XML object instead of leaving it as a String. The function also declares a variable, userMessage, which will contain the response to the user.

The `completeHandler()` function locates the text in the server response using the `text()` method. Because there is a single element in the XML document, the function can apply the method to the XML object, which is equivalent to the root (and only) element in the document.

The function tests the value of the response and sets the message string appropriately. Notice that this comparison is a string comparison.

> *The function uses the* toString() *method on the* xmlResponse.text() *expression because that expression returns an* XMLList. *In fact, because the* XMLList *consists of a single value that is text, you don't actually need to use* toString(). *You could just use the expression* xmlResponse. toString() *to find the text inside the element.*

The compared value `true` is a `String`, rather than a `Boolean` value, because all values from an XML document are treated as `String` values by default. The function could have cast the returned value as a `Boolean` variable, but I think it's simpler to use the approach shown here.

11. The final step is to add the two error-handling functions that follow:

```
function ioErrorHandler(e:IOErrorEvent):void {
  message_txt.text = e.text;
}
function securityErrorHandler(e:SecurityErrorEvent):void {
  message_txt.text = e.text;
}
```

These functions display text to the `message_txt` control in the case of either an `IOError` or a `SecurityError`. Both functions display the `text` property associated with the error.

12. Test the application in the Flash. The supplied server-side files use the username sas and password secret. Figure 9-3 shows what you should see if you provide the correct login values.

Figure 9-3. The interface after a successful login attempt

13. Publish the file and run the created HTML file through the web browser. Don't forget to enter the full server path in the address bar. Figure 9-4 shows the application with an unsuccessful login. I've purposely included the address bar in the screenshot so you can double-check the path that you've used. If you want to check the error-handling features of the application, change the name of the file and use a server path in a different domain.

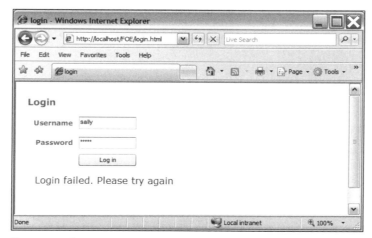

Figure 9-4. The application in a web browser showing an unsuccessful login attempt

In this example, I showed you how to integrate a simple SWF application created in Flash with a server-side page. The example used the page login.aspx. Alternatively, you could have used the login.php or login.cfm page provided with the chapter resources.

The complete code for the actions layer follows, in case you want to check it against your own file:

```
import flash.events.IOErrorEvent;
import flash.events.SecurityErrorEvent;
var sender:URLLoader;
var sendPage:URLRequest;
var sendVars:URLVariables;
initApp;
function initApp:void {
  var serverPath:String = "http://localhost/FOE/";
  var url:String = serverPath + "login.aspx";
  sender = new URLLoader();
  sendPage =  new URLRequest(url);
  sendPage.method = URLRequestMethod.POST;
  sendVars = new URLVariables();
  login_btn.addEventListener(MouseEvent.CLICK, clickHandler);
  sender.addEventListener(Event.COMPLETE, completeHandler);
  sender.addEventListener(IOErrorEvent.IO_ERROR, ioErrorHandler);
  sender.addEventListener(SecurityErrorEvent.SECURITY_ERROR,
    ➥securityErrorHandler);
}
```

297

```
function clickHandler(e:MouseEvent):void {
  var suppUsername:String = username_txt.text;
  var suppPassword:String = password_txt.text;
  if (suppUsername.length > 0 && suppPassword.length > 0) {
    message_txt.text = "";
    sendVars.username = suppUsername;
    sendVars.password = suppPassword;
    sendPage.data = sendVars;
    sender.load(sendPage);
  }
  else {
    message_txt.text = "You must enter both a username and
      ➥password before clicking the button."
  }
}
function completeHandler(e:Event):void {
  var xmlResponse:XML = XML(e.target.data);
  var userMessage:String;
  if (xmlResponse.text().toString() == "true") {
    userMessage = "Congratulations. You were successful";
  }
  else {
    userMessage = "Login failed. Please try again";
  }
  message_txt.text = userMessage;
}
function ioErrorHandler(e:IOErrorEvent):void {
  message_txt.text = e.text;
}
function securityErrorHandler(e:SecurityErrorEvent):void {
  message_txt.text = e.text;
}
```

You can find my completed Flash file login_completed.fla saved with your chapter resources.

Let's move on to the Flex version of this example.

Working through the Flex example

The Flex version of this example will achieve the same outcome as the Flash version, but use class-based code. It will work with the same server-side pages as the Flash example. I'm going to work with the VB. NET page server-side, but feel free to use the PHP or ColdFusion version.

1. Create a new Flex project and application file with the name of your choosing. Set the location to a folder in your web server. I'm using the FOE folder that I used in the previous example. This folder contains the relevant server-side file.

2. Create a new ActionScript class using the command File ➤ New ➤ ActionScript Class. Add the class to the xmlUtilities package and call it XMLLoader. The file should contain the following:

```
package xmlUtilities {
  public class XMLLoader {
    public function XMLLoader() {
    }
  }
}
```

3. Add the following import statements above the class declaration:

```
import flash.net.URLLoader;
import flash.net.URLRequest;
import flash.net.URLVariables;
import flash.net.URLRequestMethod;
import flash.events.IOErrorEvent;
import flash.events.SecurityErrorEvent;
import mx.controls.Alert;
```

These import statements reflect the classes needed for this example. The IOErrorEvent and SecurityErrorEvent classes cover error handling. The Alert class allows the application to display simple errors from the class file.

4. Add a bindable declaration above the class declaration so that all public methods and properties will be bindable in the application file.

```
[Bindable]
```

5. The code needs to declare some private variables for the URLLoader, URLRequest, and URLVariables objects used in the class file. It also needs to declare an XML object to store the server response.

Add the following declarations below the class declaration:

```
private var sender:URLLoader;
private var sendPage:URLRequest;
private var sendVars:URLVariables;
private var serverPath:String;
private var xmlResponse:XML;
```

6. You'll need to modify the constructor method to receive the server path as an argument. The method also needs to create a new URLLoader and add an event listener that responds to the complete event. It finishes by adding event handlers for the error events IOError and SecurityError.

Modify the code as shown in bold here:

```
public function XMLLoader(path:String) {
  serverPath = path;
  sender = new URLLoader();
  sender.addEventListener(Event.COMPLETE, completeHandler);
  sender.addEventListener(IOErrorEvent.IO_ERROR, IOErrorHandler);
  sender.addEventListener(SecurityErrorEvent.SECURITY_ERROR,
    ➥securityErrorHandler);
}
```

The XMLLoader() method sets the value of the serverPath private variable to the path argument that the application file will supply. It creates a URLLoader object and adds an event listener that responds when the loading operation completes successfully. The event listener calls the completeHandler() method.

The constructor method also adds event handlers to deal with the IOErrorEvent and SecurityErrorEvent events. You'll add those handler functions soon.

7. Add the first event handler, the completeHandler() method, as shown here:

```
private function completeHandler(e:Event):void {
  xmlResponse= XML(e.target.data);
  dispatchEvent(new Event(Event.COMPLETE));
}
```

This completeHandler() method assigns the returned XML content from the server-side file to the object xmlResponse, casting it to the type XML with the XML() constructor method. The method then dispatches the complete event so that the application will know that the server response is available.

8. Next, add the IOErrorHandler() method.

```
private function IOErrorHandler(e:IOErrorEvent):void{
  dispatchEvent(new IOErrorEvent (IOErrorEvent.IO_ERROR, false, true,
    ➥e.text));
}
```

This method dispatches an IOErrorEvent to inform the application that there has been an IOError. It sends the text associated with the event in the dispatched event. The application will then be able to display an appropriate error message in the TextArea control. The other two arguments, bubbles and cancelable, have been left at their default values.

9. The final event handler is the securityErrorHandler() method. Add the following private method to the class file:

```
private function securityErrorHandler(e:SecurityErrorEvent):void{
  dispatchEvent(new SecurityErrorEvent (SecurityErrorEvent.
    ➥SECURITY_ERROR, false, true, e.text));
}
```

As with the previous handler function, this function dispatches an event to the application. This time, it's a SecurityErrorEvent. This dispatchEvent() method also passes the text associated with the error.

10. The code doesn't include a function to handle the request and associated variables. You need to create a public method that the application can call. The application will send the variables as an Object, set the method property of the URLLoader, and call its load() method.

This public method, which I've named loadXML() will receive two arguments: the name of the server-side file to request and the variables to send with that request. The application will combine the server-side file name with the value of the serverPath variable to determine the full path to the file.

> *You could also pass in the full path to the* loadXML() *method, and the result would be the same. However, it's better to pass the values to the class file separately, in case the application works with more than one* URLLoader *object. That's not the situation here, but it's good practice to code so that it's easy to extend class files later if needed.*

Add the loadXML() method now.

```
public function loadXML(xmlFile:String, vars:URLVariables):void {
  try {
    sendPage = new URLRequest(serverPath + serverFile);
    sendPage.data = vars;
    sendPage.method = URLRequestMethod.POST;
    sender.load(sendPage);
  }
  catch (e:Error) {
    Alert.show("Can't contact server side file");
  }
}
```

Again, the code uses a try/catch block to provide some simple error handling. In the case of an error, the application will display the message Can't contact server side file in an Alert control.

As I said earlier, you would probably make the error handling a little more robust in a real-world application. Instead of displaying an Alert, the class file could dispatch an event to the application. You could add also some checking to make sure that the server path includes a finishing forward slash (/). If this character is missing, the full path to the server-side file won't be correct. I'll leave you to think about those areas yourself!

The loadXML() method creates a new URLRequest object, using the server path already assigned and the URL passed in as the first argument. The method assigns the variables argument to the data property of the URLRequest object and sets the method to POST the variables to the server-side page. The loadXML() method finishes by calling the load() method to make the request for the server-side file.

11. The XMLLoader class will need one public method to return the response from the server-side file. This file will return a single simple element: <loginResult>. Remember that the element will contain the text true or false. The application will apply the toString() method to locate the text inside this element when it receives the XML object from the XMLLoader object.

Add the following public response() method to the class file:

```
public function response():XML {
  return xmlResponse;
}
```

You've now finished creating the class file. I've included the completed code so that you can check what you've done against my version.

```
package xmlUtilities {
  import flash.net.URLLoader;
  import flash.net.URLRequest;
  import flash.net.URLVariables;
  import flash.net.URLRequestMethod;
  import flash.events.IOErrorEvent;
  import flash.events.SecurityErrorEvent;
  import mx.controls.Alert;
  [Bindable]
  public class XMLLoader {
    private var sender:URLLoader;
    private var sendPage:URLRequest;
    private var sendVars:URLVariables;
    private var serverPath:String;
    private var xmlResponse:XML;
    public function XMLLoader(path:String) {
      serverPath = path;
      sender = new URLLoader();
      sender.addEventListener(Event.COMPLETE, completeHandler);
      sender.addEventListener(IOErrorEvent.IO_ERROR,
        ➥IOErrorHandler);
      sender.addEventListener(SecurityErrorEvent.SECURITY_ERROR,
        ➥securityErrorHandler);
    }
    public function loadXML(serverFile:String,
      ➥vars:URLVariables):void {
      try {
        sendPage = new URLRequest(serverPath + serverFile);
        sendPage.data = vars;
      sendPage.method = URLRequestMethod.POST;
        sender.load(sendPage);
      }
      catch (e:Error) {
        Alert.show("Can't contact server side file");
      }
    }
    public function response():XML {
      return xmlResponse;
    }
    private function completeHandler(e:Event):void {
      xmlResponse = XML(e.target.data);
      dispatchEvent(new Event(Event.COMPLETE));
    }
    private function IOErrorHandler(e:IOErrorEvent):void{
      dispatchEvent(new IOErrorEvent (IOErrorEvent.IO_ERROR, false,
        ➥true, e.text));
    }
```

```
      private function securityErrorHandler(e:SecurityErrorEvent):void{
        dispatchEvent(new SecurityErrorEvent (
          ➡SecurityErrorEvent.SECURITY_ERROR, false, true, e.text));
      }
    }
  }
```

12. The next step is to create the Flex application file. Start by building the interface. Switch to the main application file and add the following interface elements inside the <mx:Application> element:

```
<mx:VBox x="10" y="10">
  <mx:Label text="Login" fontSize="14" fontWeight="bold"/>
  <mx:HBox>
    <mx:Label text="Username" fontWeight="bold" width="80"/>
    <mx:TextInput id="username_txt"/>
  </mx:HBox>
  <mx:HBox>
    <mx:Label text="Password" fontWeight="bold" width="80"/>
    <mx:TextInput id="password_txt" displayAsPassword="true"/>
  </mx:HBox>
  <mx:Button id="login_btn" label="Log in" />
  <mx:TextArea width="250" height="60" id="message_txt"/>
</mx:VBox>
```

Figure 9-5 shows how the interface should appear in Design view.

The interface includes Label controls as well as two TextInput components where the user will enter a username and a password. The Password TextInput has the displayAsPassword attribute set to true to mask the password entry.

The interface also includes a Log in button, which will trigger the request. Messages, including the response from the server, will display in the TextArea control. Feel free to make changes to this interface. However, make sure that you don't change the id settings for the components.

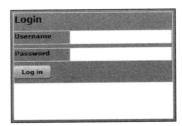

Figure 9-5. The Flex application interface for the URLLoader class example

13. As you've seen previously, a function called initApp() will set up the application. It will be called in the creationComplete attribute of the <mx:Application> element.

Modify the <mx:Application> element as shown here in bold to add the creationComplete attribute:

```
<mx:Application xmlns:mx="http://www.adobe.com/2006/mxml"
  layout="absolute" creationComplete="initApp(event)">
```

14. The initApp() function and supporting code appear in the following <mx:Script> block. Add it above the interface declarations. I'll explain it after the code.

```
<mx:Script>
  <![CDATA[
    import mx.events.FlexEvent;
    import xmlUtilities.XMLLoader;
    import flash.events.IOErrorEvent;
    import flash.events.SecurityErrorEvent;
    private var myXMLLoader:XMLLoader;
    private var serverPath:String = "http://localhost/FOE/";
    private function initApp(e:FlexEvent):void {
      myXMLLoader = new XMLLoader();
      myXMLLoader.addEventListener(Event.COMPLETE, completeHandler);
      myXMLLoader.addEventListener(IOErrorEvent.IO_ERROR,
        ➥IOErrorHandler);
      myXMLLoader.addEventListener(SecurityErrorEvent.SECURITY_ERROR,
        ➥securityErrorHandler);
      login_btn.addEventListener(MouseEvent.CLICK, clickHandler);
    }
    private function completeHandler(e:Event):void {
    }
    private function clickHandler(e:MouseEvent):void {
    }
    private function IOErrorHandler(e:IOErrorEvent):void {
    }
    private function securityErrorHandler(e:SecurityErrorEvent):
      ➥void {
    }
  ]]>
</mx:Script>
```

This <mx:Script> block starts by importing the relevant classes. The import statements include the FlexEvent class, which is necessary because this event is dispatched when the interface finishes creating. The creationComplete handler initApp() will receive this event as an argument.

The code block needs to import the XMLLoader custom class that you just created. It also needs to import the classes for the two error events IOErrorEvent and SecurityErrorEvent.

The function declares two variables, myXMLLoader, which is of the type XMLLoader, and serverPath. The serverPath variable contains the path to the application on the web server. You may need to change the value of this variable if your server path is different.

The initApp() function receives a FlexEvent as an argument. Even though the application won't use any properties of this Event, it is best practice to recognize that the function receives the Event.

The function creates a new instance of the XMLLoader class using the constructor method. It passes the serverPath variable as an argument to this function.

The initApp() function also assigns four event handlers. The first three handler functions relate to the myXMLLoader object.

The first handler is the completeHandler() function, which is called when the URLLoader receives a response from the server-side page. Second is the IOErrorHandler() function, which responds when notified of an IOError, such as a missing server-side page or incorrect file path.

The third function, securityErrorHandler(), is dispatched when a security error occurs. This error might happen if the application tries to load external content from a sandbox different from that of the SWF application's own sandbox.

The last event handler is the clickHandler() function. This function responds when the user clicks the Log in button.

The code block includes the empty handler functions for each of these events as well. Even if they don't contain code, adding the empty functions will allow you to test the application without generating an error message.

15. When the user clicks the Log in button, the application needs to validate the username and password before it calls the loadXML() method of the XMLLoader object. The validation consists only of checking that the user has entered values.

Once the application determines that entries have been made, it will call the loadXML() method. The loadXML() method passes the URL of the document to load, as well as a URLVariables object containing the entered username and password.

Modify the Log in button clickHandler() function as shown here in bold:

```
private function clickHandler(e:MouseEvent):void {
  var username:String = username_txt.text;
  var password:String = password_txt.text;
  var myVars:URLVariables = new URLVariables();
  if (username.length > 0 && password.length > 0) {
    myVars.username = username;
    myVars.password = password;
    myXMLLoader.loadXML("login.aspx", myVars);
  }
  else {
    message_txt.text = "You must enter both a username and password
      ➥before clicking the button"
  }
}
```

The clickHandler() function starts by determining the values that the user has entered in the TextArea controls. It test the length of both the username and password entries to check that the length is greater than 0.

If the function can validate these entries, it creates a new URLVariables object called myVars. It assigns the username and password properties from the entries in the TextInput controls. The function then calls the loadXML() method, passing the name of the server-side document and the URLVariables object.

The code example uses the server-side file login.aspx. If you're using a different file, you'll need to change the name of the server-side file in the loadXML() method.

If the user leaves either TextInput control blank, the message You must enter both a username and password before clicking the button displays in the TextArea at the bottom of the interface.

16. The application needs to respond when it receives a reply from the web server. The reply could be a successful response from the server-side file or notification of an error. Let's deal with a successful response first.

When the application receives a response, it will display it in the TextArea control. To have the completeHandler() function process the response, modify it as shown in bold here:

```
private function completeHandler(e:Event):void {
  var userMessage:String;
  var response:String = myXMLLoader.response().toString();
  if (response == "true") {
    userMessage = "Congratulations. You were successful";
  }
  else {
    userMessage = "Login failed. Please try again";
    }
  message_txt.text = userMessage;
}
```

This function starts by declaring two String variables: one for the message that will display in the TextArea, and a second for the response received from the server-side page. It uses the toString() method to obtain a String representation of the XML content. Because the response is a simple XML element—that is, it doesn't contain anything other than text—the toString() method returns only the text inside the element.

The function tests the response from the server and compares it against the String value true. I've stuck with strings rather than casting the returned value as a Boolean variable to keep things simple.

The completeHandler() function creates one of two messages, depending on whether the user was able to log in successfully. It finishes by displaying the message in the TextArea control at the bottom of the interface.

17. The IOErrorHandler() and securityErrorHandler() functions will deal with notifications of errors. In both cases, the text property of the event will display in the message_txt control.

Modify the handler functions as shown here in bold:

```
private function IOErrorHandler(e:IOErrorEvent):void {
  message_txt.text = e.text;
}
private function securityErrorHandler(e:SecurityErrorEvent):void {
  message_txt.text = e.text;
}
```

These changes are self-explanatory. They access the text property sent with the dispatched events.

18. Test the application. If Internet Explorer is your default browser, run the application to generate the test files and view the content directly from Flex Builder. If you're using Firefox, you will need to run the application to compile the files, and then copy them from the src folder to your web server folder. You can view the application by entering the URL in the web browser. Your URL should start with http://, so in my example it would be http://localhost.FOE/ FlexApp/.

After loading the HTML page in the browser, enter values for the username and password. The correct login values from the original server-side files are sas for the username and secret for the password.

When you click the Log in button, you should see the TextArea update with a message. Figure 9-6 shows the effect of a successful login.

Figure 9-6. The completed Flex application for the URLLoader class example

You can test if the error handlers work by changing the name of the server-side file to one that doesn't exist. You can also enter a domain outside the current SWF sandbox for further testing. Figure 9-7 shows the effect of using an incorrect file name.

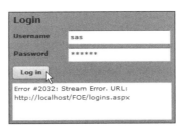

Figure 9-7. The Flex application displays an error message.

The complete code for the application file follows:

```
<?xml version="1.0" encoding="utf-8"?>
<mx:Application xmlns:mx="http://www.adobe.com/2006/mxml"
  layout="absolute"  creationComplete="initApp(event)">
  <mx:Script>
    <![CDATA[
      import mx.events.FlexEvent;
      import xmlUtilities.XMLLoader;
      import flash.events.IOErrorEvent;
      import flash.events.SecurityErrorEvent;
      private var myXMLLoader:XMLLoader;
      private var serverPath:String = "http://localhost/FOE/";
```

```
      private function initApp(e:FlexEvent):void {
        myXMLLoader = new XMLLoader(serverPath);
        myXMLLoader.addEventListener(Event.COMPLETE,
          ➥completeHandler);
        myXMLLoader.addEventListener(IOErrorEvent.IO_ERROR,
          ➥IOErrorHandler);
        myXMLLoader.addEventListener(SecurityErrorEvent.
          ➥SECURITY_ERROR, securityErrorHandler);
        login_btn.addEventListener(MouseEvent.CLICK, clickHandler);
      }
      private function completeHandler(e:Event):void {
        var userMessage:String;
        var response:String = myXMLLoader.response().toString();
        if (response == "true") {
          userMessage = "Congratulations. You were successful";
        }
        else {
          userMessage = "Login failed. Please try again";
        }
        message_txt.text = userMessage;
      }
      private function clickHandler(e:MouseEvent):void {
        var username:String = username_txt.text;
        var password:String = password_txt.text;
        var myVars:URLVariables = new URLVariables();
        if (username.length > 0 && password.length > 0) {
          myVars.username = username;
          myVars.password = password;
          myXMLLoader.loadXML("login.aspx", myVars);
        }
        else {
          message_txt.text = "You must enter both a username and
            ➥password before clicking the button"
        }
      }
      private function IOErrorHandler(e:IOErrorEvent):void {
        message_txt.text = e.text;
      }
      private function securityErrorHandler(e:SecurityErrorEvent):
        ➥void {
        message_txt.text = e.text;
      }
    ]]>
  </mx:Script>
  <mx:VBox x="10" y="10">
    <mx:Label text="Login" fontSize="14" fontWeight="bold"/>
    <mx:HBox>
      <mx:Label text="Username" fontWeight="bold" width="80"/>
      <mx:TextInput id="username_txt"/>
    </mx:HBox>
```

```
        <mx:HBox>
          <mx:Label text="Password" fontWeight="bold" width="80"/>
          <mx:TextInput id="password_txt" displayAsPassword="true"/>
        </mx:HBox>
        <mx:Button id="login_btn" label="Log in" />
        <mx:TextArea width="250" height="60" id="message_txt"/>
      </mx:VBox>
    </mx:Application>
```

You can find the resource files for this example with the other chapter resources saved as Login.mxml and XMLLoader.as.

> *As I mentioned earlier, the error handling in the Flex custom class file is not particularly robust. Feel free to modify the code to add more error handling. You might also want to modify the error-handler functions in the application file to display more user-friendly error messages.*

So far, this chapter has covered only how to work with the URLLoader class in Flash and Flex. Flex provides other approaches: using the <mx:HTTPService> element and HTTPService class. We'll turn our attention to that topic next.

Working with the <mx:HTTPService> element

Both the <mx:HTTPService> element and HTTPService class allow you to request a URL from the server and receive a response. You can optionally send arguments with the request, perhaps if you need to filter the content or provide updates to a data source. You might also wish to have the variables processed on the server in some way. For example, the Flex application may require the server to generate an e-mail or save the values in a text file.

The <mx:HTTPService> element exists in the mx.rpc.http.mxml package. As with the URLLoader class, when using the <mx:HTTPService> tag, the application must wait until it receives a response from the server before it starts to process the loaded content. The response could also be notification of a fault.

Chapter 6 covers the <mx:HTTPService> element in detail. Before we work through an example using this element, let's have a quick refresher about how to send variables with the request.

Sending variables with the <mx:HTTPService> element

As with the URLLoader class, you can send variables when you use the <mx:HTTPService> element to make a request for a server-side page. There are several different ways to send the variables with the request.

First, you can send variables at the same time that you call the send() method. If you choose this approach, you pass an Object that contains the name/value variable pairs inside the send() method call. You can see an example of this approach in the following code block:

```
<mx:Application xmlns:mx="http://www.adobe.com/2006/mxml"
  layout="absolute"
  creationComplete="xmlService.send({username:'sas'})">
```

Here, the use of the curly braces indicates the creation of an Object. The object contains one name/value pair. The variable is called username, and it has the value sas. Notice that the code uses single quotes to indicate that it is passing a String value.

You can also can use the <mx:request> element inside the <mx:HTTPService> element. The <mx:request> element lists the variables that you want to send. In the following code block, the <mx:HTTPService> element sends the same parameter, username, as shown in the previous example:

```
<mx:HTTPService id="xmlService"
  url="http://localhost/FlexApp/getAuthors.aspx">
  <mx:request>
    <username>sas</username>
  </mx:request>
</mx:HTTPService>
```

The <mx:request> element appears as a tag within the <mx:HTTPService> element. This tag uses a lowercase initial letter, unlike the uppercase letter used by most other elements.

The advantage of this approach is that it is tag-based rather than relying on an ActionScript statement. Where you have a lot of variables, using the <mx:request> element may make the application code easier to read.

A further advantage is that you can bind the variable value to other elements in the application. In the following example, the <username> element takes its value from the text property of the username_txt element:

```
<mx:request>
  <username>{username_txt.text}</username>
</mx:request>
```

We discussed the method and contentType settings earlier in the chapter, and both of the properties are available as attributes of the <mx:HTTPService> element. The following <mx:HTTPService> element uses the POST method to send the variables and structures them as an XML-formatted object. I've highlighted the relevant attributes in bold.

```
<mx:HTTPService id="xmlService" url="http://localhost/FOE/page.aspx"
  resultFormat="e4x" method="POST" contentType="application/xml" />
```

The contentType property determines the format for the variables. As I mentioned earlier, the default value of this property is application/x-www-form-urlencoded, which equates to name/value variable pairs. You can also use the setting application/xml if the URL that you request expects to receive raw XML data from the SWF application.

If you're sending variables in XML format, you'll need to format them differently. The following block shows how you might do this inside the creationComplete event of the application:

```
<mx:Application xmlns:mx="http://www.adobe.com/2006/mxml"
   layout="absolute"
   creationComplete="xmlService.send(<username>sas</username>'})">
```

The preceding code block provides an alternative to passing an Object with the method call.

Receiving a response

When you receive a server response using the <mx:HTTPService> tag, you can respond in one of two ways: either bind the response directly to UI elements or assign a result event handler. The latter option requires you to write ActionScript code; the former does not. Either way, the response appears in the lastResult property of the HTTPService element.

The following code shows how to bind a response for display in a TextArea control:

```
<mx:TextArea width="250" height="60" id="message_txt"
   text="{xmlService.lastResult.toString()}">
```

The TextArea control uses curly braces binding syntax and accesses the response using the expression xmlService.lastResult, where xmlService is the id of the <mx:HTTPService> element. It sets this as the value for the text property of the element.

As an alternative, the <mx:HTTPService> tag includes an attribute called result, which allows you to assign a result handler function to respond to the server response. In the following example, the resultHandler() function will fire when the server provides a successful response:

```
<mx:HTTPService id="xmlService" url="http://localhost/FOE/page.aspx"
   result="resultHandler(event)" resultFormat="e4x" method="POST"
   contentType="application/xml"/>
```

You would then need to write an ActionScript function called resultHandler() to process the response. An example resultHandler() function follows:

```
function resultHandler(e:Event):void {
   var loadedXML:XML= e.target.lastResult;
   //do something with the loadedXML object
}
```

The resultHandler() function receives an event as an argument. The event object allows the function to access the lastResult property of the HTTPService object, which it identifies using target.

The function declares an XML object named loadedXML to store the response. This example sets the resultFormat for the request to e4x so it can assign the response directly to an XML object.

The resultHandler() function assigns the server response to the XML object using the expression e.target.lastResult. The expression is equivalent to the root element of the loaded XML document. Because you've created an XML object, you can find specific parts of the response using E4X expressions or XML methods.

311

Handling errors

The <mx:HTTPService> element has another attribute, fault, which allows you to assign a fault handler function in case of error. You can see an example shown in bold in the following element:

```
<mx:HTTPService id="xmlService" url="http://localhost/FOE/page.aspx"
    result="resultHandler(event)" fault="faultHandler(event)"
    resultFormat="e4x" method="POST" contentType="application/xml"/>
```

Again, you would need to write an ActionScript function to respond to this event. The following is a sample faultHandler() function:

```
function faultHandler(e:FaultEvent):void {
  trace(e.fault.message);
}
```

Working through an <mx:HTTPService> element example

Let's work through the same example as in the previous exercise, where a user logs in to an application, and a server-side file checks the username and password. In this case, you'll see how to work with a tag-based approach using the <mx:HTTPService> element.

1. Create a new application file in Flex Builder and give it the name of your choosing. Make sure the application file is stored with the previous examples, in a folder on the web server.

2. Add the following interface elements:

```
<?xml version="1.0" encoding="utf-8"?>
<mx:Application xmlns:mx="http://www.adobe.com/2006/mxml"
  layout="absolute">
  <mx:VBox x="10" y="10">
    <mx:Label text="Login" fontSize="14" fontWeight="bold"/>
    <mx:HBox>
      <mx:Label text="Username" fontWeight="bold" width="80"/>
      <mx:TextInput id="username_txt"/>
    </mx:HBox>
    <mx:HBox>
      <mx:Label text="Password" fontWeight="bold" width="80"/>
      <mx:TextInput id="password_txt" displayAsPassword="true"/>
    </mx:HBox>
    <mx:HBox width="100%" horizontalAlign="center">
      <mx:Button id="login_btn" label="Log in" />
    </mx:HBox>
    <mx:TextArea width="250" height="60" id="message_txt"/>
  </mx:VBox>
</mx:Application>
```

The interface includes two TextInput controls for the user's username and password. The Password control has the displayAsPassword attribute set to true. There is a Log in button to initiate the request to the server-side page. The message_txt control will display messages to the user, including the server response.

Figure 9-8 shows how the interface should appear in the Design view of Flex Builder.

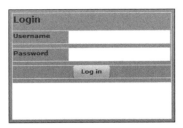

Figure 9-8. The Flex application interface for the <mx:HTTPService> element example

3. Add the following <mx:HTTPService> tag above the opening <mx:VBox> component:

```
<mx:HTTPService id="loginService"
  url="http://localhost/FOE/login.aspx" resultFormat="e4x"
  showBusyCursor="true" method="POST">
</mx:HTTPService>
```

This <mx:HTTPService> element has the id loginService. The url attribute contains the full path to the web server folder—in my case. http://localhost/FOE/. It also includes the file name login.aspx. You may need to change this value to your own web server address and update the file name if you're using either the PHP or ColdFusion version.

The code sets the value of the showBusyCursor attribute to true. This value will display a busy cursor while the request is in progress. It's handy for the user to know that the request is in progress. Unfortunately, this property isn't available when you script the HTTPService class.

The element also contains the method="POST" attribute so that the variables will be sent using the POST method. All of the server-side pages provided expect that the value will be sent using this method.

The code block includes both opening and closing tags because you'll add an <mx:request> element between them containing the username and password values. The element specifies e4x as the resultFormat because the server-side page will respond with an XML document.

4. The variables to send with the <mx:HTTPService> element will come from the user entries provided in the Username and Password controls. You'll use binding expressions to bind the values directly to the variables in the <mx:request> element.

Modify the <mx:HTTPService> tag as shown in bold here:

```
<mx:HTTPService id="loginService"
  url="http://localhost/FOE/bin-debug/login.aspx" resultFormat="e4x"
  showBusyCursor="true" method="POST">
  <mx:request>
    <username>{username_txt.text}</username>
    <password>{password_txt.text}</password>
  </mx:request>
</mx:HTTPService>
```

The changes include a new `<mx:request>` element that contains two values: `<username>` and `<password>`. The variables are bound to the `text` properties of the `username_txt` and `password_txt` controls using curly braces notation.

5. The application will send the variables with the request when the user clicks the Log in button. The code needs to include a `click` attribute in the `<mx:Button>` element. The value of this attribute will call the `send()` method of the `loginService` object.

Add the following attribute to the Log in button, shown in bold in the following line:

```
<mx:Button id="login_btn" label="Log in"
  click="loginService.send()"/>
```

6. The application will display the server-side page's response in the TextArea component. The server-side file will generate a single element, `<loginResult>`, containing either `true` or `false`. The code will bind the text inside this element to an ActionScript expression that tests the `lastResult` property of the `loginService` element.

Modify the element as shown here in bold:

```
<mx:TextArea width="250" height="60" id="message_txt"
  text="{(loginService.lastResult == 'true') ?
  'Congratulations. You were successful' :
  (loginService.lastResult == 'false') ?
  'Login failed. Please try again' : ''}"/>
```

The ActionScript expression is complicated and uses nested `if` statements in their ternary form. That's where you use the following format for an `if` statement:

```
(condition) ? response if true : response if false
```

The expression starts by comparing the value of `loginService.lastResult`. If it equals the String value `true`, the `text` property of the `message_txt` control is set to display Congratulations. You were successful.

If the value doesn't equal `true`, the expression specifies a second comparison, comparing the `lastResult` property to `false`. If the value is `false`, the TextArea displays the text Login failed. Please try again; otherwise, it displays nothing.

Why do we have two tests and two nested `if` statements? Because if we only test for a `true` value, the Login failed message will display at all other times, including when the application first loads. Seeing this message before they've done anything is likely to be confusing for the users.

7. That's it for the tag-based version of this simple application. Make sure that the server-side file you're using is saved in the bin-debug folder inside the application folder. If you're using the VB .NET version of the file, make sure you copy both `login.aspx` and the bin folder to that folder.

8. Click the Run button in Flex Builder to see how the application works. Enter the username sas and the password secret, and then click the Log in button. Figure 9-9 shows how the application should appear in a web browser after a successful login.

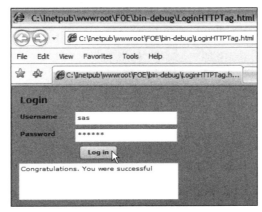

Figure 9-9. The completed Flex application for the
<mx:HTTPService> element example

Note that the error handling for this application is even less robust than the handling in the previous examples.

> *I've purposely included the address bar in Figure 9-9 so that you can see the address for the Flex application. In my case, the address of the HTML page is file-based, starting with* C:\. *You might be confused because I told you that the server-side file needs to use a URL starting with* http://.
>
> *When the Flex application moves to its final production environment, you'll be accessing it with an* http:// *path. For testing purposes, the application can use a file-based path. However, the code that refers to the server-side file inside the application must use a URL starting with* http://. *It's only the server-side page that must be processed by the web server.*

The complete code for the application follows, in case you want to check your file:

```xml
<?xml version="1.0" encoding="utf-8"?>
<mx:Application xmlns:mx="http://www.adobe.com/2006/mxml"
  layout="absolute">
  <mx:HTTPService id="loginService"
    url="http://localhost/FOE/login.aspx"
    resultFormat="e4x" showBusyCursor="true" method="POST">
    <mx:request>
      <username>{username_txt.text}</username>
      <password>{password_txt.text}</password>
    </mx:request>
  </mx:HTTPService>
```

```
<mx:VBox x="10" y="10">
  <mx:Label text="Login" fontSize="14" fontWeight="bold"/>
  <mx:HBox>
    <mx:Label text="Username" fontWeight="bold" width="80"/>
    <mx:TextInput id="username_txt"/>
  </mx:HBox>
  <mx:HBox>
    <mx:Label text="Password" fontWeight="bold" width="80"/>
    <mx:TextInput id="password_txt" displayAsPassword="true"/>
  </mx:HBox>
  <mx:HBox width="100%" horizontalAlign="center">
    <mx:Button id="login_btn" label="Log in"
    click="loginService.send()"/>
  </mx:HBox>
  <mx:TextArea width="250" height="60" id="message_txt"
    text="{(loginService.lastResult == 'true') ?
    'Congratulations. You were successful' :
    (loginService.lastResult == 'false') ?
    'Login failed. Please try again' : '' }"/>
</mx:VBox>
</mx:Application>
```

I've saved this example as LoginHTTPTag.mxml with the other chapter resource files.

Let's move on to the HTTPService class.

Working with the HTTPService class in Flex

The HTTPService class, in the mx.rpc.http package, works in a very similar way to the <mx:HTTPService> element. There are some minor differences between the two, which are covered in Chapter 6. You'll need to write ActionScript to work with the HTTPService class.

Sending variables with the HTTPService class

If you are using the HTTPService class, you need to send the variables using ActionScript by including them in the send() method call, as follows:

```
xmlService.send({username: 'sas'});
```

You can also add the variables in ActionScript using the following approach:

```
var params:Object = new Object();
params.username = "sas";
xmlService.request = params;
```

Receiving a response

When working with the HTTPService class, a successful response from the server dispatches the result event. You would need to set an event handler to deal with this response. In the following example, the appropriate line appears in bold with the other code needed to script the HTTPService class:

```
var serverPath:String = "http://localhost/FlexApp/";
var serverPage:String = serverPath + "login.apx";
var params:Object = new Object();
var xmlService:HTTPService = new HTTPService();
xmlService.url = serverPage;
xmlService.addEventListener(ResultEvent.RESULT, resultHandler);
params.username = "sas";
params.password = "secret";
xmlService.request = params;
xmlService.resultFormat = "e4x";
xmlService.method = URLRequestMethod.POST;
xmlService.send()
```

When the HTTPService dispatches the result event, the resultHandler() function processes the server reply. A successful response from the server can be accessed in the lastResult property of the HTTPService object.

In order to access this response, you would construct a function like the one shown here:

```
function resultHandler(e:Event):void {
  var loadedXML:XML= e.target.lastResult;
  //do something with the loadedXML object
}
```

The expression e.target.lastResult finds the server response. The code assigns this response to a variable called loadedXML. Because the code specifies a resultFormat of e4x, you don't need to cast the response.

Handling errors

You can also assign an event listener that responds to the fault event. The application dispatches this event when the request is not successful. The following code shows how to assign the event handler:

```
xmlService.addEventListener(FaultEvent.FAULT, faultHandler);
```

As with the result event handler, you need to assign this function before calling the send() method.

You would then need to create a faultHandler() function. A sample function follows:

```
function faultHandler(e:FaultEvent):void {
  trace(e.fault.message);
}
```

This example displays the message using a trace() statement. This approach is good for debugging, but not appropriate for a production application. The exercise in the next section uses an alternative approach.

Working through a HTTPService class example

In this final example for the chapter, you'll build the same simple application you saw earlier, but you'll do so using the HTTPService class with a custom ActionScript class. You'll work in the same folder on the web server that you've used for the previous examples.

1. Use the File ➤ New ➤ ActionScript Class command to create a new ActionScript class. Add the class to the xmlUtilities package and call it LoginService. The file should contain the following code:

    ```
    package xmlUtilities {
      public class LoginService {
        public function LoginService() {
        }
      }
    }
    ```

2. Add the following import statements underneath the package declaration. These statements reference the classes that the application will need to use, including the two events you'll capture. You can also wait and see if the statements are added automatically when you declare the variables and write additional code a little later.

    ```
    import mx.rpc.http.HTTPService;
    import mx.rpc.events.ResultEvent;
    import mx.rpc.events.FaultEvent;
    ```

3. Add a [Bindable] declaration above the class declaration. The code needs this declaration to make all of the public methods in the class file bindable in the application file.

    ```
    [Bindable]
    ```

4. Declare the following private variables below the class declaration:

    ```
    private var loginResponse:String;
    private var xmlService:HTTPService;
    ```

    The first variable, loginResponse, will store the returned XML document. The second variable, xmlService, refers to the HTTPService object that will make the request from the server-side file.

5. Modify the constructor method LoginService() as shown here:

    ```
    public function LoginService() {
      xmlService = new HTTPService();
      xmlService.addEventListener(ResultEvent.RESULT, resultHandler);
      xmlService.addEventListener(FaultEvent.FAULT, faultHandler);
    }
    ```

The constructor method creates the HTTPService object and adds an event listener that responds when the object receives a result event. This event is broadcast when the application receives the response from the server-side page. After receiving the event, the resultHandler() function will execute, processing the response. The method also adds another event listener to respond to the fault event.

6. Add the resultHandler() private method shown here:

```
private function resultHandler(e:ResultEvent):void {
  loginResult = e.target.lastResult;
  dispatchEvent(new ResultEvent(ResultEvent.RESULT));
}
```

The resultHandler() method is private because it will be needed only by the class file. The method sets the value of the loginResult XML object to the server response using the expression e.target.lastResult.

The method then dispatches the result event to the application so that it will know that the request has finished and that a result has been received.

7. You also need to add the faultHandler() method to this class file. This method follows:

```
private function faultHandler(e:FaultEvent):void {
  dispatchEvent(new FaultEvent(FaultEvent.FAULT,false, true, null,
    ➥null, e.message));
}
```

This method dispatches a FaultEvent. It passes the e.message parameter so that the application file can display the correct error message in the interface.

8. The class file needs a public method that makes the request for the server-side file. I'll call the method sendRequest(). This method will receive two arguments: the name of the file to request and the variables to send with that request.

For simplicity, the file name will need to include the server path. You could also send this in as another argument, if you want to store the value separately.

```
public function sendRequest(xmlURL:String, vars:Object):void {
  xmlService.url = xmlURL;
  xmlService.resultFormat = "e4x";
  xmlService.request = vars;
  xmlService.method = "POST";
  xmlService.send();
}
```

The sendRequest() method creates a new HTTPService object, using the URL passed in as the first argument. Because you'll be using this with a server-side file, the xmlURL variable will need to contain a full http:// path.

The public method sets the resultFormat property to e4x, as the application is expecting the server-side page to return an XML document. It assigns the vars argument to the request property of the xmlService object so it can send the variables. It also sets the method property to POST the variables to the requested page. The last line of this method calls the send() method of the HTTPService class to make the request.

9. The `LoginService` class will need one public method to return the content from the external document that is stored in the variable `loginResult`.

Add the following public getResponse() method to the class file:

```
public function getResponse():XML {
  return loginResult;
}
```

The method returns the XML object provided by the server-side page. Don't forget that you populated the object in the `resultHandler()` method that you created earlier.

That's all the code for this class file. I've included the complete file so that you can check it against what you've done.

```
package xmlUtilities {
  import mx.rpc.http.HTTPService;
  import mx.rpc.events.ResultEvent;
  import mx.rpc.events.FaultEvent;
  [Bindable]
  public class LoginService {
    private var loginResult:XML;
    private var xmlService:HTTPService;
    public function LoginService() {
      xmlService = new HTTPService();
      xmlService.addEventListener(ResultEvent.RESULT, resultHandler);
    }
    public function sendRequest(xmlURL:String, vars:Object):void {
      xmlService.url = xmlURL;
      xmlService.resultFormat = "e4x";
      xmlService.request = vars;
      xmlService.method = "POST";
      xmlService.send();
    }
    public function getResponse():XML {
      return loginResult;
    }
    private function resultHandler(e:ResultEvent):void {
      loginResult = e.target.lastResult;
      dispatchEvent(new ResultEvent(ResultEvent.RESULT));
    }
    private function faultHandler(e:FaultEvent):void {
      dispatchEvent(new FaultEvent(FaultEvent.FAULT,false, true,
        ➥null,null, e.message));
    }
  }
}
```

10. You'll use this custom class in a Flex application file, so create a new file with the name of your choosing. Add the following interface elements:

```
<?xml version="1.0" encoding="utf-8"?>
<mx:Application xmlns:mx="http://www.adobe.com/2006/mxml"
  layout="absolute">
  <mx:VBox x="10" y="10">
    <mx:Label text="Login" fontSize="14" fontWeight="bold"/>
    <mx:HBox>
      <mx:Label text="Username" fontWeight="bold" width="80"/>
      <mx:TextInput id="username_txt"/>
    </mx:HBox>
    <mx:HBox>
      <mx:Label text="Password" fontWeight="bold" width="80"/>
      <mx:TextInput id="password_txt" displayAsPassword="true"/>
    </mx:HBox>
    <mx:HBox width="100%" horizontalAlign="center">
      <mx:Button id="login_btn" label="Log in"/>
    </mx:HBox>
    <mx:TextArea width="250" height="60" id="message_txt"/>
  </mx:VBox>
</mx:Application>
```

The preceding code block creates the interface shown in Figure 9-10. This is the same interface that you saw in Figure 9-8.

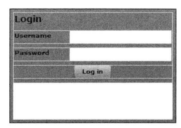

Figure 9-10. The Flex application interface for the HTTPService class example

11. The code will initialize the application by calling a function named initApp() in the creationComplete attribute of the <mx:Application> element. This function will set up the necessary variables, including a new LoginService object.

Modify the <mx:Application> element as shown here in bold:

```
<mx:Application xmlns:mx="http://www.adobe.com/2006/mxml"
  layout="absolute" creationComplete="initApp(event)">
```

This function call will pass a FlexEvent.

12. Add the following <mx:Script> block, which includes the initApp() function:

```
<mx:Script>
  <![CDATA[
    import mx.events.FlexEvent;
    import mx.rpc.events.ResultEvent;
    import mx.rpc.events.FaultEvent;
    import xmlUtilities.LoginService;
    private var myLoginService:LoginService;
    private function initApp(e:FlexEvent):void {
      myLoginService = new LoginService();
      myLoginService.addEventListener(ResultEvent.RESULT,
        ➥resultHandler);
      myLoginService.addEventListener(FaultEvent.FAULT,
        ➥faultHandler);
      login_btn.addEventListener(MouseEvent.CLICK, clickHandler);
    }
    private function resultHandler(e:ResultEvent):void {
    }
    private function faultHandler(e:FaultEvent):void {
    }
    private function clickHandler(e:MouseEvent):void {
    }
  ]]>
</mx:Script>
```

This <mx:Script> block starts by importing the relevant classes. If you forget to add these lines, the import statements should be added automatically when you refer to the classes in the remaining code.

The application will need the FlexEvent class, as this is the event type dispatched when the interface finishes creating. It imports the ResultEvent class to deal with the result event dispatched by the HTTPService element. Similarly, it imports the FaultEvent class because it needs to handle the fault event of the HTTPService element. The last import statement deals with the custom class that you just created, LoginService.

The code creates a LoginService object called myLoginService. It declares the initApp() function, which receives a FlexEvent as an argument.

The function creates a new instance of the LoginService class and then assigns the resultHandler() function to be called when the LoginService object finishes requesting the external document and receives the server response. It also assigns the faultHandler() function, which will respond if there is an error.

At the moment, neither the resultHandler() nor faultHandler() function contains any code. The code includes these function signatures to avoid errors in case you decide to run the application.

The initApp() function assigns an event listener to the login_btn instance. This listener responds to the click event of the button with the clickHandler() function. The <mx:Script> block also contains an empty clickHandler() function.

13. When the user clicks the Log in button, the application needs to check that a username and password have been provided before it calls the sendRequest() method of the LoginService object. It will do this by testing that both entries have a length greater than 0.

Modify the clickHandler() function as shown here in bold:

```
private function clickHandler(e:MouseEvent):void {
  var username:String = username_txt.text;
  var password:String = password_txt.text
  if (username.length > 0 && password.length > 0) {
    var myVars:Object = new Object();
    myVars.username = username;
    myVars.password = password;
    myLoginService.sendRequest(
      ➥"http://localhost/FOE/login.aspx", myVars);
  }
  else {
    message_txt.text = "You must enter both a username and password
      ➥before clicking the button"
  }
}
```

The clickHandler() function starts by assigning the values provided by the user to two variables: username and password. It then tests these variables to check that the length of both entries is greater than 0.

If this is the case, the user must have entered values in both TextInput controls. The function creates a new Object and assigns the username and password variables. It then calls the sendRequest() method of the LoginService object, passing the URL to request, as well as the Object containing the variables.

The URL of the server-side file contains the full path on the web server. You may need to change the path from what is shown in the code sample to one that reflects your own settings. If you're using either the PHP or ColdFusion example, you'll also need to change the file name.

If either of the TextInput controls does not contain an entry, the message You must enter both a username and password before clicking the button displays in the TextArea at the bottom of the interface.

14. The last step in building this application is to respond when a reply or fault is received from the server-side file. The application will display a successful response in the TextArea control using the resultHandler() function.

Modify this function as shown in bold:

```
private function resultHandler(e:ResultEvent):void {
  var response:String = myLoginService.getResponse().toString();
  var userMessage:String;
  if (response == "true") {
    userMessage = "Congratulations. You were successful";
  }
```

```
  else {
    userMessage = "Login failed. Please try again";
  }
  message_txt.text = userMessage;
}
```

The function starts by populating the `response` variable with a `String` representation of the server response. It finds this using the public `getResponse()` method, which returns an XML object. Because the XML object contains a single element, the `toString()` method will find the text inside that element, which is either `true` or `false`.

The function tests the response and populates a `String` variable with an appropriate message. It then displays this message in the `TextArea`.

15. Let's finish with the `faultHandler()` method. Modify it as shown in bold in the following code block:

```
private function faultHandler(e:FaultEvent):void {
  message_txt.text = e.message.toString();
}
```

16. You've now finished the Flex application file. Run the file and enter values for a username and password. If you want to test for a successful response, enter the username sas and password secret. Use other values if you want to see an unsuccessful response.

When you click the button, you should see the TextArea update, as shown in Figure 9-11. Unlike in the previous tag-based approach, you won't see a busy cursor while the request is in progress.

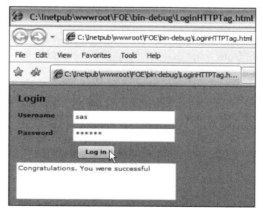

Figure 9-11. The completed Flex application for the HTTPService class example

If you want to test the error handling, change to the name of the server-side file to one that doesn't exist in the folder. Figure 9-12 shows the effect. You may wish to replace this message with a more user-friendly error message!

Figure 9-12. The Flex application displays a fault.

The complete code for the application file follows, in case you want to check it against your own application:

```xml
<?xml version="1.0" encoding="utf-8"?>
<mx:Application xmlns:mx="http://www.adobe.com/2006/mxml"
  layout="absolute"  creationComplete="initApp(event)">
  <mx:Script>
    <![CDATA[
      import mx.events.FlexEvent;
      import mx.rpc.events.ResultEvent;
      import mx.rpc.events.FaultEvent;
      import xmlUtilities.LoginService;
      private var myLoginService:LoginService;
      private function initApp(e:FlexEvent):void {
        myLoginService = new LoginService();
        myLoginService.addEventListener(ResultEvent.RESULT,
          ➥resultHandler);
        myLoginService.addEventListener(FaultEvent.FAULT,
          ➥faultHandler);
        login_btn.addEventListener(MouseEvent.CLICK, clickHandler);
      }
      private function resultHandler(e:ResultEvent):void {
        var response:String = myLoginService.getResponse().
          ➥toString();
        var userMessage:String;
        if (response == "true") {
          userMessage = "Congratulations. You were successful";
        }
        else {
          userMessage = "Login failed. Please try again";
        }
        message_txt.text = userMessage;
      }
      private function faultHandler(e:FaultEvent):void {
        message_txt.text = e.message.toString();
      }
```

325

```
          private function clickHandler(e:MouseEvent):void {
            var username:String = username_txt.text;
            var password:String = password_txt.text
            if (username.length > 0 && password.length > 0) {
              var myVars:Object = new Object();
              myVars.username = username;
              myVars.password = password;
              myLoginService.sendRequest(
                ➥"http://localhost/FOE/login.aspx", myVars);
            }
            else {
              message_txt.text = "You must enter both a username and
                ➥password before clicking the button"
            }
          }
        }
      ]]>
    </mx:Script>
    <mx:VBox x="10" y="10">
      <mx:Label text="Login" fontSize="14" fontWeight="bold"/>
      <mx:HBox>
        <mx:Label text="Username" fontWeight="bold" width="80"/>
        <mx:TextInput id="username_txt"/>
      </mx:HBox>
      <mx:HBox>
        <mx:Label text="Password" fontWeight="bold" width="80"/>
        <mx:TextInput id="password_txt" displayAsPassword="true"/>
      </mx:HBox>
      <mx:HBox width="100%" horizontalAlign="center">
        <mx:Button id="login_btn" label="Log in"/>
      </mx:HBox>
      <mx:TextArea width="250" height="60" id="message_txt"/>
    </mx:VBox>
  </mx:Application>
```

You can find the resource files for this example with the other chapter resources saved as LoginHTTPClass.mxml and LoginService.as.

Choosing the Flex approach

Flex provides you with three approaches when it comes to communicating with the server. You can work in ActionScript with the URLLoader or the HTTPService class, or you can use a tag-based approach with the <mx:HTTPService> element. How do you know which to choose?

If you prefer to take a tag-based approach or you're working with very simple content, choose the <mx:HTTPService> element. You won't need to write any code, and you'll be able to use simple binding expressions to display the content in the application interface.

However, if you prefer to work with ActionScript, you'll need to choose either the URLLoader or HTTPService class. You'll need to cast your returned content as XML before you can use E4X expressions with the URLLoader. You can specify this format specifically when working with the HTTPService class.

The URLLoader class allows you to monitor the progress of your request using the bytesLoaded and bytesTotal properties. These properties aren't available with the HTTPService class.

The URLLoader class also gives you access to a wider range of events. This can provide more detailed error handling than with the HTTPService class. So if you want a little more control in your Flex application, writing ActionScript with the URLLoader class is the best approach. Chapter 5 demonstrated how to do this.

Summary

In this chapter, I showed you how to integrate SWF applications with server-side pages. You saw examples of a server-side page in VB .NET, PHP, and ColdFusion. We worked through applications in both Flash and Flex that used the URLLoader class to send variables and receive a response from the server. You also saw how to achieve the same result with the <mx:HTTPService> element and HTTPService class.

In the next chapter, I'll show you how to work with web services in ActionScript 3.0 in both Flash and Flex.

Chapter 10

CONSUMING WEB SERVICES WITH FLEX

A web service is a remote procedure that provides results in XML format. It's a bit like running a public function on someone else's computer. The user can call the procedure without needing to know anything about the way the remote system works or the way it stores the information. When users access data from a web service, they are said to *consume* the web service.

A web service allows an organization to make its data publicly available without providing a user with direct access to its systems. Using a web service provides a layer of abstraction between a user and corporate systems.

You might use a web service in an application to look up a currency exchange rate, to access local weather information, or even as a way to connect to in-house information in a structured way. The key point is that the information is usually provided from remote computers; that is, computers running at a different location from the current application.

There are many different types of web services, including representational state transfer (REST), XML-Remote Procedure Call (XML-RPC), Simple Object Access Protocol (SOAP), and JavaScript Object Notation Remote Procedure Call (JSON-RPC). These represent different ways for users to access the remote service.

SWF applications built in Flex can access SOAP web services using the `<mx:WebService>` element and WebService class. In this chapter, I'll go through both of these approaches and we'll work through two examples, showing different ways to consume the same web service.

The web service we'll consume in the examples is a currency conversion service. We'll build an application that retrieves the rate and converts an amount.

Flash doesn't have access to the WebService class. However, there are some alternative ways that you can use a SWF application built in Flash to consume a web service. That's the topic for the next chapter, so skip ahead if you're particularly interested in Flash.

You can download the resources for the chapter from http://www.friendsofed.com.

Before we explore how to consume a web service in a Flex application, it's important to understand some background information. The first section in this chapter explains some of the concepts associated with web services and some of the terms that you're likely to come across.

Understanding web services

As I mentioned, there are many different standards or protocols for working with web services, including REST, SOAP, XML-RPC, and JSON-RPC. By the broadest definition, you could also consider an RSS feed to be a web service.

All of these approaches provide access to information in a different way. Each uses a different vocabulary of XML to return the content.

One of the most popular protocols for web services is SOAP. It is also the most relevant for this book because it is the only protocol supported by Flash and Flex. Because the WebService class in Flex works with SOAP web services, we'll start with that topic.

Understanding SOAP web services

SOAP is a communication protocol that uses XML to describe web services. It uses a system of messages. SOAP messages occur in two directions, and are requests made to and responses received from a web service.

The SOAP protocol comes in different versions, and the latest is version 1.2. It describes the specific XML vocabulary required to make the request and provide the response. If you're interested in finding out more about SOAP, you can read about SOAP 1.2 at the W3C web site in the following pages:

- **SOAP primer**: http://www.w3.org/TR/2003/REC-soap12-part0-20030624/
- **Messaging framework**: http://www.w3.org/TR/2003/REC-soap12-part1-20030624/
- **Adjuncts**: http://www.w3.org/TR/2003/REC-soap12-part2-20030624/

SWF applications built in Flex can access SOAP web services using the WebService class. Flex applications can use the <mx:WebService> element and WebService class to create the SOAP message for the request automatically. They can also decode the SOAP response from the web service.

In order to be able to use a web service in a Flex application, you must be able to specify a Web Services Description Language (WSDL) file. The WSDL file provides the details of the functions the web service provides, how to access those functions, and how the returned data will be provided.

The functions available at the web service are described as *operations* within the WSDL file. This file describes which parameters each operation requires, as well as the relevant data types. It also describes which return values each operation will provide and their data types. As well as built-in data types, the WSDL file can also define custom data types.

Understanding the role of WSDL

WSDL is a vocabulary of XML, so you can view the contents of a WSDL file by loading the URL into a web browser. Figure 10-1 shows a sample WSDL file.

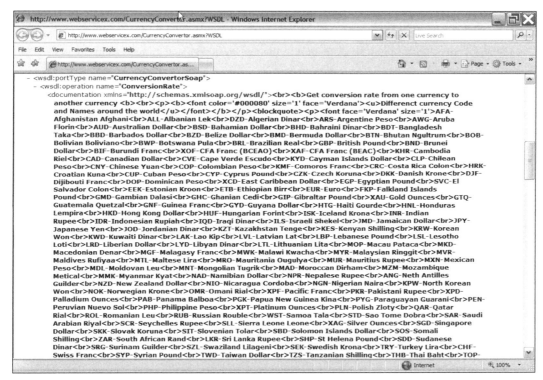

Figure 10-1. Viewing a WSDL file in a web browser

This WSDL file is for a currency conversion web service and is at the URL http://www.webservicex. net/CurrencyConvertor.asmx?WSDL.

A WSDL file contains a set of definitions. It defines the data types used for the operations, the messages that it can receive and send, the operations available, and the communication protocols that the web service uses.

As far as developers are concerned, the most important parts within the WSDL file are the <portType> elements. These elements contain details about the operation request and response, including the name of the operation.

In Figure 10-1, you can see that the operation displayed is called ConversionRate. The <documentation> element provides a description of the operation with supporting information.

The WSDL file indicates that the ConversionRate operation requires that the following element is sent with the request:

```
<wsdl:part name="parameters" element="tns:ConversionRate"/>
```

This argument is defined as part of the tns namespace, and it represents a custom data type. Further digging in the WSDL file reveals that the tns namespace is associated with the http://www. webserviceX.NET/ URL.

The WSDL file defines the ConversionRate data type as a complex element made up of FromCurrency and ToCurrency values. Each element can appear only once in the data type. This means that the user needs to provide two arguments when calling the ConversionRate operation.

The following code block shows the definition of the ConversionRate data type from the WSDL file:

```
<s:element name="ConversionRate">
  <s:complexType>
  <s:sequence>
  <s:element minOccurs="1" maxOccurs="1" name="FromCurrency"
    type="tns:Currency" />
  <s:element minOccurs="1" maxOccurs="1" name="ToCurrency"
    type="tns:Currency" />
  </s:sequence>
  </s:complexType>
</s:element>
```

You'll notice that this definition also specifies that both the FromCurrency and ToCurrency elements are of the type tns:Currency. The WSDL file defines this as a simple type element containing a list of abbreviations for acceptable currencies. The relevant element in the WSDL file follows, but I've included only the first two values in the list:

```
<s:simpleType name="Currency">
  <s:restriction base="s:string">
    <s:enumeration value="AFA"/>
    <s:enumeration value="ALL"/>
  </s:restriction>
</s:simpleType>
```

For developers, this data type means that they must send the correct abbreviation when they query the web service. The abbreviation must be one of the values in the <s:enumeration> elements.

The web service returns a single element described in the following <message> element:

```
<wsdl:output message="tns:ConversionRateSoapOut"/>
```

The WSDL defines the ConversionRateSoapOut message as a <ConversionRateResponse> element.

```
<wsdl:message name="ConversionRateSoapOut">
  <wsdl:part name="parameters" element="tns:ConversionRateResponse"/>
</wsdl:message>
```

The element is a complex type element made up of a single element called ConversionRateResult, which is of the type double. The following code block shows the details of this element:

```
<s:element name="ConversionRateResponse">
  <s:complexType>
    <s:sequence>
    <s:element minOccurs="1" maxOccurs="1"
      name="ConversionRateResult" type="s:double"/>
    </s:sequence>
  </s:complexType>
</s:element>
<s:element name="double" type="s:double"/>
```

You can see that finding your way through a WSDL file can be very complicated! Luckily, Flex can decode the contents of the file so that you don't need to understand it in any detail.

The <mx:WebService> element and WebService ActionScript 3.0 class provide all the functionality that you need to work with SOAP web services in Flex.

Using Flex to consume a web service

You can use the <mx:WebService> element and WebService class to make requests of a SOAP web service in any Flex application. You'll need to provide the WSDL of the web service, the name of any operations that you want to call, and the parameters required by those operations. The SOAP web service will then provide a response, which is either the returned value or a fault.

You can use a tag-based or scripted approach. I'll show you both approaches, starting with an overview of the <mx:WebService> element.

Working with the <mx:WebService> element

The <mx:WebService> element consumes SOAP web services and provide a response to a Flex application. To consume a web service with the <mx:WebService> element, you must take the following steps:

1. Create the <mx:WebService> element, providing a valid wsdl attribute.
2. Specify the web service operation(s) and identify the parameters to send.
3. Call the send() method of the web service.
4. Process the response from the web service.

We'll look at each of these steps in turn.

Creating the web service request

You can create a web service request using the <mx:WebService> element. You'll need to give the element an id and specify the URL for the WSDL file in the wsdl attribute, as shown here:

```
<mx:WebService id="wsRequest" wsdl="urlToTheWSDL">
```

You may also want to display a busy cursor while the request is taking place. You can do so using the following showBusyCursor attribute:

```
<mx:WebService id="wsRequest" wsdl="urlToTheWSDL"
  showBusyCursor="true">
```

This attribute is useful as it informs the user that the request is in progress. It is available only to the element, and you can't set this property in the WebService class with ActionScript.

Once you've set up the `<mx:WebService>` tag, you need to specify which operation to call from the web service.

Specifying the operation

Each type of remote procedure available in the web service is called an *operation*, and you need to specify which operations you want to call from the web service. As I showed you earlier, it's possible to identify the operation names from the WSDL file. Even though you might add a single `<mx:WebService>` element, it's possible for the application to call multiple operations within that web service.

You add each operation that you want to access using an `<mx:operation>` element between the opening and closing `<mx:WebService>` elements. You then specify the arguments for that operation with the `<mx:request>` element. Every argument that you want to send for a specific operation appears inside the `<mx:request>` element, as shown here:

```
<mx:operation name="operationName">
  <mx:request>
    <param1>Value 1</param1>
    <param2>Value 2</param2>
  </mx:request>
</mx:operation>
```

The values that you send with an operation frequently come from UI components in the application. When working with a tag-based approach, it's often easiest to access them with binding expressions. The following code shows how you might use bindings when specifying the arguments for the operation:

```
<mx:operation name="operationName">
  <mx:request>
    <param1>{controlID.boundProperty}</param1>
    <param2>{controlID.boundProperty}</param2>
  </mx:request>
</mx:operation>
```

Once you've added the operation, you need to make the request.

Making the request

You call the send() method of the web service to make the request. You'll need to refer to the id of the `<mx:WebService>` element and the operation name, as shown here:

```
wsRequest.operationName.send();
```

It's important to include the operation name, as it's possible to add multiple operations inside the <mx:WebService> element.

If you need the response to be available when the application loads, you can add a call to the send() method to the creationComplete event of the <mx:Application> element, as shown here:

```
<mx:Application xmlns:mx="http://www.adobe.com/2006/mxml"
    layout="absolute" creationComplete="myWS.doSomething.send()">
```

You could also make the request in the click attribute of a button, as you can see in the following line:

```
<mx:Button id="click_btn" label="Call web service"
    click="myWS.doSomething.send()"/>
```

Requesting the web service will result in a response that contains either the results of the request or an error message.

Receiving the response

The web service will respond to the request in one of two ways: it will provide a valid response, or it will notify the application that a fault occurred. You can specify handlers for the result of an operation by adding the result attribute to the opening element, as shown here:

```
<mx:operation name="operationName" result="resultHandler(event)">
```

You can track fault events from the <mx:WebService> element, as shown in the following code block:

```
<mx:WebService id="wsRequest" wsdl=" urlToTheWSDL"
    showBusyCursor="true" result="resultHandler(event)"
    fault="faultHandler(event)"/>
```

You'll need to write ActionScript functions of the same name. In the preceding example, the resultHandler() function receives a ResultEvent as an argument, while the faultHandler() function receives a FaultEvent.

If you want to avoid writing ActionScript, you can also bind the response—whether it's a result or fault—directly to another component.

Accessing the reply

As with the <mx:HTTPService> element, you can identify the returned results from the web service by accessing the lastResult property of the operation. If the request returns a single parameter, it's also possible to access the response using the toString method:

```
wsRequest.operationName.lastResult.toString();
```

If the response returns more than one parameter, you can use the name of the returned parameter to identify which value to display.

```
wsRequest.operationName.lastResult.returnedParam;
```

335

Again, you must use the operation name to specify which result you're identifying. This is still the case, even if you've included only one operation in the <mx:WebService> element.

You'll process the response in the resultHandler() function either with ActionScript or by using a binding expression in another component. A simple binding expression follows:

```
<mx:TextInput text="{wsRequest.operation.lastResult.toString()}"/>
```

You'll see examples of both approaches in this chapter.

Understanding the resultFormat of an operation

The web service provides a result in the lastResult property of the operation. By default, the data that the web service returns is represented as a simple tree of ActionScript objects. You can also use E4X expressions to access the results; in this case, you'll need to declare the resultFormat of the operation as e4x.

```
<mx:operation name="operationName" resultFormat="e4x">
```

The resultFormat indicates how you'll access the response from the web service. In E4X expressions, the lastResult property is equivalent to the root element, so you wouldn't include it in the path. If you accept the default resultFormat setting, you'll need to include the name of the root element in the path.

Be very careful before using a resultFormat of e4x, as you will probably need to deal with namespaces in the response. If the web service response contains a default namespace, you'll need to write some additional ActionScript declaring the namespace.

For example, the following opening element of a web service response contains the default namespace http://www.webserviceX.NET/. The default namespace doesn't have a prefix and appears in bold in the following code block:

```
<ConversionRateResponse xmlns=http://www.webserviceX.NET/
    xmlns:soap=http://schemas.xmlsoap.org/soap/envelope/
    xmlns:xsi="http://www.w3.org/2001/XMLSchema-instance"
    xmlns:xsd="http://www.w3.org/2001/XMLSchema">
```

To work with the result using E4X expressions, you would need to specify that you wanted to use the default namespace in an <mx:Script> block, as shown here:

```
<mx:Script>
  <![CDATA[
    private namespace webserviceX = "http://www.webserviceX.NET/";
    use namespace webserviceX;
  ]]>
</mx:Script>
```

Handling errors

You can handle errors from the web service in the `faultHandler()` function. This function receives a `FaultEvent` as an argument, and you can access the `fault` property of the event. If you wanted to see a `String` representation of the error, you would use the following code:

```
FaultEvent.fault.faultString;
```

You can add this property to the `fault` attribute of the `<mx:WebService>` element, as shown in the following line:

```
<mx:WebService id="wsRequest" wsdl="myWSDL"
  fault="mx.controls.Alert.show(event.fault.faultString)">
```

This example displays the error message in an Alert control.

That's enough of the theory. We'll work through an example so you can see the different ways to consume a web service.

Working through a tag-based example

This example demonstrates how to consume a web service that provides currency conversion services. The WSDL file for the web service is located at http://www.webservicex.net/CurrencyConvertor.asmx?WSDL. Figure 10-1, earlier in the chapter, shows this WSDL file viewed in a web browser.

We'll use the `ConversionRate` operation. This operation takes two parameters: the abbreviations of the currencies to convert from and to. These parameters are called `FromCurrency` and `ToCurrency`. The WSDL file provides a long list of currency abbreviations that you can use. The operation returns a double number called `ConversionRate`, but because it returns only a single value, you can use the `toString()` method to access it.

1. Start by creating a Flex project with the name and location of your choosing. Create a new application file with the following interface:

```
<?xml version="1.0" encoding="utf-8"?>
<mx:Application xmlns:mx="http://www.adobe.com/2006/mxml"
  layout="absolute">
  <mx:VBox x="10" y="10">
    <mx:Label text="Currency converter" fontSize="14"
      fontWeight="bold"/>
    <mx:HBox>
      <mx:Label text="From currency" fontWeight="bold" width="150"/>
      <mx:ComboBox id="from_cbo"></mx:ComboBox>
    </mx:HBox>
    <mx:HBox>
      <mx:Label text="To currency" fontWeight="bold" width="150"/>
      <mx:ComboBox id="to_cbo"></mx:ComboBox>
    </mx:HBox>
    <mx:HBox>
      <mx:Label text="Amount" fontWeight="bold" width="150"/>
      <mx:TextInput id="amount_txt"/>
    </mx:HBox>
```

```
      <mx:HBox width="100%" horizontalAlign="right">
        <mx:Button label="Convert" id="convert_btn"/>
      </mx:HBox>
      <mx:Spacer height="20"/>
      <mx:HBox>
        <mx:Label text="Converted amount" fontWeight="bold"
          width="150"/>
        <mx:TextInput id="convertedAmount_txt"/>
      </mx:HBox>
    </mx:VBox>
</mx:Application>
```

The application contains two ComboBox controls, which you'll populate with names of the currencies available for conversion. The data associated with each name will be the currency abbreviation.

The interface also contains a TextInput control, so that the users can enter the amount of currency that they wish to convert. There is a Convert button to carry out the operation, and a second TextInput control to display the converted amount.

Figure 10-2 shows how the interface appears when you run the application in a web browser.

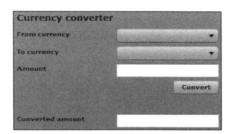

Figure 10-2. The currency converter interface

2. You need to add the list of currencies to convert from and to. You can see the full list of all abbreviations available to the web service at http://www.webservicex.com/CurrencyConvertor. asmx?op=ConversionRate. However, for simplicity, this example uses a small number of these currencies. Feel free to expand on the list if you like.

Modify the from_cbo element as shown here in bold:

```
<mx:ComboBox id="from_cbo" prompt="Select from currency">
  <mx:dataProvider>
    <mx:Array>
      <mx:Object label="Australia dollars" data="AUD"/>
      <mx:Object label="British pound" data="GBP" />
      <mx:Object label="Canadian dollar" data="CAD" />
      <mx:Object label="Euro" data="EUR" />
      <mx:Object label="Singapore dollar" data="SGD" />
      <mx:Object label="South African rand" data="ZAR"/>
      <mx:Object label="US dollar" data="USD"/>
    </mx:Array>
  </mx:dataProvider>
</mx:ComboBox>
```

The <mx:ComboBox> control includes a prompt showing a default value to the user. The code also has an <mx:dataProvider> element containing an Array of values. Each value is an <mx:Object> element containing label and data properties. The label will display in the ComboBox, while the abbreviation provides the data.

3. Make the same modifications to the to_cbo control, adding a prompt and <mx:dataProvider> element.

```
<mx:ComboBox id="to_cbo" prompt="Select to currency">
  <mx:dataProvider>
    <mx:Array>
      <mx:Object label="Australia dollars" data="AUD"/>
      <mx:Object label="British pound" data="GBP" />
      <mx:Object label="Canadian dollar" data="CAD" />
      <mx:Object label="Euro" data="EUR" />
      <mx:Object label="Singapore dollar" data="SGD" />
      <mx:Object label="South African rand" data="ZAR"/>
      <mx:Object label="US dollar" data="USD"/>
    </mx:Array>
  </mx:dataProvider>
</mx:ComboBox>
```

The code populates both ComboBox controls with the same list of currencies. You may wish to add your own currency if it isn't covered here.

> *I could have used a more streamlined approach to populating both ComboBox controls with the introduction of an ActionScript Array and a binding expression. However, in this case, I wanted to show a purely tag-based approach, rather than introducing scripting. You'll see how to populate the controls with ActionScript in this chapter's second example.*

Figure 10-3 shows the interface after populating the ComboBox controls with a list of currencies. In the figure, I've expanded the first ComboBox.

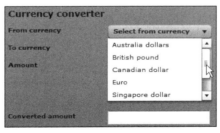

Figure 10-3. Populating the ComboBox controls with currency values

4. The user will enter the amount to convert in a TextInput control. You need to add some validation for the Amount value to make sure that the user enters a valid number before the application carries out the conversion. If you don't do this, you'll generate errors when you try to multiply a nonnumeric value by the conversion rate returned from the web service.

Add the following `<mx:NumberValidator>` element below the opening `<mx:Application>` tag:

```
<mx:NumberValidator id="amountValidator"
  source="{amount_txt}" property="text"
  trigger="{convert_btn}" triggerEvent="click"
  required="true" invalidCharError="Please enter a number"/>
```

The NumberValidator checks that the entry in the Amount TextInput control is a number. The required property indicates that the control must have an entry before the user's entry is considered valid.

The validation occurs when the user clicks the Convert button, because the code specifies the click event of the bound convert_btn control as the trigger. If the entry contains invalid characters, the application displays the message Please enter a number.

Figure 10-4 shows the effect of an invalid entry in the Amount field. The control is highlighted with a red border, and the error message appears when the user moves the mouse over this area.

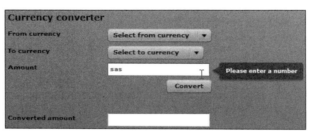

Figure 10-4. The application validates the entry in the Amount TextInput control.

5. You'll make the web service request using an `<mx:WebService>` tag. Add the following tag above the opening `<mx:VBox>` element:

```
<mx:WebService id="currencyService"
  wsdl="http://www.webservicex.net/CurrencyConvertor.asmx?WSDL"
  showBusyCursor="true"
  fault="mx.controls.Alert.show(event.fault.faultString)">
  <mx:operation name="ConversionRate">
    <mx:request>
      <FromCurrency>{from_cbo.selectedItem.data}</FromCurrency>
      <ToCurrency>{to_cbo.selectedItem.data}</ToCurrency>
    </mx:request>
  </mx:operation>
</mx:WebService>
```

The code creates an `<mx:WebService>` element with the id of currencyService. This web service uses the WSDL file that I provided earlier. When requesting the service, the application will show a busy cursor while the request is in progress. The web service includes a fault handler that displays the faultString property in an Alert control.

The web service identifies a single operation: ConversionRate. This operation requires two parameters: FromCurrency and ToCurrency. These values are bound to the data properties of the selected items in the two ComboBox controls.

6. The web service request will occur when the user clicks the Convert button. Clicking the button also invokes the NumberValidator to check that the conversion amount is valid. The conversion will stop if this amount is invalid.

Modify the Button element as shown here in bold:

```
<mx:Button label="Convert" id="convert_btn"
  click="currencyService.ConversionRate.send()"/>
```

When the user clicks the button, the application calls the send() method of the currencyService web service operation ConversionRate.

7. The last step in completing the application is to display the converted amount in the Converted amount TextInput control.

Modify the convertedAmount_txt control as shown in the following code. The new attribute, text, is shown in bold.

```
<mx:TextInput id="convertedAmount_txt"
  text="{String(Number(currencyService.ConversionRate.lastResult.
➡toString()) * Number(amount_txt.text))}"/>
```

Unfortunately, this binding expression looks cumbersome and a little difficult to interpret. That's because the code binds the results of a calculation to the text property of the TextInput control. The expression must treat the values as numbers during the calculation, but treat them as String data to display the result in the TextArea control.

As always, the binding expression appears inside curly braces. The expression finds the returned rate and casts it as a Number using the following expression:

```
Number(currencyService.ConversionRate.lastResult.toString())
```

The returned rate is found by converting the lastResult property using the toString() method.

The code casts the expression as a Number because, even though the WSDL file indicates that the data type is double, the web service content is returned as an object. The code needs to convert this to a String to access the returned value.

The following expression finds the amount to convert. The expression treats the value entered in the Amount control as a Number.

```
Number(amount_txt.text)
```

The bound expression multiplies both of these numbers together and casts the result as a String so it can be bound to the text property of the TextInput control.

> *You can omit the String casting, and the example will still work. However, it's best practice to explicitly cast the data type rather than relying on Flex to do it for you.*

8. You can now run the completed application. Select two currencies, and enter an amount for the conversion. Figure 10-5 shows the result of a successful currency conversion.

Figure 10-5. The completed application

You can also test the error-handling capability of the application. Figure 10-6 shows the results of clicking the Convert button without selecting either currency.

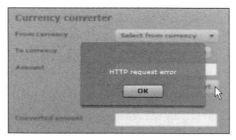

Figure 10-6. Displaying an error in the web service request

The application displays an Alert control with an error message. In this case, it says HTTP request error. You could also include a more descriptive message in the faultHandler() function.

The complete code for this application follows:

```xml
<?xml version="1.0" encoding="utf-8"?>
<mx:Application xmlns:mx="http://www.adobe.com/2006/mxml"
  layout="absolute">
  <mx:NumberValidator id="amountValidator"
    source="{amount_txt}" property="text"
    trigger="{convert_btn}" triggerEvent="click"
    required="true" invalidCharError="Please enter a number"/>
  <mx:WebService id="currencyService"
    wsdl="http://www.webservicex.net/CurrencyConvertor.asmx?WSDL"
    showBusyCursor="true"
    fault="mx.controls.Alert.show(event.fault.faultString)">
    <mx:operation name="ConversionRate">
      <mx:request>
        <FromCurrency>{from_cbo.selectedItem.data}</FromCurrency>
        <ToCurrency>{to_cbo.selectedItem.data}</ToCurrency>
      </mx:request>
```

```
      </mx:operation>
   </mx:WebService>
   <mx:VBox x="10" y="10">
     <mx:Label text="Currency converter" fontSize="14"
       fontWeight="bold"/>
     <mx:HBox>
       <mx:Label text="From currency" fontWeight="bold" width="150"/>
       <mx:ComboBox id="from_cbo" prompt="Select from currency">
         <mx:dataProvider>
           <mx:Array>
             <mx:Object label="Australia dollars" data="AUD"/>
             <mx:Object label="British pound" data="GBP" />
             <mx:Object label="Canadian dollar" data="CAD" />
             <mx:Object label="Euro" data="EUR" />
             <mx:Object label="Singapore dollar" data="SGD" />
             <mx:Object label="South African rand" data="ZAR"/>
             <mx:Object label="US dollar" data="USD"/>
           </mx:Array>
         </mx:dataProvider>
       </mx:ComboBox>
     </mx:HBox>
     <mx:HBox>
       <mx:Label text="To currency" fontWeight="bold" width="150"/>
       <mx:ComboBox id="to_cbo" prompt="Select to currency">
         <mx:dataProvider>
           <mx:Array>
             <mx:Object label="Australia dollars" data="AUD"/>
             <mx:Object label="British pound" data="GBP" />
             <mx:Object label="Canadian dollar" data="CAD" />
             <mx:Object label="Euro" data="EUR" />
             <mx:Object label="Singapore dollar" data="SGD" />
             <mx:Object label="South African rand" data="ZAR"/>
             <mx:Object label="US dollar" data="USD"/>
           </mx:Array>
         </mx:dataProvider>
       </mx:ComboBox>
     </mx:HBox>
     <mx:HBox>
       <mx:Label text="Amount" fontWeight="bold" width="150"/>
       <mx:TextInput id="amount_txt"/>
     </mx:HBox>
     <mx:HBox width="100%" horizontalAlign="right">
       <mx:Button label="Convert" id="convert_btn"
         click="currencyService.ConversionRate.send()"/>
     </mx:HBox>
     <mx:Spacer height="20"/>
     <mx:HBox>
       <mx:Label text="Converted amount" fontWeight="bold"
         width="150"/>
```

```
        <mx:TextInput id="convertedAmount_txt"
          text="{String(Number(currencyService.ConversionRate.
          ➥lastResult.toString()) * Number(amount_txt.text))}"/>
      </mx:HBox>
    </mx:VBox>
  </mx:Application>
```

You can find the completed file saved as CurrencyConverterTag.mxml with the chapter resources.

Before we work though a scripted version of this example, let's explore the WebService class.

Working with the WebService class

The WebService class is in the mx.rpc.soap.mxml package. It works in a very similar way to the <mx:WebService> tag, except that the showBusyCursor property isn't available to the class. The WebService class works with the Operation class, which describes the operations available to the web service.

Let's look at the properties, methods, and events of the WebService class. Then I'll cover some relevant points about web service operations.

Properties of the WebService class

Table 10-1 shows the most commonly used properties of the WebService class.

Table 10-1. Properties of the WebService class

Property	Data type	Description	Default value
concurrency	String	Indicates how to handle multiple calls to the same service. Choose from multiple, single, and last.	multiple
description	String	Provides the description of the service.	
headers	Array	Returns the SOAP headers registered for the web service.	
port	String	Specifies the port to use with the web service.	
ready	Boolean	Indicates whether the web service is ready for requests.	
service	String	Specifies which remote operation the web service should use.	
wsdl	String	Specifies the location for the WSDL for the web service.	

For simple web services, you'll most commonly use only the wsdl property to set the location of the WSDL file for the web service. For that reason, I won't go into detail about the other properties, with the exception of concurrency.

The concurrency property determines how to deal with multiple requests to the web service. The default value of multiple indicates that the application can call the web service more than once. A value of single means that only one request can be made at a time and that a fault is generated when more than one request occurs. The value last means that a new request cancels any earlier request. You would change from the default value only if you wanted to restrict the application from making multiple requests.

The WebService class also has a number of methods.

Methods of the WebService class

Table 10-2 shows the main methods of the WebService class.

Table 10-2. Methods of the WebService class

Method	Parameters	Description	Returns
canLoadWSDL()		Determines if the web service is ready to load the WSDL file	Boolean
disconnect()		Disconnects from the web service and removes any pending requests	Nothing
getOperation()	name: String	Returns the operation specified from the web service	AbstractOperation
loadWSDL()	uri: String	Loads the WSDL for the web service	Nothing
WebService()	Constructor that creates a new web service	Nothing	

When working with simple web services, you'll most likely use only the constructor and loadWSDL() methods. You can either pass the URL of the WSDL file with the loadWSDL() method or set the wsdl property prior to calling the method.

Let's move onto the events dispatched by the WebService class.

Events of the WebService class

The WebService tag dispatches a number of events, as summarized in Table 10-3.

Table 10-3. The events dispatched by the WebService class

Event	Type	Description
fault	FaultEvent	Dispatched when a WebService call fails
invoke	InvokeEvent	Dispatched when the WebService call is invoked, providing an error isn't encountered first
load	LoadEvent	Dispatched when the WSDL loads successfully
result	ResultEvent	Dispatched when a WebService call returns successfully

Of these, you're most likely to use the fault and result events.

Before we move on, it's worth looking briefly at the Operation class, which works with the WebService class when consuming a web service.

Understanding the Operation class

The Operation class is in the mx.rpc.soap package. It describes the operation at the web service, and it's an integral part of requesting a web service. It's important to understand the methods, properties, and events of the Operation class.

Properties of the Operation class

Table 10-4 shows the most important properties of the Operation class.

Table 10-4. Properties of the Operation class

Property	Data type	Description	Default value
arguments	Object	Contains the arguments for the operation.	
ignoreWhitespace	Boolean	Determines if whitespace should be ignored when processing a SOAP request or response.	true
lastResult	Object	Contains the result of the last call to the operation.	
multiplePartsFormat	String	Determines the type of the result object where the web service defines multiple parts in the output message.	array
name	String	The name of the operation.	
resultFormat	String	The encoding for the Operation result. The choices are object, e4x, and xml.	object
service	AbstractService	Provides access to the service that hosts the operation.	

Most of these properties are self-explanatory, but a few need a little more explanation:

- arguments: The arguments property contains the parameters that will be passed to the operation when the application calls the send() method. If the send() method also includes its own parameters, the arguments property is ignored.

- multiplePartsFormat: The multiplePartsFormat property has the possible values object and array. The value object indicates that the lastResult will be an Object containing properties that correspond to each output part. A value of array means that lastResult is treated as an array. The output part values are added to the Array in the order they occur in the SOAP response.

- resultFormat: The resultFormat property determines how the result from the web service is provided to the application. The default value, object, means that the XML content is placed into an object structure as detailed in the WSDL document. Using e4x means that you can use E4X expressions to access the content. The value xml is used for ActionScript 2.0–type XML documents.

The Operation class also has a number of methods.

Methods of the Operation class

Table 10-5 shows the main methods of the Operation class.

Table 10-5. Methods of the Operation class

Method	Parameters	Description	Returns
cancel()	id: String	Cancels the last request or the request with the id passed to the method. Prevents the result or fault method from being dispatched.	AsyncToken
clearResult()	fireBindingEvent: Boolean	Sets the result property to null. Useful when the result is a large object that is no longer being used.	AsyncToken
Operation()	webService: AbstractService, name: String	Constructor method. Creates a new Operation.	Nothing
send()	arguments: *	Executes the operation, passing any arguments inside the method with the call.	AsyncToken

These methods are self-explanatory, so let's move on to the events of the Operation class.

Events of the Operation class

The Operation class dispatches the events summarized in Table 10-6.

Table 10-6. The events dispatched by the Operation class

Event	Type	Description
fault	FaultEvent	Dispatched when an Operation call fails.
header	HeaderEvent	Dispatched when an Operation call returns with SOAP headers in the response. A HeaderEvent is dispatched for each SOAP header.
result	ResultEvent	Dispatched when an AbstractOperation call returns successfully.

These events work in the same way as for the web service. You set an event listener for each event and respond appropriately when they are dispatched. It's possible to set a listener for a result and fault on both the web service and the operation.

The fault event of the WebService responds to a web service failure where the fault isn't handled by the operation itself. If the operation handles the fault, it will dispatch its own fault event.

Next, let's look at the process that you'll need to follow to consume a web service using ActionScript.

Consuming a web service with ActionScript

The steps to consume a web service in ActionScript are much the same as those used in the tag-based approach.

1. Create an instance of the WebService class, providing a valid wsdl property.
2. Optionally, add a [Bindable] metatag if you want to bind the results of the web service to other controls.
3. Specify the web service operation and identify the arguments to send.
4. Call the send() method of the web service operation.
5. Process the response from the web service.

Let's work through the process in more detail.

Creating the web service request

To start the process, you would create a new WebService object using the constructor method, as shown here:

```
var wsRequest:WebService = new WebService();
```

If you want to bind the results from a web service request made with ActionScript, you'll need to use the [Bindable] metatag when you declare the object, as shown here:

```
[Bindable]
var wsRequest:WebService = new WebService();
```

This metatag will allow you to use binding expressions in curly braces for the bound properties of your other components. For example, you might want to bind the lastResult directly to the text property of another component.

You can use the loadWSDL() method to specify the URL for the WSDL file, as follows:

```
wsRequest.loadWSDL("urlToTheWSDL");
```

You can also set the wsdl property first and call the loadWSDL() method without passing the URL as an argument.

```
wsRequest.wsdl = "urlToTheWSDL";
wsRequest.loadWSDL();
```

Specifying the operation

It's a little more complicated to specify the operation in ActionScript compared with using the <mx:WebService> element. You can add an operation by creating an Operation object, as shown here:

```
var wsRequest:WebService = new WebService();
var wsOperation: Operation;
wsOperation = wsRequest["operationName"];
```

An Operation represents the operation on the web service. As you can see, you need to declare an Operation object first, and then associate it with the web services request, passing a String for the name of the operation.

You can set the arguments at the same time using the arguments property. In this case, each of the arguments for the operation must be created as properties of an Object. You can then set that Object as the arguments property of the web service request, as shown here:

```
var args = new Object();
args.param1 = "value 1";
args.param2 = "value 2";
wsOperation.arguments = args;
```

It's also possible to pass the arguments inside the call to the send() method, which you'll see in the next example.

Making the request

In ActionScript, it's simple to make the request for the web service. You use the name of the web service and call the send() method.

```
wsRequest.send();
```

You can also call the operation directly as a method of the web service, as shown in the next line:

```
wsRequest.wsOperation();
```

If you use the second approach, you can pass the arguments directly with the operation or with the send() method of the operation. The following two lines are equivalent:

```
wsRequest.wsOperation("value 1", "value 2");
wsRequest.wsOperation.send("value 1", "value 2");
```

Remember that passing arguments directly with the operation overrides any arguments set as the arguments property of the operation.

Receiving the response

The addEventListener() method assigns event handlers for the result and fault events. You would use the method as shown in the following code block:

```
wsRequest.addEventListener(ResultEvent.RESULT, resultHandler);
wsRequest.addEventListener(FaultEvent.FAULT, faultHandler);
```

The result event handler function, resultHandler(), receives a ResultEvent as an argument. The fault handler function receives a FaultEvent. You can use properties of each event to access information from the web service.

You can also assign event handlers to the operation itself. This process allows you to respond directly to any errors that occur in the operation itself, rather than from the web service.

```
wsOperation.addEventListener(ResultEvent.RESULT, resultHandler);
wsOperation.addEventListener(FaultEvent.FAULT, faultHandler);
```

Accessing the reply

You access the reply from the web service in much the same way as you do in the tag-based approach. You need to use the lastResult property of the operation. If the operation returns a single value, you can access the response with the toString() method, as you saw earlier.

```
wsRequest.operationName.lastResult.toString();
```

You can also use the name of the returned parameter to identify which value to display from the response.

```
wsRequest.operationName.lastResult.returnedParam;
```

As I mentioned earlier, it's important to consider the lastResult property of the operation. By default, the web service returns data as a simple tree of ActionScript objects. If you want to override this setting, you can declare the resultFormat of the operation as e4x so you can use E4X expressions.

```
wsOperation.resultFormat = "e4x";
```

It's important to remember that in E4X expressions, the `lastResult` property is equivalent to the root element, so you wouldn't include it in the path. If you accept the default `resultFormat` setting, you'll need to include the name of the root element in the path.

You'll also need to consider the effect of namespaces if you're using a `resultFormat` of e4x. As I mentioned earlier, if the web service response contains a default namespace, you'll need to indicate that you wish to use the namespace with the following ActionScript:

```
private namespace webserviceX = " http://www.webserviceX.NET/";
use namespace webserviceX;
```

Understanding returned data types

One advantage of using the `WebService` class is that many of the built-in data types specified in the WSDL file are converted to ActionScript 3.0 data types. For example, if the WSDL file specifies a return value that uses the data type `xs:int`, Flex recognizes this value as an `int` data type once the content is loaded.

This operates differently from a `URLLoader` object or an `HTTPService` object, where all element and attribute values are treated as `String` values. Bear in mind, though, that custom data types won't have an equivalent value in ActionScript.

Table 10-7 shows how the data types listed in the WSDL document convert to ActionScript 3.0 data types.

Table 10-7. ActionScript conversions of SOAP data types

SOAP data type	ActionScript data type
xs:string	String
xs:int	int
xs:float	Number
xs:boolean	Boolean
xs:date	Date

In our example, the returned data type is double, which doesn't have an ActionScript 3.0 equivalent. This means that the value will be treated as a `String`.

Handling errors

As you saw earlier, you can handle errors from both the web service and the operation using a fault event handler function. Both functions receive a FaultEvent as an argument, and you can access the fault property of the event. You can see the fault message using the `faultString` property, as shown here:

```
FaultEvent.fault.faultString;
```

We'll work through the same example that you saw earlier using a scripted approach. This time, we'll use a custom class to handle the web service request.

Working through a scripted example

We'll revisit the example from earlier in the chapter using ActionScript. We'll use the same interface but work with a custom class to access the web service.

1. Start by creating an ActionScript class in the project you created earlier using File ➤ New ➤ ActionScript Class. Give the class the name CurrencyConverter and add it to the package xmlUtilities.

   The file should contain the following code. Don't worry if Flex Builder has used a slightly different arrangement for the opening curly braces.

   ```
   package xmlUtilities {
     public class CurrencyConverter{
       public function CurrencyConverter () {
       }
     }
   }
   ```

2. Modify the class file to make it bindable by adding a [Bindable] metatag above the class declaration. This metatag makes all public methods of the class file available for use in binding expressions in the application file.

   ```
   [Bindable]
   public class CurrencyConverter{
   ```

3. If you would like, you can add the following import statements below the package declaration. These statements reference the class files that the application will need to use. They will also be added automatically as you complete the class file. If you choose to skip this step, please double-check that all of the import statements are present when you've finished creating this class.

   ```
   import mx.rpc.soap.WebService;
   import mx.rpc.soap.Operation;
   import mx.rpc.events.ResultEvent;
   import mx.rpc.events.FaultEvent;
   ```

4. Add the following private variable declarations underneath the class file declaration.

   ```
   private var ws:WebService;
   private var wsOperation:String;
   private var rate:Number;
   ```

   The ws object refers to the WebService object. The wsOperation variable refers to the operation on the web service. The rate Number stores the rate returned by the operation.

5. Now it's time to create the constructor method for the CurrencyConverter class. Modify the constructor as shown here in bold:

```
public function CurrencyConverter() {
  ws = new WebService();
  ws.wsdl = "http://www.webservicex.com/CurrencyConvertor.asmx?WSDL";
  ws.loadWSDL();
  ws.addEventListener(ResultEvent.RESULT,
    ➥wsResultHandler);
  ws.addEventListener(FaultEvent.FAULT, wsFaultHandler);
}
```

The constructor method starts by creating a new WebService object. It then sets the value of the wsdl property to the URL for the web service. It calls the loadWSDL() method of the ws object to load this WSDL file.

The method finishes by adding event handlers. It adds a result and fault event handler to the web service. You'll add these private methods next.

6. Add the following private methods:

```
private function wsResultHandler(e:ResultEvent):void {
  rate = e.target[wsOperation].lastResult.toString();
  dispatchEvent(new ResultEvent(ResultEvent.RESULT));
}
private function wsFaultHandler(e:FaultEvent):void {
  dispatchEvent(new FaultEvent(FaultEvent.FAULT, false, true,
    ➥e.fault));
}
```

The wsResultHandler() method sets the rate variable from the returned result. It uses the wsOperation, which you'll set when the application specifies the operation to call. Notice that the code refers to the operation using e.target[wsOperation], because it can't use the String value wsOperation as part of a path created with dot notation.

The method then dispatches a new ResultEvent. The wsFaultHandler() method dispatches a new FaultEvent with default values for arguments and includes the fault object so the user can see the provided faultString.

7. The next step in building the class file is to provide a public method that will call the operation on the web service. Add the callWS() method now.

```
public function callWS(operation:String, fromCurr:String,
  ➥toCurr:String):void {
  wsOperation = operation;
  ws[wsOperation].send(fromCurr, toCurr);
}
```

The method takes the operation name, from-currency value, and to-currency value as arguments. It calls the operation using the send() method and passing the values. Again, you'll notice the use of the expression ws[operation] to deal with the operation name.

8. The class file will provide two public methods to the user to access the rate, depending on whether the user provides an amount to convert. The first public method, getRate(), will return only the rate. The second method, convert(), will accept a value and perform a conversion of this value based on the returned rate. It will return the converted amount.

Add these methods now.

353

```
public function getRate():Number {
  return rate;
}
public function convert(amount:Number):Number {
  return rate * amount;
}
```

That's it for the content in the class file. The complete code follows, so you can check your version against mine.

```
package xmlUtilities {
  import mx.rpc.soap.WebService;
  import mx.rpc.soap.Operation;
  import mx.rpc.events.FaultEvent;
  import mx.rpc.events.ResultEvent;
  [Bindable]
  public class CurrencyConverter {
    private var ws:WebService;
    private var wsOperation:String;
    private var rate:Number;
    public function CurrencyConverter() {
      ws = new WebService();
      ws.wsdl = "http://www.webservicex.com/
        ➥CurrencyConvertor.asmx?WSDL";
      ws.loadWSDL();
      ws.addEventListener(ResultEvent.RESULT, wsResultHandler);
      ws.addEventListener(FaultEvent.FAULT, wsFaultHandler);
    }
    public function callWS(operation:String, fromCurr:String,
      ➥toCurr:String):void {
      wsOperation = operation;
      ws[wsOperation].send(fromCurr, toCurr);
    }
    public function getRate():Number {
      return rate;
    }
    public function convert(amount:Number):Number {
      return rate * amount;
    }
    private function wsResultHandler(e:ResultEvent):void {
      rate = e.target[wsOperation].lastResult.toString();
      dispatchEvent(new ResultEvent(ResultEvent.RESULT));
    }
    private function wsFaultHandler(e:FaultEvent):void {
      dispatchEvent(new FaultEvent(FaultEvent.FAULT, false, true,
        ➥e.fault));
    }
  }
}
```

9. Now you need to build an application that will use this class to query the web service. Create a new application file with the name of your choosing. I've called my file CurrencyConverterClass.

10. Modify the file to display the following interface:

```
<?xml version="1.0" encoding="utf-8"?>
<mx:Application xmlns:mx="http://www.adobe.com/2006/mxml"
  layout="absolute">
  <mx:VBox x="10" y="10">
    <mx:Label text="Currency converter" fontSize="14"
      fontWeight="bold"/>
    <mx:HBox>
      <mx:Label text="From currency" fontWeight="bold" width="150"/>
      <mx:ComboBox id="from_cbo" prompt="Select from currency"/>
    </mx:HBox>
    <mx:HBox>
      <mx:Label text="To currency" fontWeight="bold" width="150"/>
      <mx:ComboBox id="to_cbo" prompt="Select to currency" />
    </mx:HBox>
    <mx:HBox>
      <mx:Label text="Amount" fontWeight="bold" width="150"/>
      <mx:TextInput id="amount_txt"/>
    </mx:HBox>
    <mx:HBox width="100%" horizontalAlign="right">
      <mx:Button label="Convert" id="convert_btn"/>
    </mx:HBox>
    <mx:Spacer height="20"/>
    <mx:HBox>
      <mx:Label text="Converted amount" fontWeight="bold"
        width="150"/>
      <mx:TextInput id="convertedAmount_txt"/>
    </mx:HBox>
  </mx:VBox>
</mx:Application>
```

Figure 10-7 shows how this interface appears.

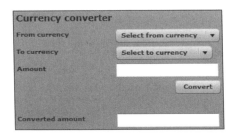

Figure 10-7. The Currency Converter application interface

It's very similar to the first exercise, except that you've added prompts to the ComboBox components from the beginning.

355

11. Add a creationComplete attribute to the opening <mx:Application> element, as shown in bold in the following line:

```
<mx:Application xmlns:mx="http://www.adobe.com/2006/mxml"
  layout="absolute" creationComplete="initApp(event)">
```

The initApp() function will set up the application after the interface has finished creating.

12. Add the following <mx:Script> block beneath the opening <mx:Application> element. The script block contains the initApp() function, as well as other ActionScript that you'll need to set up the application.

```
<mx:Script>
  <![CDATA[
    import mx.events.FlexEvent;
    import mx.rpc.events.ResultEvent;
    import mx.rpc.events.FaultEvent;
    import xmlUtilities.CurrencyConverter;
    import mx.controls.Alert;
    import mx.events.ValidationResultEvent;
    private var myCC: CurrencyConverter;
    private var currencyList:Array = new Array();
    private function initApp(e:FlexEvent):void {
      myCC = new CurrencyConverter();
      myCC.addEventListener(ResultEvent.RESULT, resultHandler);
      myCC.addEventListener(FaultEvent.FAULT, faultHandler);
    }
    private function resultHandler(e:ResultEvent):void{
    }
    private function faultHandler(e:FaultEvent):void {
    }
  ]]>
</mx:Script>
```

This <mx:Script> block starts by importing the classes you'll need to refer to in the application. Again, you can allow Flex to add these classes automatically if you prefer.

These classes include the FlexEvent class, needed for the creationComplete handler; the ResultEvent and FaultEvent, needed for the server response; and the CurrencyConverter customer class that you created in the first part of the exercise.

The second-to-last import statement references the class for the Alert control, which you'll use to display user messages. The final import statement refers to the class ValidationResultEvent, which you'll need for the <mx:NumberValidator> you'll add a little later.

The code includes the declaration of the new CurrencyConverter object called myCC. It also declares a currencyList Array, which you'll use to populate the currencies in the ComboBox controls.

The initApp() function follows. It receives a FlexEvent as an argument and returns nothing. It creates a new CurrencyConverter object. It adds event listeners for the result and fault events of the CurrencyConverter object. The code also includes empty function declarations for these two handler functions.

13. The next task is to populate the ComboBox controls with the list of currency values. You need to assign values to the countryList Array and then associate this Array as the dataProvider property for both ComboBox controls.

Modify the initApp() function as shown in bold here:

```
private function initApp(e:FlexEvent):void {
  myCC = new WebServiceConsumer();
  myCC.addEventListener(ResultEvent.RESULT, resultHandler);
  myCC.addEventListener(FaultEvent.FAULT, faultHandler);
  populateCurrencies();
}
```

The new line calls the populateCurrencies() function, which you'll add next.

14. Add the populateCurrencies() function:

```
private function populateCurrencies():void {
  currencyList.push({label: "Australia dollars", data: "AUD"});
  currencyList.push({label: "British pound", data: "GBP"});
  currencyList.push({label: "Canadian dollar", data: "CAD"});
  currencyList.push({label: "Euro", data: "EUR"});
  currencyList.push({label: "Singapore dollar", data: "SGD"});
  currencyList.push({label: "South African rand", data: "ZAR"});
  currencyList.push({label: "US dollar", data: "USD"});
  from_cbo.dataProvider = currencyList;
  to_cbo.dataProvider = currencyList;
}
```

This function adds values to the currencyList Array using the push() method. Each line adds an Object to the Array, consisting of a label and data property. This example uses the same values that were used in the first exercise.

Once the Array is populated with the seven currencies, it sets the currencyList as the dataProvider for both the from_cbo and to_cbo controls. If you test the application at this point, you'll see that both controls contain a list of currencies.

15. The application will use a number validator to ensure that the user enters a valid number value into the Amount field. The application will proceed with the conversion only if the entry is valid, so it will use a slightly different process than the one used in the first example.

Add the following <mx:NumberValidator> below the closing </mx:Script> tag:

```
<mx:NumberValidator id="amountValidator"
  source="{amount_txt}" property="text"
  trigger="{convert_btn}" triggerEvent="click"
  required="false" invalidCharError="Please enter a number"
  valid="callCC(event)" invalid="convertedAmount_txt.text = ''"/>
```

This NumberValidator doesn't require an entry in the amount_txt control. If there is no entry, only the exchange rate will display. Otherwise, the application will calculate the converted amount.

When the user makes an entry, if the entry includes nonnumeric characters, the error message Please enter a number displays. Validation occurs when the user clicks the Convert button. If the entry is valid, the application calls the callCC() method, passing a ValidationResultEvent. If the entry isn't valid, the application clears any entries in the convertedAmount_txt control.

In this version of the application, clicking the Convert button doesn't call the web service. Instead, it calls the validator, which in turn calls the web service if the amount_txt entry is either blank or a valid number.

Figure 10-4, earlier in the chapter, shows the effect of an invalid entry in the Amount field.

16. To respond to the valid event of the `<mx:NumberValidator>`, you'll need to add the `callCC()` function that you referenced earlier.

```
private function callCC(e:ValidationResultEvent):void {
  var fromCurrencyIndex:int = from_cbo.selectedIndex;
  var toCurrencyIndex:int = to_cbo.selectedIndex;
  if (fromCurrencyIndex!= -1 && toCurrencyIndex != -1) {
  myCC.callWS("ConversionRate", from_cbo.selectedItem.data,
    ➥to_cbo.selectedItem.data);  }
  else {
    Alert.show("Select currencies to convert before clicking the
      ➥Convert button");
  }
}
```

This function creates variables for the selected From currency index (`fromCurrencyIndex`), and the selected To currency index (`toCurrencyIndex`). It tests that the user has selected both currencies by comparing the selectedIndex properties with the value -1.

If an index is selected for both ComboBox components, the function calls the `callWS()` method of the CurrencyConverter object, passing the operation name and the from-currency and to-currency arguments.

If the user hasn't selected currencies, the else block displays an Alert control with the message Select currencies to convert before clicking the Convert button. Figure 10-8 shows the message that the user will see in this case.

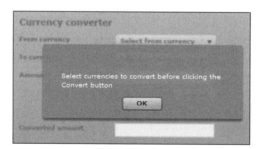

Figure 10-8. Clicking the Convert button without selecting currency values generates an alert.

17. Once the call to the web service is made, the result and fault event handlers need to be configured to deal with the server response. Modify the result handler as shown here:

```
private function resultHandler(e:ResultEvent):void{
  var amtToConvert:String = amount_txt.text;
  if (amtToConvert.length > 0) {
    convertedAmount_txt.text =
      ➥String(myCC.convert(Number(amtToConvert)));
  }
  else {
    convertedAmount_txt.text = String(myCC.getRate());
  }
}
```

The resultHandler() function receives a ResultEvent object as an argument. It starts by identifying the entry in the amount_txt control. If there is an entry in this TextInput component, the application will convert the supplied value into the new currency. It does so by calling the convert() public method of the CurrencyConverter class, passing the amount cast as a Number.

The application assigns this value to the text property of the convertedAmount_txt control. Notice that it uses the String() constructor to cast the returned calculation as a String.

If the user has not entered an amount to convert, the application calls the getRate() method of the CurrencyConverter. It places the call inside the String() constructor method to cast it appropriately before assigning it to the text property of the TextInput control.

18. The application also needs to respond to a fault in the call to the web service. It will do this by displaying an Alert control with the relevant error message.

Modify the fault handler as shown in the following code block:

```
private function faultHandler(e:FaultEvent):void {
  Alert.show(e.fault.faultString);
}
```

The faultHandler() function receives a FaultEvent as an argument. It displays the faultString property of the passed fault object in an Alert control. Figure 10-9 shows the effect of this function.

Figure 10-9. The application displays an alert when notified of a fault.

I generated the error by changing the value of the wsdl property to a nonexistent URL. You could assign your own custom error message instead, if you want to display something more descriptive.

Well done—you've completed the application file. The complete code follows, so you can check it against your own version:

```
<?xml version="1.0" encoding="utf-8"?>
<mx:Application xmlns:mx="http://www.adobe.com/2006/mxml"
  layout="absolute" creationComplete="initApp(event)">
  <mx:Script>
    <![CDATA[
      import mx.events.FlexEvent;
    import mx.rpc.events.ResultEvent;
      import mx.rpc.events.FaultEvent;
      import xmlUtilities.CurrencyConverter;
      import mx.controls.Alert;
      import mx.events.ValidationResultEvent;
      private var myCC:CurrencyConverter;
      private var currencyList:Array = new Array();
      private function initApp(e:FlexEvent):void {
        myCC = new CurrencyConverter();
        myCC.addEventListener(ResultEvent.RESULT, resultHandler);
        myCC.addEventListener(FaultEvent.FAULT, faultHandler);
        populateCurrencies();
      }
      private function populateCurrencies():void {
        currencyList.push({label: "Australia dollars", data: "AUD"});
        currencyList.push({label: "British pound", data: "GBP"});
        currencyList.push({label: "Canadian dollar", data: "CAD"});
        currencyList.push({label: "Euro", data: "EUR"});
        currencyList.push({label: "Singapore dollar", data: "SGD"});
        currencyList.push({label: "South African rand",
          ➥data: "ZAR"});
        currencyList.push({label: "US dollar", data: "USD"});
        from_cbo.dataProvider = currencyList;
        to_cbo.dataProvider = currencyList;
      }
      private function resultHandler(e:ResultEvent):void{
        var amtToConvert:String = amount_txt.text;
        if (amtToConvert.length > 0) {
          convertedAmount_txt.text =
            ➥String(myCC.convert(Number(amtToConvert)));
        }
        else {
          convertedAmount_txt.text = String(myCC.getRate());
        }
      }
      private function faultHandler(e:FaultEvent):void {
        Alert.show(e.fault.faultString);
      }
```

```
      private function callCC(e:ValidationResultEvent):void {
        var fromCurrencyIndex:int = from_cbo.selectedIndex;
        var toCurrencyIndex:int = to_cbo.selectedIndex;
        if (fromCurrencyIndex != -1 && toCurrencyIndex != -1) {
          myCC.callWS("ConversionRate", from_cbo.selectedItem.data,
            ➥to_cbo.selectedItem.data);
        }
        else {
          Alert.show("Select currencies to convert before clicking
            ➥the Convert button");
        }
      }
    }
  ]]>
</mx:Script>
<mx:NumberValidator id="amountValidator"
  source="{amount_txt}" property="text"
  trigger="{convert_btn}" triggerEvent="click"
  required="false" invalidCharError="Please enter a number"
  valid="callCC(event)" invalid="convertedAmount_txt.text = ''"/>
<mx:VBox x="10" y="10">
  <mx:Label text="Currency converter" fontSize="14"
    fontWeight="bold"/>
  <mx:HBox>
    <mx:Label text="From currency" fontWeight="bold" width="150"/>
    <mx:ComboBox id="from_cbo" prompt="Select from currency"/>
  </mx:HBox>
  <mx:HBox>
    <mx:Label text="To currency" fontWeight="bold" width="150"/>
    <mx:ComboBox id="to_cbo" prompt="Select to currency"/>
  </mx:HBox>
  <mx:HBox>
    <mx:Label text="Amount" fontWeight="bold" width="150"/>
    <mx:TextInput id="amount_txt"/>
  </mx:HBox>
  <mx:HBox width="100%" horizontalAlign="right">
    <mx:Button label="Convert" id="convert_btn"/>
  </mx:HBox>
  <mx:Spacer height="20"/>
  <mx:HBox>
    <mx:Label text="Converted amount" fontWeight="bold"
      width="150"/>
    <mx:TextInput id="convertedAmount_txt"/>
  </mx:HBox>
</mx:VBox>
</mx:Application>
```

19. Test the application and select conversion values. Enter an amount to convert and click the Convert button. You should see the converted amount in the interface, as shown in Figure 10-10. You can also test the application without entering an amount to convert.

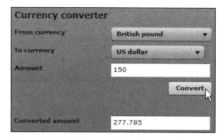

Figure 10-10. The completed application showing a sample conversion

You can find the completed files for this exercise saved with the other chapter resources.

As I explained earlier, the showBusyCursor property isn't available to the WebService class. You might have noticed that, when you clicked the Convert button, there was nothing in the interface to indicate that the call was in progress. You might wish to extend the example to deal with this situation, perhaps by displaying a message or image to the user. I'll leave that up to you.

There is one more approach you can use to consume a web service with Flex: the Web Service Introspection wizard.

Using Flex Builder to manage web services

The Web Service Introspection wizard manages the process of consuming a web service. The wizard generates the ActionScript classes you need to consume that web service. You can see an example of how to use the wizard in the Flex article at http://www.adobe.com/devnet/flex/articles/flex_ws.html. The example that we'll work through here demonstrates that the Web Service Introspection wizard makes connecting to a SOAP web service very easy.

> *A word of warning here. I'm certain that the wizard works well with simple data types such as* String *and* Number *types. However, I had difficulty getting the wizard to work with a custom data type for the web service in the example that you'll see shortly. In the end, I made some modifications to the classes generated to switch from using a custom data type to work with a* String *type.*

Let's see how to use the Web Service Introspection wizard to connect to the currency conversion web service.

Working through the Web Service Introspection wizard

You can access the Web Service Introspection wizard by choosing File ➤ Import ➤ Web Service (WSDL). In the first step of the wizard, you need to choose a location for the generated classes, as shown in Figure 10-11. In this example, I've chosen the same location used for the earlier examples in this chapter. Feel free to select a different source for your generated files if you wish.

Figure 10-11. Selecting the source folder for the generated classes

After clicking Next, you'll be asked for the location of the WSDL file for the web service. Figure 10-12 shows the settings for our example.

I've specified that I'll get the details directly from the web service and provided the location of the WSDL file. If you want to use this example outside the Flex environment, the web service will need to have a cross-domain policy file allowing access to the SWF application. Luckily, the web service chosen here provides the policy file.

In the final step of the wizard, you need to select the operation and port. The wizard will identify the names of all services and operations available at the web service. In Figure 10-13, you can see that the service CurrencyConvertor is available. In fact, no other services are available at the web service used in the example.

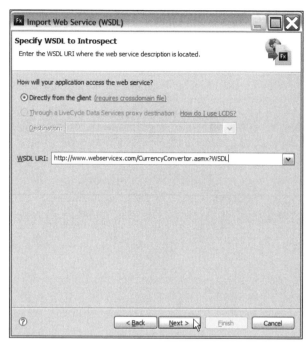

Figure 10-12. Providing the WSDL file location

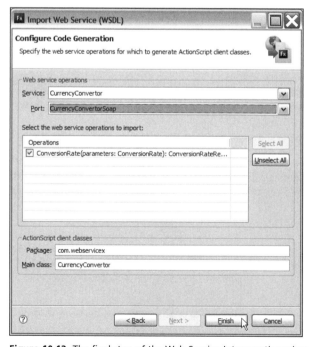

Figure 10-13. The final step of the Web Service Introspection wizard

The wizard also asks for the port to use. This setting equates to the method of connection for the web service. In the case of this web service, you can access the operation in three different ways: by using SOAP, by using an HTTP GET request, or by using an HTTP POST request.

In Figure 10-13, you can see that I've left the CurrencyConverterSoap option selected. I've also specified that I want the operation ConversionRate. No other operations are available at this web service.

The wizard specifies that it will create the classes in the com.webservicex package and that the main class will be CurrencyConverter. Click Finish to generate the required classes. Figure 10-14 shows all of the classes generated by the wizard.

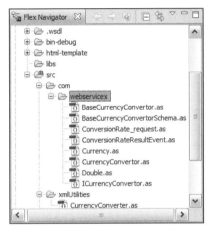

Figure 10-14. The classes generated by the Web Service Introspection wizard

Flex Builder generates a lot of classes to consume this web service! The main class that you need to work with is the CurrencyConverter.as class. This class makes all of the web service calls, so you won't need to use the WebService class.

Managing web services

Once you've worked through the wizard, you can manage an application's web services using the Manage Web Services dialog box, as shown in Figure 10-15. Choose Data ➤ Manage Web Services to open this dialog box.

Figure 10-15. Managing existing web services

The Manage Web Services dialog box allows you to add a new web service, update an existing WSDL, or delete a web service. If you choose the update option, you'll be taken back to step 3 of the wizard to specify the service, port, and operation. Flex Builder will then regenerate the classes for the web service.

Consuming the web service

Before we proceed with the examples, you'll need to make some changes to the generated classes. When I tried to use the generated code, I came across some difficulties with the Currency custom data type. In the end, the only way I could solve the problem was to change the data type of the two currencies sent to the web service from the Currency type to the String type.

I made the changes in the following locations, and you'll need to do the same if you want to work through the examples yourself:

- Within the CurrencyConverter.as file, modify the public function conversionRate. Change this line:

```
public function conversionRate(fromCurrency:Currency,toCurrency:
➥Currency):AsyncToken
```

to read as follows:

```
public function conversionRate(fromCurrency:String,toCurrency:
➥String):AsyncToken
```

- Make the same change in the BaseCurrencyConverter.as and ICurrencyConverter.as files.
- In the CurrencyRate_request.as file, change the variable declarations in the ConversionRate_request() method as shown in bold here:

```
public function ConversionRate_request() {}
  public var FromCurrency:String;
  public var ToCurrency:String;
}
```

Be aware that if you regenerate the classes using the wizard, you'll overwrite these changes.

Now that we've addressed these difficulties, I can show you how to use the generated classes to consume the currency converter web service. You have two choices about how to do this: you can either use MXML tags or write ActionScript. I'll demonstrate both approaches using a cut-down version of the previous example. This version will show the conversion rate for a single exchange.

Using MXML tags with the generated classes

In this example, we'll build an application that shows the conversion rate for a single exchange, Australia dollars (AUD) to British pounds (GBP). I've purposely chosen a very simple example so you can see how to use the generated classes in as few steps as possible.

1. Start by creating a new application file. I called mine CurrencyConversionWizardTag.mxml.

2. Add the following interface elements:

```
<mx:VBox x="10" y="10">
  <mx:Button label="Show rate" id="convert_btn" />
  <mx:Label text="Conversion rate" fontWeight="bold" width="150"/>
  <mx:TextInput id="rate_txt" />
</mx:VBox>
```

Figure 10-16 shows the interface that this code creates.

When a user clicks the Show rate button, the relevant exchange rate appears in the TextInput control.

Figure 10-16.
The simplified single currency application interface

3. Modify the opening `<mx:Application>` element to include the namespace for the new classes. The modification appears in bold.

```
<mx:Application xmlns:mx="http://www.adobe.com/2006/mxml"
  layout="absolute" xmlns:srv="com.webservicex.*">
```

4. Add the new `<svc:CurrencyConverter>` element, as shown in the following code block:

```
<srv:CurrencyConvertor id="myService">
  <srv:conversionRate_request_var>
    <srv:ConversionRate_request FromCurrency="AUD" ToCurrency="GBP"/>
  </srv:conversionRate_request_var>
</srv:CurrencyConvertor>
```

The element has the id `myService` and contains a `<srv:conversionRate_request_var>` element. The arguments for the web service request appear in a `<srv:ConversionRate_request>` element. These are the `FromCurrency` and `ToCurrency` attributes. As explained earlier, I changed these elements to be a `String` data type.

> The code to make the connection came from comments in the `CurrencyConverter.as` file. However, the sample code provided was incorrect. The comments indicated that I should use the following code:
>
> ```
>         <srv:CurrencyConvertor id="myService">
>           <srv:ConversionRate_request_var>
>             <srv:ConversionRate_request
>                FromCurrency=myValue,ToCurrency=myValue/>
>           </srv:ConversionRate_request_var>
>         </srv:CurrencyConvertor>
> ```
>
> When I tried to do so, I got a number of errors caused by the incorrect casing of the elements. For example, the sample code indicated that I should use `<srv:ConversionRate_request_var>`, when the actual element was `<srv:conversionRate_request_var>`.
>
> The arguments were also incorrectly specified in the `<srv: ConversionRate_request>` element. They were not written as attributes of the element. Instead of writing `<srv:ConversionRate_request FromCurrency=myValue,ToCurrency=myValue/>`, the correct approach was to use `<srv:ConversionRate_request  FromCurrency="myValue" ToCurrency="myValue"/>`. Luckily, Flex Builder provides code hinting for the custom classes, so you can determine the correct code.
>
> If you try to use the Web Service Introspection wizard, be aware that you may need to modify the sample code provided in the main class file.

5. The application will call the web service in response to the click of the Show rate button. Modify the element to add a click attribute, as shown here in bold:

```
<mx:Button label="Show rate" id="convert_btn"
  click="myService.conversionRate_send()"/>
```

Clicking the button calls the conversionRate_send() method of the myService web service. Again, the sample code provided in CurrencyConverter.as used incorrect casing for this element, so be aware that you may need to change the supplied example if you use the wizard with your own examples.

6. In order to display the exchange rate, the application will need to bind the returned result to the TextInput control. Change the control as shown in bold here:

```
<mx:TextInput id="rate_txt"
  text="{myService.conversionRate_lastResult.toString()}"/>
```

The code binds the text property of the TextInput control to the returned result. The application finds the exchange rate using the conversionRate_lastResult property to which you've applied the toString() method. This line wasn't provided in the code sample from Adobe, but again, code hinting helped to locate the correct property.

7. The final stage is to test the application. Run the application. You'll see the text NaN displayed in the TextInput control.

Figure 10-17. The completed application showing the current exchange rate

Click the Show rate button to call the web service. Unfortunately, because we're using a scripted approach, there is no way to show a busy cursor while the request takes place. After a short wait, you should see the returned exchange rate, as shown in Figure 10-17.

You might want to add an if statement to the binding to hide the initial NaN value. I'll leave that up to you.

You can find this file saved as CurrencyConversionWizardTag.mxml with your chapter resources. The complete application code follows, in case you wish to check your own version:

```
<?xml version="1.0" encoding="utf-8"?>
<mx:Application xmlns:mx="http://www.adobe.com/2006/mxml"
  xmlns:srv="com.webservicex.*" layout="absolute">
  <srv:CurrencyConvertor id="myService">
    <srv:conversionRate_request_var>
      <srv:ConversionRate_request FromCurrency="AUD"
        ToCurrency="GBP"/>
    </srv:conversionRate_request_var>
  </srv:CurrencyConvertor>
  <mx:VBox x="10" y="10">
    <mx:Button label="Show rate" id="convert_btn"
      click="myService.conversionRate_send()"/>
    <mx:Label text="Conversion rate" fontWeight="bold" width="150"/>
    <mx:TextInput id="rate_txt"
      text="{myService.conversionRate_lastResult.toString()}"/>
  </mx:VBox>
</mx:Application>
```

Let's move onto a scripted version of the previous example.

Scripting the generated classes

Again, we'll create a simple application that shows the conversion rate between Australia dollars (AUD) and British pounds (GBP).

1. Create a new application file. In this case, I called mine CurrencyConversionWizardScript. mxml.

2. Add the interface elements shown earlier in Figure 10-16.

```
<mx:VBox x="10" y="10">
  <mx:Button label="Show rate" id="convert_btn" />
  <mx:Label text="Conversion rate" fontWeight="bold" width="150"/>
  <mx:TextInput id="rate_txt" />
</mx:VBox>
```

Clicking the Show rate button displays the relevant exchange rate in the TextInput control.

3. Modify the opening <mx:Application> element to include a creationComplete attribute, as shown here in bold:

```
<mx:Application xmlns:mx="http://www.adobe.com/2006/mxml"
  layout="absolute" creationComplete="initApp(event)">
```

When the application finishes creating the interface, it calls the initApp() function, which sets up the web service.

4. Add the following <mx:Script> block above the opening <mx:VBox> element:

```
<mx:Script>
  <![CDATA[
    import com.webservicex.*;
    import mx.events.FlexEvent;
    private var myService:CurrencyConvertor= new CurrencyConvertor();
    private function initApp(e:FlexEvent):void {
      myService.addconversionRateEventListener(resultHandler);
    }
    private function resultHandler(e:ConversionRateResultEvent):void {
    }
  ]]>
</mx:Script>
```

The code block starts by importing all of the generated classes using the following statement:

```
import com.webservicex.*;
```

The code block also imports the FlexEvent class so the application can correctly recognize the type of event passed to the initApp() function. It declares a variable myService of the type CurrencyConverter.

The initApp() function receives a FlexEvent as an argument and adds an event handler to the myService element. It uses the method addconversionRateEventListener(). The event has one argument, which is the name of the handler function.

369

The resultHandler() function receives a ConversionRateResultEvent as an argument. The code block includes the function signature, but the function itself is empty. Again, the instructions in the CurrencyConverter.as file are a little lacking. The addconversionRateEventListener() method was incorrectly cased in the sample code.

5. The application will call the web service in response to the click of the Show rate button, so you need to add an event handler that responds to the click event.

Modify the initApp() method as shown here in bold:

```
private function initApp(e:FlexEvent):void {
  myService.addconversionRateEventListener(resultHandler);
  convert_btn.addEventListener(MouseEvent.CLICK, clickHandler);
}
```

You'll also need to add the clickHandler() function that follows:

```
private function clickHandler(e:MouseEvent):void{
  myService.conversionRate("AUD", "GBP");
}
```

Clicking the button calls the clickHandler() function. This function contains a single line, which calls the conversionRate() method of the myService web service. This method includes the two conversion currencies as arguments. Because of the changes I made, the method call passes these as String values.

6. In order to display the exchange rate, the application will need to display the returned result in the TextInput control.

Modify the resultHandler() function as shown here:

```
private function resultHandler(e:ConversionRateResultEvent):void {
  rate_txt.text = e.result.toString();
}
```

The new line sets the text property of the TextInput to the returned result. The function finds the exchange rate using the expression e.result.toString(). As with the previous example, this line wasn't provided in the code sample from Adobe.

7. Run the application. Click the Show rate button to call the web service. You should see the returned exchange rate, as shown earlier in Figure 10-17.

The complete code for the application follows, and you can find this saved in the file CurrencyConversionWizardScript.mxml.

```
<?xml version="1.0" encoding="utf-8"?>
<mx:Application xmlns:mx="http://www.adobe.com/2006/mxml"
  layout="absolute" creationComplete="initApp(event)">
  <mx:Script>
    <![CDATA[
      import com.webservicex.*;
      import mx.events.FlexEvent;
      private var myService:CurrencyConvertor=
        ➥new CurrencyConvertor();
```

```
        private function initApp(e:FlexEvent):void  {
          myService.addconversionRateEventListener(resultHandler);
          convert_btn.addEventListener(MouseEvent.CLICK,
            ➥clickHandler);
        }
        private function clickHandler(e:MouseEvent):void{
          myService.conversionRate("AUD", "GBP");
        }
        private function resultHandler(e:ConversionRateResultEvent):
          ➥void {
          rate_txt.text = e.result.toString();
        }
      ]]>
    </mx:Script>
  <mx:VBox x="10" y="10">
    <mx:Button label="Show rate" id="convert_btn" />
    <mx:Label text="Conversion rate" fontWeight="bold" width="150"/>
    <mx:TextInput id="rate_txt" />
  </mx:VBox>
</mx:Application>
```

You can see that using the generated classes requires less code than was used in the previous exercises. You might find this approach easier than the examples I showed earlier. However, there were also some difficulties associated with the custom data type Currency and the supplied sample code. If you choose to use the Web Service Introspection wizard, you might need to modify the generated content and sample code.

Summary

In this chapter, I explained web services and showed you how to consume them in Flex with both the <mx:WebService> element and WebService class. We worked through two examples that illustrated each approach. The first showed how to use a tag-based approach, and the second demonstrated a class-based approach.

I also showed you how to work with the Web Service Introspection wizard. We generated custom classes to consume the web service and used them in both a tag-based and scripted approach. I also provided some warnings about using this approach.

In the next chapter, you'll learn how to consume a web service in Flash. That will prove a little more challenging, as Flash can't access the WebService class.

Chapter 11

CONSUMING WEB SERVICES WITH FLASH

As you learned in the previous chapter, a web service is a remote procedure that pro-vides its results in XML format. A user *consumes* a web service by identifying which operations are available and providing the correct parameters. After a successful request, the web service sends back a response in XML format.

In the previous chapter, I showed you how to use Flex to consume a currency conversion web service. In this chapter, I'll show you how to repeat the process using Flash.

As you saw, Flex can access SOAP web services using the WebService class. The great advantage of this class is that it can assemble the SOAP requests for you automati-cally based on a Web Services Definition Language (WSDL) file. You'll remember from the last chapter that this file provides information about a web service, includ-ing how to consume it.

Unfortunately for Flash users, the WebService class from Flex isn't available to Flash. This deficiency has caused great frustration to designers and developers alike. With Flash, two alternatives are available:

- Consume the web service using the URLLoader class.
- Use the ActionScript 2.0 WebServiceConnector component to consume the web service.

This chapter covers both approaches. As always, you can download the resources for the chapter from http://www.friendsofed.com.

Consuming web services with the URLLoader class

It's possible to use the URLLoader class to consume a web service in Flash. However, you need to be able to understand the WSDL file for the web service so you can determine the location of the web service, the operation name, and the values you need to send with the request. Then you can make the request by writing the appropriate ActionScript 3.0.

Unlike working with the WebService class in Flex, using the URLLoader in Flash is a manual process. You'll need to understand the web service thoroughly and write appropriate code. Using this process can be extremely frustrating if you're working with SOAP web services, because you'll need to decipher the WSDL file for the web service and assemble the SOAP request yourself. Luckily, in addition to using SOAP, some web services also allow you to use GET and POST requests, which simplifies the process greatly. We'll explore both approaches in this section.

In broad steps, you need to work through the following sequence to use the URLLoader class to consume a web service:

1. Create an instance of the URLLoader class.
2. Create a URLRequest object, passing the location of the web service.
3. Add an event handler listening for the complete event.
4. Create the request, identifying the arguments to pass.
5. Set other properties of the URLLoader if required, such as the method and contentType.
6. Call the web service using the load() method.
7. Handle the response from the web service.

The following code block shows an example of using the HTTP POST method to consume a web service:

```
var loader:URLLoader = new URLLoader();
var request:URLRequest = new URLRequest("URLToWebService");
var args:URLVariables= new URLVariables();
loader.addEventListener("complete", completeHandler);
args.Variable1 = "Value1";
args.Variable2 = "Value2";
request.data = args;
request.method = URLRequestMethod.POST;
loader.load(request);
function completeHandler(e:Event):void {
  var loadedXML:XML= XML(e.target.data);
  trace("loaded: " + loadedXML.toXMLString());
}
```

The first two lines of the code block tackle steps 1 and 2 of the process. The code also declares a URLVariables object at this point. Next, the code adds the event handler that responds to the complete event, as described in step 3 of the process.

The two lines that follow show how to assign variables to the args object. Step 4 is demonstrated as the code then assigns these variables to the data property of the URLRequest. The code then sets the method property of the request, taking care of step 5.

The code block finishes by calling the load() method of the loader object, as described in step 6. The last lines detail a sample completeHandler() function, which is step 7 of the process.

Before we work through examples, you need to have a good understanding of the WSDL file for the web service.

Understanding the WSDL file

In this section, we'll walk through consuming the web service with a WSDL file at http://www.webservicex.com/CurrencyConvertor.asmx?WSDL, so you may want to load this URL into a web browser and have a look. You can find a fuller discussion of the WSDL file in Chapter 10.

For your Flash application, the most important parts of the WSDL file are the methods that you can use for its consumption. You can see the methods for consuming the web service if you work through the file and look for the <wdsl:PortType> elements. In our case, you'll see the following elements:

```
<wsdl:portType name="CurrencyConvertorSoap">
<wsdl:portType name="CurrencyConvertorHttpGet">
<wsdl:portType name="CurrencyConvertorHttpPost">
```

These elements indicate that a SWF application can access the web service using any of these three methods: SOAP, GET, or POST. Let's look at all three methods, starting with GET.

Using GET to consume a web service

You can use an HTTP GET request to consume a web service if the service provides that method of access. The GET method sends name/value pairs in the query string, and each pair is separated by an ampersand character. Here is an example of variables sent with a GET request:

```
http://www.myurl.com?var1=value1&var2=value2&var3=value3
```

The variable pairs appear after the question mark (?) character at the end of the URL. In the case of a web service, you use the URL for the operation, *not* the URL of the WSDL file. You can find this address in the following elements:

```
<wsdl:port name="CurrencyConvertorHttpGet"
  binding="tns:CurrencyConvertorHttpGet">
  <http:address
    location="http://www.webservicex.com/CurrencyConvertor.asmx"/>
</wsdl:port>
```

Here, the address is http://www.webservicex.com/CurrencyConvertor.asmx. The following elements describe the location of the web service within this URL:

```
<wsdl:binding name="CurrencyConvertorHttpGet"
  type="tns:CurrencyConvertorHttpGet">
<http:binding verb="GET"/>
<wsdl:operation name="ConversionRate">
  <http:operation location="/ConversionRate"/>
  <wsdl:input>
    <http:urlEncoded/>
  </wsdl:input>
  <wsdl:output>
    <mime:mimeXml part="Body"/>
  </wsdl:output>
</wsdl:operation>
</wsdl:binding>
```

The line in bold indicates the web service is accessed by adding the ConversionRate folder to the web service location. Putting these elements together indicates that the web service is at the following location:

```
http://www.webservicex.com/CurrencyConvertor.asmx/ConversionRate
```

You will need to send any parameters for this web service as part of the URL. The WSDL file indicates that the GET web service needs two parameters, as shown in the following elements:

```
<wsdl:message name="ConversionRateHttpGetIn">
  <wsdl:part name="FromCurrency" type="s:string"/>
  <wsdl:part name="ToCurrency" type="s:string"/>
</wsdl:message>
```

You need to send the FromCurrency and ToCurrency values. These are both String types. At the beginning of the WSDL file, you can see a list of acceptable values in the <s:simpleType name="Currency"> element.

If you wanted to convert British pounds to US dollars, you would use the FromCurrency value GBP and the ToCurrency value USD. You would need to append these values to the URL, as shown here:

```
http://www.webservicex.com/CurrencyConvertor.asmx/ConversionRate
  ➥?FromCurrency=GBP&ToCurrency=USD
```

Compared to the alternatives, consuming a web service using the GET method in Flash is by far the easiest of all options shown in this chapter. Even so, you can see from the preceding content that decoding the WSDL file to find the relevant elements is quite a difficult process. I guess you know why Flash designers and developers are unhappy that they don't have access to the WebService class!

It's harder to use a POST method to consume a web service or to assemble a SOAP request manually. In a GET request, all you need to do is to modify the URL for the web service to include the parameters to send. In a POST request, you need to assemble the parameters in a URLVariables object and change the method property for the URLLoader object.

In a SOAP web service, you must create the XML content for the request yourself. In my experience, this is harder than it looks!

> *Don't forget that consuming a web service loads data from a source in a different security sandbox from the SWF application. If you want to test the example outside Flash, the web service will need to provide a cross-domain policy file allowing access to the SWF. Where no policy file exists, you'll need to proxy the content locally using a server-side file. You can find out more about Flash Player 10 security in Chapter 5.*

Let's work through a simple example of how to consume the currency converter web service using a GET request. As in the previous chapter, this exercise consumes the web service that converts from one currency to another. The user will provide both the from and to currencies, as well as an amount to convert. We'll use the GET method to consume the web service, and the application will use procedural code. If you prefer a class-based approach, feel free to modify the code.

Working through a GET example

The WSDL file for this web service is at http://www.webservicex.com/CurrencyConvertor.asmx?WSDL. You can find a full discussion of this WSDL file at the start of Chapter 10.

1. Open the starter file ccStarter.fla. Figure 11-1 shows the interface.

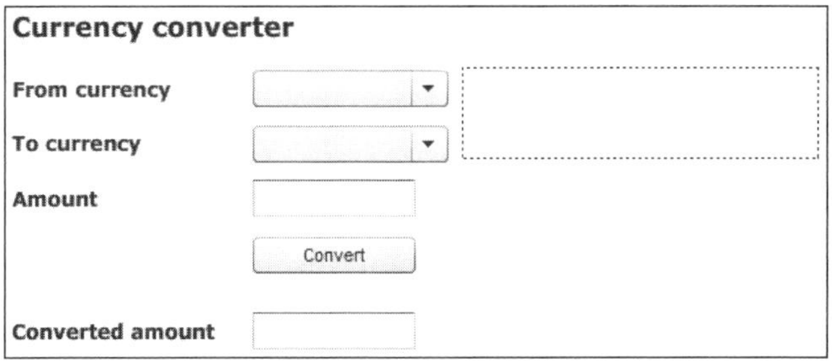

Figure 11-1. The interface for the currency converter application

The application contains two ComboBox components, which the application will populate with a list of currencies. It contains a TextInput control for the user to enter an amount, as well as a Convert button and TextInput control in which to display the results. To the right of the components is a dynamic text field for displaying messages to the user.

2. Start by configuring the ComboBox controls, in a function called initApp(). Add a new layer called actions and enter the following code:

```
import fl.data.DataProvider;
initApp();
stop();
function initApp():void {
  populateCurrencies();
}
```

The code starts by importing the DataProvider class. This is necessary because the application will use a DataProvider object to populate the ComboBox controls. The code then calls the initApp() function and includes a stop() action. The initApp() function follows. It contains one line: a call to the populateCurrencies() function, which will load the ComboBox components. You'll add this function next.

3. The following populateCurrencies() function adds currencies to both ComboBox components. Add it now.

```
function populateCurrencies():void {
  var dp:DataProvider = new DataProvider();
  dp.addItem({label: "Choose...", data: "0"});
  dp.addItem({label: "Australia dollars", data: "AUD"});
  dp.addItem({label: "British pound", data: "GBP"});
  dp.addItem({label: "Canadian dollar", data: "CAD"});
  dp.addItem({label: "Euro", data: "EUR"});
  dp.addItem({label: "Singapore dollar", data: "SGD"});
  dp.addItem({label: "South African rand", data: "ZAR"});
  dp.addItem({label: "US dollar", data: "USD"});
  from_cbo.dataProvider = dp;
  to_cbo.dataProvider = dp;
}
```

This function starts by declaring a new DataProvider object called dp. The next eight lines populate this object using the addItem() method. Each new item is an object containing a label property and a data property.

Except for the first item, all other items use an abbreviation for the data value. This abbreviation is required by the web service. The first item contains a String representation of the value 0. I've purposely made this value a String to be consistent with the other values.

As with the Flex examples in the previous chapter, I've chosen only a small subset of the currencies available to the web service. If you want to see a complete list of all currencies available, open the WSDL file in a web browser and look for the <s:simpleType name="Currency"> element near the top of the file. Feel free to add other elements if your country is not represented.

4. Test the application now, and you should see the two ComboBox controls populated with a list of currencies. Figure 11-2 shows how the application should appear at this point.

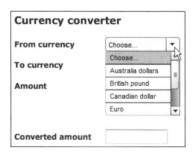

Figure 11-2. The application showing a populated ComboBox control

The name of the currency displays in the ComboBox. The data property of each value contains the abbreviation for that currency.

5. The next task is to configure the Convert button to call the web service. Add the following event listener function to the initApp() function:

```
function initApp():void {
  populateCurrencies();
  convert_btn.addEventListener(MouseEvent.CLICK, clickHandler);
}
```

The addEventListener() method adds the handler function. Clicking the button will call the clickHandler() function, which follows. Add this function to the actions layer.

```
function clickHandler(e:MouseEvent):void {
  var fromCurrency:String = from_cbo.selectedItem.data;
  var toCurrency:String = to_cbo.selectedItem.data;
  var convertAmount:String = amount_txt.text;
  if (from_cbo.selectedIndex > 0 && to_cbo.selectedIndex > 0) {
    if (convertAmount.length > 0) {
      if (! isNaN(Number(convertAmount))) {
        message_txt.text = "Good to go!"
      }
      else {
        message_txt.text = "Enter a number to convert";
      }
    }
    else {
      message_txt.text = "Enter an amount to convert"
    }
  }
  else {
    message_txt.text = "Select both a 'from' and 'to' currency";
  }
}
```

You'll modify this function shortly. To start with, the function tests entries from the user. The first two lines find the selected data values from the ComboBox components and the amount_ txt control.

The function checks that the user has selected values for both ComboBox controls. It does this by comparing the selectedIndex with 0, which is the selectedIndex of the Choose… item in each ComboBox. If the user hasn't made a selection, the selectedIndex value will be 0.

If the user has selected a value, the code checks that there is an entry in the amount_txt TextInput control. It checks the length of the entry to make sure it is greater than 0. If so, the function checks to see that the value entered in the amount_txt control is numeric.

At each stage of the function, a message displays in the message_txt dynamic text field. You'll replace the Good to go! message with the code to call the web service in the next step.

6. At this point, test the application to make sure that you're seeing the correct messages. Figure 11-3 shows the message that should appear if the user clicks the Convert button without making any selections. You should also test for a blank or nonnumeric Amount entry.

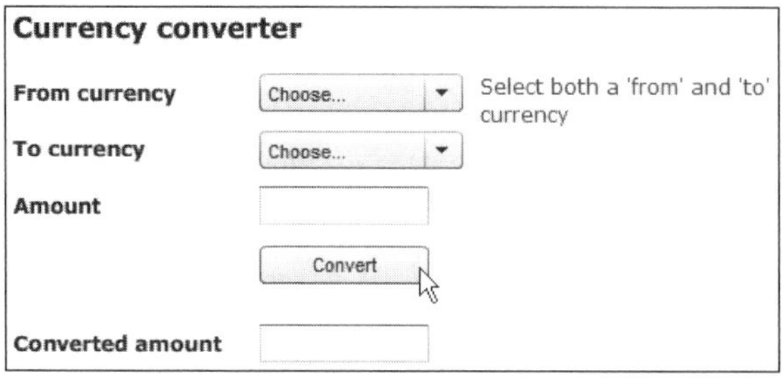

Figure 11-3. The clickHandler() function displays an error message.

7. Next, you need to modify the clickHandler() function to call the web service. In this example, it will send the values to the web service using GET by modifying the URL.

Replace the message_txt.text = "Good to go!" line in the clickHandler() function with the following lines, which clear any existing message and call the webServiceGET() function:

```
message_txt.text = "";
webServiceGET(fromCurrency, toCurrency);
```

The second line calls the webServiceGET() function, passing the fromCurrency and toCurrency values.

Add the following webServiceGet() function. I'll explain it after the listing.

```
function webServiceGET():void {
  var requestURL:String = "http://www.webservicex.net/
    ➥CurrencyConvertor.asmx/ConversionRate?
    ➥FromCurrency=" + from + "&ToCurrency=" + to;
  var wsRequest:URLRequest = new URLRequest(requestURL);
  var webService:URLLoader = new URLLoader();
  webService.addEventListener(Event.COMPLETE, completeHandler);
  webService.addEventListener(IOErrorEvent.IO_ERROR, ioErrorHandler);
  webService.addEventListener(HTTPStatusEvent.HTTP_STATUS,
    ➥httpStatusHandler);
  webService.load(wsRequest);
  message_txt.text = "Contacting web service";
}
```

The function starts by declaring a String variable for the location of the web service. The location is at http://www.webservicex.net/CurrencyConvertor.asmx/ConversionRate, as I explained earlier in the chapter. The URL also includes the variables to send. They are listed as name/value pairs after the question mark (?).

The function then declares a URLRequest object called wsRequest, passing the requestURL value as an argument. It also declares a URLLoader object called webService.

The function adds three event listeners to the webService: one for the complete event; one for the ioerror event, in case there is a problem with the web service; and one for the httpStatus event, following the progress of the call. I've added the third event listener to show you the types of messages that the web service can return.

The function calls the load() method of the webService object, passing the URLRequest. It finishes by displaying the message Contacting web service to the user.

The function doesn't need to set the method of the URLLoader to GET, because that's the default method. It doesn't need to create a URLVariables object to pass the variables, because the variables are added to the end of the web service URL.

8. Add the event handler functions that follow:

```
function completeHandler(e:Event):void {
  var returnedXML:XML = new XML(e.target.data);
  var rate:Number = Number(returnedXML.toString());
  var convertedAmount:Number = Number(amount_txt.text) * rate;
  result_txt.text = String(convertedAmount);
}
function ioErrorHandler(e:ErrorEvent):void {
  message_txt.text = "Error contacting web service: " + e.text;
}
function httpStatusHandler(e:HTTPStatusEvent):void {
  message_txt.text = "httpStatus " + e.toString();
}
```

The first function, completeHandler(), processes the web service response and calculates the converted amount. It finds the returned value as an XML object using the expression XML(e.target.data). The web service returns the following XML document structure:

```
<?xml version="1.0" encoding="utf-8"?>
<double xmlns="http://www.webserviceX.NET/">0.8947</double>
```

The completeHandler() function finds the rate by using the toString() method to return only the numeric portion of the XML document. It casts this value as a Number using Number(). It then finds the converted amount by multiplying the user-supplied amount, cast as a Number, by the returned rate. Remember that the application has already dealt with nonnumeric responses before it called the web service.

The converted amount is cast as a String so the code can assign it to the text property of the result_txt control.

The ioErrorHandler() function will respond to errors in the web service. It displays the message Error contacting web service with the text value of the error. You can test this function a little later by using an incorrect URL for the web service.

The final function responds when the web service sends back an HTTP status message. This message indicates the status of the request. You've seen these types of messages when a 404 File Not Found error occurs while loading a web page. When the call completes, the status of the request will display in the message_txt control. A successful request will provide a status of 200.

9. Test the application. Choose two currencies, enter an amount to convert, and click the Convert button. Figure 11-4 shows a sample conversion from British pounds to US dollars.

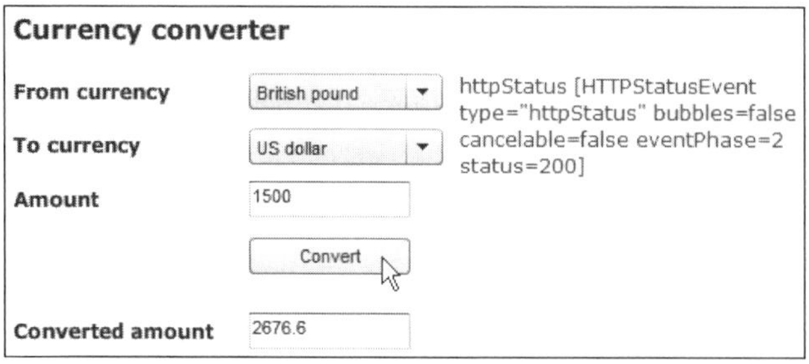

Figure 11-4. The completed currency converter application

The application displays the HTTP status message to the right. Notice that it includes a status property with a value of 200. The message also indicates the other properties of the HTTPStatusEvent, such as its type and whether it is cancelable.

The application also displays the converted amount at the bottom of the screen. Notice that this amount doesn't round to two decimal places, so you may want to fix that yourself.

The complete code for this application follows, and you can find it saved in the file ccGet.fla with the chapter resources:

```
import fl.data.DataProvider;
initApp();
stop();
function initApp():void {
  populateCurrencies();
  convert_btn.addEventListener(MouseEvent.CLICK, clickHandler);
}
function populateCurrencies():void {
  var dp:DataProvider = new DataProvider();
  dp.addItem({label: "Choose...", data: "0"});
  dp.addItem({label: "Australia dollars", data: "AUD"});
  dp.addItem({label: "British pound", data: "GBP"});
  dp.addItem({label: "Canadian dollar", data: "CAD"});
  dp.addItem({label: "Euro", data: "EUR"});
  dp.addItem({label: "Singapore dollar", data: "SGD"});
  dp.addItem({label: "South African rand", data: "ZAR"});
  dp.addItem({label: "US dollar", data: "USD"});
  from_cbo.dataProvider = dp;
  to_cbo.dataProvider = dp;
}
```

```
function clickHandler(e:MouseEvent):void {
  var fromCurrency:String = from_cbo.selectedItem.data;
  var toCurrency:String = to_cbo.selectedItem.data;
  var convertAmount:String = amount_txt.text;
  if (from_cbo.selectedIndex > 0 && to_cbo.selectedIndex > 0) {
    if (convertAmount.length > 0) {
      if (! isNaN(Number(convertAmount))) {
        message_txt.text = "";
        webServiceGET(fromCurrency, toCurrency);
      }
      else {
        message_txt.text = "Enter a number to convert";
      }
    }
    else {
      message_txt.text = "Enter an amount to convert"
    }
  }
  else {
    message_txt.text = "Select both a 'from' and 'to' currency";
  }
}
function webServiceGET(from:String, to:String):void {
  var requestURL:String = "http://www.webservicex.net/
    ➥CurrencyConvertor.asmx/ConversionRate?
    ➥FromCurrency=" + from + "&ToCurrency=" + to;
  var wsRequest:URLRequest = new URLRequest(requestURL);
  var webService:URLLoader = new URLLoader();
  webService.addEventListener(Event.COMPLETE, completeHandler);
  webService.addEventListener(IOErrorEvent.IO_ERROR, ioErrorHandler);
  webService.addEventListener(HTTPStatusEvent.HTTP_STATUS,
    ➥httpStatusHandler);
  webService.load(wsRequest);
    message_txt.text = "Contacting web service";
}
function completeHandler(e:Event):void {
  var returnedXML:XML = new XML(e.target.data);
  var rate:Number = Number(returnedXML.toString());
  var convertedAmount:Number = Number(amount_txt.text) * rate;
  result_txt.text = String(convertedAmount);
}
function ioErrorHandler(e:ErrorEvent):void {
  message_txt.text = "Error contacting web service: " + e.text;
}
function httpStatusHandler(e:HTTPStatusEvent):void {
  message_txt.text = "httpStatus " + e.toString();
}
```

As I mentioned earlier, requesting a web service using GET is probably the simplest approach for consuming web services with Flash. Let's turn our attention to the POST method next.

Consuming a web service with POST

When you consume a web service using the POST method, you send the variables required for the service using the POST HTTP method. The process is the same as sending a form to the server for processing. In this method, the variables are sent with the page request, rather than being added to the query string, as in the GET method. The next example re-creates the same functionality of the first example using a POST request.

Working through a POST example

We'll consume the same web service and send the variables using the POST method. If you work through the WSDL file, you'll see that the example needs to use the same URL as in the previous example, but without the added variable values. The URL for the POST request follows:

```
http://www.webservicex.net/CurrencyConvertor.asmx/ConversionRate
```

1. Open the starter file ccPOSTstart.fla. As this example is similar to the previous one, this starter file already includes some code on the actions layer. In fact, the code is identical to the application at the end of step 5 in the previous example.

   The code populates the ComboBox controls and adds a click event handler for the Button control. It also tests that the user has made the required entries.

   The code at this point follows, and you can refer back to the previous example for a full explanation:

```
import fl.data.DataProvider;
initApp();
stop();
function initApp():void {
  populateCurrencies();
  convert_btn.addEventListener(MouseEvent.CLICK, clickHandler);
}
function populateCurrencies():void {
  var dp:DataProvider = new DataProvider();
  dp.addItem({label: "Choose...", data: "0"});
  dp.addItem({label: "Australia dollars", data: "AUD"});
  dp.addItem({label: "British pound", data: "GBP"});
  dp.addItem({label: "Canadian dollar", data: "CAD"});
  dp.addItem({label: "Euro", data: "EUR"});
  dp.addItem({label: "Singapore dollar", data: "SGD"});
  dp.addItem({label: "South African rand", data: "ZAR"});
  dp.addItem({label: "US dollar", data: "USD"});
  from_cbo.dataProvider = dp;
  to_cbo.dataProvider = dp;
}
function clickHandler(e:MouseEvent):void {
  var fromCurrency:String = from_cbo.selectedItem.data;
  var toCurrency:String = to_cbo.selectedItem.data;
  var convertAmount:String = amount_txt.text;
  if (from_cbo.selectedIndex > 0 && to_cbo.selectedIndex > 0) {
    if (convertAmount.length > 0) {
      message_txt.text = "Good to go!";
    }
```

```
    else {
      message_txt.text = "Enter an amount to convert"
    }
  }
  else {
    message_txt.text = "Select both a 'from' and 'to' currency";
  }
}
```

2. Replace the line message_txt.text = "Good to go!" in the clickHandler() function with a call to the webServicePOST() function.

Add the following lines to the clickHandler(), as shown in bold here:

```
function clickHandler(e:MouseEvent):void {
  var fromCurrency:String = from_cbo.selectedItem.data;
  var toCurrency:String = to_cbo.selectedItem.data;
  var convertAmount:String = amount_txt.text;
  if (from_cbo.selectedIndex > 0 && to_cbo.selectedIndex > 0) {
    if (convertAmount.length > 0) {
      message_txt.text = "";
      webServicePOST(fromCurrency, toCurrency);
    }
    else {
      message_txt.text = "Enter an amount to convert"
    }
  }
  else {
    message_txt.text = "Select both a 'from' and 'to' currency";
  }
}
```

The lines clear any existing text from the message_txt control and call the webServicePOST() function, passing the conversion currencies.

3. Add the webServicePOST() function shown here to the actions layer:

```
function webServicePOST(from:String, to:String):void {
  var requestURL:String = "http://www.webservicex.net/
    ➥CurrencyConvertor.asmx/ConversionRate";
  var wsRequest:URLRequest = new URLRequest(requestURL);
  var webService:URLLoader = new URLLoader();
  var args:URLVariables= new URLVariables();
  webService.addEventListener(Event.COMPLETE, completeHandler);
  webService.addEventListener(IOErrorEvent.IO_ERROR, ioErrorHandler);
  webService.addEventListener(HTTPStatusEvent.HTTP_STATUS,
    ➥httpStatusHandler);
  args.FromCurrency = from;
  args.ToCurrency = to;
  wsRequest.method = URLRequestMethod.POST;
  wsRequest.data = args;
  webService.load(wsRequest);
  message_txt.text = "Contacting web service";
}
```

The function works in much the same way as the `webServiceGET()` function in the previous exercise. It starts by declaring a `String` variable called `requestURL` for the location of the web service. It then creates `URLRequest` and `URLLoader` objects. This time, however, the function also creates a `URLVariables` object, because the variables aren't included in the URL for the web service.

The function adds three event handlers for the `complete`, `ioError`, and `httpStatus` events. You'll add those functions in the next step.

The function adds the from and to currencies as properties of the `URLVariables` object. The object uses the names `FromCurrency` and `ToCurrency`.

The function also sets the method to `URLRequestMethod.POST` to POST the variables to the web service. It finishes by adding the args object as the data property of the request and calling the `load()` method of the `webService` object. The last line displays the message Contacting web service in the dynamic text field.

4. You now need to add the event handler functions to deal with the response. There are three functions to add: `completeHandler()`, `ioErrorHandler`, and `httpStatusHandler`. These functions follow:

```
function completeHandler(e:Event):void {
    var returnedXML:XML = new XML(e.target.data);
    var rate:Number = Number(returnedXML.toString());
    var convertedAmount:Number = Number(amount_txt.text) * rate;
    result_txt.text = String(convertedAmount);
}
function ioErrorHandler(e:ErrorEvent):void {
    message_txt.text = "Error contacting web service: " + e.text;
}
function httpStatusHandler(e:HTTPStatusEvent):void {
    message_txt.text = "httpStatus " + e.toString();
}
```

These functions are exactly the same as those used in the previous example. You can find a complete explanation earlier in the chapter, at step 8 in the GET example.

5. Test the file and enter currencies to convert. You should see the same outcome as shown earlier in Figure 11-4.

You can see that this example is a little more complicated than the GET example. The completed code for the application follows, and you can also find it in the resource file ccPOST.fla.

```
import fl.data.DataProvider;
initApp();
stop();
function initApp():void {
    populateCurrencies();
    convert_btn.addEventListener(MouseEvent.CLICK, clickHandler);
}
function populateCurrencies():void {
    var dp:DataProvider = new DataProvider();
    dp.addItem({label: "Choose...", data: "0"});
```

```
    dp.addItem({label: "Australia dollars", data: "AUD"});
    dp.addItem({label: "British pound", data: "GBP"});
    dp.addItem({label: "Canadian dollar", data: "CAD"});
    dp.addItem({label: "Euro", data: "EUR"});
    dp.addItem({label: "Singapore dollar", data: "SGD"});
    dp.addItem({label: "South African rand", data: "ZAR"});
    dp.addItem({label: "US dollar", data: "USD"});
    from_cbo.dataProvider = dp;
    to_cbo.dataProvider = dp;
}
function clickHandler(e:MouseEvent):void {
  var fromCurrency:String = from_cbo.selectedItem.data;
  var toCurrency:String = to_cbo.selectedItem.data;
  var convertAmount:String = amount_txt.text;
  if (from_cbo.selectedIndex > 0 && to_cbo.selectedIndex > 0) {
    if (convertAmount.length > 0) {
      if (! isNaN(Number(convertAmount))) {
        message_txt.text = "";
        webServicePOST(fromCurrency, toCurrency);
      }
      else {
        message_txt.text = "Enter a number to convert";
      }
    }
    else {
      message_txt.text = "Enter an amount to convert"
    }
  }
  else {
    message_txt.text = "Select both a 'from' and 'to' currency";
  }
}
function webServicePOST(from:String, to:String):void {
  var requestURL:String = "http://www.webservicex.net/
    ➥CurrencyConvertor.asmx/ConversionRate";
  var wsRequest:URLRequest = new URLRequest(requestURL);
  var webService:URLLoader = new URLLoader();
  var args:URLVariables= new URLVariables();
  webService.addEventListener(Event.COMPLETE, completeHandler);
  webService.addEventListener(IOErrorEvent.IO_ERROR, ioErrorHandler);
  webService.addEventListener(HTTPStatusEvent.HTTP_STATUS,
    ➥httpStatusHandler);
  args.FromCurrency = from;
  args.ToCurrency = to;
  wsRequest.method = URLRequestMethod.POST;
  wsRequest.data = args;
  webService.load(wsRequest);
    message_txt.text = "Contacting web service";
}
```

```
function completeHandler(e:Event):void {
  var returnedXML:XML = new XML(e.target.data);
  var rate:Number = Number(returnedXML.toString());
  var convertedAmount:Number = Number(amount_txt.text) * rate;
  result_txt.text = String(convertedAmount);
}
function ioErrorHandler(e:ErrorEvent):void {
  message_txt.text = "Error contacting web service: " + e.text;
}
function httpStatusHandler(e:HTTPStatusEvent):void {
  message_txt.text = "httpStatus " + e.toString();
}
```

In this example, you saw how to consume a web service using POST. The example is quite similar to the previous GET example, except that you pass the variables in a different way.

The final method of consuming a web service is by using a SOAP request.

Consuming a SOAP web service with the as3webservice extension

It would be possible to re-create the previous example using a SOAP request; however, the process of assembling the SOAP request correctly is quite a challenge. It involves creating the correct XML document and adding headers; it can be quite a convoluted process. Working through such an example is beyond the scope of an introductory book.

As an alternative, I'll introduce you to an open source extension that can consume a web service for you. Instead of assembling the request manually, you need to provide only the URL, and the class library will generate the correct SOAP request and process the response.

The as3webservice extension is an open source web service class library for Flash. It uses ActionScript 3.0 to mimic the functionality of the WebService class available to Flex applications. You need to provide the URL for the web service's WSDL file, as well as the operation name and arguments. The class library builds the SOAP request and handles the response.

Without getting into too much detail, the library consists of the following three classes:

- The WebService class handles the call to the web service, including the creation of the SOAP request.
- The Operation class manages the operation at the web service.
- The OperationEvent is a custom event class dispatched by the Operation class.

You'll need all three classes to create an application that consumes a web service.

From experience, I can tell you that the extension is easy to use and greatly simplifies the process of consuming web services from Flash. Details of the class library are at http://www.wellconsidered. be/blog/as3-webservice-component/. You can download the extension from Google Code at http:// code.google.com/p/as3webservice/. Both web sites include sample code for using the extension.

> *A word of caution here: we'll use the* as3webservice *class library in the following example; however, this class library is a work in progress. The author of the extension explained that the library isn't complete, and he adds functionality as people request it.*
>
> *At the time of writing, it was possible to use the extension to consume the currency conversion web service for this example. You may get different results with other web services. If you find that to be the case, I encourage you to contact the author of the classes, Pieter Michels, via his web site.*

Let's see how to use the as3webservice class library in an example.

Working through an as3webservice example

In this example, we'll consume the same web service that you've seen throughout the chapter using the as3webservice class library.

1. The first step is to download and install the as3webservice extension from the Google Code site. Switch to the Source tab, click Browse, and save the file as3webservice.mxp from the trunk ➤ build folder.

2. You'll need the Adobe Extension Manager to install the extension. If you don't have the Extension Manager, download it from http://www.adobe.com/exchange/em_download/ and install the software.

3. Make sure Flash is not open and double-click the extension to install it to Flash. Once the installation is complete, open the ccSoapStart.fla resource file in Flash.

   Check the Components panel. You should see the wellconsidered components, as shown in Figure 11-5. If you can't see them, you may need to refresh the panel. Click the panel menu on the right side and choose Reload, as shown in Figure 11-5.

   Figure 11-5. The Components panel showing the wellconsidered classes

4. Before you can consume the web service, you'll need to drag a copy of all three wellconsidered classes—Operation, OperationEvent, and WebService—to the Library panel. Figure 11-6 shows the Library panel for the ccSoapStart.fla file. As I pointed out earlier, you'll need all three classes in order to consume a web service.

5. This example is similar to the previous two examples, so the starter file already includes some code on the actions layer. The code brings the application to the same stage as at the end of step 5 in the first example, so we'll pick up from that point.

   Modify the message_txt.text = "Good to go!" line in the clickHandler() function as shown in bold in the following code block:

   Figure 11-6. The Library panel showing the well-considered classes

```
function clickHandler(e:MouseEvent):void {
  var fromCurrency:String = from_cbo.selectedItem.data;
  var toCurrency:String = to_cbo.selectedItem.data;
  var convertAmount:String = amount_txt.text;
  if (from_cbo.selectedIndex > 0 && to_cbo.selectedIndex > 0) {
    if (convertAmount.length > 0) {
      if (! isNaN(Number(convertAmount))) {
        message_txt.text = "";
        webServiceSOAP(fromCurrency, toCurrency);
      }
      else {
        message_txt.text = "Enter a number to convert";
      }
    }
    else {
      message_txt.text = "Enter an amount to convert"
    }
  }
  else {
    message_txt.text = "Select both a 'from' and 'to' currency";
  }
}
```

The new lines clear any message showing in the message_txt control and call the webServiceSOAP() function, which you'll add shortly.

6. The application needs to include import statements for the three wellconsidered classes contained in the extension. Add the following lines at the top of the actions layer:

```
import be.wellconsidered.services.WebService;
import be.wellconsidered.services.Operation;
import be.wellconsidered.services.events.OperationEvent;
```

You can find the names of these classes from the Library panel.

7. Add the webServiceSOAP() function that follows:

```
function webServiceSOAP(from:String, to:String):void {
  var wsdlURL:String = "http://www.webservicex.net/
    ➥CurrencyConvertor.asmx?WSDL";
  var ws = new be.wellconsidered.services.WebService(wsdlURL);
  var op:Operation = new Operation(ws);
  op.addEventListener(OperationEvent.COMPLETE, completeHandler);
  op.addEventListener(OperationEvent.FAILED, failedHandler);
  op.ConversionRate(from, to);
  message_txt.text = "Contacting web service";
}
```

This function creates a new instance of the wellconsidered WebService class, passing the URL for the WSDL file as an argument. Notice that I used the fully qualified name of the WebService class to avoid any name confusion with existing classes. The function also creates a new Operation for the class called op.

The `webServiceSOAP()` function adds two event listeners: one for the complete event and one for the `failed` event. These events are both part of the `OperationEvent` class.

The function calls the operation `ConversionRate`, passing the from and to currencies as arguments. It finishes by displaying a message to the user that says Contacting web service.

8. The last step is to add the two handler functions that follow:

```
function completeHandler(e:OperationEvent):void {
  var returnedXML:XML = new XML(e.data);
  var rate:Number = Number(returnedXML.toString());
  var convertedAmount:Number = Number(amount_txt.text) * rate;
  result_txt.text = String(convertedAmount);
}
function failedHandler(e:OperationEvent):void {
  message_txt.text = "Error contacting web service : " + e.data.text;
}
```

These functions work in much the same way as you saw in the previous examples. The `completeHandler()` function receives an `OperationEvent` object as an argument and locates the returned XML document using the expression `e.data`. It determines the exchange rate by using the `toString()` method of the XML object.

The function uses the same calculations that you saw previously. Please refer back to the first example if you need an explanation.

The `failedHandler()` function responds in the case of an error. It also receives an `OperationEvent` as an argument. The function displays an error message to the user saying Error contacting web service:, along with the text associated with the error.

9. Test the application. You should be able to select two currencies, enter an amount to convert, click the Convert button, and see the converted amount. You can see an example of how the application should look in Figure 11-4, earlier in the chapter.

You can find this application saved in the file `ccSoap.fla` with your chapter resources. The complete code follows, in case you want to check your work:

```
import be.wellconsidered.services.WebService;
import be.wellconsidered.services.Operation;
import be.wellconsidered.services.events.OperationEvent;
import fl.data.DataProvider;
initApp();
stop();
function initApp():void {
  populateCurrencies();
  convert_btn.addEventListener(MouseEvent.CLICK, clickHandler);
}
function populateCurrencies():void {
  var dp:DataProvider = new DataProvider();
  dp.addItem({label: "Choose...", data: "0"});
  dp.addItem({label: "Australia dollars", data: "AUD"});
  dp.addItem({label: "British pound", data: "GBP"});
  dp.addItem({label: "Canadian dollar", data: "CAD"});
```

```
            dp.addItem({label: "Euro", data: "EUR"});
            dp.addItem({label: "Singapore dollar", data: "SGD"});
            dp.addItem({label: "South African rand", data: "ZAR"});
            dp.addItem({label: "US dollar", data: "USD"});
            from_cbo.dataProvider = dp;
            to_cbo.dataProvider = dp;
        }
        function clickHandler(e:MouseEvent):void {
            var fromCurrency:String = from_cbo.selectedItem.data;
            var toCurrency:String = to_cbo.selectedItem.data;
            var convertAmount:String = amount_txt.text;
              if (from_cbo.selectedIndex > 0 && to_cbo.selectedIndex > 0) {
              if (convertAmount.length > 0) {
                if (! isNaN(Number(convertAmount))) {
                    message_txt.text = "";
                    webServiceSOAP(fromCurrency, toCurrency);
                }
                else {
                  message_txt.text = "Enter a number to convert";
                }
              }
              else {
                message_txt.text = "Enter an amount to convert"
              }
            }
            else {
              message_txt.text = "Select both a 'from' and 'to' currency";
            }
        }
        function webServiceSOAP(from:String, to:String):void {
            var wsdlURL:String = "http://www.webservicex.net/
              ➥CurrencyConvertor.asmx?WSDL";
            var ws = new be.wellconsidered.services.WebService(wsdlURL);
            var op:Operation = new Operation(ws);
            op.addEventListener(OperationEvent.COMPLETE, completeHandler);
            op.addEventListener(OperationEvent.FAILED, failedHandler);
            op.ConversionRate(from);
            message_txt.text = "Contacting web service";
        }
        function completeHandler(e:OperationEvent):void {
            var returnedXML:XML = new XML(e.data);
            var rate:Number = Number(returnedXML.toString());
            var convertedAmount:Number = Number(amount_txt.text) * rate;
            result_txt.text = String(convertedAmount);
        }
        function failedHandler(e:OperationEvent):void {
          message_txt.text = "Error contacting web service: " + e.data.text;
        }
```

So far in the book, you've seen some ActionScript 3.0 approaches to consuming a web service. Unfortunately, Flash doesn't have access to the same functionality that is available in Flex in the WebService class, so consuming a web service is a much more cumbersome process.

There is an ActionScript 2.0 alternative that uses a data component. As with other Flash components, this one can help to simplify the process of building SWF applications. You can drag the component onto the stage and configure it using panel settings instead of by writing ActionScript. I'll cover this topic next.

Consuming a SOAP web service with the WebServiceConnector component

Flash can work with SOAP requests using the ActionScript 2.0 WebServiceConnector data component. You need to provide the URL to the WSDL file, and the component will generate the SOAP request for you. You can also script the WebServiceConnector class, but that's beyond the scope of this book.

In order to work with the WebServiceConnector component, you must create an ActionScript 2.0 Flash file. Each WebServiceConnector component can work with only one operation at the web service, but you can call the same operation more than once. You need to add extra WebServiceConnector components if you're calling more than one operation in your application.

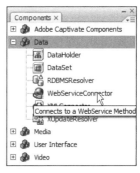

You can find the WebServiceConnector in the Data section of the Components panel of an ActionScript 2.0 document, as shown in Figure 11-7.

As with the other ActionScript 2.0 data components, the WebServiceConnector component has no visual appearance in a compiled Flash movie.

Figure 11-7. The Data section of the Components panel in an Action-Script 2.0 document

Configuring the WebServiceConnector

You configure the WebServiceConnector component using the Component Inspector panel. When you select the component in the application, you'll see three tabs in the Component Inspector:

- The Parameters tab configures the component and includes the location of the WSDL file and operation name.
- The Bindings tab indicates how user interface components interact with the WebService-Connector.
- The Schema tab shows the structure for operation arguments and returned values.

We'll start by covering the Parameters tab.

Adding parameters

To begin, you must enter the settings for the web service in the Parameters tab of the Component Inspector panel. Figure 11-8 shows the panel.

Figure 11-8. The WebServiceConnector parameters in the Component Inspector

Table 11-1 provides a summary of the parameters in this tab.

Table 11-1. The settings listed in the Parameters tab of the Component Inspector

Parameter	Type	Purpose
WSDLURL	String	Provides the URL of the WSDL document for the web service.
operation	String	Contains the name of the remote procedure or method within the SOAP port specified in the WSDL file.
multipleSimultaneousAllowed	Boolean (default: False)	Determines whether to allow multiple calls. A false value means that a call won't proceed if one if already in progress.
suppressInvalidCall	Boolean (default: False)	Determines whether to suppress a call if there are invalid parameters. A true value will prevent the component from being triggered if the parameters are invalid.

The most important parameter here is WSDLURL. As the name suggests, it is the path to the WSDL file for the web service. You can either type the URL yourself or copy and paste it from another location. I find that I'm less likely to make a mistake if I copy and paste from the address bar of a web browser. If you've added the WSDL URL previously, it will appear in a drop-down list in the Value column.

When you enter the URL, Flash tries to locate the WSDL file. If it finds a valid WSDL document, it will populate the operation setting with all available procedures for the web service. However, you may need to wait a few seconds before you can see these operation names.

You normally don't need to change the last two settings, multipleSimultaneousAllowed and suppressInvalidCall, in the Parameters tab.

Determining the arguments for the operation

Once you've selected an operation, the Schema tab of the Component Inspector will identify any parameters required by the web service operation. The tab also shows the structure of the results. Figure 11-9 shows the Schema tab after selecting the ConversionRate operation for the web service.

In this case, the Schema tab identifies that the operation requires two parameters: FromCurrency and ToCurrency. Both parameters are a String data type. The web service returns a single value, called results. It is a Number data type.

You can find out more about each parameter by selecting it and viewing the details in the field below. Figure 11-10 shows the details of the FromCurrency argument.

Adding parameter bindings

You'll need to add bindings in two different cases:

- You'll need to bind any UI components that provide values for the arguments for a web service operation.
- You'll also need to bind the results to display in the interface.

The currency conversion example requires a from and to currency as parameters. In the next example, you'll see how to add a binding from a ComboBox to each parameter.

To add a binding that provides an argument to the web service, click the Add binding (+) button in the Schema tab. Select a parameter from the params object, as shown in Figure 11-11.

Click OK to add the binding. You'll be able to see the details of the binding in the Bindings tab of the Component Inspector, as shown in Figure 11-12.

When configuring a binding for an argument to a web service operation, you'll need to set the direction to in, as the component is sending the value to the parameter. In the bound to section, select the component that will supply the value for this parameter. You need to click inside the bound to Value column so you can see a magnifying glass icon. Clicking the magnifying glass icon displays the Bound To dialog box, as shown in Figure 11-13.

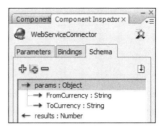

Figure 11-9. The Schema tab available after selecting an operation

Figure 11-10. Details of the FromCurrency argument for the ConversionRate operation

Figure 11-11. Adding a parameter binding

Figure 11-12. Selecting a component for the binding

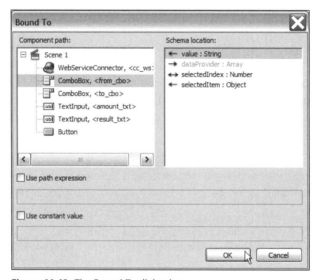

Figure 11-13. The Bound To dialog box

Select the component that will supply the value to the parameter. In Figure 11-13, I've selected the from_cbo control. The Schema location list on the right side of the dialog box shows the available properties for binding. The figure shows that value is selected.

If necessary, you can specify a fixed value for any parameters that won't vary. You would need to do that to send a developer token or ID with your request. For example, to consume the Amazon web service, you need to apply for a developer token, which is an alphanumeric value a bit like a personal identification number (PIN). Each time you consume the Amazon web service, you need to send the Amazon developer ID with the request. To add this to your application, instead of selecting a component in the Bound To dialog box, check the Use constant value check box and enter the value.

> *Bear in mind that storing a fixed value within Flash is not very secure. If you are concerned about security, a better approach is to request the value from a server-side file or load the token with the page hosting the Flash movie.*

You can also specify a formatter in the Bindings tab if you need to format the value before sending it to the web service. You might do this if you need to add some extra text with the user-entered value, or if you need to access more than one value from the data provider of a component, perhaps a DataGrid.

Triggering the web services call

You need to trigger the call to the web service in order to generate the request for the web service. You can use the Behaviors panel to generate the ActionScript, or you can add the code yourself. You would choose the latter option if you wanted to add extra ActionScript—possibly some validation of a user entry.

When you work with web services, you'll often add the trigger to a Button instance. Select the Button control and bring up the Behaviors panel with the Shift+F3 shortcut. Click the Add Behavior button, which looks like a plus sign (+). Select Data ➤ Trigger Data Source. This brings up the Trigger Data Source dialog box, as shown in Figure 11-14. Remember that we're working with an ActionScript 2.0 component here; the Trigger Data Source option won't appear in ActionScript 3.0 documents.

You'll need to select the WebServiceConnector component to trigger. You can insert a reference to this component with either a relative or an absolute path, by selecting the corresponding radio button in the Trigger Data Source dialog box. I normally choose the default setting of Relative to create a relative path, in case I need to rearrange my movie timelines later.

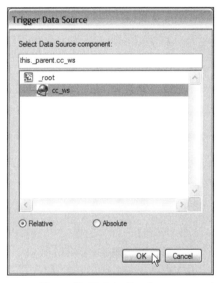

Figure 11-14. Selecting the component to trigger

In the case of a Button instance, Flash adds the following code, assuming WSCInstanceName is the name you gave to the component:

```
on (click) {
    // Trigger Data Source Behavior
    // Macromedia 2003
    this._parent.WSCInstanceName.trigger();
}
```

As I mentioned, you could also type this ActionScript yourself, as you'll see in the final exercise in this chapter.

Binding the results

Once you've triggered the component, you'll need to bind the results of your web service to one or more components to display the results. Make sure the WebServiceConnector component is selected and click the Add binding button in the Bindings tab of the Component Inspector.

Select one of the results elements. These elements are the values returned by the web service. Figure 11-15 shows the selection of a Number element, which is the only result returned from the web service.

Figure 11-15. Adding a binding for the results

You'll need to set the direction for this binding to out, as the value comes *out* of the WebServiceConnector. You must also select a component, as shown in Figure 11-16.

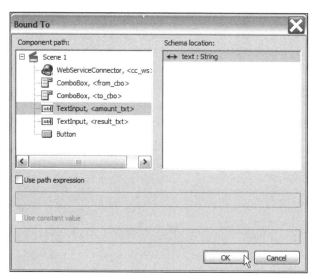

Figure 11-16. Binding a result to a component

Figure 11-16 shows a simple binding from the Number result to the text property of a TextInput component. This binding displays the returned result in the TextInput control. If you want to bind the results to a data-aware UI component, such as the List, ComboBox, or DataGrid, you'll most likely select a result with an Array data type.

Accessing the results in ActionScript

You can also use ActionScript to work with the results. In order to do this, you'll need to add a function that listens for the result event. This event is dispatched when the WebServiceConnector receives a response from the web service.

The response is in the results property of the WebServiceConnector. You can access this property by finding the target property of the object passed to the handler function. Be careful not to confuse the result event with the results property.

The following code block demonstrates how you might assign a handler function and deal with the results. Remember that this code block uses ActionScript 2.0, because we're working with a version 2.0 data component.

```
var myListener:Object = new Object();
myListener.result = function(e:Object):Void {
  //do something with e.target.results;
};
cc_ws.addEventListener("result", myListener);
```

This example uses an anonymous function to respond to the result event. You can also assign a named function, as shown here:

```
var myListener:Object = new Object();
myListener.result = myFunction;
cc_ws.addEventListener("result", myListener);
function myFunction(e:Object):Void {
  //do something with e.target.results;
}
```

Whichever approach you take, you will access the results property with the expression e.target.results, where e represents the Object passed to the event listener.

Viewing the Web Services panel

You can see a list of web services that you've worked with through the Web Services panel. Display the panel by choosing Window ➤ Other Panels ➤ Web Services. Figure 11-17 shows the Web Services panel displaying details of the ConversionRate operation.

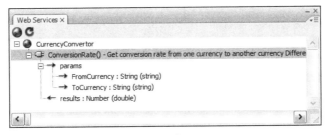

Figure 11-17. The Web Services panel

You can expand each web service listed in the panel to see a list of available operations, as well as the schema for the params and results. This dialog box provides an alternative to viewing the Component Inspector.

You can refresh all web services within the panel by clicking the Refresh Web Services button at the top of the panel. You might need to do this if you've entered a WSDL URL but can't see any operations listed in the Parameters tab of the Component Inspector.

You can also manage the web services in the list by clicking the Define Web Services button at the top left of the panel. This button has an icon that looks like a globe. Clicking the button displays the Define Web Services dialog box, as shown in Figure 11-18.

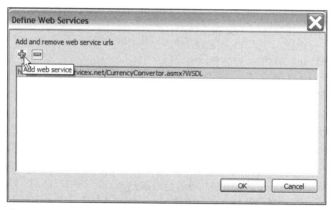

Figure 11-18. The Define Web Services dialog box

You can use the plus and minus buttons at the top of the dialog box to add and remove the URLs for the WSDL documents for each web service. Click OK to return to the Web Services panel.

You can also use the Web Services panel menu to carry out other tasks. For example, Figure 11-19 shows how to view the WSDL document in a web browser

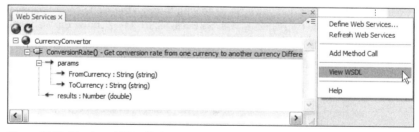

Figure 11-19. Viewing a WSDL file in a web browser

The WebServiceConnector component will become clearer when we work through a simple example. In the next exercise, we'll re-create the currency converter example that you saw earlier.

Working through a WebServiceConnector example

In this exercise, we'll use the WebServiceConnector component to consume the currency conversion service we've been working with in this chapter. The WSDL file for this web service is at `http://www.webservicex.com/CurrencyConvertor.asmx?WSDL`.

1. Open the starter file `ccStarterComponent.fla` in Flash. This is an ActionScript 2.0 document. The interface is identical to the one in the previous examples, and you can see it in Figure 11-1 earlier in the chapter.

2. Drag a WebServiceConnector component to the application. You can place it anywhere you like, as it does not have a visual appearance. Give the component the instance name `cc_ws`.

3. Select the WebServiceConnector component and open the Component Inspector panel. In the WSDLURL field of the Parameters tab, enter the URL for the WSDL: `http://www.webservicex.com/CurrencyConvertor.asmx?WSDL`. Wait for the operation field to populate, and then select the ConversionRate operation.

4. The next task is to populate the ComboBox components with currencies. Add a new layer called actions and enter the following ActionScript 2.0 code:

```
initApp();
stop();
function initApp():Void {
  populateCurrencies();
}
function populateCurrencies():Void {
  var dp:Array= new Array();
  dp.addItem({label: "Choose...", data: "0"});
  dp.addItem({label: "Australia dollars", data: "AUD"});
  dp.addItem({label: "British pound", data: "GBP"});
  dp.addItem({label: "Canadian dollar", data: "CAD"});
  dp.addItem({label: "Euro", data: "EUR"});
  dp.addItem({label: "Singapore dollar", data: "SGD"});
  dp.addItem({label: "South African rand", data: "ZAR"});
  dp.addItem({label: "US dollar", data: "USD"});
  from_cbo.dataProvider = dp;
  to_cbo.dataProvider = dp;
}
```

The code starts by calling the `initApp()` function and includes a `stop()` action. The `initApp()` function has a single line, which calls the `populateCurrencies()` function. Notice that, because the code is in ActionScript 2.0, it's necessary to capitalize the first letter of the return type Void.

The `populateCurrencies()` function is almost the same as the one used earlier, except that it uses an Array to populate the ComboBox controls. There is no DataProvider class in ActionScript 2.0.

401

5. Test the application now. You should see the two ComboBox controls populated with a list of currencies, as shown in Figure 11-20.

Figure 11-20. Populating the ComboBox components in the application

6. The application will trigger the WebServiceConnector when the user clicks the Convert button. You'll need to add a function that responds to the click event of the button. Add the following line to the initApp() function:

```
convert_btn.onRelease = clickHandler;
```

Notice that the code uses ActionScript 2.0 notation to reference the clickHandler() function with onRelease.

7. Add the clickHandler() function that follows to the actions layer:

```
function clickHandler():Void {
  if (from_cbo.selectedIndex <> 0 && to_cbo.selectedIndex <> 0) {
    if (amount_txt.text.length > 0) {
      if (! isNaN(amount_txt.text)) {
        message_txt.text = "Contacting web service";
        cc_ws.trigger();
      }
      else {
        message_txt.text = "Enter a valid number to convert";
      }
    }
    else {
      message_txt.text = "Enter an amount to convert";
    }
  }
  else {
    message_txt.text = " Select both a 'from' and 'to' currency";
  }
}
```

The function tests that both currencies have been selected. If so, it then tests that the user has entered an amount to convert. The next if statement checks that the entry is numeric.

If all entries are present and correct, the function calls the trigger() method of the WebServiceConnector. If there are missing or incorrect entries, the function displays an appropriate error message.

8. Now you need to bind the values from the ComboBox components to the params of the web service. Select the WebServiceConnector component and display the Bindings tab of the Component Inspector. Click the Add binding button and select FromCurrency : String. Click OK.

Make sure that the binding direction is set to in. Click in the bound to Value column, and click the magnifying glass icon. Choose the from_cbo control and select the value: String property. Click OK.

Repeat this process for the to_cbo ComboBox. Figure 11-21 shows how the Component Inspector Bindings tab should appear at this point.

Figure 11-21. Configuring the bindings for the web service operation

9. Because the application will perform a calculation with the returned value from the web service, you'll need to write the ActionScript to access the result. Start by adding a listener to the WebServiceConnector. Place the following ActionScript 2.0 code in the initApp() function:

```
var ccListener:Object = new Object();
ccListener.result = resultHandler;
cc_ws.addEventListener("result", ccListener);
```

The code adds an event listener that responds to the result event from the WebServiceConnector. When the application receives a result, it will call the resultHandler() function.

10. Add the following resultHandler() function to the actions layer:

```
function resultHandler(e:Object):Void {
  var amtToConvert:Number = Number(amount_txt.text);
  var rate:Number = Number(e.target.results);
  message_txt.text = "";
  result_txt.text = String(amtToConvert*rate);
}
```

This ActionScript 2.0 function finds the values of the amount to be converted and the conversion rate. It finds the rate using the expression e.target.results. It multiplies these values and displays the value in the results_txt TextInput control. The function also clears any existing messages.

11. Test the movie. Select two currencies to convert and click the Convert button. You should see the converted amount displayed in the `result_txt` TextInput control. Figure 11-22 shows a sample conversion.

Figure 11-22. The completed WebServiceConnector sample application

As with the other examples, you may want to format the returned result to two decimal places. I'll leave that up to you!

You can find the completed file saved as `ccComponent.fla` with your chapter resources. The ActionScript for the completed application follows. Again, remember that this is ActionScript 2.0 code, unlike the other examples in the chapter.

```
initApp();
stop();
function initApp():Void {
  var ccListener:Object = new Object();
  populateCurrencies();
  convert_btn.onRelease = clickHandler;
  ccListener.result = resultHandler;
  cc_ws.addEventListener("result", ccListener);
}
function populateCurrencies():Void {
  var dp:Array= new Array();
  dp.addItem({label: "Choose...", data: "0"});
  dp.addItem({label: "Australia dollars", data: "AUD"});
  dp.addItem({label: "British pound", data: "GBP"});
  dp.addItem({label: "Canadian dollar", data: "CAD"});
  dp.addItem({label: "Euro", data: "EUR"});
  dp.addItem({label: "Singapore dollar", data: "SGD"});
  dp.addItem({label: "South African rand", data: "ZAR"});
  dp.addItem({label: "US dollar", data: "USD"});
  from_cbo.dataProvider = dp;
  to_cbo.dataProvider = dp;
}
function clickHandler():Void {
  if (from_cbo.selectedIndex <> 0 && to_cbo.selectedIndex <> 0) {
    if (amount_txt.text.length > 0) {
```

```
            if (! isNaN(amount_txt.text)) {
                message_txt.text = "Contacting web service";
                cc_ws.trigger();
            }
            else {
              message_txt.text = "Enter a valid number to convert";
            }
          }
          else {
            message_txt.text = "Enter an amount to convert";
          }
        }
        else {
          message_txt.text = " Select both a 'from' and 'to' currency";
        }
      }
      function resultHandler(e:Object):Void {
        var amtToConvert:Number = Number(amount_txt.text);
        var rate:Number = Number(e.target.results);
        message_txt.text = "";
        result_txt.text = String(amtToConvert*rate);
      }
```

In this exercise, we created a simple currency converter application using the WebServiceConnector component. The WebServiceConnector component created the SOAP request and sent through currency values from two ComboBox controls. The Flash application received a conversion value, which it used to calculate a converted amount.

As you can see, using the WebServiceConnector component to consume a web service in Flash is significantly easier than the ActionScript 3.0 approaches. You can see why Flash designers and developers are disappointed that they don't have access to the ActionScript 3.0 WebService class that is available to Flex applications.

Summary

In this chapter, I showed you different ways that you can consume a web service in Flash. Unfortunately, Flash doesn't have access to the WebService class available to Flex applications. Instead, you can choose from a variety of different approaches, and I showed you how to consume a currency conversion web service using an HTTP GET and POST. I also showed you an open source extension that provides functionality for consuming a SOAP web service.

In the second half of the chapter, we looked at how to work with the WebServiceConnector data component. You saw how to use this ActionScript 2.0 component to consume the same currency conversion web service.

In the final two chapters of the book, we'll work through case studies showing how to combine what you've learned so far into real-world examples. The next chapter will cover a Flash case study where we'll consume the Flickr web service. In the final chapter, we'll consume the kuler RSS feed from the Adobe web site using Flex.

Chapter 12

FLASH CASE STUDY

The final two chapters of this book take you through case studies so you can apply what you've learned throughout the book in real-world applications. In this chapter, we'll build an application that queries Flickr and displays the photos that it finds. We'll use the Flickr web service to locate and display photographs and related information.

As you probably know, Flickr provides access for people to store their photos. It also allows users to view these photos and find out more about the photographer. You can access the images at Flickr in a number of different ways: by searching using a keyword, by viewing photos marked as interesting, and by seeing the most recent photos uploaded.

The application that we'll build will provide all of this functionality for locating images in Flickr. It will search by keyword, display recently uploaded images, and display interesting photos. You'll be able to view a collection of thumbnails from each search and click to see a large version of each one. You'll also be able to view the image at the Flickr web site and find out more about the photographer.

In this chapter, we'll use Flash to build the Flickr application. We'll use a function-based approach for the ActionScript code, rather than working with custom classes. In the next chapter, we'll create an application using custom classes in Flex.

As usual, all of the resources for this chapter are available for download at http://www.friendsofed.com.

Before working through the example, you should have an idea of how Flickr works and the ways in which developers can access Flickr content.

Understanding Flickr

Flickr is a web site that hosts images and videos. It creates an online community that allows photographers to share their work with the rest of the world. It allows photographers to provide details about themselves and their images.

The web site organizes images using tags to provide topic information. Visitors to the site can search for images by keyword or browse through collections of images. Figure 12-1 shows an example of a search for the word *sunset*.

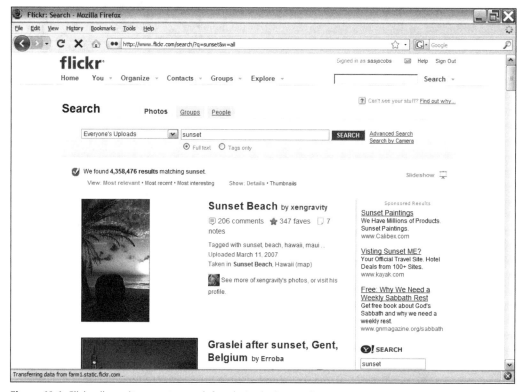

Figure 12-1. Flickr allows site users to search for photos by keyword.

Users of the Flickr site can store both public and private images. The application that we build in this chapter will access only publicly available photos.

Flickr offers an application programming interface (API) that allows developers to interact with its content. The API provides information about the procedures that developers can call at Flickr. Developers request content in a number of different ways, and the details are supplied as an XML document. Essentially, this provides access to Flickr as a web service.

Before you can get started, you'll need to apply for a Flickr key.

Applying for a Flickr key

Before you can access any of the developer functionality, you need to apply for a Flickr key. This is an alphanumeric string that you need to pass with all of your requests. You can apply for the key at `http://www.flickr.com/services/api/keys/apply/`.

When you apply, you'll be prompted whether your use of Flickr is commercial or noncommercial. For our example, choose the noncommercial option. After you make the request, Flickr will provide you with the key immediately. My key is a 32-character string, but I'm not going to provide you with those details. You'll need your own key to work through the example.

It's possible to query the Flickr web service in several different ways.

Making a Flickr request

You can request information from Flickr using the REST, XML-RPC, or SOAP web service protocol. As you saw in the previous chapter, consuming a SOAP web service in Flash is a little difficult, so we'll stick with the REST format. REST allows you to modify your request by making changes to the URL that you query. You can select the Flickr operation by changing the URL used in the request. You can send parameters for each request by adding name/value pairs to the end of the URL.

The format for each REST request to Flickr is as follows:

```
http://api.flickr.com/services/rest/?method=methodName&var1=value1
```

You need to replace the `methodName` variable with the actual method name from the Flickr API. You will pass additional values with each request as name/value pairs. For example, you may want to specify how many results to return or provide a search term.

You must include your Flickr key with each request. This value is shown in bold in the following URL with the variable name api_key:

```
http://api.flickr.com/services/rest/?method=methodName
  ➥&api_key=add_key_here";
```

You'll replace the value add_key_here in the URL with your own Flickr key.

In order to make a successful request, you need to understand the Flickr API.

Understanding the Flickr API

You can view the Flickr API at `http://www.flickr.com/services/api/`. The API lists all of the operations that are possible at the Flickr web service, and you'll see that many operations are available.

In this chapter, we'll focus on the following operations:

- `flickr.photos.getRecent`: Corresponds to a request for recently uploaded images.
- `flickr.interestingness.getList`: Corresponds to a request for interesting images.
- `flickr.photos.search`: Corresponds to a request for images that match a search term.
- `flickr.people.getInfo`: Corresponds to a request for information about photographers.

You can see that each operation is named in a specific way that describes its purpose.

409

Understanding the returned photo XML document

The `flickr.photos.getRecent`, `flickr.interestingness.getList`, and `flickr.people.getInfo` operations return the following XML structure:

```
<photos page="2" pages="89" perpage="10" total="881">
  <photo id="2867482474" owner="21766629@N07" secret="90f2218d57"
    server="3232" farm="4" title="IMG_0047 copy" ispublic="1"
    isfriend="0" isfamily="0"/>
</photos>
```

This response describes the photos identified by the request. The root of the response is the `<photos>` element. This element contains attributes to describe which page of photos is being viewed (page), how many pages there are in total (pages), how many images display per page (perpage), and the total number of images returned (total).

The response will normally contain multiple `<photo>` elements; I've shown only one here for the sake of brevity. As you can see, each `<photo>` element contains its own of attributes. Table 12-1 summarizes the purpose of each of these attributes.

Table 12-1. Flickr `<photo>` element attributes

Attribute	Description
id	The ID of the photo at Flickr. This attribute is used to generate the URL for the image.
owner	The Flickr code or user ID identifying the photo owner. You can look up this value to find out more about the owner.
secret	A code allowing access to the image that is used to generate the URL for the image.
server	The server containing the photo. This value is used to create the URL for the image.
farm	The number of the server farm at Flickr. This value is used in accessing the image URL.
title	The title for the photo.
ispublic	Indicates whether the image is available publicly. A value of 1 means that this image is publicly available.
isfriend	Indicates whether the image is available to friends.
isfamily	Indicates whether the image is available to family.

The `flickr.people.getInfo` operation returns an XML document with a different structure.

Understanding the returned people XML document

The `flickr.people.getInfo` operation provides information in the following XML format:

```
<person nsid="12037949754@N01" isadmin="0" ispro="0" iconserver="122"
  iconfarm="1">
  <username>bees</username>
  <realname>Cal Henderson</realname>
  <mbox_sha1sum>eea6cd28e3d0003ab51b0058a684d94980b727ac</mbox_sha1sum>
  <location>Vancouver, Canada</location>
  <photosurl>http://www.flickr.com/photos/bees/</photosurl>
  <profileurl>http://www.flickr.com/people/bees/</profileurl>
  <photos>
    <firstdate>1071510391</firstdate>
    <firstdatetaken>1900-09-02 09:11:24</firstdatetaken>
    <count>449</count>
  </photos>
</person>
```

The <person> element contains several attributes. The isadmin attribute indicates whether the person is an administrator. The ispro attribute indicates whether the person is a professional member. The iconserver and iconfarm attributes are used to build the URL for the user's buddy icon.

The child elements provide information about the person, and most are self-explanatory. The <mbox_sha1sum> element contains an SHA1 digest of the user's e-mail address This element is a representation of the address that does not reveal the actual e-mail address.

Information about this user's photographs is available in the <photos> element. The <firstdate> element contains the Unix date stamp of the first photo contributed by this user. The <firstdatetaken> element contains the MySQL date and time of the first photo taken by the user. The <count> element indicates how many photos the user has at Flickr.

Let's look at each of the Flickr API operations we'll use in the example in a little more detail.

Finding recent photos

The flickr.photos.getRecent operation returns a list of the latest public photos uploaded to Flickr. The images returned by this operation change very quickly. You're likely to see very different images each time you make a request, even if your requests occur close together. As with the other operations, you'll need to provide your API key to access the flickr.photos.getRecent operation.

You can request additional information about each image, such as the date the image was taken and when it was last updated, but we won't do that in the sample application. It's also possible to specify how many photos to return per page. If you leave out this value, Flickr returns 100 photos with each request. In our application, we'll return ten records at a time by specifying the name/value pair per_page=10 as part of the requested URL. The photos are organized into pages, so you can also request a specific page number to see more photos. You use the page variable in the URL to specify which page to view.

The Flickr URL that we'll request for this operation will look something like the following:

```
http://api.flickr.com/services/rest/?api_key=API_KEY_HERE
    ➥&method=flickr.photos.getRecent&per_page=10&page=1&ts=dateTimeStamp
```

You'll replace the text API_KEY_HERE with your own key.

You'll notice that I've also added a dateTimeStamp variable at the end of the URL. The dateTimeStamp variable will be a unique value made up of the current date and time. The dateTimeStamp variable isn't required by Flickr, but it will help to ensure that the web browser doesn't cache the results, by forcing it to request new details from the server each time. Many developers will be familiar with this trick to prevent caching of web page content.

The next operation to examine is finding interesting photos.

Finding interesting photos

The flickr.interestingness.getList operation returns a list of photos for the current day that are marked as interesting. Interestingness is determined by Flickr in several different ways: by analyzing where the click-throughs come from; by examining the photo comments; by analyzing who marks the photo as a favorite; and by looking at its tags. You'll need to provide your API key with this request.

You can specify a date to retrieve interesting photos from different dates. You can also specify a date by providing a date variable that uses the date format of *YYYY-MM-DD* for its value. As with the getRecent operation, you can request additional photo information, specify the number of images to display per page, and specify the page number to return.

A sample URL for this operation follows:

```
http://api.flickr.com/services/rest/?api_key=API_KEY_HERE
  ➥&method=flickr.interestingness.getList&per_page=10&page=1
  ➥&ts=dateTimeStamp
```

Again, I've included a dateTimeStamp value to avoid caching.

We will also search for photos.

Searching for photos

The final operation that displays photos is flickr.photos.search. This operation returns a list of photos matching the supplied search criteria. As usual, you need to provide your API key with the request. You can specify the number of images per request, and the page number to return. You also need to provide a value for the text variable. This is the user's search criteria.

The operation provides a lot of options and, rather than reproducing them all of them here, I encourage you to view the details at www.flickr.com/services/api/flickr.photos.search.html. We're not going to specify any additional search options in the sample application.

The URL for this request will look something like the following:

```
http://api.flickr.com/services/rest/?api_key=API_KEY_HERE
  ➥&method=flickr.photos.search&text=SEARCH_CRITERIA&per_page=10
  ➥&page=1&ts=dateTimeStamp
```

You will need to replace the text SEARCH_CRITERIA with your own search keywords. Multiple keywords are separated by commas.

The fourth operation that we will use returns information about photo owners. We'll look at that now.

Finding owner information

The `flickr.people.getInfo` operation returns information about a specific photo owner. You must provide your API key and the `user_id` of the owner who you want to research.

Your request for this operation will look something like the following:

```
http://api.flickr.com/services/rest/?api_key=API_KEY_HERE
    ➥&method=flickr.people.getInfo&user_id=userID
```

You'll need to replace userID with the ID of the relevant owner. You'll find this value with each of the photos you display. In fact, in our application, you'll need to display photos before you can request information about photo owners.

Once you've made a request, you'll need to deal with the response from Flickr.

Receiving a Flickr response

Each time our application makes a request, it will receive the standard Flickr REST response. When a successful request is made, the requested information appears inside this standard response.

The standard response from Flickr is an XML document with the root element <rsp>. The root element contains a stat attribute, which indicates whether the request was successful.

You will receive the following response to a successful request:

```
<?xml version="1.0" encoding="utf-8" ?>
<rsp stat="ok">
  <!-- XML document -->
</rsp>
```

The stat value of ok indicates that you've successfully completed the request. The comment <!-- XML document --> will be replaced by the returned information. In our case, this will be either a photos XML document or a person XML document.

If your request isn't successful, you'll see a value of fail for the stat attribute, as shown here:

```
<?xml version="1.0" encoding="utf-8" ?>
<rsp stat="fail">
  <err code="[error-code]" msg="[error-message]" />
</rsp>
```

The returned XML document will provide an error code and message to help you understand where you've gone wrong. You can display any error message by accessing the msg attribute of the <err> element.

The first step in processing any response from Flickr will be to check for a stat value of ok.

In our application, we'll receive two types of results: one for photos and one for the owner details. Let's deal with the photos first.

Receiving photo information

When your results describe a list of photos, the XML document returned inside the root element will contain a <photos> element with one or more <photo> child elements. The structure will look something like the following block:

```
<?xml version="1.0" encoding="utf-8" ?>
<rsp stat="ok">
  <photos page="2" pages="89" perpage="10" total="881">
    <photo id="2867482474" owner="21766629@N07" secret="90f2218d57"
      server="3232" farm="4" title="IMG_0047 copy" ispublic="1"
      isfriend="0" isfamily="0"/>
  </photos>
</rsp>
```

You've seen the photo XML document structure earlier in the chapter. In this example, I've shown only one <photo> element, but you're more likely to see multiple elements. Our application will return ten results per request, so the <photos> element will contain ten <photo> child elements.

Receiving person information

If you request details of an owner, you'll receive a response similar to the following XML document:

```
<?xml version="1.0" encoding="utf-8" ?>
<rsp stat="ok">
  <person nsid="12037949754@N01" isadmin="0" ispro="0"
    iconserver="122" iconfarm="1">
    <username>bees</username>
    <realname>Cal Henderson</realname>
    <mbox_sha1sum>eea6cd28e3d0003ab51b0058a684d94980b727ac
    </mbox_sha1sum>
    <location>Vancouver, Canada</location>
    <photosurl>http://www.flickr.com/photos/bees/</photosurl>
    <profileurl>http://www.flickr.com/people/bees/</profileurl>
    <photos>
      <firstdate>1071510391</firstdate>
      <firstdatetaken>1900-09-02 09:11:24</firstdatetaken>
      <count>449</count>
    </photos>
  </person>
</rsp>
```

The details appear within a <person> element. You can access the person's username, real name, location, and Flickr URLs. Again, you've seen this structure earlier in the chapter.

Finding the URL of a photo

You might have noticed that the <photo> element doesn't contain a URL for the image. We'll need this URL if our application is to display the image.

Flickr requires you to build the URL dynamically from the information provided in each <photo> element. You can find out more about how to build the URL at http://www.flickr.com/services/api/misc.urls.html. For the purposes of this example, it's enough to know that you can use the following format for the image URL:

    http://farm{farm-id}.static.flickr.com/{server-id}/{id}_{secret}.jpg

Each of the dynamic values is marked in curly braces and comes from an attribute in the <photo> element. The farm_id comes from the farm attribute of the <photo> element. You can find the server-id, id, and secret values in the same way. You could access the following photo:

    <photo id="2867482474" owner="21766629@N07" secret="90f2218d57"
      server="3232" farm="4" title="IMG_0047 copy" ispublic="1"
      isfriend="0" isfamily="0"/>

with this URL:

    http://farm**4**.static.flickr.com/**3232/21766629@N07_90f2218d57**.jpg

I've marked the dynamic portions of the URL in bold.

You can also add a suffix before the .jpg file extension to specify which image size to view. For example, to find a small square with a size of 75 pixels by 75 pixels using the previous photo element, use the _s suffix in the URL, as follows:

    http://farm4.static.flickr.com/3232/21766629@N07_90f2218d57**_s.**jpg

Table 12-2 shows the available suffix options.

Table 12-2. Suffix options for Flickr photo sizes

Suffix	Description
s	Small square, 75×75
t	Thumbnail, 100 on longest side
m	Small, 240 on longest side
-	Medium, 500 on longest side
b	Large, 1024 on longest side (only exists for very large original images)
o	Original image—a JPG, GIF, or PNG, depending on source format

Finding the page containing the photo

Our application will also identify the page containing the photo being viewed. This will allow the user to click a button and jump to the image on the Flickr web site.

You can find the location of the page at Flickr by creating a URL made up of the owner and photo id, as shown in the following line. The dynamic portions appear in bold.

```
http://www.flickr.com/photos/owner/photo id
```

Well, that's enough background information about Flickr for us to get started with the application. Let's build the application now.

Building the application

This SWF application, built in Flash, will allow users to access and display photos from Flickr. Users will be able to do the following:

- Search for a photo by entering a keyword
- View recent photos
- View interesting photos for the current day

The application will display the images in pages of ten photographs. Once users have made a request, they will be able to page through the groups of ten images. In addition, they will be able to view a large-sized version of each image, see its title, and click a button to view the image at the Flickr web site.

Let's start with the application interface.

Working through the interface

Figure 12-2 shows the interface for the application. A starter file containing this interface is provided with the chapter resources.

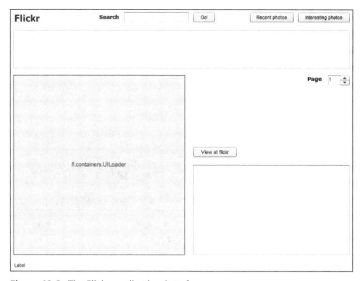

Figure 12-2. The Flickr application interface

As you can see, this interface is simple. Feel free to make it look a little better.

The interface contains several options across the top: a Search box, a Recent photos button, and an Interesting photos button. Selecting any of these options creates a request for Flickr.

A successful response from Flickr will display ten images in the TileList control at the top of the screen. It's possible for a user to click an item in the TileList control to create some kind of interaction. In our case, clicking an image will display a large-sized version of the image.

> *The TileList control provides a grid of columns and rows, usually containing images. You normally populate this control by setting its* dataProvider *property. The contents for each item in the control are identified by a* source *property in the data provider.*

The application includes a NumericStepper component, which will allow the user to scroll through each page of image results. By default, each request will show the first page of results, but it will be possible for the user to view subsequent pages by scrolling through the NumericStepper.

Clicking the image in the TileList will display a large-sized version in a UILoader container. The UILoader component is useful if you want to retrieve content from a remote location to display in a SWF application. You can display SWF, JPG, PNG, and GIF files in the control. As we want to display Flickr JPG files, this control is perfect for our application.

Once a large image displays, its title will appear in a Label control underneath the UILoader. The user will also be able to click a View at flickr button to jump to the image at the Flickr web site. Later, we'll add controls that will display information about photo owners.

For debugging purposes, I've included a TextArea control at the bottom right of the interface. We'll use this to load the XML document from Flickr, so we can see the outcome of our request. Obviously, we'll remove this control before we publish the application on a web site.

Now that you understand the interface, let's set up the application.

Setting up the application

Follow these steps to set up the application:

1. Open the starter file FlickrStarter.fla from the chapter resources. It contains the interface discussed in the previous section and shown in Figure 12-2.

2. Add a new layer to the Flash file and call it actions. Open frame 1 of the layer in the Actions panel with the F9 shortcut key, and add the following code:

```
var strFlickrURL:String = "http://api.flickr.com/services/rest/
    ➥?api_key=API_KEY_HERE";
var xmlRequest:URLRequest;
var xmlLoader:URLLoader;
var xmlResults:XML;
var currentPhoto:Object;
var flickrRequestURL:String;
var currentPageNumber:int;
initApp();
stop();
function initApp():void {
}
```

This code sets up the application. We'll work through it line by line.

The first line creates a variable for the base URL for all Flickr REST web services. It contains the URL for the web service, as well as the api_key variable. Make sure you replace the text API_KEY_HERE with your own Flickr key.

The code also declares a number of variables that we'll use throughout the application. These variables are not declared within functions, so they have timeline scope; in other words, their values are available to all functions.

The xmlRequest variable is the URLRequest object that we'll use to make the request. We also have an xmlLoader object that we'll use to load the external content. The xmlResults variable will contain the returned XML document from Flickr.

The currentPhoto object will store some of the most important properties of each photo. These properties include the base URL for the image, the owner ID, and the photo ID.

The flickrRequestURL variable will identify the URL for the operation. Because we're working with a REST web service, all arguments for the web service operation will be passed by generating an appropriate URL.

Finally, the currentPageNumber variable will keep track of which page of results the application has loaded. We'll need to do this to provide paging functionality for the user.

The code starts by calling the initApp() function. After calling this function, the code includes a stop() action. The code block also includes the signature for the initApp() function which we'll populate in the next step.

3. Let's create the initApp() function now. The purpose of this function is to set up the application before the user starts.

Initially, the initApp() function will set up the URLLoader object and its event listener. When the xmlLoader object finishes loading the external content, it will call the completeHandler() function. The completeHandler() function will display the loaded XML content in the message_txt TextArea. It will also load the TileList control with the requested thumbnails from Flickr.

Add the following initApp() function to the bottom of the actions layer:

```
function initApp():void {
  xmlLoader = new URLLoader();
  xmlLoader.addEventListener(Event.COMPLETE, completeHandler);
}
```

Add the function signature for the completeHandler() function as well. We'll fill in the details of this function a little later on.

```
function completeHandler(e:Event):void {
}
```

With the setup complete, we're ready to begin adding functionality.

Getting the recent photos list

We'll start by requesting the recent photos list.

1. Our first step in retrieving recently uploaded photos is to respond when the user clicks the Recent photos button. We need to add an event listener to the initApp() function, as shown in bold in the following code block:

```
function initApp():void {
    xmlLoader = new URLLoader();
    xmlLoader.addEventListener(Event.COMPLETE, completeHandler);
    recent_btn.addEventListener(MouseEvent.CLICK, recentClickHandler);
}
```

When the user clicks the Recent photos button, the application calls the recentClickHandler() function.

2. Add the recentClickHandler() handler function that follows:

```
function recentClickHandler(e:MouseEvent):void {
    flickrRequestURL = strFlickrURL + "&method=
        ➥flickr.photos.getRecent&per_page=10";
    getPhotos(1);
}
```

This function creates the URL for the REST request and stores it in the flickrRequestURL variable. The URL starts with the base URL that we defined at the top of the actions layer.

The function then adds the method variable with the relevant operation as its value. In this case, that operation is flickr.photos.getRecent. The URL also indicates that we're requesting ten photos per page with per_page=10.

The flickrRequestURL variable doesn't contain the finished variable for the REST request. We'll also add the page number to request, as well as a timestamp to prevent caching. We'll add those values in the getPhotos() function a little later.

The recentClickHandler() function finishes by calling the getPhotos() function. This function will finish creating the URL for the web service request. It receives one argument, which is the number of the page to display. In this case, the recentClickHandler() function passes a value of 1, as we want to see the first page of results.

3. Add the following getPhotos() function. I'll explain it after the code.

```
function getPhotos(pageNum:int):void {
    var dateTimeStamp:Date = new Date();
    var requestURL:String;
    currentPageNumber = pageNum;
    requestURL = flickrRequestURL + "&page=" +
        ➥String(currentPageNumber) + "&ts=" + dateTimeStamp;
    xmlRequest = new URLRequest(requestURL);
    xmlLoader.load(xmlRequest);
}
```

As I mentioned, this function receives the page number to request as an argument. This value will be useful when we're paging through the results a little later, as we'll be able to call the function again, passing a different page number.

The getPhotos() function creates a new dateTimeStamp variable, which will contain the current date and time. Using the current date and time is one way to create a unique random number. As I mentioned previously, adding a random number to a URL is one way to prevent caching of the results from Flickr in the web browser.

The getPhotos() function declares a new variable, requestURL, which will store the final URL for the web service request. It also sets the value of the currentPageNumber variable to the passed-in page number. Because this variable has timeline scope, the value is set for all functions in the application.

The function creates the request URL from the flickrRequestURL variable created in the recentClickHandler() function. It adds the page variable as well as the ts variable, which contains the random number.

When completed, the requestURL variable will look something like the following. You can trace the value if you want to see it for yourself.

```
http://api.flickr.com/services/rest/?api_key= API_KEY_HERE
    ➥&method=flickr.photos.getRecent&per_page=10&page=0&
    ➥ts=Thu Sep 18 14:15:03 GMT+0800 2008
```

The value API_KEY_HERE will be replaced by your own key. The ts variable will contain a different date and time value, depending on when you create this application.

The function finishes by creating a new URLRequest object from the requestURL variable. It passes this object to the load() method of the xmlLoader object. It's the last line of the function that actually makes the request to Flickr.

4. We'll need to finish creating the completeHandler() function referred to in the initApp() function so we can process the results from Flickr. Remember that this function is called when the URLLoader object dispatches the complete event after a successful request.

   Initially, we'll use the function to display the returned XML content from Flickr in the TextArea control. This step is a useful tool to see the structure of the XML document returned, but you wouldn't do it in a production environment.

   Modify the completeHandler() function as shown in bold here:

   ```
   function completeHandler(e:Event):void {
     xmlResults = XML(e.target.data);
     message_txt.text = xmlResults.toXMLString();
   }
   ```

   The first new line assigns the data property of the URLLoader object to the xmlResults object. We've used e.target to identify the URLLoader and cast the String value returned as an XML object. The completeHandler() function then displays a String representation of the contents in the message_txt TextArea control using the toXMLString() method.

5. Test the application and click the Recent photos button. Figure 12-3 shows what you should see. Notice the returned XML document in the TextArea control. If you can see this document, your application is working correctly.

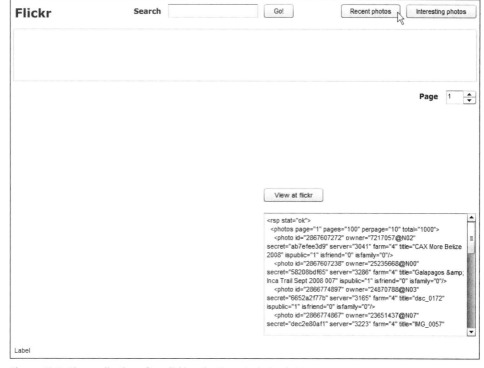

Figure 12-3. The application after clicking the Recent photos button

The application makes the request for recent photos at Flickr. It receives an XML document in response, which is visible in the TextArea control. The response is the standard photo XML document that you saw earlier in the chapter.

Figure 12-3 shows that the stat attribute of the root element ‹rsp› has a value of ok. This indicates that we have a successful response from Flickr.

6. We'll populate the TileList control with thumbnails derived from each of the ‹photo› elements in the returned XML document. You'll recall from the discussion in the "Finding the URL of a photo" section earlier in the chapter that we must create this URL dynamically from attributes in the ‹photo› element.

We'll create a DataProvider object containing the details of each photo. This object will provide the source for the images in the TileList control.

Because we're working with the DataProvider class, you'll need to add the following import statement to the top of the actions layer:

```
import fl.data.DataProvider;
```

7. We'll need to loop through each ‹photo› element in the returned XML document so we can build its URL dynamically in order to display the image in the TileList control.

Once we've identified the photo's URL, we can set this value as the source property in the DataProvider for the TileList. This process will display the image as an item in the TileList. You could also add a label property to display a text caption for each image, but we're not going to do that in this application.

421

Modify the completeHandler() function as shown in the following code block. As there are a number of changes, you might want to enter all of the code inside the function again.

```
function completeHandler(e:Event):void {
  var dp:DataProvider = new DataProvider();
  var imageURL:String;
  xmlResults = XML(e.target.data);
  if (xmlResults.@stat == "ok") {
    for each (var photoXML:XML in xmlResults.photos.photo) {
      imageURL = "http://farm" + photoXML.@farm +
        ➥".static.flickr.com/";
      imageURL += photoXML.@server;
      imageURL += "/" + photoXML.@id;
      imageURL += "_" + photoXML.@secret;
      dp.addItem({source: imageURL + "_s.jpg",
        ➥largeURL: imageURL + "_b.jpg", title: photoXML.@title,
        ➥owner: photoXML.@owner, photoID: photoXML.@id});
    }
    images_tl.dataProvider = dp;
    images_tl.setStyle("contentPadding", 10);
    message_txt.text = xmlResults.toXMLString();
  }
  else {
    message_txt.text = "Error:" + xmlResults.err.@msg;
  }
}
```

The completeHandler() function starts by declaring a new DataProvider object called dp, which we'll use to populate the TileList. Each item in the DataProvider will be an object containing a number of relevant properties. In addition to the source property, we'll store other information about each image, such as the URL for the large-sized image, the owner, and the photo's ID.

Using an object simplifies the process of accessing image information compared with constructing E4X expressions later on. It will be easier for us to view more information about each image when it is clicked in the TileList.

The completeHandler() function also declares a variable called imageURL for the base URL for each image. We'll use this variable to store the dynamic URL for the image. We won't include the .jpg image extension in the variable so we can use it to construct the URL for both small and large-sized images. Remember that it's possible to specify the image size by adding a suffix before the file extension.

After assigning the data property of the URLLoader to the xmlResults object, the function tests the stat attribute of the root element. This attribute indicates if we have made a successful request by comparing the value to ok.

If the request was successful, the code works through each <photo> element using a for each loop. Notice that the code specifies the XMLList to loop through by using the E4X expression xmlResults.photos.photo. This expression identifies each of the individual <photo> elements within the <photos> element.

The next few lines generate the base URL for the image. Revisit the "Finding the URL of a photo" section earlier in this chapter if you're not sure how I created the photo URL.

After creating the base URL in the imageURL variable, the function uses the addItem() method of the DataProvider object to add an object for each photo. This object assigns the URL of a small image, found by adding the suffix _s.jpg to the URL, to the source property. This small image will display in the TileList control.

The dp object also contains a largeURL property, obtained by adding the suffix _b to the base image URL. The object contains a title, owner, and photoID property for each photo. These properties will come in handy when we want to display more information about a selected photo, including the large image.

Once the dp object is created, the function sets it as the dataProvider property for the TileList. The function also adds some contentPadding to the TileList to add margins. It finishes by displaying a String representation of the XML object in the message_txt control using toXMLString().

If the request is not successful, the function displays the error message from Flickr in the message_txt control. The E4X expression uses the msg attribute of the returned <err> element.

8. Test the application now. Click the Recent photos button, and you should see the TileList populate with recent photos, as shown in Figure 12-4. The TileList should display ten images.

Figure 12-4. Populating the TileList with recent photos

Displaying a large image and title

The next step in building the application is to display a large image and title when the user clicks a thumbnail image.

1. In order to display a full-sized image in the UILoader control, we need to add an event listener that responds when the user clicks an image in the TileList. This event listener will also need to display the title below the large image.

   Because we'll be tracking a ListEvent, we need to add the following import statement to the top of the actions layer:

   ```
   import fl.events.ListEvent;
   ```

2. We'll assign the event listener for the TileList ItemClick event with the following line, which you should add to the initApp() function:

   ```
   images_tl.addEventListener(ListEvent.ITEM_CLICK, itemClickHandler);
   ```

   When a user clicks an image in the TileList, the itemClickHandler() function will be called.

423

3. Now you can add the `itemClickHandler()` function shown here:

```
function itemClickHandler(e:ListEvent):void {
  currentPhoto = images_tl.getItemAt(e.index);
  title_txt.text = currentPhoto.title;
  image_uil.source = currentPhoto.largeURL;
}
```

This function assigns the clicked item from the TileList data provider to the `currentPhoto` object. It does so by using the `getItemAt()` method with the number of the photograph clicked, found with the expression `e.index`.

The function can then use the properties of the `currentPhoto` object to identify the title and URL for the large-sized image. The second line assigns the `title` property to the `text` property of the `title_txt` label. The third line of the function assigns the `largeURL` property of the `currentPhoto` object to the `source` of the `image_uil` UILoader control. This line will display the large image in the interface.

Before continuing, let's clear the current text displaying in the label so users don't see the word Label before a large photo displays. In the Parameters panel, remove the Label value from the text field.

4. Test the application, click the Recent photos button, and then click an image in the TileList. Figure 12-5 shows how the interface should appear when you click an image from the TileList. You can see the large-sized version of the clicked image below the thumbnails. You can also see a title below the image.

Figure 12-5. Displaying the large image and details

5. We want the user to be able to view this image at Flickr by clicking the View at flickr button. To accomplish this, add the following event listener line to the initApp() function:

```
view_btn.addEventListener(MouseEvent.CLICK, viewClickHandler);
```

This line responds when the user clicks the View at flickr button by calling the viewClickHandler() function.

6. Add the following viewClickHandler() function to the actions layer:

```
function viewClickHandler(e:MouseEvent):void {
  var photoPageURL:String;
  photoPageURL = "http://www.flickr.com/photos/" +
    ➥currentPhoto.owner + "/" + currentPhoto.photoID;
  navigateToURL(new URLRequest(photoPageURL), "_blank");
}
```

This function creates the URL for the page displaying this photo at Flickr. The function starts by declaring a variable for this URL called photoPageURL. It creates the URL from the owner and id attributes of the <photo> element. We stored this information in the DataProvider object. If you're not sure how to create the URL, see the "Finding the page containing the photo" section earlier in this chapter.

7. Test the application and click the View at flickr button. You should see the image at the Flickr web site, as shown in Figure 12-6. Viewing the photo at Flickr allows a user to view comments on the image, see more information about the image, and find out about the owner of the image.

Figure 12-6. Viewing the image at Flickr

425

Adding paging functionality

The next task is to allow the user to move from one page of results to another.

1. The application will control paging by using the NumericStepper control. The application will also need to cap the number of pages that the user can view by using the pages attribute from the <photos> element. If we don't do this, users will get an error if they try to go to a page higher than the last page available from Flickr.

   At the moment, the NumericStepper has its default maximum value of 10. We'll need to change this to be the total number of pages available from Flickr.

   Add a new variable called totalPages with the other variable declarations at the top of the actions layer. The new line appears in bold.

   ```
   var currentPageNumber:int;
   var totalPages:int;
   ```

2. Populate this variable by making the following changes to the completeHandler() function. Again, the new lines appear in bold; the complete function isn't shown in the following code block:

   ```
   function completeHandler(e:Event):void {
     var dp:DataProvider = new DataProvider();
     var imageURL:String;
     xmlResults = XML(e.target.data);
     if (xmlResults.@stat == "ok") {
       totalPages = xmlResults.photos.@pages;
       page_step.maximum = totalPages;
       page_step.minimum = 1;
       for each (var photoXML:XML in xmlResults.photos.photo) {
   ```

   The first new line determines the total number of pages available by using the E4X expression xmlResults.photos.@pages. The second new line sets this value as the maximum property of the NumericStepper. The third new line sets the minimum value in the NumericStepper to 1.

3. Now we need to respond when the user clicks the NumericStepper to change the page number. Add an event listener to the NumericStepper that will respond when the selected value changes. The user can either use the up and down buttons or type a new value in the control.

   Add the following line to the initApp() function:

   ```
   page_step.addEventListener(Event.CHANGE, stepperChangeHandler);
   ```

   This line ensures that the application calls the stepperChangeHandler() function when the value in the NumericStepper changes.

4. Add the stepperChangeHandler() function to the actions layer.

   ```
   function stepperChangeHandler(e:Event):void {
     if (e.target.value != currentPageNumber){
     getPhotos(e.target.value);
     }
   }
   ```

This function is very simple. It checks that the selected value in the NumericStepper is not equal to the currentPageNumber variable. If this is the case, the function calls the getPhotos() function, passing the value selected in the NumericStepper as the new page number.

5. Test the application again. Figure 12-7 shows how to use the NumericStepper control to select different pages in the application. As you choose a different value, you should see the thumbnails refresh in the TileList control. Once you've changed the selected page, you should be able to click any of the new images to see their details below.

Figure 12-7. Choosing different pages with the NumericStepper control

Making cosmetic changes to the interface

Before moving on, we need to make some cosmetic changes to clean up the interface a little.

1. The application should hide the View at flickr button until an image is selected from the TileList. It should also disable the NumericStepper until the user has made a request for Flickr images, and reset its value to 1 with each new request.

   Add the following two lines to the initApp() function. I've added them at the bottom of the function, but it really doesn't matter where they are placed.

   ```
   page_step.enabled = false;
   view_btn.visible = false;
   ```

   These lines disable the NumericStepper control and hide the view_btn control when the application first loads. If you test the application, you won't see the View at flickr button at first, and the NumericStepper won't be enabled. These pieces of functionality don't make sense unless the interface displays images.

2. We'll enable the NumericStepper once we've made a successful request for images. Add the following bold line to the completeHandler() function. I've included the existing line that you should add the new line above.

   ```
   page_step.enabled = true;
   message_txt.text = xmlResults.toXMLString();
   ```

   The line sets the enabled property of the NumericStepper to true.

3. We want to display the View at flickr button once a photo has been clicked in the TileList. When the user sees the large-sized image, this button will also appear.

   Add the following line to the itemClickHandler() function:

   ```
   view_btn.visible = true;
   ```

427

4. Finally, we'll reset the NumericStepper when we make a new request. This will make sure that the control displays the correct page number. In our case, this number will be 1, representing the first page of results.

Add the following line to the `recentClickHandler()` function:

```
page_step.value = 1;
```

The line sets the value in the NumericStepper back to 1.

5. Test the application and click the Recent photos button. The View at flickr button should become visible only after you click a photo in the TileList. The NumericStepper should be enabled only after you've requested the recent photos.

Viewing interesting photos

The next stage in building this application is to enable the Interesting photos button. We've actually done most of the work already, so we'll need to make only minor changes to add this functionality.

1. To enable the Interesting photos button, all we need to do is to add an event listener and handler function. Add the following line to the `initApp()` function:

```
interesting_btn.addEventListener(MouseEvent.CLICK,
    ➥interestingClickHandler);
```

We'll call the `interestingClickHandler()` function when the user clicks the Interesting photos button.

2. Add the `interestingClickHandler()` function now.

```
function interestingClickHandler(e:MouseEvent):void {
    flickrRequestURL = strFlickrURL +
    ➥"&method=flickr.interestingness.getList&per_page=10";
    getPhotos(1);
    page_step.value = 1;
}
```

This function is very similar to the `recentClickHandler()` function. The only difference is that it calls a different method—in this case, `flickr.interestingness.getList`. It calls the `getPhotos()` function to request the interesting photos from Flickr. The function also resets the NumericStepper back to 1 because we're starting with the first page.

3. Test the application again. You should be able to click the Interesting photos button to display interesting photos in the TileList control. You should be able to click one of the photos to see a large-sized version, as well as the title. Figure 12-8 shows how the application might appear when you've done so.

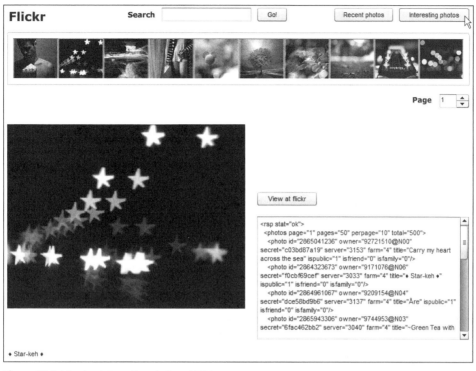

Figure 12-8. Viewing interesting photos at Flickr

Searching Flickr

The application also needs to search Flickr when the user enters a keyword and clicks the Go! button.

1. In order to carry out a search of Flickr, the application will need to call the flickr.photos. search operation. It will need to send the user's search term with the request.

We'll add an event listener that responds when the user clicks the Go! button. Add the following line to the initApp() function to indicate that the searchClickHandler() function should be called in this case.

```
search_btn.addEventListener(MouseEvent.CLICK, searchClickHandler);
```

2. Now add the searchClickHandler() function to the actions layer.

```
function searchClickHandler(e:MouseEvent):void {
  flickrRequestURL = strFlickrURL + "&method=flickr.photos.search&
    ➥per_page=10&text=" + search_txt.text;
  getPhotos(1);
  page_step.value = 1;
}
```

This function creates a URL that calls the `flickr.photos.search` operation, providing the search text as one of the variables. As with the other examples, we're retrieving ten photos at a time.

The function then calls the `getPhotos()` function, passing a value of 1 so that the first page displays. It finishes by resetting the value in the NumericStepper to 1.

3. Test the application again. You should be able to enter a search term and see the relevant photos. Figure 12-9 shows an example of searching for the term flower. You can see that I've clicked one of the images to display a large-sized photo.

Figure 12-9. Using the search functionality in the application

Showing owner information

Let's finish the application by showing details of each owner.

1. The application should display the details about each photo owner, including the username, real name, and location. It should also provide a link to view the owner's Flickr profile.

We'll need to modify the interface slightly. Add four new Label controls to the right of the UILoader. Give them the instance names username_txt, owner_txt, location_txt, and url_txt, respectively. Figure 12-10 shows how I've arranged the new controls.

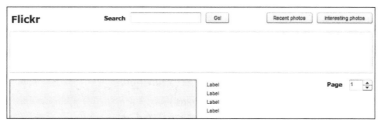

Figure 12-10. The new Label controls in the interface

After you're happy with the position of the controls, remove the Label value from the text field of each Label in the Parameters panel. This ensures that text Label won't be visible before we load a large-sized image.

2. Modify the itemClickHandler() function to call a new function, showOwnerDetails(), as listed in bold here:

```
function itemClickHandler(e:ListEvent):void {
  currentPhoto = images_tl.getItemAt(e.index)
  title_txt.text = currentPhoto.title;
  image_uil.source = currentPhoto.largeURL;
  view_btn.visible = true;
  showOwnerDetails(currentPhoto.owner);
}
```

The new line calls the showOwnerDetails() function, passing the owner details from the currentPhoto object. This value is a String indicating the owner ID at Flickr.

3. Add the showOwnerDetails() function that follows:

```
function showOwnerDetails(ownerID:String):void {
  var xmlOwnerRequest:URLRequest;
  var xmlOwnerLoader:URLLoader = new URLLoader();
  var dateTimeStamp:Date = new Date();
  var ownerRequest:String = strFlickrURL +
    ➥"&method=flickr.people.getInfo&user_id=" + ownerID +
    ➥"&ts=" + dateTimeStamp;
  xmlOwnerLoader.addEventListener(Event.COMPLETE, ownerCompleteHandler);
  xmlOwnerRequest = new URLRequest(ownerRequest);
  xmlOwnerLoader.load(xmlOwnerRequest);
}
```

This function requests the owner details from Flickr. It starts by declaring a URLRequest and URLLoader object. It also creates a new dateTimeStamp variable that we'll use to avoid caching of results in the web browser. The final variable is the String that we'll pass to the URLRequest.

The ownerRequest variable contains the base Flickr URL that we created at the top of the actions layer. It adds the name of the method to call—in this case, flickr.people.getInfo. It also passes the user_id argument with the request. As with the other URLs, this String includes a dateTimeStamp variable at the end.

431

The function adds an event listener that will respond when the application receives a response. When Flickr replies, the application will call the ownerCompleteHandler() function.

The showOwnerDetails() function creates a new URLRequest from the ownerRequest variable and calls the load() method of the xmlOwnerLoader object.

4. Add the following ownerCompleteHandler() function:

```
function ownerCompleteHandler(e:Event):void {
  var xmlOwnerDetails:XML = XML(e.target.data);
  if (xmlOwnerDetails.@stat == "ok") {
    username_txt.text = xmlOwnerDetails.person.username;
    owner_txt.text = xmlOwnerDetails.person.realname;
    location_txt.text = xmlOwnerDetails.person.location;
    url_txt.htmlText = "<a href='" + xmlOwnerDetails.person.
      ➥profileurl + "' target='_blank'><font color='#0000FF'>
      <u>View flickr profile</u></font></a>";
  }
  else {
    message_txt.text = "Error:" + xmlResults.err.@msg;
  }
}
```

This function processes the response from Flickr and populates an XML object with the results provided. Note that it casts the data property of the URLLoader as an XML object so we can apply E4X expressions.

The function checks the stat attribute to make sure that it has a value of ok. If so, the function populates the Label controls that we added earlier with the relevant elements from the loaded owner XML content. The application uses E4X expressions to target these elements within the <person> element.

The function populates the url_txt control a little differently from the approach used in the other controls. In this case, the application creates a clickable Label control by assigning the <profileurl> element to the htmlText property of the Label. This element contains the full URL to the owner's Flickr profile.

The ownerCompleteHandler() function uses the value to create a hyperlink. It also uses HTML 3.2 tags to provide underlining and a blue color.

If the request is not successful, the relevant error message appears in the message_txt control.

5. To test the new functionality, run the application and find some Flickr photos. You can search for a keyword, view the recent photos, or see interesting photos. When the TileList populates, click one of the images. You should see the user details appear to the right of the image, as shown in Figure 12-11. When you click the View flickr profile link, you should see the owner's Flickr profile page in a web browser, as shown in Figure 12-12.

Figure 12-11. Viewing the photo owner details

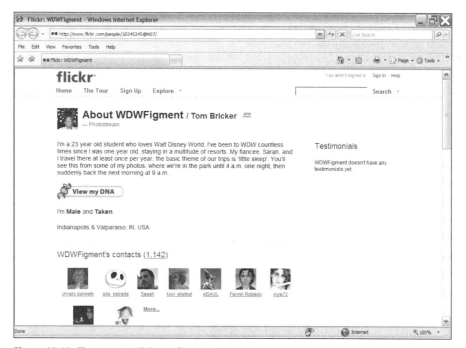

Figure 12-12. The owner's Flickr profile page

Well, that's it for the sample application. Congratulations on getting this far. I hope you found building this application a useful exercise, and I hope it gave you some tips for working with XML documents.

I've included the code for the application in case you want to check it against your own code.

```
import fl.data.DataProvider;
import fl.events.ListEvent;
var strFlickrURL:String = "http://api.flickr.com/services/rest/
    ➥?api_key=API_KEY_HERE";
var xmlRequest:URLRequest;
var xmlLoader:URLLoader;
var xmlResults:XML;
var currentPhoto:Object;
var flickrRequestURL:String;
var currentPageNumber:int;
var totalPages:int;
initApp();
stop();
function initApp():void {
  xmlLoader = new URLLoader();
  recent_btn.addEventListener(MouseEvent.CLICK, recentClickHandler);
  interesting_btn.addEventListener(MouseEvent.CLICK,
    ➥interestingClickHandler);
  search_btn.addEventListener(MouseEvent.CLICK, searchClickHandler);
  xmlLoader.addEventListener(Event.COMPLETE, completeHandler);
  images_tl.addEventListener(ListEvent.ITEM_CLICK, itemClickHandler);
  view_btn.addEventListener(MouseEvent.CLICK, viewClickHandler);
  page_step.addEventListener(Event.CHANGE, stepperChangeHandler);
  page_step.enabled = false;
  view_btn.visible = false;
}
function completeHandler(e:Event):void {
  var dp:DataProvider = new DataProvider();
  var imageURL:String;
  xmlResults = XML(e.target.data);
  if (xmlResults.@stat == "ok") {
    totalPages = xmlResults.photos.@pages;
    page_step.maximum = totalPages;
    page_step.minimum = 1;
    for each (var photoXML:XML in xmlResults.photos.photo) {
      imageURL = "http://farm" + photoXML.@farm +
        ➥".static.flickr.com/";
      imageURL += photoXML.@server;
      imageURL += "/" + photoXML.@id;
      imageURL += "_" + photoXML.@secret;
      dp.addItem({source: imageURL + "_s.jpg", largeURL:
        ➥imageURL + "_b.jpg", title: photoXML.@title,
        ➥owner: photoXML.@owner, photoID: photoXML.@id});
    }
```

```
      images_tl.dataProvider = dp;
      images_tl.setStyle("contentPadding", 10);
      page_step.enabled = true;
      message_txt.text = xmlResults.toXMLString();
    }
    else {
      message_txt.text = "Error:" + xmlResults.err.@msg;
    }
  }
  function recentClickHandler(e:MouseEvent):void {
    flickrRequestURL = strFlickrURL +
      ➥"&method=flickr.photos.getRecent&per_page=10";
    getPhotos(1);
    page_step.value = 1;
  }
  function interestingClickHandler(e:MouseEvent):void {
    flickrRequestURL = strFlickrURL +
      ➥"&method=flickr.interestingness.getList&per_page=10";
    getPhotos(1);
    page_step.value = 1;
  }
  function searchClickHandler(e:MouseEvent):void {
    flickrRequestURL = strFlickrURL +
      ➥"&method=flickr.photos.search&per_page=10&text=" +
      ➥search_txt.text;
    getPhotos(1);
    page_step.value = 1;
  }
  function getPhotos(pageNum:int):void {
    var dateTimeStamp:Date = new Date();
    var requestURL:String;
    currentPageNumber = pageNum;
    requestURL = flickrRequestURL + "&page=" +
      ➥String(currentPageNumber) + "&ts=" + dateTimeStamp;
    xmlRequest = new URLRequest(requestURL);
    xmlLoader.load(xmlRequest);
  }
  function itemClickHandler(e:ListEvent):void {
    currentPhoto = images_tl.getItemAt(e.index);
    title_txt.text = currentPhoto.title;
    image_uil.source = currentPhoto.largeURL;
    view_btn.visible = true;
    showOwnerDetails(currentPhoto.owner);
  }
  function viewClickHandler(e:MouseEvent):void {
    var photoPageURL:String;
      photoPageURL = "http://www.flickr.com/photos/" +
        ➥currentPhoto.owner + "/" + currentPhoto.photoID;
      navigateToURL(new URLRequest(photoPageURL), "_blank");
  }
```

```
            function stepperChangeHandler(e:Event):void {
               if (e.target.value != currentPageNumber){
                     getPhotos(e.target.value);
                  }
            }
            function showOwnerDetails(ownerID:String):void {
               var xmlOwnerRequest:URLRequest;
               var xmlOwnerLoader:URLLoader = new URLLoader();
               var dateTimeStamp:Date = new Date();
               var ownerRequest:String = strFlickrURL +
                  ➥"&method=flickr.people.getInfo&user_id=" + ownerID +
                  ➥"&ts=" + dateTimeStamp;
               xmlOwnerLoader.addEventListener(Event.COMPLETE, ownerCompleteHandler);
               xmlOwnerRequest = new URLRequest(ownerRequest);
               xmlOwnerLoader.load(xmlOwnerRequest);
            }
            function ownerCompleteHandler(e:Event):void {
               var xmlOwnerDetails:XML = XML(e.target.data);
               if (xmlOwnerDetails.@stat == "ok") {
                  username_txt.text = xmlOwnerDetails.person.username;
                  owner_txt.text = xmlOwnerDetails.person.realname;
                  location_txt.text = xmlOwnerDetails.person.location;
                  url_txt.htmlText = "<a href='" + xmlOwnerDetails.person.
                     ➥profileurl + "' target='_blank'><font color='#0000FF'>
                     <u>View flickr profile</u></font></a>";
               }
               else {
                  message_txt.text = "Error:" + xmlResults.err.@msg;
               }
            }
```

You can find the completed Flash file saved as FlickrCompleted.fla with the chapter resources. Note that this version doesn't include an API key, so you'll need to edit the strFlickrURL variable at the top of the actions layer to include your own. Replace API_KEY_HERE with your own API key in the Flash file in order to make the example work correctly.

Summary

In this example, I showed you how to build a simple SWF application in Flash that queries Flickr in various ways. You saw how to view recent and interesting photos, as well as how to add Flickr search functionality.

Note that Adobe has created a Flickr ActionScript 3.0 library that provides access to all the functionality available through the Flickr API. You can find this library at http://code.google.com/p/as3flickrlib/ if you want to explore it further.

In the final chapter of this book, I'll work through a Flex XML application. This application will work with Adobe Kuler to query it and display color swatches.

Chapter 13

FLEX CASE STUDY

Welcome to the last chapter of this book. In this chapter, we'll build a SWF application using Flex Builder. This application will work with Adobe Kuler. Kuler is built into Flash CS4, but it isn't as easily accessed by Flex Builder.

The application will display color themes taken from the Kuler web site. It will request the highest rated and most popular themes. It will also enable users to search the themes for a specific keyword.

In this example, our application will display the five color swatches associated with each theme. We'll need to build a custom component so we can add the swatches to a DataGrid. We'll also create a custom class to handle the loading and parsing of the Kuler feed. As a bonus, you'll learn how to work with XML documents and E4X expressions that include namespaces.

As usual, all of the resources for this chapter are available for download at http://www.friendsofed.com.

Before working through the example, you should have an idea of how Kuler works and the ways in which developers can access Kuler content.

Understanding Adobe Kuler

The Adobe Kuler web site allows users to share color themes. Visitors to the site can browse or search for existing color themes, as well as upload their own to share with other users. The Adobe Kuler site is at http://www.adobe.com/products/kuler/, as shown in Figure 13-1.

439

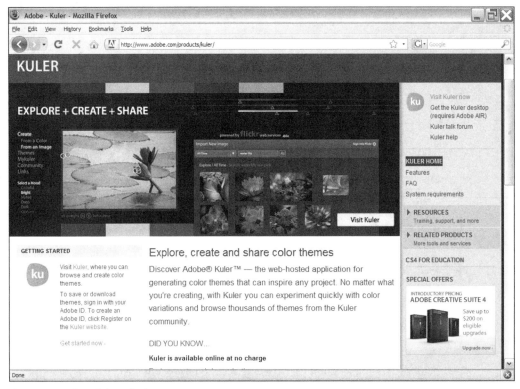

Figure 13-1. The Adobe Kuler home page

Adobe has made the Kuler content available to developers as a series of RSS 2.0 feeds. This functionality allows developers to display Kuler content in their own web applications. The Kuler feeds provide information about the highest rated, most popular, newest, and random color themes. Users can also search among the themes in various ways.

RSS is a standard XML vocabulary used to provide web site content for syndication. There are different versions of the specification. You can find out more about the version 2 specification at `http://www.rssboard.org/rss-specification`.

Developers can request a specific feed by starting with a base URL and adding name/value variable pairs that indicate what they want to view. You'll see how to change the URL of the feed shortly. The developer web site and supporting documentation is at `http://learn.adobe.com/wiki/display/kulerdev/Home`.

The following rules apply to Adobe Kuler feeds:

- They are available only for noncommercial uses. Commercial users need to contact Adobe to make other arrangements.

- Developers need an API key to consume each feed. The key is available only to developers with an existing Adobe ID.

- Developers must display the Kuler API logo in any application that they develop.

Applying for a Kuler key

Before building the application in this chapter, you'll need to apply for an Adobe Kuler API key. You can do this at http://kuler.adobe.com/api/. You'll need to sign in with your Adobe ID first and fill in a form. The API key will be e-mailed to you, and you'll need to verify it by clicking the link in the e-mail message.

Once you have a Kuler API key, you're ready to start consuming the RSS feeds.

Understanding the Kuler feeds

Information about all of the Kuler feeds is available through the API web site at http://kuler-api.adobe.com/. Click the B. Feeds link on the left side of the page to learn more about each feed. You can request a predetermined feed, such as a list of highest rated themes, or provide search criteria to retrieve a set of custom results in the feed.

In this chapter, we'll focus on the highest rated and most popular existing feeds, and allow the user to search all Kuler themes by keyword.

Accessing an existing feed

The URL for all feeds starts with http://kuler-api.adobe.com/. To return a list of items in either the highest rated or most popular feed, you need to add the following parameters to the base URL:

```
rss/get.cfm?listType=[listType]&startIndex=[startIndex]
&itemsPerPage=[itemsPerPage]&timeSpan=[timeSpan]&key=[key]
```

The order of the parameters in the URL doesn't matter. Table 13-1 explains these parameters.

Table 13-1. Parameters to pass when requesting a Kuler feed

Parameter name	Required/ optional	Description	Default value
listType	Optional	Determines the type of list to request. Choose from recent, popular, rating, or random.	recent
startIndex	Optional	Determines the first item to display, starting from 0.	0
itemsPerPage	Optional	Determines the maximum number of items to display on each page. Choose values from 1 to 100.	20
timeSpan	Optional	Determines the number of days from which to retrieve values. A value of 0 retrieves all themes without a time limit.	0
key	Required	Provides the developer API key obtained for the request.	

The following examples show how you can use these parameters to request feeds:

- Return the most recent feeds, starting from the tenth record:

    ```
    http://kuler-api.adobe.com/rss/get.cfm?key=your_key
    ➥&listType=recent&startIndex=10
    ```

- Find the most popular feeds for the previous seven days:

    ```
    http://kuler-api.adobe.com/rss/get.cfm?key=your_key
    ➥&listType=popular&timeSpan=7
    ```

- Retrieve the highest rated items, ten per page:

    ```
    http://kuler-api.adobe.com/rss/get.cfm?key=your_key&listType=rating
    ➥&itemsPerPage=10
    ```

In all of the examples, you would need to replace the text your_key with the developer key provided by Adobe.

In our application, we'll pass the listType, startIndex, itemsPerPage, and key parameters. Because we won't include a timeSpan, no time limit will be imposed on the results.

Searching Kuler

You can search the Kuler themes by using the following URL:

```
http://kuler-api.adobe.com/rss/search.cfm?
➥searchQuery=[searchQuery]&startIndex=[startIndex]
➥&itemsPerPage=[itemsPerPage]&key=[key]
```

Table 13-2 shows the meaning of each of the parameters.

Table 13-2. Search parameters for Kuler themes

Parameter name	Required/ optional	Description	Default value
searchQuery	Optional	Determines the search criteria. Either a String value or one of the predetermined items listed in Table 13-3. A String search looks for the search term in theme titles, tags, author names, theme IDs, author IDs, and hex values.	
startIndex	Optional	Determines the first item to display, starting from 0, which is the first list item.	0
itemsPerPage	Optional	Determines the maximum number of items to display on each page. Choose values from 1 to 100.	20
key	Required	Provides the developer API key obtained for the request.	

As you can see, most of the parameters are the same as in the previous request types. However, the searchQuery parameter requires a little more explanation.

The easiest way to use the searchQuery parameter is by including a keyword or phrase as the value, and that's what we'll do in our application. You can also add a filter to search in particular areas. These are explained in Table 13-3.

Table 13-3. Predefined Kuler search items

Filter	Description
themeID	Searches on the provided theme ID
userID	Searches on the provided user ID
email	Searches on the provided e-mail address
tag	Searches on the provided tag
hex	Searches on the provided hex color value, in the format ABCDEF or 0xABCDEF
title	Searches on the provided theme title

You can apply any of these filters by preceding your search term with the relevant word. For example, to search theme tags for the word *sand*, you would use the following name/value pair in the URL:

    searchQuery=tag:sand

The following examples show how to search Kuler themes:

- Search using the word *orange* and returning 100 items per page:

      http://kuler-api.adobe.com/rss/search.cfm?key=your_key
        ➥&searchQuery=orange&itemsPerPage=100

- Search for all themes tagged with the word *sand*, starting from the tenth record:

      http://kuler-api.adobe.com/rss/search.cfm?key=your_key
        ➥&searchQuery=tag:sand&startIndex=10

Again, you would replace your_key with the developer key provided by Adobe.

> *It's possible to retrieve other information from Kuler, such as a thumbnail of a theme or comments about a theme. However, for the purposes of this application, we won't cover these areas. Feel free to research them yourself if you would like to include them in your application.*

Once you've made a successful request for a Kuler RSS 2.0 feed, you'll need to deal with the response.

Receiving a Kuler response

All Kuler responses conform to the RSS 2.0 XML vocabulary. As I mentioned earlier, you can find details about this vocabulary at http://www.rssboard.org/rss-specification. Each feed contains additional items outside the specification, from the Kuler namespace http://kuler.adobe.com/kuler/API/rss/. These items are prefixed with the name kuler.

A sample Kuler RSS feed for the highest rated items follows. I've included only a single <item> element, but, in reality, you would see one <item> element for each theme returned.

```
<rss version="2.0" xmlns:xs=http://www.w3.org/2001/XMLSchema
  xmlns:kuler="http://kuler.adobe.com/kuler/API/rss/"
  xmlns:rss="http://blogs.law.harvard.edu/tech/rss">
  <channel>
    <title>kuler highest rated themes</title>
    <link>http://kuler.adobe.com/</link>
    <description>highest-rated themes on kuler (1 to 10 of 106069)
    </description>
    <language>en-us</language>
    <pubDate>Wed, 01 Oct 2008 05:31:44 PST</pubDate>
    <lastBuildDate>Wed, 01 Oct 2008 05:31:44 PST</lastBuildDate>
    <docs>http://blogs.law.harvard.edu/tech/rss</docs>
    <generator>Kuler Services</generator>
    <managingEditor>kulerfeedback@adobe.com</managingEditor>
    <webMaster>kulerfeedback@adobe.com</webMaster>
    <recordCount>106069</recordCount>
    <startIndex>0</startIndex>
    <itemsPerPage>10</itemsPerPage>
    <item>
      <title>Theme Title: Buddha in Rain</title>
      <link>http://kuler.adobe.com/index.cfm#themeID/242145</link>
      <guid>http://kuler.adobe.com/index.cfm#themeID/242145</guid>
      <enclosure xmlns="http://www.solitude.dk/syndication/
        enclosures/">
        <title>Buddha in Rain</title>
        <link length="1" type="image/png">
          <url>http://kuler-api.adobe.com/kuler/themeImages/
            theme_242145.png</url>
        </link>
      </enclosure>
      <description>&lt;img src="http://kuler-api.adobe.com/kuler/
        themeImages/theme_242145.png" /&gt;&lt;br /&gt;
         Artist: lr&lt;br /&gt; ThemeID: 242145&lt;br /&gt;
        Posted: 08/23/2008&lt;br /&gt; Tags: bath, buddha, cleanse,
        night, quest, thoughts, thunder, turbulence &lt;br /&gt;
        Hex: FF8000, FFD933, CCCC52, 8FB359, 192B33</description>
      <kuler:themeItem>
        <kuler:themeID>242145</kuler:themeID>
        <kuler:themeTitle>Buddha in Rain</kuler:themeTitle>
```

```
<kuler:themeImage>http://kuler-api.adobe.com/kuler/
  themeImages/theme_242145.png</kuler:themeImage>
<kuler:themeAuthor>
  <kuler:authorID>50963</kuler:authorID>
  <kuler:authorLabel>lr</kuler:authorLabel>
</kuler:themeAuthor>
<kuler:themeTags>bath, buddha, cleanse, night, quest,
  thoughts, thunder, turbulence</kuler:themeTags>
<kuler:themeRating>4</kuler:themeRating>
<kuler:themeDownloadCount>770</kuler:themeDownloadCount>
<kuler:themeCreatedAt>20080823</kuler:themeCreatedAt>
<kuler:themeEditedAt>20080912</kuler:themeEditedAt>
<kuler:themeSwatches>
  <kuler:swatch>
    <kuler:swatchHexColor>FF8000</kuler:swatchHexColor>
    <kuler:swatchColorMode>cmyk</kuler:swatchColorMode>
    <kuler:swatchChannel1>0.0</kuler:swatchChannel1>
    <kuler:swatchChannel2>0.5</kuler:swatchChannel2>
    <kuler:swatchChannel3>1.0</kuler:swatchChannel3>
    <kuler:swatchChannel4>0.0</kuler:swatchChannel4>
    <kuler:swatchIndex>0</kuler:swatchIndex>
  </kuler:swatch>
  <kuler:swatch>
    <kuler:swatchHexColor>FFD933</kuler:swatchHexColor>
    <kuler:swatchColorMode>cmyk</kuler:swatchColorMode>
    <kuler:swatchChannel1>0.0</kuler:swatchChannel1>
    <kuler:swatchChannel2>0.15</kuler:swatchChannel2>
    <kuler:swatchChannel3>0.8</kuler:swatchChannel3>
    <kuler:swatchChannel4>0.0</kuler:swatchChannel4>
    <kuler:swatchIndex>1</kuler:swatchIndex>
  </kuler:swatch>
  <kuler:swatch>
    <kuler:swatchHexColor>CCCC52</kuler:swatchHexColor>
    <kuler:swatchColorMode>cmyk</kuler:swatchColorMode>
    <kuler:swatchChannel1>0.0</kuler:swatchChannel1>
    <kuler:swatchChannel2>0.0</kuler:swatchChannel2>
    <kuler:swatchChannel3>0.6</kuler:swatchChannel3>
    <kuler:swatchChannel4>0.2</kuler:swatchChannel4>
    <kuler:swatchIndex>2</kuler:swatchIndex>
  </kuler:swatch>
  <kuler:swatch>
    <kuler:swatchHexColor>8FB359</kuler:swatchHexColor>
    <kuler:swatchColorMode>cmyk</kuler:swatchColorMode>
    <kuler:swatchChannel1>0.2</kuler:swatchChannel1>
    <kuler:swatchChannel2>0.0</kuler:swatchChannel2>
    <kuler:swatchChannel3>0.5</kuler:swatchChannel3>
    <kuler:swatchChannel4>0.3</kuler:swatchChannel4>
    <kuler:swatchIndex>3</kuler:swatchIndex>
  </kuler:swatch>
```

445

```
                    <kuler:swatch>
                      <kuler:swatchHexColor>192B33</kuler:swatchHexColor>
                      <kuler:swatchColorMode>cmyk</kuler:swatchColorMode>
                      <kuler:swatchChannel1>0.5</kuler:swatchChannel1>
                      <kuler:swatchChannel2>0.15</kuler:swatchChannel2>
                      <kuler:swatchChannel3>0.0</kuler:swatchChannel3>
                      <kuler:swatchChannel4>0.8</kuler:swatchChannel4>
                      <kuler:swatchIndex>4</kuler:swatchIndex>
                    </kuler:swatch>
                  </kuler:themeSwatches>
                </kuler:themeItem>
                <pubDate>Wed, 01 Oct 2008 05:31:44 PST</pubDate>
            </item>
          </channel>
        </rss>
```

You'll notice that there are several namespaces in the root <rss> element. As I mentioned, we're particularly interested in the kuler namespace. We'll need to declare this namespace in ActionScript 3.0 before we can access any of the elements prefixed with kuler.

Information about the returned results appears in the <channel> element. It's possible to access the name of the feed in the <title> element, as well as a description of the feed in the <description> element. The <description> element shows which themes are included in the responses, as well as the total number of records available.

Each of the themes appears in an <item> element. Each item has a theme title and link. It also includes a <kuler:themeItem> element. This element contains the information that we'll need to access about each theme.

Each <kuler:themeItem> element has a child <kuler:themeSwatches> element. Within this child element are five <kuler:swatch> elements—one for each color in the theme. You can access the hexadecimal color for each of these elements using the <kuler:swatchHexColor> child element. We'll need this element in order to display the correct color swatch in our application.

Navigating the returned XML document will be a little more difficult than in the Flash application created in the previous chapter. In this Flex application, we'll need to take into account the kuler namespace whenever we work with E4X expressions. Our expressions will appear to be more complicated than the ones you've seen so far in this book.

Well, that's enough background information about Kuler for us to get started with the application. Let's create the Flex application.

Building the application

To recap, we'll build a Flex application that will allow users to access color themes from Kuler. We'll allow the user to choose which type of themes to display, and then list the returned themes in groups of ten in a DataGrid component. We'll use a custom ItemRenderer component to display the color swatches associated with each theme in the DataGrid.

The users will be able to do the following with the Kuler API:

- Search Kuler themes by entering a keyword
- View the highest rated themes
- View the most popular themes

They will be able to see each of the results in groups of ten themes, and page through the remaining results using a NumericStepper control.

We'll display the returned XML document in a TextArea control. However, you wouldn't normally display this information in a real-world application. It's for debugging purposes only.

We'll start with the application interface.

Working through the interface

Figure 13-2 shows the interface for the application. A starter file containing this interface is provided with the chapter resources. We'll work through that file soon.

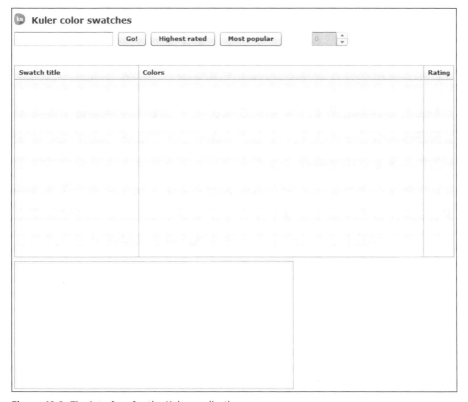

Figure 13-2. The interface for the Kuler application

As with the previous case study, this interface is very simple. Feel free to make any changes you wish, but remember that you must display the Kuler logo to conform to Adobe's requirements.

The interface provides several options for accessing Kuler feeds. The users can enter a search term and click Go! to retrieve results. They can also select the highest rated or most popular themes by clicking the corresponding buttons. All of these options generate a URL that requests a Kuler RSS feed.

When the Kuler service responds, the RSS feed XML document will display in the TextArea control at the bottom of the application. The DataGrid will populate with the title of the swatch, thumbnails of the five colors, and the theme rating.

The RSS feed provides an image that you can use to display thumbnails of the theme. However, this image is quite small. For our application, we'll show larger-sized thumbnails in the DataGrid. We'll do this by using a custom ItemRenderer within the Colors column of the DataGrid. This column will also display the hexadecimal value for the color.

A NumericStepper control will allow the user to scroll through each page of theme results. When a request is initially made, the first page of results will display. Clicking the NumericStepper will allow the user to view the themes on subsequent pages.

Let's set up this application in Flex Builder.

Setting up the application

In our application, we'll work with the following three files:

- The main application file containing the interface
- A custom class file that handles the loading and parsing of the Kuler RSS feed
- A custom component that will be used as the ItemRenderer for the DataGrid component

The process for setting up the application follows:

1. Start by creating a new Flex project with the name of your choosing. Add the starter file KulerStarter.mxml from the chapter resources to this project. You can copy the entire MXML file from its location and paste it into the Flex Navigator view.

2. Create a new folder called assets in the project and copy the file ku_18pxBugOnly.gif there. This file is the Kuler logo that we must display in our application.

3. The starter file KulerStarter.mxml creates the interface. It contains the following code:

```
<?xml version="1.0" encoding="utf-8"?>
<mx:Application xmlns:mx="http://www.adobe.com/2006/mxml"
  layout="absolute" backgroundColor="white"
  backgroundGradientAlphas="100,100">
  <mx:VBox x="10" y="10">
    <mx:HBox>
      <mx:Image source="assets/ku_18pxBugOnly.gif"/>
      <mx:Label text="Kuler color swatches" fontSize="14"
        fontWeight="bold"/>
      <mx:Label id="searchType_txt" fontSize="14" fontWeight="bold"
        width="231"/>
    </mx:HBox>
```

```
      <mx:HBox>
        <mx:TextInput id="search_txt"/>
        <mx:Button label="Go!" id="search_btn"/>
        <mx:Button label="Highest rated" id="highest_btn"/>
        <mx:Button label="Most popular" id="popular_btn"/>
        <mx:Label id="page_txt" text="Page" visible="false"/>
        <mx:NumericStepper id="page_ns" enabled="false"/>
      </mx:HBox>
      <mx:Label id="loading_lbl" color="#FF0000"/>
      <mx:DataGrid id="swatches_dg" height="300">
        <mx:columns>
          <mx:DataGridColumn headerText="Swatch title" width="200">
          </mx:DataGridColumn>
          <mx:DataGridColumn headerText="Colors" width="460">
          </mx:DataGridColumn>
          <mx:DataGridColumn headerText="Rating" width="50">
          </mx:DataGridColumn>
        </mx:columns>
      </mx:DataGrid>
      <mx:TextArea id="content_txt" width="450" height="200"/>
   </mx:VBox>
</mx:Application>
```

You'll notice that in addition to the controls described in the previous section, the application includes a hidden Label control with the id of page_txt, which we'll use to display messages to the user. There is another control named loading_lbl, which we'll use to display a message when a feed is requested.

The final Label control, called searchType_txt, will show information to the user about the type of results that are currently displayed. This will be either the name of a preset feed or the custom search criteria that the user has entered.

> *Feel free to modify the width settings for the DataGrid and TextArea for the application. You can also choose a different Kuler logo by visiting* http://learn.adobe.com/wiki/display/kulerdev/ A.+Kuler+API+Documentation.

Creating the custom class file

We'll create a custom class file that will manage the request for the loading and parsing of the Kuler feed.

1. Create the class file by choosing File ➤ New ➤ ActionScript Class. Add the class to the xmlUtilities package and name it KulerLoader.as.

   Flex Builder will create the class file in a new xmlUtilities folder. The class file should contain the following content. Don't worry if the brackets are spaced a little differently than in my example.

```
package xmlUtilities {
  public class KulerLoader {
    public function KulerLoader {
    }
  }
}
```

2. The first task here is to make the class bindable. Add the following declaration above the class declaration:

```
[Bindable]
```

This declaration will allow us to use any of the public methods in binding expressions within our application file.

3. We'll also need to declare some variables and constants for use in the class file. Add the following declarations immediately below the class declaration:

```
private var xmlAllContent:XML;
private var xmlLoader:URLLoader;
private var swatchElements:XMLList;
private var swatchElementsCollection: ArrayCollection;
private var kulerNS:Namespace =
  ➥new Namespace("http://kuler.adobe.com/kuler/API/rss/");
private const API_KEY:String = "your_key_here";
private const KULER_BASE_URL:String =
  ➥"http://kuler-api.adobe.com/rss/";
```

We'll use these variables in the class file. The xmlAllContent object will store the loaded XML document from Kuler. We'll use the xmlLoader object to request the RSS feed.

The swatchElements XMLList object will store all of the <item> elements from the XML document. We'll use the swatchElementsCollection object to store an array of objects containing the relevant properties of each of the themes. Because of the hierarchical nature of the RSS feed, it will be much easier if we use E4X expressions to extract the information we need and store it in a flat structure within an ArrayCollection made up of Object objects.

Because the RSS feed includes the Kuler namespace http://kuler.adobe.com/kuler/API/rss/, we'll need to declare a Namespace object so that we can construct E4X expressions correctly. I've called this namespace KulerNS.

The final two declarations are the constants that we'll use in the class file. The first constant is API_KEY, which will provide the key value for each request. Replace the text your_key_here with your Kuler developer key from Adobe.

The second constant is the base URL for all Kuler feeds. You'll remember from earlier in the chapter that all feeds start with the URL http://kuler-api.adobe.com. We've added rss to the end of the URL, as all of the feeds we'll request in this application include rss as part of their path.

4. After adding these private variables, check that Flex Builder has added the following import statements at the top of the file:

```
import flash.net.URLLoader;
import mx.collections.ArrayCollection;
```

You should add any import statements that are missing.

5. We'll turn our attention now to the constructor method KulerLoader(). This method will instantiate a KulerLoader object by creating a URLLoader object and adding event listeners that respond to the complete, HTTPStatus, IOError, and SecurityError events.

   Modify the KulerLoader() constructor method as shown in bold here:

```
public function KulerLoader() {
  xmlLoader = new URLLoader();
  xmlLoader.addEventListener(Event.COMPLETE, completeHandler);
  xmlLoader.addEventListener(HTTPStatusEvent.HTTP_STATUS,
    ➥httpStatusHandler);
  xmlLoader.addEventListener(IOErrorEvent.IO_ERROR, ioErrorHandler);
  xmlLoader.addEventListener(SecurityErrorEvent.SECURITY_ERROR,
    ➥securityHandler);
}
```

   You can see the naming convention that I've used to name each of the handler functions.

6. After adding the code, check that Flex Builder has added the following import statements. If they don't appear in your class file, you'll need to add them yourself.

```
import flash.events.HTTPStatusEvent;
import flash.events.IOErrorEvent;
import flash.events.SecurityErrorEvent;
```

7. We'll also need to add the completeHandler() method that follows:

```
private function completeHandler(e:Event):void {
  xmlAllContent = XML(e.target.data);
  dispatchEvent(new Event(Event.COMPLETE));
}
```

   This method is private because it does not need to be accessed from the application file. The method starts by assigning the loaded Kuler XML document to the xmlAllContent object. It finds the document using e.target.data and casts the returned String as an object of type XML.

   The method also dispatches a complete event to the Flex application file. It does this with the dispatchEvent() method. The main application file will include an event handler to respond when the KulerLoader object dispatches this event.

8. Add the following handlers for the other events that we identified:

```
private function httpStatusHandler(e:HTTPStatusEvent):void {
  dispatchEvent(new HTTPStatusEvent(HTTPStatusEvent.HTTP_STATUS,
    ➥false, false, e.status));
}
private function ioErrorHandler(e:IOErrorEvent):void {
  dispatchEvent(new IOErrorEvent(IOErrorEvent.IO_ERROR, false,
    ➥false, e.text));
}
private function securityHandler(e:SecurityErrorEvent):void {
  dispatchEvent(new SecurityErrorEvent(SecurityErrorEvent.
    ➥SECURITY_ERROR, false, false, e.text));
}
```

These handlers all dispatch an event of the same type that they received to the application file. For example, the httpStatusHandler() method receives an HTTPStatusEvent as an argument and dispatches an HTTPStatusEvent to the application.

In each of the methods, we've passed the appropriate arguments when dispatching the event. You can see these arguments and their default values as tool tips as you start entering the constructor method.

When creating the new events, we've mostly passed the default values for each of the arguments. But, in some cases, we've passed a value from the originating event. This allows us to pass along an error message or value from the initial event. For example, the httpStatusHandler() method passes the status value from the original event when it dispatches the new HTTPStatusEvent to the application file. We identified the original value by using e.status as the status argument when we created the new HTTPStatusEvent.

9. The custom class file needs a public method that will request the Kuler RSS feed. We'll call this method getKulerFeed(). The role of this method is to prepare the URL to request and call the load() method of the URLLoader class to load the feed. The loaded feed will then be handled by the completeHandler() method.

Before we create the getKulerFeed() method, we'll declare a new event called the loadError event. This event will have an Event type but will use a custom name. We'll dispatch the loadError event if the load() method of the URLLoader class fails.

Add the following event declaration above the class declaration:

```
[Event(name="loadError", type="flash.events.Event")]
```

We've declared an event with the name loadError of the type flash.events.Event. We'll dispatch the loadError event if the load() method fails inside the new getKulerFeed() method.

10. Add the new method now, as shown in the following code:

```
public function getKulerFeed(feedPath:String, startIndex:int):void {
  var kulerURL:String;
  kulerURL = KULER_BASE_URL + feedPath + "&startIndex=" +
    ➥String(startIndex) + "&key=" + API_KEY + "&itemsPerPage=10";
  try {
    xmlLoader.load(new URLRequest(kulerURL));
  }
  catch (e:Error) {
    dispatchEvent(new Event("loadError"));
  }
}
```

The getKulerFeed() function handles the loading of the external feed. It receives two arguments: feedPath, which provides details of the URL to request, and startIndex, which indicates the starting point for the request.

Remember that all URLs have the same base, but differ in the additional arguments that they require. The feedPath variable contains these arguments. The "Understanding the Kuler feeds" section earlier in this chapter provides information about all of the arguments that you can use.

The getKulerFeed() function starts by declaring a variable called kulerURL, which will store the complete URL for the feed. The full URL begins with the KULER_BASE_URL constant and adds the additional URL details, feedPath, passed with the function call. The kulerURL variable also includes the startIndex name/value pair, which will take its value from the startIndex argument.

In addition to the passed-in arguments, the kulerURL variable adds a name/value pair for the Kuler API key. This variable is called key, and it uses the value stored in the API_KEY constant.

The URL finishes with the itemsPerPage variable. This variable has a fixed value of 10, meaning that the application will display ten records at a time. You could also pass this value as an argument to the function, but I've chosen not to do that here. This enhancement might be one you add yourself later.

After creating the URL, the call to the load() method of the URLLoader object appears in a try/catch block. If there is an error when calling this method, the KulerLoader object dispatches a loadError event—the event we declared earlier. We'll add a listener for this event in the application file a little later, when we add the other event listeners.

11. We also need another public method in the class file that returns the loaded XML document. We'll use this method to display a String representation of the XML document in the TextArea component of the application.

Add the following public getXML() method to the class file:

```
public function getXML():XML {
  return xmlAllContent;
}
```

This method returns the xmlAllContent XML object. Remember that we load the XML document into this object in the completeHandler() method.

Getting the highest rated themes

The next task in creating the application is to request a Kuler feed. We'll start with the highest rated Kuler themes.

1. Open the starter file KulerStarter.mxml in your project. You should have copied this resource file to your project earlier. We'll start by configuring the Highest rated button.

2. We'll need to set up the application. We'll do so by calling a function in the creationComplete attribute of the <mx:Application> tag.

Start by adding this attribute to the opening <mx:Application> element, as shown in bold here:

```
<mx:Application xmlns:mx="http://www.adobe.com/2006/mxml"
  layout="absolute" backgroundColor="white"
  backgroundGradientAlphas="100,100"
  creationComplete="initApp(event)">
```

When the interface finishes creating, the application will call the initApp() function, passing a FlexEvent object. In the next step, we'll create this function and add the code we need to make the application work.

3. Add an `<mx:Script>` block containing the following code:

```
<mx:Script>
  <![CDATA[
    import xmlUtilities.KulerLoader;
    private var myKulerXML:KulerLoader;
    private function initApp(e:FlexEvent):void {
      myKulerXML = new KulerLoader();
      myKulerXML.addEventListener(Event.COMPLETE, completeHandler);
      myKulerXML.addEventListener(HTTPStatusEvent.HTTP_STATUS,
        ➡httpStatusHandler);
      myKulerXML.addEventListener(IOErrorEvent.IO_ERROR,
        ➡ioErrorHandler);
      myKulerXML.addEventListener(SecurityErrorEvent.SECURITY_ERROR,
        ➡securityHandler);
      myKulerXML.addEventListener("loadError", errorHandler);
    }
    private function completeHandler(e:Event):void {
    }
    private function httpStatusHandler(e:HTTPStatusEvent):void {
    }
    private function ioErrorHandler(e:IOErrorEvent):void {
    }
    private function securityHandler(e:SecurityErrorEvent):void {
    }
    private function errorHandler(e:Event):void {
    }
  ]]>
</mx:Script>
```

This `<mx:Script>` block imports the KulerLoader custom class that we just created. It also declares a new KulerLoader object called myKulerXML.

The initApp() function follows. In this function, we create the KulerLoader object using the constructor method. We also add several event listeners that respond to the various events dispatched by the custom class. The code block also includes empty handler functions, which we'll complete a little later.

4. After you've entered this code, check that Flex Builder has added the following import statement at the top of the code block:

```
import mx.events.FlexEvent;
```

If the import statement doesn't appear, you will need to add it with the others at the top of the code block.

5. Let's add some code to the handler functions so we can display errors in the case of loading problems. We'll display the error messages in the loading_lbl control, so modify the handler functions as shown here in bold:

```
private function httpStatusHandler(e:HTTPStatusEvent):void {
  loading_lbl.text = "HTTP Status error " + String(e.status);
}
private function ioErrorHandler(e:IOErrorEvent):void {
  loading_lbl.text = "IOError " + e.text;
}
private function securityHandler(e:SecurityErrorEvent):void {
  loading_lbl.text = "Security error " + e.text;
}
private function errorHandler(e:Event):void {
  loading_lbl.text = "There was an error loading the Kuler feed";
}
```

The first three error handler functions display a message with a property from the event object. You'll remember that we dispatched these properties when we called the dispatchEvent() method to create the events in the custom class.

In the case of the HTTPStatusEvent object, we display the status code from the server. This is a value of data type int that indicates how the server responded to the request. For example, the value might be a 404 status, meaning that the file wasn't found. A successful request will have a status of 200. A little later, we'll remove the message for successful requests.

The IOError and SecurityError handler functions both display the text property associated with the event object. The errorHandler() function displays the static text There was an error loading the Kuler feed. Remember that the loadError event is dispatched if the call to the load() method of the URLLoader fails in the try/catch block of the custom class.

6. Now we need to configure the completeHandler() function. Initially, we'll just display the returned XML document in the TextArea control so you can see what is returned by the Kuler web site.

   Modify the completeHandler() function as shown in bold here:

```
private function completeHandler(e:Event):void {
  content_txt.text = e.target.getXML().toXMLString();
}
```

   When the myKulerXML object receives the XML document response from the Kuler web site, it will call the getXML() method to return the XML document. It displays this document in the TextArea with the toXMLString() method.

7. Before we can test the application, we need to configure the Highest rated button. We'll add a handler when a user clicks this button to request the highest rated themes.

   Add the following event listener to the initApp() function:

```
highest_btn.addEventListener(MouseEvent.CLICK, highestHandler);
```

8. When the user clicks the Highest rated button, it calls the highestHandler() function. Add this function to the <mx:Script> block now:

```
private function highestHandler(e:Event):void {
  startFeed("get.cfm?listtype=rating","- highest rating");
}
```

The highestHandler() function calls the startFeed() function, passing the correct name/value pair to add to the base URL for the Kuler feeds. Remember that the starting URL for all Kuler feeds is the same, and that we request each feed by manipulating the final URL and including query string variables.

We'll call the startFeed() function with every different type of request that we make to the Kuler web site because the only change will be to the URL. We'll also pass a string value that will tell the users what type of result they are viewing. In this example, it's the text – highest rating. We'll eventually display the text in the searchType_txt TextBox control.

9. We'll also need to add the startFeed() function to the <mx:Script> block. However, before we do so, we'll declare a variable that stores the feed URL. This step will allow us to keep track of the last requested feed. When we add the paging functionality a little later, we'll be able to repeat the request for the last feed using this variable.

Add the following feedURL variable below the declaration of the myKulerXML object:

```
private var feedURL:String;
```

10, The next step is to add the startFeed() function. Add the following function to the <mx:Script> block:

```
private function startFeed(feedURL:String, feedDisplayText:String):
➥void {
showFeed(feedURL);
searchType_txt.text = feedDisplayText;
}
```

This function receives the feed URL as an argument, along with the text describing the request, stored in the feedDisplayText argument. The function then calls the showFeed() function, which we'll add shortly, passing the feedURL argument. It finishes by displaying the feedDisplayText value in the searchType_txt control.

11. Now we need to add the showFeed() function that follows:

```
private function showFeed(feed:String):void {
  loading_lbl.text = "Loading Kuler feed";
  feedURL = feed;
  myKulerXML.getKulerFeed(feedURL, 0);
}
```

The showFeed() function will be called with every different type of feed request. The function receives a String variable, which provides the last part of the feed URL. The custom class file will add this value to the end of the base URL for all feeds.

The function displays the text Loading Kuler feed in the loading_lbl control. It assigns the passed-in feed variable to the feedURL variable we added earlier. Finally, the function calls the getKulerFeed() method, passing the feedURL variable and a value of 0 to indicate that we're requesting the first record from the feed.

12. We're ready to test the application. With the functionality we have added so far, we should be able to request the first ten records from the highest rated feed. When the application receives the XML document from the Kuler web site, it will display a `String` representation in the TextArea control.

Run the application and click the Highest rated button. Initially, you should see the loading message as the application requests the feed. Figure 13-3 shows what should appear after the feed successfully loads.

Figure 13-3. Loading the first feed

The Label control at the top of the screen indicates that we are working with the highest rating feeds. The Label control above the DataGrid provides the HTTP status of the request. It indicates that we have a status of 200, which means that the server successfully provided the page.

The TextArea control at the bottom of the screen displays the RSS feed provided by Adobe. If you look at the `<description>` element, you'll see that the feed includes records 1 to 10 of 106880.

Scroll through the feed XML document to see its structure. You should see ten `<item>` elements.

13. It's a small point, but the user shouldn't see the HTTP status error message for a successful request. We'll modify the `httpStatusHandler()` function so that it displays error messages only where the status is not equal to 200.

Change the `httpStatusHandler()` function as shown in bold here:

```
private function httpStatusHandler(e:HTTPStatusEvent):void {
  var httpStatus:int = e.status;
  if (e.status != 200) {
    loading_lbl.text = "HTTP Status error " + String(e.status);
  }
}
```

If you test the application again, you will see only the message Loading Kuler feed in the Label control. We'll remove that value a little later on.

Displaying the theme

Now that we have access to the RSS feed, it's time to think about how to display the feed details in the DataGrid. You can see that the component has three columns: Swatch title, Colors, and Rating. We'll use item renderers to display the values from the feed correctly, and you'll see how this works shortly.

Before we can display the values in the DataGrid, we need to retrieve them from the RSS feed. We'll extract the values and add them to an `ArrayCollection` object.

We'll be able to store a flat structure in the `ArrayCollection` object from the hierarchical structure of the RSS file. Doing so will allow us to assign the `ArrayCollection` object as the data provider for the DataGrid.

The `ArrayCollection` is more suitable as a data provider than an `Array`, as it supports two-way data binding. The `ArrayCollection` object also has access to additional methods for manipulating the object content.

If you examine each of the `<item>` elements in the feed, you'll notice that structure is complex. The following is a simplified version of the structure, which includes only the elements that we want to access from the feed: title, rating, and colors.

```
<item>
  <kuler:themeItem>
    <kuler:themeTitle>Buddha in Rain</kuler:themeTitle>
    <kuler:themeRating>4</kuler:themeRating>
    <kuler:themeSwatches>
      <kuler:swatch>
        <kuler:swatchHexColor>FF8000</kuler:swatchHexColor>
      </kuler:swatch>
      <kuler:swatch>
        <kuler:swatchHexColor>FFD933</kuler:swatchHexColor>
      </kuler:swatch>
```

```
          <kuler:swatch>
            <kuler:swatchHexColor>CCCC52</kuler:swatchHexColor>
          </kuler:swatch>
          <kuler:swatch>
            <kuler:swatchHexColor>8FB359</kuler:swatchHexColor>
          </kuler:swatch>
          <kuler:swatch>
            <kuler:swatchHexColor>192B33</kuler:swatchHexColor>
          </kuler:swatch>
        </kuler:themeSwatches>
      </kuler:themeItem>
    </item>
```

Notice that some of the elements include the prefix `kuler:` to indicate that they are part of the Kuler namespace `http://kuler.adobe.com/kuler/API/rss/`. We declared this value as a `Namespace` object called `kulerNS` at the start of the class file. We'll need to use this `Namespace` when constructing E4X expressions to retrieve theme values.

The `<kuler:themeTitle>` element is a child of the `<kuler:themeItem>` element, which in turn is a child of each `<item>` element. We can retrieve the theme title with a relatively simple E4X expression. If there were no namespaces involved, we could simply use the expression `item.themeItem.themeTitle`. However, because two of the elements are prefixed with the Kuler namespace, we'll need to prefix them with `kulerNS::` to access them correctly. So the resulting E4X expression for the `<kuler:themeTitle>` element will be `item.kulerNS::themeItem.kulerNS::themeTitle`.

Accessing the `<kuler:themeRating>` element works in the same way. The E4X expression that we'll need is `item.kulerNS::themeItem.kulerNS::themeRating`.

To access each of the `<kuler:swatchHexColor>` elements, we'll need a more complicated E4X expression. Without namespaces, the expression would be as follows:

```
item.themeItem.themeSwatches.swatch[i].swatchHexColor
```

Because there are five swatches, we'll replace the `i` value with a number from 0 to 4. However, because all elements except `<item>` are within the Kuler namespace, we'll need to use the following E4X expression:

```
item.kulerNS::themeItem.kulerNS::themeSwatches.kulerNS::swatch[0].
➥kulerNS::swatchHexColor
```

The expression looks more difficult to understand than it really is. We'll need to use this expression five times—once for each of the swatches. Let's see how this works in the class file.

1. Switch to the custom class file KulerLoader.as and add the following public method, getSwatches(). I'll explain it after the code.

```
public function getSwatches():ArrayCollection {
  var title:String;
  var col1:String;
  var col2:String;
  var col3:String;
  var col4:String;
  var col5:String;
  var rating:String;
  swatchElements = xmlAllContent.channel.item;
  swatchElementsCollection = new ArrayCollection();
  for each (var item:XML in swatchElements) {
    title = item.kulerNS::themeItem.kulerNS::themeTitle;
    rating = item.kulerNS::themeItem.kulerNS::themeRating;
    col1 = "0x" + item.kulerNS::themeItem.kulerNS::themeSwatches.
      ➡kulerNS::swatch[0].kulerNS::swatchHexColor;
    col2 = "0x" + item.kulerNS::themeItem.kulerNS::themeSwatches.
      ➡kulerNS::swatch[1].kulerNS::swatchHexColor;
    col3 = "0x" + item.kulerNS::themeItem.kulerNS::themeSwatches.
      ➡kulerNS::swatch[2].kulerNS::swatchHexColor;
    col4 = "0x" + item.kulerNS::themeItem.kulerNS::themeSwatches.
      ➡kulerNS::swatch[3].kulerNS::swatchHexColor;
    col5 = "0x" + item.kulerNS::themeItem.kulerNS::themeSwatches.
      ➡kulerNS::swatch[4].kulerNS::swatchHexColor;
    swatchElementsCollection.addItem({label: title, rating:rating,
      ➡color1: col1, color2: col2, color3: col3, color4: col4,
      ➡color5: col5});
  }
  return swatchElementsCollection;
}
```

This method returns an ArrayCollection object populated with the title, rating, and five swatch colors for each theme. It starts by declaring variables for each of these properties. It then identifies each of the <item> elements using the E4X expression xmlAllContent. channel.item. Remember that each theme is inside an <item> element.

The method creates the ArrayCollection object. We declared the object at the start of the class file. It uses a for each loop to work through each of the <item> elements. Within the loop, we access the relevant elements using the E4X expressions you've just seen.

At the end of the loop, the method uses addItem() to add the values to the swatchElementsCollection object. Each element in the ArrayCollection is an Object with the properties label, rating, color1, color2, color3, color4, and color5. For the colors, we've added the prefix 0x to the beginning of the supplied number so we can use the values to display the colors a little later. The method finishes by returning the swatchElementsCollection to the application.

2. Switch back to the application file. We'll display the values from each `<item>` in the feed within the DataGrid component. Let's start by displaying the title and rating in the first and third column of the DataGrid.

Modify the `<mx:DataGrid>` element as shown in bold in the following code block:

```
<mx:DataGrid id="swatches_dg" height="300">
  <mx:columns>
    <mx:DataGridColumn headerText="Swatch title" width="200"
      dataField="label">
      <mx:itemRenderer>
        <mx:Component>
          <mx:Label />
        </mx:Component>
      </mx:itemRenderer>
    </mx:DataGridColumn>
    <mx:DataGridColumn headerText="Colors" width="460">
    </mx:DataGridColumn>
    <mx:DataGridColumn headerText="Rating" width="50"
      dataField="rating">
      <mx:itemRenderer>
        <mx:Component>
          <mx:Label width="100%" textAlign="center" />
        </mx:Component>
      </mx:itemRenderer>
    </mx:DataGridColumn>
  </mx:columns>
</mx:DataGrid>
```

The first and third columns use a `dataField` property as well as an `<mx:itemRenderer>` element. The item renderer determines how the value will display in the column. In both cases, the item renderer component is an `<mx:Label>` control. By default, Flex assigns the data from the data field to the `text` property of this control.

3. Nothing will display in the DataGrid until we assign the swatches as its data provider. Modify the `completeHandler()` function to add the following line, shown in bold:

```
private function completeHandler(e:Event):void {
  content_txt.text = e.target.getXML().toXMLString();
  showSwatches();
}
```

4. The new line calls the showSwatches() function, which we'll add now.

```
private function showSwatches():void {
  swatches_dg.dataProvider = myKulerXML.getSwatches();
  loading_lbl.text = "";
}
```

This function calls the `getSwatches()` method that we just added to the custom class file. It assigns the returned `ArrayCollection` object as the `dataProvider` property of the DataGrid. It also clears the text in the `loading_lbl` control so that the user no longer sees the message Loading Kuler feed.

461

5. Run the application again and click the Highest rated button. You should see that the DataGrid populates with the title and rating for each feed, as shown in Figure 13-4.

Figure 13-4. Populating two columns in the DataGrid

6. The middle column in the DataGrid will display the five colors associated with each theme. In order to show these colors, we'll need to create a custom component to use as the item renderer for the column.

Create the new component using File ➤ New ➤ MXML Component. The new component is called ColorSwatch and it is based on the VBox component. It has a Width setting of 460 and a Height setting of 90. Figure 13-5 shows the settings for this component. After you have added the settings, click Finish to create the component.

Flex Builder should create the following code in the component:

```
<?xml version="1.0" encoding="utf-8"?>
<mx:VBox xmlns:mx="http://www.adobe.com/2006/mxml" width="460"
  height="90">
</mx:VBox>
```

Figure 13-5. The settings for the ColorSwatch component

7. The component will contain five <mx:Canvas> controls, which we'll use to display the swatch color. We'll use the hexadecimal value as the backgroundColor property of the controls. The component will also contain five labels to display the color value below the swatch.

We'll need to send in the color values from the data provider of the DataGrid. Remember that we called these properties color1, color2, color3, color4, and color5 when we created the ArrayCollection object in the custom class file.

Modify the custom component as shown in the following code block. The new lines appear in bold.

```
<?xml version="1.0" encoding="utf-8"?>
<mx:VBox xmlns:mx="http://www.adobe.com/2006/mxml" width="460"
  height="90">
  <mx:HBox>
    <mx:Spacer width="10"/>
    <mx:Canvas id="swatch1" width="50" height="50"
      backgroundColor="{data.color1}" borderStyle="solid"
      borderColor="#000000"/>
    <mx:Spacer width="20"/>
```

```
        <mx:Canvas id="swatch2" width="50" height="50"
          backgroundColor="{data.color2}" borderStyle="solid"
          borderColor="#000000"/>
        <mx:Spacer width="20"/>
        <mx:Canvas id="swatch3" width="50" height="50"
          backgroundColor="{data.color3}" borderStyle="solid"
          borderColor="#000000"/>
        <mx:Spacer width="20"/>
        <mx:Canvas id="swatch4" width="50" height="50"
          backgroundColor="{data.color4}" borderStyle="solid"
          borderColor="#000000"/>
        <mx:Spacer width="20"/>
        <mx:Canvas id="swatch5" width="50" height="50"
          backgroundColor="{data.color5}" borderStyle="solid"
          borderColor="#000101"/>
        <mx:Spacer width="10"/>
      </mx:HBox>
      <mx:HBox>
        <mx:Label id="colorName1_lbl" width="80" textAlign="center"
          text="{data.color1}"/>
        <mx:Label id="colorName2_lbl" width="80" textAlign="center"
          text="{data.color2}"/>
        <mx:Label id="colorName3_lbl" width="80" textAlign="center"
          text="{data.color3}"/>
        <mx:Label id="colorName4_lbl" width="80" textAlign="center"
          text="{data.color4}"/>
        <mx:Label id="colorName5_lbl" width="80" textAlign="center"
          text="{data.color5}"/>
      </mx:HBox>
    </mx:VBox>
```

The custom component uses <mx:HBox> and <mx:Spacer> elements to lay out the <mx:Canvas> and <mx:Label> controls. It assigns the colors to display to the backgroundColor property of each Canvas control and to the text property of the Label controls. We reference these properties using a curly braces binding expression that starts with the text data.. For example, to access color1, we use the expression {data.color1}.

8. To use the custom component as the item renderer in the DataGrid, we need to modify the relevant column, as shown here in bold:

```
<mx:DataGridColumn headerText="Colors" width="460"
  itemRenderer="ColorSwatch">
</mx:DataGridColumn>
```

The change adds the itemRenderer property to the <mx:DataGridColumn> and sets its value to the name of the custom control ColorSwatch.

9. Run the application and click the Highest rated button. This time, you should see the second column populated with color swatches, as shown in Figure 13-6.

Each of the colors displays as the background for the Canvas controls in the custom component. The color value also displays below each Canvas in a Label control.

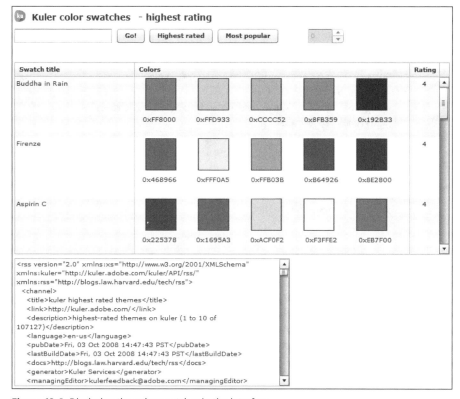

Figure 13-6. Displaying the color swatches in the interface

Adding paging functionality

At the moment, we can see only the first ten items when we view the highest rated themes. We'll need to make several changes in order to allow the user to page through the other results.

1. The first task is to modify the custom class so we can determine how many pages there are in total for the current request. Switch to the KulerLoader.as file and add the following getPages() public method:

```
public function getPages():int {
    var totalRecords:int = int(xmlAllContent.channel.recordCount);
    var pages:int = Math.ceil(totalRecords/10);
    return pages;
}
```

The getPages() method determines the total number of records from the <recordCount> element that we find with the E4X expression xmlAllContent.channel.recordCount. It then divides this value by ten and rounds up to determine the total number of pages. Remember that we're displaying ten items at a time. The method finishes by returning the calculated number of pages.

465

2. Switch back to the application file and modify the completeHandler() file as shown here in bold:

```
private function completeHandler(e:Event):void {
  var numPages:int = myKulerXML.getPages();
  content_txt.text = e.target.getXML().toXMLString();
  if (numPages == 0) {
    loading_lbl.text = "There are no matching Kuler themes";
    page_ns.enabled = false;
  }
  else {
    loading_lbl.text = "";
    page_ns.enabled = true;
    page_ns.minimum = 1;
    page_ns.maximum = numPages;
    showSwatches();
  }
}
```

The first change to this function is that it adds a new variable called numPages, which stores the number of pages returned by the public getPages() method we just created. The change also adds an if else block to the function.

If the number of pages to display equals 0—in other words, no records were returned—the application will display the message There are no matching Kuler themes. It will also disable the NumericStepper control, as there are no additional pages to display.

When more than 0 pages are returned, the application will clear the loading message from the loading_lbl control. It will enable the NumericStepper so that the user can use it to page through the results. The function also sets the minimum and maximum values of this control.

3. We'll also need to make some changes to the startFeed() function, which is called when a feed is first requested. At this point, the NumericStepper should display a value of 1. We need to do this in case the user has changed the value to a higher number when viewing an earlier feed. The function also disables the NumericStepper while the new feed loads.

Modify the startFeed() function as shown in bold in the following code block:

```
private function startFeed(feedURL:String, feedDisplayText:String)
  ➥:void {
  page_ns.value = 1;
  page_ns.enabled = false;
  showFeed(feedURL);
  searchType_txt.text = feedDisplayText;
}
```

4. We also need to modify the showFeed() function to pass the requested page number to the getKulerFeed() method of the KulerLoader object. At the moment, it's passing a value of 1.

Modify the showFeed() function as shown here in bold:

```
private function showFeed(feed:String):void {
  var startIndex:int = (page_ns.value -1)* 10;
  loading_lbl.text = "Loading Kuler feed";
  feedURL = feed;
  myKulerXML.getKulerFeed(feedURL, startIndex);
  swatches_dg.dataProvider = [];
}
```

The first change is the calculation of a startIndex variable. The results in a Kuler feed are numbered from 0 onward. The first result in a group of pages will be one less than the value in the NumericStepper multiplied by ten.

For example, if the NumericStepper displays a value of 2, the first record we'll need to access is record 10. We find this by number taking one from the NumericStepper value to give us one and multiplying this by ten to give us the starting index of 10.

We also need to modify the call to the getKulerFeed() method to pass the new startIndex variable.

Finally, the application should clear the DataGrid while the new feed is requested. We do this by assigning the dataProvider property to an empty array using the expression [].

5. The final change to introduce paging to the application is to add a listener to the NumericStepper control. This listener will respond when the user changes the page value.

Add the following line to the initApp() function:

```
page_ns.addEventListener(NumericStepperEvent.CHANGE,
  ➥nsChangeHandler);
```

When the user changes the value in the NumericStepper, the application will call the nsChangeHandler function.

6. Check that Flex Builder has added the following import statement:

```
import mx.events.NumericStepperEvent;
```

If not, add the line yourself.

7. We also need to add the following nsChangeHandler() function to respond when the value in the NumericStepper changes:

```
private function nsChangeHandler(e:NumericStepperEvent):void {
  swatches_dg.dataProvider = [];
  page_ns.enabled = false;
  showFeed(feedURL);
}
```

This function starts by clearing the DataGrid prior to making another request. It does this using the same method that you saw earlier.

The function also disables the NumericStepper while the request is in progress. The last line of the function calls the showFeed() function again, passing the feedURL variable. Remember that this variable will store the last requested feed type, so we'll repeat the same request.

As you saw earlier, the showFeed() function will calculate the starting point for the results from the value in the NumericStepper control.

467

8. Run the application and click the Highest rated button. The NumericStepper should be enabled after the application receives the feed. Choosing a different page should clear the DataGrid and disable the NumericStepper while the new feed loads. When the selected page displays, the NumericStepper should be enabled again.

Figure 13-7 shows the application displaying page 4 of the highest rated feeds.

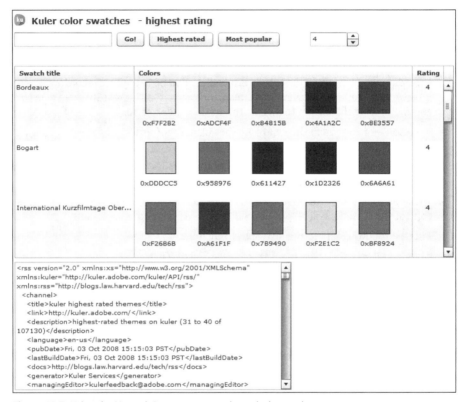

Figure 13-7. Using the NumericStepper to page through the results

We've almost finished the application. The next step is to show the most popular themes.

Displaying the most popular schemes

We can display the most popular schemes for the past 30 days with only minor changes to the application.

1. First, we need to add the following event listener to the initApp() function in the main application file:

```
popular_btn.addEventListener(MouseEvent.CLICK, popularHandler);
```

2. We also need to add the popularHandler() function that follows:

```
private function popularHandler(e:Event):void {
  startFeed("get.cfm?listtype=popular", "- most popular");
}
```

This handler function passes the new feed URL to the startFeed() function. At that point, the startFeed() function will configure the NumericStepper and pass the new URL to the showFeed() function. This function will make the request for the new feed.

3. Run the application and click the Most popular button. Figure 13-8 shows what you should see.

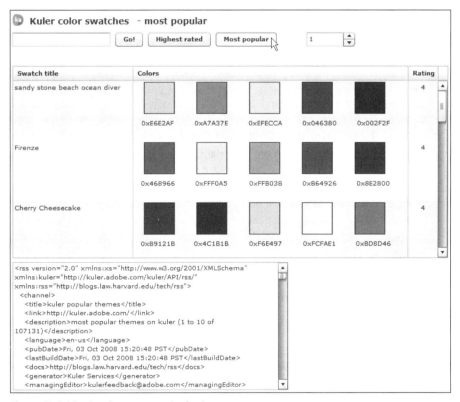

Figure 13-8. Viewing the most popular feeds

After viewing the first page, you should be able to use the NumericStepper control to view the other pages.

Searching Kuler

The final step in completing this application is to enable the search functionality. We'll use the generic Kuler search that searches theme titles, tags, author names, theme IDs, author IDs, and hex values for the provided keyword. Again, because of the way we've set up the application, this process is very simple.

1. Start by adding the following event listener to the initApp() function:

```
search_btn.addEventListener(MouseEvent.CLICK, searchHandler);
```

2. When the user clicks Go!, the application will call the searchHandler() function. Add this function now.

```
private function searchHandler(e:Event):void{
  if (search_txt.text.length > 0) {
    startFeed("search.cfm?searchQuery=" + search_txt.text,
      ➥"- search for term '" + search_txt.text + "'");
  }
  else {
    loading_lbl.text = "Enter a search term";
  }
}
```

The function tests that the user has entered a value in the search_txt control by comparing the length of the text property with 0. If a value has been entered, the function calls the startFeed() function, passing a new URL that includes the search term. It also passes the text search for term with the search text, so that users can see their search criteria.

If a search term has not been entered, the user will see the text Enter a search term in the loading_lbl control.

3. The final change is to modify the startFeed() function to clear the text from the search box. Change the function as shown in bold here:

```
private function startFeed(feedURL:String, feedDisplayText:String)
  ➥:void {
  page_ns.value = 1;
  page_ns.enabled = false;
  showFeed(feedURL);
  searchType_txt.text = feedDisplayText;
  search_txt.text = "";
}
```

4. The application is complete. Run it, enter a search term, and click Go!. You should see the first page of results display. If your search returned more than one page, you should be able to display the other pages using the NumericStepper. Figure 13-9 shows a sample search for the term sand.

> If you want to use this application on your web site, you'll probably want to remove the TextArea control first.

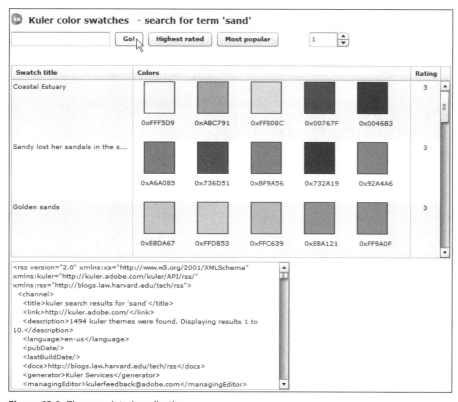

Figure 13-9. The completed application

Reviewing the completed code

You can find the completed code files saved with the chapter resources as KulerCompleted.mxml, ColorSwatch.mxml, and KulerLoader.as. I've also included the completed files here, so you can check your code. Don't forget that you'll need to edit the custom class file KulerLoader.as to add your own developer key. Replace the text your_key_here with your own API key value.

KulerLoader.as

The first file I'll show is KulerLoader.as.

```
package xmlUtilities {
  import flash.events.Event;
  import flash.events.HTTPStatusEvent;
  import flash.events.IOErrorEvent;
  import flash.events.SecurityErrorEvent;
  import flash.net.URLLoader;
  import flash.net.URLRequest;
  import mx.collections.ArrayCollection;
  [Bindable]
  [Event(name="loadError", type="flash.events.Event")]
```

```
public class KulerLoader {
  private var xmlAllContent:XML;
  private var xmlLoader:URLLoader;
  private var swatchElements:XMLList;
  private var swatchElementsCollection: ArrayCollection;
  private var kulerNS:Namespace =
    ➥new Namespace("http://kuler.adobe.com/kuler/API/rss/");
  private const API_KEY:String = "api_key_here";
  private const KULER_BASE_URL:String =
    ➥"http://kuler-api.adobe.com/rss/";
  public function KulerLoader() {
    xmlLoader = new URLLoader();
    xmlLoader.addEventListener(Event.COMPLETE, completeHandler);
    xmlLoader.addEventListener(HTTPStatusEvent.HTTP_STATUS,
      ➥httpStatusHandler);
    xmlLoader.addEventListener(IOErrorEvent.IO_ERROR,
      ➥ioErrorHandler);
    xmlLoader.addEventListener(SecurityErrorEvent.SECURITY_ERROR,
      ➥securityHandler);
  }
  public function getKulerFeed(feedPath:String, startIndex:int)
    ➥:void {
    var kulerURL:String;
    kulerURL = KULER_BASE_URL + feedPath + "&key=" + API_KEY +
      ➥"&startIndex=" + String(startIndex) + "&itemsPerPage=10";
    try {
      xmlLoader.load(new URLRequest(kulerURL));
    }
    catch (e:Error) {
      dispatchEvent(new Event("loadError"));
    }
  }

  public function getXML():XML {
    return xmlAllContent;
  }

  public function getSwatches():ArrayCollection {
    var title:String;
    var col1:String;
    var col2:String;
    var col3:String;
    var col4:String;
    var col5:String;
    var rating:String;
```

```
        swatchElements = xmlAllContent.channel.item;
        swatchElementsCollection = new ArrayCollection();
        for each (var item:XML in swatchElements) {
          title = item.kulerNS::themeItem.kulerNS::themeTitle;
          rating = item.kulerNS::themeItem.kulerNS::themeRating;
          col1 = "0x" + item.kulerNS::themeItem.kulerNS
            ➥::themeSwatches.kulerNS::swatch[0].kulerNS::swatchHexColor;
          col2 = "0x" + item.kulerNS::themeItem.kulerNS
            ➥::themeSwatches.kulerNS::swatch[1].kulerNS::swatchHexColor;
          col3 = "0x" + item.kulerNS::themeItem.kulerNS
            ➥::themeSwatches.kulerNS::swatch[2].kulerNS::swatchHexColor;
          col4 = "0x" + item.kulerNS::themeItem.kulerNS
            ➥::themeSwatches. kulerNS::swatch[3].kulerNS::swatchHexColor;
          col5 = "0x" + item.kulerNS::themeItem.kulerNS
            ➥::themeSwatches. kulerNS::swatch[4].kulerNS::swatchHexColor;
          swatchElementsCollection.addItem({label: title,
            ➥ rating:rating, color1: col1, color2: col2, color3: col3,
            ➥ color4: col4, color5: col5});
        }
        return swatchElementsCollection;
      }
      public function getPages():int {
        var totalRecords:int = int(xmlAllContent.channel.recordCount);
        var pages:int = Math.ceil(totalRecords/10);
        return pages;
      }
      private function completeHandler(e:Event):void {
        xmlAllContent = XML(e.target.data);
        dispatchEvent(new Event(Event.COMPLETE));
      }
      private function httpStatusHandler(e:HTTPStatusEvent):void {
        dispatchEvent(new HTTPStatusEvent(HTTPStatusEvent.HTTP_STATUS,
          ➥false, false, e.status));
      }
      private function ioErrorHandler(e:IOErrorEvent):void {
        dispatchEvent(new IOErrorEvent(IOErrorEvent.IO_ERROR, false,
          ➥false, e.text));
      }
      private function securityHandler(e:SecurityErrorEvent):void {
        dispatchEvent(new SecurityErrorEvent(
          ➥SecurityErrorEvent.SECURITY_ERROR, false, false, e.text));
      }
    }
  }
}
```

ColorSwatch.mxml

The ColorSwatch.mxml custom component follows:

```
<?xml version="1.0" encoding="utf-8"?>
<mx:VBox xmlns:mx="http://www.adobe.com/2006/mxml" width="460"
  height="90">
  <mx:HBox>
    <mx:Spacer width="10"/>
    <mx:Canvas id="swatch1" width="50" height="50"
      backgroundColor="{data.color1}" borderStyle="solid"
      borderColor="#000000"/>
    <mx:Spacer width="20"/>
    <mx:Canvas id="swatch2" width="50" height="50"
      backgroundColor="{data.color2}" borderStyle="solid"
      borderColor="#000000"/>
    <mx:Spacer width="20"/>
    <mx:Canvas id="swatch3" width="50" height="50"
      backgroundColor="{data.color3}" borderStyle="solid"
      borderColor="#000000"/>
    <mx:Spacer width="20"/>
    <mx:Canvas id="swatch4" width="50" height="50"
      backgroundColor="{data.color4}" borderStyle="solid"
      borderColor="#000000"/>
    <mx:Spacer width="20"/>
    <mx:Canvas id="swatch5" width="50" height="50"
      backgroundColor="{data.color5}" borderStyle="solid"
      borderColor="#000101"/>
    <mx:Spacer width="10"/>
  </mx:HBox>
  <mx:HBox>
    <mx:Label id="colorName1_lbl" width="80" textAlign="center"
      text="{data.color1}"/>
    <mx:Label id="colorName2_lbl" width="80" textAlign="center"
      text="{data.color2}"/>
    <mx:Label id="colorName3_lbl" width="80" textAlign="center"
      text="{data.color3}"/>
    <mx:Label id="colorName4_lbl" width="80" textAlign="center"
      text="{data.color4}"/>
    <mx:Label id="colorName5_lbl" width="80" textAlign="center"
      text="{data.color5}"/>
  </mx:HBox>
</mx:VBox>
```

KulerCompleted.mxml

Finally, you can see the completed code for the application file, KulerCompleted.mxml.

```
<?xml version="1.0" encoding="utf-8"?>
<mx:Application xmlns:mx="http://www.adobe.com/2006/mxml"
  layout="absolute"  backgroundColor="white"
  backgroundGradientAlphas="100,100"
  creationComplete="initApp(event)">
  <mx:Script>
    <![CDATA[
      import mx.events.NumericStepperEvent;
      import mx.events.FlexEvent;
      import xmlUtilities.KulerLoader;
      private var myKulerXML:KulerLoader;
      private var feedURL:String;
      private function initApp(e:FlexEvent):void {
        myKulerXML = new KulerLoader();
        myKulerXML.addEventListener(Event.COMPLETE, completeHandler);
        myKulerXML.addEventListener(HTTPStatusEvent.HTTP_STATUS,
          ➥httpStatusHandler);
        myKulerXML.addEventListener(IOErrorEvent.IO_ERROR,
          ➥ioErrorHandler);
        myKulerXML.addEventListener(SecurityErrorEvent.
          ➥SECURITY_ERROR, securityHandler);
        myKulerXML.addEventListener("loadError", errorHandler);
        search_btn.addEventListener(MouseEvent.CLICK, searchHandler);
        highest_btn.addEventListener(MouseEvent.CLICK,
          ➥highestHandler);
        popular_btn.addEventListener(MouseEvent.CLICK,
          ➥popularHandler);
        page_ns.addEventListener(NumericStepperEvent.CHANGE,
          ➥nsChangeHandler);
      }
      private function completeHandler(e:Event):void {
        var numPages:int = myKulerXML.getPages();
        content_txt.text = e.target.getXML().toXMLString();
        if (numPages == 0) {
          loading_lbl.text = "There are no matching Kuler themes";
          page_ns.enabled = false;
        }
        else {
          loading_lbl.text = "";
          page_ns.enabled = true;
          page_ns.minimum = 1;
          page_ns.maximum = numPages;
          showSwatches();
        }
      }
```

```
private function httpStatusHandler(e:HTTPStatusEvent):void {
  var httpStatus:int = e.status;
  if (e.status != 200) {
  loading_lbl.text = "HTTP Status error " + String(e.status);
  }
}
private function ioErrorHandler(e:IOErrorEvent):void {
  loading_lbl.text = "IOError " + e.text;
}
private function securityHandler(e:SecurityErrorEvent):void {
  loading_lbl.text = "Security error " + e.text;
}
private function errorHandler(e:Event):void {
  loading_lbl.text = "There was an error loading the
    ➥Kuler feed";
}
private function searchHandler(e:Event):void{
  if (search_txt.text.length > 0) {
    startFeed("search.cfm?searchQuery=" + search_txt.text,
      ➥"- search for term '" + search_txt.text + "'");
  }
  else {
    loading_lbl.text = "Enter a search term";
  }
}
private function highestHandler(e:Event):void {
  startFeed("get.cfm?listtype=rating","- highest rating");
}
private function popularHandler(e:Event):void {
  startFeed("get.cfm?listtype=popular", "- most popular");
}
private function startFeed(feedURL:String,
  ➥feedDisplayText:String):void {
  page_ns.value = 1;
  page_ns.enabled = false;
  showFeed(feedURL);
  searchType_txt.text = feedDisplayText;
  search_txt.text = "";
}
private function nsChangeHandler(e:NumericStepperEvent):void {
  swatches_dg.dataProvider = [];
  page_ns.enabled = false;
  showFeed(feedURL);
}
private function showFeed(feed:String):void {
  var startIndex:int = (page_ns.value -1)* 10;
  loading_lbl.text = "Loading Kuler feed";
  feedURL = feed;
  myKulerXML.getKulerFeed(feedURL, startIndex);
  swatches_dg.dataProvider = [];
}
```

```
        private function showSwatches():void {
          swatches_dg.dataProvider = myKulerXML.getSwatches();
          loading_lbl.text = "";
        }


    ]]>
  </mx:Script>
  <mx:VBox x="10" y="10">
    <mx:HBox>
      <mx:Image source="assets/ku_18pxBugOnly.gif"/>
      <mx:Label text="Kuler color swatches" fontSize="14"
        fontWeight="bold"/>
      <mx:Label id="searchType_txt"  fontSize="14" fontWeight="bold"
        width="231"/>
    </mx:HBox>
    <mx:HBox>
      <mx:TextInput id="search_txt"/>
      <mx:Button label="Go!" id="search_btn"/>
      <mx:Button label="Highest rated" id="highest_btn"/>
      <mx:Button label="Most popular" id="popular_btn"/>
      <mx:Label id="page_txt" text="Page" visible="false"/>
      <mx:NumericStepper id="page_ns" enabled="false"/>
    </mx:HBox>
    <mx:Label id="loading_lbl" color="#FF0000"/>
    <mx:DataGrid id="swatches_dg" height="300">
      <mx:columns>
        <mx:DataGridColumn headerText="Swatch title" width="200"
          dataField="label">
                  <mx:itemRenderer>
                      <mx:Component>
                          <mx:Label />
                      </mx:Component>
                  </mx:itemRenderer>
          </mx:DataGridColumn>
              <mx:DataGridColumn headerText="Colors" width="460"
          itemRenderer="ColorSwatch">
          </mx:DataGridColumn>
        <mx:DataGridColumn headerText="Rating" width="50"
          dataField="rating">
                  <mx:itemRenderer>
                      <mx:Component>
                          <mx:Label width="100%"
                            textAlign="center" />
                      </mx:Component>
                  </mx:itemRenderer>
              </mx:DataGridColumn>
      </mx:columns>
    </mx:DataGrid>
    <mx:TextArea id="content_txt" width="450" height="200"/>
  </mx:VBox>
</mx:Application>
```

Summary

Well, that's it for the chapter and for the book. In this chapter, we worked through a Flex case study that processed the Kuler feeds from Adobe. The application allowed you to view the highest rated themes and the most popular themes, and to search themes using a keyword.

When the feed loaded, each of the individual themes displayed in a DataGrid component. We created a custom component to show the five color swatches for each theme. The application also allowed users to view other pages of themes.

I hope that you enjoyed this case study and that it helped you to understand the role of namespaces in XML. Good luck with your XML endeavors in Flash and Flex!

INDEX